Hacking
MythTV

Hacking
MythTV

Jarod Wilson, Ed Tittel, Matt Wright, and Justin Korelc

Wiley Publishing, Inc.

Hacking MythTV

Published by
Wiley Publishing, Inc.
10475 Crosspoint Boulevard
Indianapolis, IN 46256
www.wiley.com

ISBN-13: 978-0-470-03787-4
ISBN-10: 0-470-03787-3

Manufactured in the United States of America

10 9 8 7 6 5 4 3 2 1

1B/RQ/QY/QW/IN

For general information on our other products and services or to obtain technical support, please contact our Customer Care Department within the U.S. at (800) 762-2974, outside the U.S. at (317) 572-3993 or fax (317) 572-4002.

Library of Congress Cataloging-in-Publication Data:

Hacking MythTV / Jarod Wilson ... [et al.].
   p. cm.
 ISBN-13: 978-0-470-03787-4 (paper/website)
 ISBN-10: 0-470-03787-3 (paper/website)
 1. MythTV. 2. Multimedia systems. 3. Interactive multimedia—Authoring programs.
 4. Interactive television. 5. Computer hackers. I. Wilson, Jarod, 1977-
 QA76.575H33 2006
 006.7—dc22
                         2006019599

About the Authors

Jarod Wilson has been an avid Linux user since circa 1997, when he was first introduced to Red Hat Linux 4.2 in a UNIX Operating Systems course in college. One spring about three years ago, Jarod was between jobs and discovered the MythTV project, and loved it so much he decided to help try to make it accessible to as many people as possible, and thus was born his MythTV on Fedora HOW-TO, dubbed Fedora Myth(TV)ology, which he still maintains to this day (when time permits). Professionally, every job he's held since college has incorporated daily use of Linux. Jarod recently left high-performance computing cluster vendor Linux Networx, where he was an on-site field service engineer for a large customer, for a job at the very company from whence his first taste of Linux came. Jarod currently works in Red Hat's Enterprise Kernel Group as a senior software engineer, focused on kernel testing, but also contributes time and effort to Red Hat's Fedora Core Linux community distribution.

Ed Tittel's passion for media was kindled right out of undergraduate school, way back in 1973, when he had the extremely good fortune to be hired as a studio engineer at the Library of Congress. Not only did Bob Carneal and John Howell teach Ed the basics of good audio engineering and careful audition of the resulting sounds, they also taught him the importance of careful design and quality implementation. Since then, Ed has gone through numerous iterations of building a great entertainment center, and has really enjoyed learning how to meld a PC into that mix. Ed's interest in media PCs began with his last ExtremeTech book on Windows Media Center PCs, but his excitement peaked when he realized that MythTV offered an open-ended, more flexible, and client-server based implementation of the kind of functionality that MCE offers, kicked up several notches. In working on this book, Ed refreshed his knowledge of the first real operating system he ever learned (the second Berkeley Software Distribution, aka 2BSD, circa 1979), and learned to appreciate how far Linux has come and how little UNIX has really changed.

Matt Wright is a longtime home theater PC (HTPC) enthusiast and computer fiend. He's been working full-time in the industry for nearly five years, and is a regular contributor to (and resident expert at) HTPCnews.com, one of the most popular HTPC online destinations. Matt also contributed two chapters and chunks of several more to Wiley's *Building the Ultimate Home Theater PC* (Wiley, 2005) and consults regularly with professional and individual clients on HTPC topics, hardware, and technology.

Justin Korelc, at six years of age, asked his father how he could learn to use a computer. Instead of being given an obvious or easy answer, Justin's father sat him down at the console, handed him a copy of K&R's classic *The C Programming Language*, and gave him a gentle introduction to basic shell input/output. This proved instrumental in Justin's personal and professional growth, starting with a migration from BSD UNIX to Linux in his teenage years, which eventually led him to write about his experiences. Today, Justin works as a freelance author writing articles and occasional book chapters for a variety of online and traditional publishers. Although his primary focus targets Linux and open-source software, he is also quite knowledgeable in the areas of hardware, network protocols, and a variety of unusual programming concepts, most of which center around security topics.

Credits

Executive Editor
Chris Webb

Development Editors
Sara Shlaer and Brian Herrmann

Production Editor
William A. Barton

Copy Editor
Luann Rouff

Editorial Manager
Mary Beth Wakefield

Production Manager
Tim Tate

Vice President and Executive Group Publisher
Richard Swadley

Vice President and Executive Publisher
Joseph B. Wikert

Project Coordinator
Ryan Steffen

Graphics and Production Specialists
Jennifer Mayberry, Barbara Moore,
Lynsey Osborn, Alicia B. South

Quality Control Technician
Brian H. Walls

Media Development Specialists
Angela Denny
Kit Malone
Travis Silvers

Proofreading and Indexing
Techbooks

Cover Design
Anthony Bunyan

Contents

Part II: Installing and Configuring MythTV   79

Chapter 4: Downloading, Installing, and Configuring
Linux for MythTV 81

Part IV: Advanced MythTV Hacks   **273**

Acknowledgments

Jarod Wilson

First and foremost, thank-you to Isaac Richards, the founding father and lead developer of MythTV. Thanks also to everyone else who has contributed code to the project, helped a new user on the mailing list or chat, helped with documentation, or even simply recommended the project to a friend. Thanks to everyone who has e-mailed me with corrections, updates, or words of encouragement for my own little corner of the MythTV universe, `http://wilsonet.com/mythtv/`. And, of course, I would like to thank my wife and kids for putting up with all the time I've spent on this book and on MythTV in general over the years.

Ed Tittel

Because Jarod has so thoroughly thanked Isaac Richards for his pioneering work with MythTV, I want to thank Isaac for leading me to this subject and providing great information, guidance, and input as well. I'd also like to thank Justin Korelc for his efforts on this book, which occasionally went way beyond the call of duty in building the best book that we could envision. To Matt Wright, my thanks for chipping in on a challenging project and for hanging in when life stepped in your way. And finally, my profound and copious thanks to Kim Lindros, of Gracie Editorial, for stepping in closer to the end of this project than she probably should have, and for straightening the rest of us out and making us fly right! Also, our thanks to Sara Shlaer, Brian Herrmann, and the rest of the great staff at Wiley, plus Chris Webb, for helping us put another good media PC book into play.

Justin Korelc

Thank you, Father, for teaching me to fish. You are smarter, wiser, and more clever than I could have known then, and I hope my future children will idolize me as I do you. Thank you, Mother, for encouraging my intellectual development and creative growth, and for your unwavering support when both artistic and scientific progress went completely awry. Without your influence I might never have investigated myself or the world around me, and I'd be lost without your guidance.

Thanks also to you, Marion, my girlfriend, my confidante, and my best friend. Your unconditional love and support helps me to triumph over adversity, and our loving relationship has shaped my personal growth in more positive ways than any combination of past life experiences.

I extend my deepest gratitude to the following individuals: Ed Tittel, editor, occasional co-author, and guiding light through the darkness of uncertainty; Jarod Wilson, whose personal efforts to make MythTV accessible to the greater public has led to this great opportunity; and

Isaac Richards, for his vision and insight into the world of real convergence technology. You are a true champion of the people, Mr. Richards.

A special thanks goes to the following: Toby Digby, one of few people I know who can keep pace with my unbridled technical creativity and constant ability to think outside the box; Kim Lindros, for pulling this all together (and your boundless patience) despite a few setbacks and challenges; and the great people at Wiley for taking a chance on an unknown author. Perhaps most important, I give special thanks to the open-source community for empowering the end-user

Introduction

MythTV is an open-source, Linux-based multimedia management system that supports listening to and viewing sound, movies, TV, digital photos, and more. As an open-source project, MythTV is by no means a one-man show, but MythTV's originator, Isaac Richards, describes his impetus for its development as follows:

> I got tired of the rather low-quality cable box that AT&T Broadband provides with their digital cable service. It's slow to change channels, ridden with ads, and the program guide is a joke. So, I figured it'd be fun to try and build a replacement. Yes, I could have just bought a TiVo, but I wanted to have more than just a PVR — I want a web browser built in, a mail client, maybe some games. Basically, I want the mythical convergence box that's been talked about for a few years now.
>
> From the "Background" page at `www.mythtv.org/modules.php?name= MythInfo`.

Over time, his quest for "the mythical convergence box" — which really means a device that combines TV, (DVD) movies, all kinds of music, radio, photographs, and other forms of entertainment or lifestyle activities (MythTV even includes a plug-in to manage cooking recipes) — has spawned a veritable do-it-yourself digital entertainment management tool that anyone who's somewhat Linux savvy can download and install at no charge, and then extend and customize beyond belief. Though you'll hear MythTV often described as a personal video recorder (PVR), there's really an awful lot more to it than that, particularly for those who seek to take fullest advantage of its capabilities.

But MythTV is also very much a do-it-yourself phenomenon. This means people must be willing to find and assemble the parts necessary to build a PC on which to run MythTV, and then go out and grab all the software pieces and parts (of which there are more than a few) to install, configure, and get MythTV set up and running. Then there's the constant tinkering required to make of it exactly what you want it to be. Sounds like work, doesn't it?

In fact, you may be wondering why on earth anybody would want to go to that much trouble. Well, for one thing, though you may run into a little trouble here or there, it's really not that difficult. In addition, some people actually revel in this kind of thing (including, obviously, this book's intrepid and interested authors). What you get at the end of the process is what really makes the whole thing worthwhile: MythTV is every bit as capable (and in some ways, more capable) than comparable products such as Windows XP Media Center Edition 2005. And you can take the base installation and customize it to your heart's content, which makes it infinitely better to those who care about such things.

All of this said, there is one potential gotcha about working with MythTV. It not only runs on top of Linux, it uses the operating system both heavily and fully. Thus, if you want to work with MythTV you should be reasonably familiar with Linux. In fact, you should be unafraid of installing a big and feature-laden runtime environment — namely, MythTV and its constituent elements, plus plug-ins, and add-ons — onto a Linux-based PC.

What Do You Need to Run MythTV?

We answer the foregoing question in much greater detail in several chapters in this book, but for now, let's just say a MythTV-capable PC is a personal computer that can run Linux and MythTV software, along with its various baggage, and can also acquire, store, manage, and play all kinds of entertainment material. This includes television, music, DVD movies, and digital photos. Some PC hardware (usually part of a TV tuner card) even enables these devices to access radio transmissions from over the air; but because Internet access (a key source of program guides, broadcast/play schedules, and descriptive information about music, movies, TV shows, and other programming material) is *absolutely essential* for any capable entertainment PC (including MythTV PCs), it's also easy to select and listen to any of the thousands of radio stations that stream onto the Internet without a radio receiver of any kind.

Basically, to get started with MythTV, you need two kinds of ingredients: a home theater PC (HTPC), and a collection of software components that includes a suitable Linux distribution, the MythTV core distribution, a bunch of other odds and ends, and whatever plug-ins or add-ons you decide to add to the basic MythTV environment. In a nutshell, this book tells you how to make sure your PC is up to the task, and how (and where) to get the software components you'll need, as well as what to do with them to get your system up and running. And though we stick to KnoppMyth and Fedora Core Linux implementations, our lead author, Jarod Wilson, points out that intrepid souls can build MythTV implementations around FreeBSD (complete) and Mac OS X (partial, at least) as well.

There's no requirement that a home theater PC run Linux along with MythTV to create a workable digital entertainment system. Enthusiasts of various types will argue that Windows Media Center Edition (usually just called MCE) or the Mac OS (a variant of UNIX itself these days) work as well or better than MythTV, not to mention other multimedia environments such as Sage TV that will happily run on either Linux or Windows. We picked MythTV as the focus for this book not because it's the only game in town — it's definitely not, not by a long shot — but because we like the way it's built and maintained, enjoy the way it works, and appreciate the way we can tweak it and play with it as much as we want. A lot of other people apparently feel the same way, and we hope this book helps you join their swelling ranks.

Why Build Your Own MythTV PC?

This is a question you'll want to answer before buying this book and again before beginning the build process for your own MythTV PC. At one time, the answer might have been simple: to save money. Today, however, with numerous HTPCs available for under $1,000 (albeit in tower cases and not terribly well suited for the kind of quiet operation a home entertainment center sometimes demands), you probably can't really save that much money by doing it yourself.

To us (and we hope the majority of readers of this book), the best answers to this question are as follows:

- To learn and understand more about how entertainment PCs work in general, and how MythTV PCs work in particular

- To invest the care, time, and effort necessary to construct a quiet, good-looking MythTV PC with the functionality that's right for you

- Because you like to do things yourself, and don't mind spending time, money, and energy to achieve the result you want

Jarod Wilson also reports that he finds that a lot of people take on MythTV as a first significant Linux project, and find it to be a great learning experience. Inevitably, this first taste also leads to more Linux use in other ways as well.

For your authors, these factors were bolstered by one more: all of us had a burning desire to reduce the number of remote controls cluttering our living rooms. At one point, one of us had six remotes to deal with for his entertainment center; now, with a sleek, quiet MythTV PC at the heart of a digital entertainment system, he only needs one remote regularly (a MythTV-compatible remote that also drives other infrared, or IR, multimedia gear).

What's in This Book

This book is the result of lead author Jarod Wilson's two-plus years of playing around with MythTV, followed by six intense months of building, tweaking, and taking care of up to half a dozen home-built MythTV PCs. The book falls into five parts, each of which addresses part of the HTPC equation for MythTV:

- Part I introduces MythTV and explains how to select (or build) a suitable PC on which to run this software, as well as how to download software and otherwise prepare for MythTV installation. It also covers the ins and outs of working with MythTV sound and picture, from the standpoint of adding, installing, and configuring compatible sound and TV cards in your MythTV PC.

- Part II deals with installing and configuring MythTV, starting with basic Linux installation and the drivers and other software components that are involved in putting a working MythTV PC together. After that, you'll tackle installing and setting up your remote control, and then configuring the many aspects of MythTV that must be tweaked and prodded to match your PC's hardware components and capabilities. As the triumphant conclusion to this part, you go through the motions to ensure that your MythTV works properly, and start scheduling TV recordings (among other things).

- Part III deals with the extensions to MythTV's core functionality called *plug-ins*, which add so much to its overall capabilities. This includes self-describing items such as MythDVD, MythGallery, MythMusic, MythVideo, and more, all of which you can peruse and explore to determine whether you want to make them part of your MythTV experience.

- Part IV takes you deep into MythTV's inner workings and explains related hacks — time-honored ways to tweak, adjust, and improve basic software capabilities — you can (and probably should) apply to your MythTV environment. This includes tips on how to hack MythTV's look and feel, ways to boost its performance and responsiveness, ways to further extend MythTV's behavior and characteristics, and finally how to troubleshoot the occasional problems that can crop up on a MythTV system.

- Part V is supplementary material, and includes information and pointers to all kinds of additional details, news, information, tutorials, and other resources available online. Topics covered include information, sources, and documentation for key MythTV-friendly Linux distributions, along with a compendium of MythTV resources and sources, plus a cornucopia of Linux system diagnostics and monitoring tools.

This book is best read from start to finish in order. However, it was also written to be used as a reference manual for the core code in a MythTV installation, plus all the various plug-ins and add-ons. It should also help interested readers figure out what to install, hardware-wise, to get music, movies, and TV working on their systems, and how to make best use of them within the MythTV environment. Feel free to skip around if you don't want to take each step in the complete journey involved in selecting, purchasing, assembling, testing, and installing all the software and components that go into crafting a carefully customized MythTV installation. After an initial read-through, we expect the book will serve best as a reference as you go through the steps involved in constructing your own MythTV PC.

Who This Book Is For

This book is aimed at the intermediate to advanced computer user, preferably one who knows how to use a screwdriver and insert and remove PC components. If you are a beginner or a PC hardware novice, this book may not be for you. If you understand the basic pieces and parts in a modern PC, and aren't afraid to take one apart or (more important) put one together, please dive right in.

That said, you should also know something about Linux, or be willing to learn *a lot* about that subject as you also dig into the details related to MythTV. In particular, you will find this book a lot easier to follow if you know what a package is (it's a collection of software components designed to work with an installer program, used to add individual programs or entire runtime environments, such as MythTV, to a working Linux installation). You should also know about the hierarchy of Linux users, how to work with the command line and some kind of command shell (preferably bash), and how to run programs as root or by invoking superuser privileges. Finally, some basic knowledge of typical Linux file systems and file organization will greatly help you put the information in this book into context. Those who lack such background should probably consult a book such as Dee-Ann LeBlanc's excellent *Linux For Dummies*, 7th Edition (Wiley 2006), or perhaps Jon "maddog" Hall's equally good (and potentially more relevant) *Red Hat Fedora Linux3 For Dummies* (Wiley 2005). Of course, one great thing about Linux is that there's no end to the books and other documentation available on that subject, so feel free to investigate and use other sources and resources as well.

You will need to purchase at least $500 worth of components and software to put a workable MythTV PC together, and a completely realistic budget is more like $900 (the same is true if you plan to buy a MythTV-ready system instead). If you can't afford that kind of money, it's better to wait until you've got enough funds to start building or buying, though that shouldn't stop you from reading as much as you want in this book and/or from other sources.

How to Use This Book

You'll want to begin by reading as much of this book, in the order in which chapters are presented, as you can (if you're already familiar with a topic in Part I or Part II, feel free to skim over those parts). You'll definitely want to read all of Parts I, II, and IV, to get a sense of what's involved in planning, obtaining, assembling, installing, and testing a MythTV system.

Once you start your own construction process, you'll want to return to the chapters in Part I to bone up on the components you'll be selecting, and buying or downloading. Then you'll want to refer regularly to Part II to help you plan and install MythTV. After your system is up and running, you'll find Part IV invaluable in helping you make the most of your MythTV system, and in keeping it working trouble-free.

All along the way, you should find the information, references, and resources in Part V at least of interest, if not of definite and immediate help. We tried throughout to include numerous sources for community input, Q&A, and outright support to help you over any rough spots you may encounter.

Conventions Used in This Book

This book uses several notification icons that point out important information such as cautions, quick tips, and cross-references. Specifically, four types of icons appear in this book:

 Provides valuable information that will help you avoid a disaster

 Recommendations to save time, reduce cost, or ensure the best possible results for your HTPC

 Pointers to other parts of the book, or to Internet sites, where you can find more information about the subject at hand

 Items of information to which you should pay particular attention, or which refer you to additional details on subjects explored in the main text

Companion Web Sites

For links, updates, and news about recent developments, product or software releases, and other material relevant to building a MythTV PC, please visit this book's companion Web site at www.wiley.com/compbooks/extremetech. We're asking readers to share their favorite resources, and promise to include the best of those in updates to the companion site on a timely basis. In addition, don't forget to check out the information all over MythTV.org (www.mythtv.org) or lead author Jarod Wilson's excellent Fedora Myth(TV)ology site (www.wilsonet.com/mythtv) either.

It's a Hit, Not a Myth!

We sincerely hope that the ultimate result of reading this book is the proliferation of more PCs running MythTV in the world at large. If you put such a system together, we think you'll find (as we have) that a MythTV PC makes an outstanding addition to — or even cornerstone for — a modern home entertainment center. If you build a working MythTV system, you'll find a lot of ways to enjoy the fruits of your labor. That much we can promise!

Introducing MythTV

MythTV is a powerful, open-ended Linux-based software environment you can use to build a great multimedia system. And when we say multimedia, we really mean it: Out of the gate, with only official plug-ins installed, MythTV can handle music, DVD video, TV, Web browsing, digital photos, and online weather information. Not only that, you can tweak and customize MythTV until the cows come home, or until you get tired of fiddling about.

Chapter 1 provides a complete description of MythTV's contents and capabilities and explains its architecture and requirements. Consider it your formal introduction to this multimedia system's many facets and functions.

Chapter 2 walks you through the long and sometimes tricky process of pulling together all the pieces and parts required to build a working MythTV installation. We hope you won't be daunted by the element count involved, so please take comfort from the handholding, detailed instructions, and advice we dispense at each stop on the list of ingredients.

Chapter 3 digs into MythTV's audio and video capabilities, starting with a review of its sound capabilities for stereo and multi-channel speaker rigs. The next subject is working with a display device — probably a TV set, though it may be a conventional TV (standard-definition television, or SDTV) or high-definition TV (HDTV). This means we tackle how you can use MythTV to record and play back television programs, and make the most of both standard and high-definition signals and displays.

By the time you finish this part of the book, you'll have a pretty good idea about what MythTV is and what it can do. You'll also be able to gather all of the ingredients you'll need for a basic MythTV installation.

part

in this part

Chapter 1
What is MythTV?

Chapter 2
Fundamental Linux Concepts for MythTV

Chapter 3
MythTV Sound and Picture

What Is MythTV?

MythTV is an extensible third-party software package (see the side-bar titled "The Linux Package") that converts a mild-mannered Linux desktop into a full-fledged personal entertainment system. Its capabilities include graphics and photo display, music management and playback, DVD playback, and, of course, TV capture and playback. The package may get its name from its television capabilities, but there's a lot more to it than that. It offers a built-in Digital Video Recorder (DVR) and integrates a customizable user-driven interface and underlying audio and video decoding and encoding capabilities with device support necessary to work with sound, images, movies, and TV programs. In fact, DVR boxes (including a suitably equipped PC running MythTV) can take analog or digital inputs and store or manipulate such data streams before sending them out to other components via numerous outputs: RCA, S-Video, Component video, Composite video, S/PDIF (the Sony-Philips digital interface format often used for handling multi-channel sound), and so forth.

The MythTV framework provides an alternative to manufactured Personal Video Recorders (PVRs) — and perhaps more directly, to Windows Media Center PCs — solutions currently available for sale in today's home entertainment marketplace. Not only does MythTV deliver much of the same capabilities, it also picks up where such pre-fabricated packages often leave off. Much of the motivation behind MythTV is to help users build an ultimate entertainment convergence box — a device that handles all the functions of several common though usually discrete communications or playback devices.

MythTV can do numerous things, including (but not limited to) the following: Store live television feeds directly to the disk volumes of your choosing, and burn captures in real time straight to DVD using compatible DVD-ROM burners. It can help you browse the Internet, peruse RSS news feeds, and obtain local program guide listings and detailed weather information from online sources. You can use it to provide background sound as an MP3 jukebox, to proffer itself as an Xmame arcade emulator, or display vivid eye candy in a slide show of digital images. You can use its Voice over IP (VoIP) phone and videophone modules to integrate Internet telephony devices and services. You can also combine multiple capture cards on multiple computers, and create varied client/server arrangements by setting up a MythTV master computer with multiple MythTV slave backends (making more entertainment available to multiple users and displays than you might have thought a PC-based environment could handle).

in this chapter

- ☑ What is MythTV?
- ☑ How MythTV compares to other PC-TV systems
- ☑ Basic MythTV requirements
- ☑ Hardware considerations

The Linux Package

In Linux, a software package is generally little more than a single archive containing one or more files and the necessary rules for installing the package contents on the target computer. The most commonly used utility for packages on the Linux platform is called the *Red Hat Package Manager,* and such files end in an .rpm extension. Unlike shrink-wrapped or downloaded software packages for the Windows platform, sometimes Linux packages are incomplete — that is, they rely on third-party dependencies developed independently from the software package contents. This is easily resolved through a comprehensive package management utility such as Yellow Dog Updater, Modified (YUM) in Fedora Core, or Yet Another Set-up Tool (YaST) under the SUSE distribution.

Given even a modest bill of materials, a well-designed MythTV PC can easily best the capabilities of most commercial Personal Video Recorder (PVR) gear, but the strongest lure to using the MythTV framework is the freedom of personal choice it offers: You are the one who gets to decide what does and doesn't go into your project build.

Let's be very clear about what MythTV definitely *is not*: MythTV is not intended as a fast and cost-effective replacement for TiVo, ReplayTV, or similar video recording units. MythTV only offers the software foundation upon which a DVR is built; the hardware elements are entirely up to you, the system architect and designer. After all is said and done, the bottom line on building a MythTV box from scratch will lose to commercial, turnkey white box options purely on a cost basis (although such devices usually require for-a-fee monthly subscriptions).

Commercial applications such as Windows Media Center Edition may claim advantages primarily in the areas of initial cost and ease of use, owing to volume of production and corporate sponsorship for research and development. That said, MythTV's open-source origins and licensing explains why it dominates the categories of flexibility, capability, and extensibility. MythTV is also the nexus for a broad and varied community of developers around the world. Plus — for those of you concerned about such things — there's no need to worry about voiding any warranties by tinkering under MythTV's hood (short of messing with system components and their individual warranties).

This chapter takes you through the fundamental concepts and components that define a digital video recorder, explaining how MythTV fits that definition and why it outshines all other forms of video cataloging and playback software and hardware products.

A Few Essential Terms

In the Linux world, jargon is an essential element of communication. Thus, understanding the significance of this potentially valuable appendix depends on decoding the jargon that makes up its very title:

- **Distro** is an abbreviation for *distribution*, or, more properly, *Linux distribution* or *code distribution*—namely, the collection of elements necessary to install, configure, and make Linux or related software run. Some distributions are binary (and thus target specific processor architectures); others are source code, and require access to the proper compiler or other code generators needed to create binary code; and still others include a mix of binary and source code elements. The distribution typically represents the kernel for the version of Linux you intend to install and run, and thus establishes the foundation for whatever type of system you wish to build. For this book, though other distributions are indeed feasible for use with MythTV, we concentrate on two specific Linux distributions: Fedora Core 5 and KnoppMyth, a specially tailored version of Knoppix.

- **Download** is the term normally used for a file, or collection of files, that you grab from a Web site or FTP server. Ultimately, all noncommercial Linux distributions may be obtained by grabbing their associated downloads (commercial versions usually require users to possess a valid account and password to download such for-a-fee software). The same thing is true for all other kinds of MythTV components, including the primary MythTV core, MythTV Plug-ins, and MythTV Themes, among numerous other elements you will copy to your machine in the process of installing, configuring, and, ultimately, extending MythTV on your system.

- **Docs** is short for documentation, but covers a multitude of vehicles typical in the Linux world. This includes the ubiquitous and often informative Q&A documents known as FAQs (lists of *Frequently Asked Questions*), plus another genre of technical advice and information known as the HOW-TO. It also includes a lot of manuals (*man pages* in Linux), references, guides, tutorials, and other kinds of information and advice to help turn novices into more experienced (and self-sufficient) Linuxheads.

Understanding DVRs

Before delving further into what defines MythTV, it is important to understand what a Digital Video Recorder does, for those not already "in the know." Often mistakenly used interchangeably with the term Personal Video Recorder (PVR), a Digital Video Recorder (DVR) describes a class of devices capable of recording from virtually any format and storing it digitally. DVRs represent a natural progression away from antiquated VCRs that were once key elements in a typical array of home theater equipment. PVRs share many of the same characteristics of a DVR: Most (but not necessarily all) of them make digital recordings, and many provide all kinds of program selection, scheduling, and playback functions as well. We prefer the term DVR because we look at it as a component of a larger-scale multimedia playback, capture, and management system, rather than focusing purely on the video (or TV) component of a multi-faceted set of media types.

Some of the advantages of a DVR over a VCR are immediate and clear: freedom of component selection (and from being tied to vendor-specific products and services); larger storage potential; the capability to capture from a wide variety of input sources; and the capability to write using a variety of formats and multiple types of media. Many of the remaining advantages are not so obvious, and reveal themselves only in how you leverage this technology and apply your knowledge.

The MythTV initiative is largely designed by and for the do-it-yourself community, and its freely modifiable open-source development grants creative license to anyone with enough know-how and drive for such an undertaking. The rewards come from the completion of a custom-tailored media center that rivals commercial offerings in terms of features and functionality — where it doesn't outright surpass them. In fact, roll-your-own motivation inspired MythTV's author, Isaac Richards, to begin the monumental task of developing the framework in April of 2002. If DIY is a staple acronym of your verbal diet, MythTV is definitely for you.

MythTV is essentially a suite of applications to aid you in designing and implementing a fully customized entertainment and communications center. Consider it enabling software for building the ultimate Home Theater Personal Computer (HTPC) — or, in the apt words of MythTV's author, a "mythical [home] convergence box." Video capture and playback is only part of what MythTV is about — and does not adequately define MythTV or address its full capabilities.

Convergence technology speaks to a tendency to merge consumer commodities that approach one another in feature sets or functionality to perform similar tasks inside a single system or framework. As an example, consider your cable service provider's communications infrastructure, whereby services are often rolled into a single so-called *triple-play package* that combines television, Internet, and telephony in a single offering. MythTV converges nicely by providing the building blocks necessary to engineer a perfectly capable communications center that can browse the Internet, check e-mail, play games, obtain current weather information, display digital telephone caller identification on screen, handle radio, movies, music, and TV programs, and much more. This enables users to harness common communications devices and find synergies that increase their usability.

The "myth" in MythTV reminds you of unfulfilled promises from key industry players to deliver uncompromised home entertainment convergence. Each vendor inevitably attempts to tie end users into its own proprietary platforms and services, often limiting how much freedom and flexibility users may exercise to enhance or personalize them. With MythTV, nearly everything is designed to be personalized, from themed interfaces to the modular plug-in framework used for optional features such as MythWeather and MythNews (RSS news feeds).

MythTV can perform many of the same duties as garden-variety commercial offerings, and some tasks that such products cannot, including the following:

- Pause, fast-forward, and rewind real-time television programs.
- Watch recordings at variable rates to adjust audio pitch.
- Analyze recorded shows and eliminate them from playback.
- Transcode live television feed into various formats.
- Remotely service content to multiple clients from a central server.
- Centralize programs to provide a common view to all clients.

- Administer system functions via a Web-enabled interface.

- Utilize multiple capture cards to perform multiple parallel recordings.

- Obtain free program guide information directly over the Internet.

- Provide optional functionality via an extensible plug-in framework.

- Remotely control the box using infrared and/or radio frequency.

- Display a fully customizable interface with a themed menu system.

- Provide Picture-in-Picture support for multiple tuner cards.

- Encode and decode various audio and video formats.

- Categorize and visualize various audio formats.

- Create a slide show from a gallery of pictures.

- Enable phone and videophone capability (SIP).

As of this writing, the current version of MythTV supports the following plug-ins:

- **MythBrowser** — A small browser window module

- **MythDVD** — A DVD-management module

- **MythGame** — A frontend for the Xmame arcade emulator

- **MythGallery** — An image gallery management module

- **MythMusic** — A music player collection management module

- **MythNews** — An RSS news feed reader module

- **MythPhone** — A SIP phone and video phone module

- **MythVideo** — A video management module

- **MythWeather** — A local weather forecast module

- **MythWeb** — A Web interface module for MythTV

This book aims to bring MythTV to a much broader audience of do-it-yourself hobbyists and weekend project warriors, based largely upon information available from the online MythTV community and the personal experiences and insights of the contributing authors. Particularly useful resources that make this book what it is come from the MythTV project Web site and the documented experiences of Jarod Wilson, maintainer of perhaps the most comprehensive MythTV HOW-TO coverage to date, and the keen insight of HTPCnews.com moderator Matt Wright. You may want to peruse the online copy of Wilson's Fedora-centric MythTV installation guide (the same one that serves as a basis for this book). Point your favorite browser to http://wilsonet.com/mythtv/fcmyth.php for details.

How MythTV Compares to Other PC-TV Systems

When put under the microscope, innumerable differences between MythTV and alternative PVR solutions pop up. Only the most distinctive differences are covered here, to help you differentiate among available DVR offerings.

Apples and oranges are the currency of distinction for a side-by-side comparison of MythTV and the many similar (though entirely different) alternative media center implementations. In the case of MythTV, this means only the third-party add-on software; that is, neither operating system nor hardware are included. Barring any obvious architectural differences (such as the well-defined client/server architecture underlying the MythTV framework), MythTV is similar to Windows Media Center Edition in that it provides additional support for multimedia playback to an existing platform (such as Linux or Windows). Openly available on the market are complete solutions such as TiVo or ReplayTV, although their continued operation requires periodic subscription fees. A handful of these units are detailed in the paragraphs that follow.

First and foremost, commercial solutions such as TiVo and ReplayTV generally involve a one-time cost to purchase the relevant PVR or DVR hardware. Next follows a subscription service fee for the duration of account ownership (either an annual fee or monthly billing). Overall costs must be calculated on the basis of initial hardware costs, plus service charges over its useful lifetime. Remember too that you're explicitly tied to the hardware choices that the vendor makes, and that any DIY upgrades are likely to void warranty coverage.

However, a prefab unit offers tremendous savings in time and expense over the careful research, system assembly, and software configuration necessary to implement a working MythTV system. By reading this book you express interest in this fast-growing home entertainment sector, but you may not be inherently disposed to devote free time to building your own system.

In addition, you must recognize that in and of itself, MythTV is an incomplete solution. It's merely a framework for building a multimedia home entertainment system, and lacks any of the hardware you'll need to finish the job. Like Windows XP Media Center Edition (MCE), MythTV provides a viable basis for personal entertainment systems. As such, it can't compare directly to more focused products such as the TiVo and ReplayTV units.

Windows MCE can't begin to compare to MythTV on many levels. First, MythTV is free to anybody who wants to download, own, or redistribute it, for any number of installations. Second, MythTV is merely a third-party extension to an existing Linux desktop environment. Windows MCE is an entire operating system (Windows XP, to be exact) with various multimedia underpinnings and a graphical user interface overlay. Third, end-users are at liberty to modify, compile, and redistribute MythTV — as with KnoppMyth, a Knoppix CD-ROM based distribution.

On the upside, a self-made MythTV DVR system is more rewarding beyond anything a TiVo, ReplayTV, or other commercial unit can offer. The enriching experience of learning a new operating system, playing with new hardware, and using existing technology in creative new ways is a reward all by itself. The satisfaction of building something truly useful and beneficial for your entertainment center is another.

There is no restriction on hardware: You have the freedom to build massive storage volumes of virtually any kind (internal and external), a choice of networking equipment (wireless or wired), and the freedom to pick and choose precisely what components go into your system build. Because it's your show, you get to call the shots.

Again, the downside is made crystal clear in regard to time spent on research, building the system, and working out bugs or problems before your MythTV system is ready to be put to work.

HACKmyth represents one of few ready-made solutions for MythTV, and further expands upon the notion of convergence technology by incorporating a variety of wireless home automation features as an essential ingredient. At present, HACKmyth Version 3 is out of production and into the mainstream market as a solution to home automation control. The HACKmyth product line features many mainstream products, including a handful of plug-in appliance modules, and is one of only a few outlets for prefab MythTV systems.

Potential customers are directed to the vendor Web site (`www.hackmyth.com`) for additional information.

Freevo is one of few products that compares directly to MythTV in that it too is a third-party extension to the Linux working environment. Though the project appears quite mature, a quick browse through the features list indicates that the complexity of the Freevo code base leaves MythTV unequalled. For instance, there currently appears to be no means to configure multiple recording units as used in MythTV's master and slave backend systems (although it does support multiple cards).

Curious readers are directed to the Freevo vendor Web site at `http://freevo.source forge.net`.

Some MythTV System Terminology

- **Frontend Systems** — The MythTV frontend system delivers content and control to the user (see Figure 1-1). It's the colorful interface that provides a window to access all configurable aspects of MythTV appearance, behavior, and control. This is usually referred to as the On-Screen Display (OSD) or simply the menu system.

  Configuration settings are accessed through a hierarchy of entries categorized by similar functionality. This lends MythTV a more-or-less universally accepted interface that makes transitioning to MythTV from similar video recording solutions relatively simple. The frontend application also serves as a launch pad for MythTV plug-ins, and provides a modular and adaptive framework for customizers.

- **Backend Systems** — Single capture card configurations are their own master backend and are simply called backend systems. When multiple tuner cards are involved, a master/slave relationship is established in an abstracted layer that operates between the MythTV frontend (user interface) and the actual video codecs. (Codec, a combination of the words coder and decoder, describes an application capable of encoding a stream or signal-based communications.)

  The backend system is responsible for the timely scheduling of recording tasks, obtaining and cataloging DataDirect or XMLTV program guides, and handling the complex interaction between user interface and hardware.

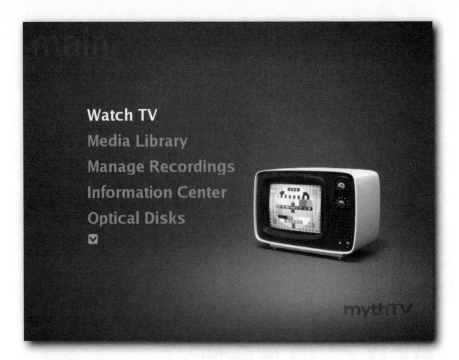

FIGURE 1-1: The MythTV frontend

- **Master Backend Systems** — A Master Backend System (MBE) coordinates the collective scheduling and interoperation of backend systems using multiple tuner cards. It may reside on a single machine with multiple cards or exist as one machine on a network with other tuner cards. Behind the scenes, a scheduler on the MBE maintains a running track record of idle states throughout the entire MythTV network of Slave Backends (SBEs). The MBE then delegates recording tasks among the available SBE systems.

  This lends scalability to MythTV capture systems whereby multiple tuner cards work together to record multiple sources following varying schedules. This also enables SBE systems to be awakened or put to sleep at the MBE's sole discretion. Using MythTV in a multiple capture system topology requires Network Interface Cards (NICs) with Wake-on-LAN (WoL) capability to enable remote initialization and shutdown, so plan in advance.

  This unique configuration is especially beneficial to consumers of multiple video feed types, such as satellite and cable television, VCR and DVD players, and the like.

  The MythTV Master backend architecture is detailed in the following wiki: `http://wiki.cs.uiuc.edu/cs427/MythTV+Architecture+Styles+and+Patterns`

- **Slave Backend Systems** — Slave Backend (SBE) systems are units designated to batch recording jobs in keeping with the MBE master schedule. These units can hibernate to conserve energy and heat output by exploiting lapses in activity until the MBE wakes a subservient SBE for its scheduled recording duty.

As stated, NICs with WoL functionality are required for multiple capture system configurations.

The MythTV Slave backend architecture is detailed in the following wiki: `http://wiki.cs.uiuc.edu/cs427/MythTV+Architecture+Styles+and+Patterns`

Basic MythTV Requirements

Proper research is vital to ensuring timely and efficient MythTV construction. Poor planning and inadequate product information will certainly lead to unnecessary delays and hang-ups. To ensure a relatively trouble-free experience, make sure that all components are chosen on the basis of possessing workable Linux driver software and documented reliability.

As stated on the MythTV Web site (`http://mythtv.org`), the absolute bare-minimum requirements to get a functional base system up and running are as follows:

- **500 MHz or better CPU** (low-cost AMD Sempron, XP, and Duron processors are suitable)

- **TV tuner or capture card that supports Video4Linux (V4L)** — The Hauppauge line of PVR cards has a great reputation for working well with Linux, and comes highly recommended as the tuner of choice. As a basic model, the Hauppauge PVR-150MCE Original Equipment Manufacturer (OEM) edition offers great value at minimal cost by ditching retail packaging, the remote control, and cables. OEM products generally pass savings onto you, the consumer, by skimping on the accessories or packaging, which makes a great alternative to paying full price for extra features you neither want nor need.

Video4Linux supplies the software interface between the operating system and the encoder card under Linux. Online lists detail the currently supported hardware for V4L use, but you must establish a mailing list account to view this information. Join the `www.redhat.com` Video4Linux Mailing List at `https://listman.redhat.com/mailman/listinfo/video4linux-list`. After you sign up, you can read the (private) Red Hat Video4Linux Mailing List at `www.redhat.com/mailman/private/video4linux-list/`.

The following wiki provides information about V4L and compatible hardware under its Supported Hardware heading: `www.linuxtv.org/v4lwiki/index.php/Main_Page`

- **Compatible video card with TV-out**

- **XMLTV for obtaining program information** (`http://membled.com/work/apps/xmltv/`)

- **MySQL for storing program information** (www.mysql.com/) — MySQL is a reliable, fast database that supports a symbolic query language. It's designed to store all kinds of information, and enjoys good market share across various multiple platforms (especially Linux, but versions for many other operating systems are also available). MySQL is integral to MythTV's operation — for storing program guide listings, among other information — but its ease of installation makes setup a snap. Consult your chosen Linux distribution documentation about package management, and for instructions on adding MySQL to your system's runtime environment.

- **FreeType for rendering on-screen fonts** (www.freetype.org/)

- **Qt** (www.trolltech.com/) The Qt class library is a cross-platform collection of functions and definitions for developing graphical user interfaces on both Linux and Windows platforms. Qt is required for building many applications that tie into the MythTV framework.

- **LAME (libmp3lame) for compressing audio streams** (http://lame.source forge.net)

Using MythMusic on a MythTV system also requires the following libraries and applications:

- MAD MP3 decoder and ID3 library (www.mp3dev.org/mp3/)

- Ogg Vorbis high-quality MP3 alternative format (www.vorbis.com/)

- FLAC lossless encoding of audio streams (http://flac.sourceforge.net/)

- libcdaudio for obtaining FreeDB information (http://libcdaudio.source forge.net/)

- cdparanoia for ripping CD information (www.xiph.org/paranoia/)

Not listed on the MythTV Web site, but absolutely required for a working MythTV installation, are the following:

- **Current version of a Linux distribution** (kernel version 2.6.x or better) — See the section "Suggested Linux Distributions" later in this chapter for more information on selecting a distribution.

- **Linux Infra-Red Remote Control Daemon** — If you want to use a remote control with your MythTV system, you'll also need the Linux Infra-Red Remote Control Daemon (LIRC). LIRC supplies the Linux interface to IrDA technology found in electronic component remote controls. Visit the Linux Infra-Red Remote Control Daemon Web site at www.lirc.org/.

- **IVTV or BTTV driver support (card-specific)** — See the following sections for more information on IVTV and BTTV.

IVTV MPEG-2 CODEC

The IVTV project goal, as stated in the IVTV FAQ, is to "provide a 'clean room' Linux Open Source driver implementation for video capture cards based on the iCompression iTVC15 or Conexant CX23415/CX23416 MPEG Codec." In short, IVTV drivers rank among the best and most widely used MPEG-2 codecs for Linux. A lot of the better capture-card products on the market bundle and use the IVTV driver software as part of their product offerings. See the following sites for more information:

- IVTV Vendor Web Site — `http://ivtv.sourceforge.net`
- IVTV Product Support Page — `http://ivtvdriver.org/index.php/Supported_hardware`
- IVTV TV-Out How-To — `http://ivtv.writeme.ch/tiki-index.php?page=TvOutHowto`

BTTV MPEG-2 CODEC

Another popular driver solution caters to the BrookTree Technologies BT848 and BT878 chipsets, both of which are known to work fairly well under Linux. Driver support appears in the 2.2.0 kernel version of Linux and continues to show up in the latest 2.6.x versions. Many popular vendor cards use this chipset; consult online resources for compatibility listings according to exact make and model.

The following list shows cards known to be compatible with the BTTV driver:

- Euresys Picolo Tetra
- Spirit TV Tuner
- AVerMedia AVerTV DVB-T 771
- AVerMedia AVerTV DVB-T 761
- MATRIX Vision Sigma-SQ
- MATRIX Vision Sigma-SLC
- APAC Viewcomp 878(AMAX)
- DVICO FusionHDTV DVB-T Lite
- V-Gear MyVCD
- Super TV Tuner
- Tibet Systems "Progress DVR" CS16
- Kodicom 4400R (master)
- Kodicom 4400R (slave)

To learn about new hardware that may have been added recently, please check the following BTTV-supported cards list: `www.linuxtv.org/v4lwiki/index.php/CardlistPre.BTTV`.

For additional information on BTTV, try the following sites:

- BTTV Web Site — `http://linux.bytesex.org/v4l2/bttv.html`
- BTTV Wiki — `www.linuxtv.org/v4lwiki/index.php/Bttv_devices_%28bt848%2C_bt878%29`
- Enabling support for your Bt8×8 hardware in Linux — `www.linux.com/howtos/BTTV/hw.shtml`
- Linux BTTV Video How-To — `www.faqs.org/docs/Linux-mini/BTTV.html#ss4.5`
- Linux BTTV Audio How-To — `www.linuxtv.org/v4lwiki/index.php/Btaudio`

MythTV Packages

MythTV is bundled in a myriad of package schemes, primarily as a base set of packages (`mythplugins`, `myththemes`, and the `mythtv` itself) to be installed on an existing Linux distribution, though specialty distributions roll a functional operating system with MythTV specifically tailored to Linux video capture. Because this book explicitly deals with MythTV as a package system, with a walkthrough for specific Linux operating system setup and operation, alternative options are mentioned only in passing.

And You May Also Want . . .

The following elements are not required, but are highly recommended additions:

- **Xmame, Xmess, and Arcade Emulation** — Both Xmame and Xmess are applications adapted from an original pair of arcade game emulation programs, the Multiple Arcade Machine Emulator (MAME) and Multi Emulator Super System (MESS). Xmame and Xmess are born of the long-lost arcade game nostalgia and nurture the inner child within every geek. Using the MythGames plug-in, Xmame functionality provides endless hours of low-resolution entertainment. The Xmame and Xmess Web site is `http://x.mame.net/`.
- **MythTV Upcoming CGI Script** — The MythTV Upcoming CGI Script details current recordings scheduled under MythTV without requiring connection to the `mythbackend` daemon process. Queries are made directly to the MySQL database kept by MythTV. Though not essential to the operation of MythTV, this script does merit one-time mention as a useful potential addition to any MythTV system. The MythTV Upcoming CGI Script Web site is `www.webdez.net/hacks/mythtv-upcoming`.

Hardware Considerations

A typical DVR system need not be a formidable powerhouse in terms of performance. For example, in certain TiVo boxes the power plant is nothing more than a relatively paltry 50 to 250 MHz PowerPC processor with a measly 16 to 32 MB of on-board memory. The key concept here is the continental divide between a desktop computer and a DVR solution; a DVR uses a subset of typical desktop hardware resources. Depending upon desired quality of capture and playback, a core clock speed of 500 MHz is adequate, but 1 GHz or better is preferable. Thus, it's entirely feasible to cobble a MythTV system together from remnants of yesteryear's technology.

As a general rule, buying the latest in advanced hardware ingredients when working with Linux does not sit high on the list of priorities. That's because the driver development cycle for the open-source community faces a different set of challenges than does the Windows community. Some hardware vendors closely guard the ingredients to their secret sauces, and the very nature of open source violates their rights to such secrecy. Occasionally, though, a vendor does show support either directly or by indirect participation (providing closed-source binary-only drivers), or driver support is simply reverse-engineered into existence (as is the case with forcedeth Ethernet drivers for Linux).

That said, many recent distributions of Linux support a surprising number of new technologies without major omissions, challenging this notion. However, just because support is there doesn't justify the costs that some of these items can involve. We recommend taking a cost-benefit trade-off approach in picking hardware components, spending most on what matters most to you, and cutting back on things that may not be as important (such as skimping a bit on hard disks to spend more on a more capable graphics card, for example).

MythTV boasts support for many PVR cards from various manufacturers, as well as support for High-Definition TV (HDTV) and Digital Video Broadcasting (DVB; European) capture cards (since release version 0.17). The tuner card should do most of the heavy lifting, so we recommend that you purchase a card that provides on-board MPEG-2 decoding. This way, the CPU is better utilized for auxiliary system tasks that are less subject to interruptions from the video encoding and decoding processes.

Do Your Hardware Homework

It's always smart to research hardware specifications thoroughly before you make any purchases. That's the best way to ensure minimal fuss and downtime during the construction phase. One of the most important component choices you'll face is your TV tuner card (or cards, if you also decide to build in over-the-air HDTV capability); among other choices you must consider are regional dependencies that relate to broadcast technologies and signals (such as NTSC in North America versus PAL/SECAM throughout much of the rest of the world). Network cards, though non-essential, contain chipsets that may not be identified or even supported under Linux — especially where 802.11 b and g wireless gear is concerned. That's why a short but important list of resources devoted to this subject appears at the end of this chapter.

Several online resources such as the PVR Hardware Database provide short listings of MythTV-compatible hardware builds from various users. Google is a huge treasure trove of MythTV user experiences, so this is but one of many resources you might wish to consult: http://pvrhw.goldfish.org/tiki-pvrhwdb.php.

Well-informed research, conducted well in advance of any purchase, is vital to successful construction of a MythTV system. Newcomers to Linux will soon discover the tremendous learning curve involved in configuring, building, and maintaining a functional system, but those who persevere will also discover the rewards of a fully customizable operating system. Recent distributions cater to the curious Windows user base by streamlining and simplifying the installation process and creating graphical interfaces for virtually every task. However, actual administration of a Linux box differs vastly from Windows.

Keep your general design scheme in mind and observe how that influences the hardware choices you make. While horizontal cases fit nicely amid entertainment center gear, they can prevent using oversized components or those that require extra room. For example, try cramming a passively cooled GeForce 6600 card with overarching heat pipes such as the Gigabyte GV-N66256DP into a slim profile case such as the Silverstone LC04 and you'll immediately understand what we're getting at when you realize you can't fit the cover over the heat pipes. Plenty of add-in cards come in Low-Profile (LP) formats that work well within horizontal cases, or where space may be at a premium for one reason or another. For example, Hauppauge offers the PVR-150-MCE LP in a tiny form factor.

Make your most essential hardware purchases to meet compatibility and consumption requirements. When you find yourself weighing certain options, determine the most essential capability you seek from your own personally tailored MythTV system. Which is more relevant to your needs: extreme processing capability or expansive storage? Do you want to record one or more programs while watching another program (which requires multiple tuner cards, or a dual tuner card such as the Hauppauge PVR-500MCE), or is a single tuner in your system enough to meet your needs?

In addition, consider carefully any features you may not need but for which you may still pay extra. As an example, the Hauppauge PVR-150MCE card doubles as an FM radio tuner in addition to on-board MPEG-2 decoding. Don't need FM radio? Get the new Hauppauge model that comes without it, and save $18 or more. Tuner cards arrive in a variety of configurations at distributors and retail outlets; some have multiple tuners per card, others lack integrated audio encoding. Know what you want, and what you're buying.

Occasionally, a given tuner card is sold in OEM form. This means you pay only for the bare essentials; none of the mark-up for retail packaging, accessory parts, and sometimes cabling (where applicable). Again as an example, the aforementioned PVR-150MCE from Hauppauge ships in OEM form, minus the remote, cables, and adapter found in the more expensive retail version. The price difference may be negligible, as you'll have to buy another remote control, but that's a plus if you think the stock Hauppauge remote is too restrictive for your needs (indeed, we did, and opted for SnapStream's Firefly and Logitech's Harmony 680 remotes instead).

For ambitious system builders operating on less restrictive budgets, options that offer comprehensive airflow management, functional case design and construction, and acoustic noise reducing materials are plentiful. Conversely, you can choose a case that doesn't integrate much acoustic dampening, and add in such materials as you build your system. For example, Antec carries a line of NoiseKiller products—thin silicon rubber screw gaskets and shims molded to fit specific fan diameters (80 and 120 mm), or standard ATX power supplies that, when installed properly between component and case, provide superb sound deadening.

Likewise, various types of sound-dampening foam pads are available to help limit noise from your MythTV PC. Acousti Products offers various noise-dampening products, including a dense, adhesive-backed foam sheeting called AcoustiPack that comes in various kits, some designed for the end-user to cut to fit a PC case, others pre-cut to fit specific case makes and models. The company also offers ultra-quiet fans, fan mounting kits, and even cases with AcoustiPack dampening already installed. Visit them at www.acoustiproducts.com.

Visit Mike Chin's outstanding Silent PC Review Web site (www.silentpcreview.com) for more information about quiet PC components and good noise-dampening products and techniques.

Component Recommendations

In the sections that follow, we walk through the key components you'll want to consider—and ultimately, select—for your MythTV PC. Though we may mention specific vendors with whom we've had good experiences, don't be bashful about doing your own research to come up with other options. You'll find sites such as HTPCnews.com, PCAlchemy.com, Quietpcusa.com, EndPCNoise.com, Subzeropcs.com, and Siliconacoustics.com all to be of great value in helping you narrow down your options because all cater to the home theater and/or quiet PC buyer.

Computer Cases

Many contributing factors distinguish a good case design from a bad one, and these factors are unique to your MythTV build. Motherboard form factors such as ATX and mini-ITX require entirely different chassis with completely incompatible dimensions, for example. It might make more sense to consider specialty components such as slim-line optical drives and low-profile memory where mini-ITX dimensions are concerned, but the premium for these specialized components may not appeal to budget-oriented consumers. Therefore, the more standard ATX form factor makes the most sense from an economic standpoint, accommodates more types and quantities of hardware, and yields the most abundant off-the-shelf equipment for timely, cost-effective system builds.

Antec (www.antec.com) is a leading manufacturer and innovative producer of computer-related hardware, encompassing everything from consumer-grade to enterprise-level enclosures, power supplies, and an increasing variety of silencing accessories. We've had great results using the Antec P-180 as a workstation, and it would make a formidable master-backend server for multi-client environments. The P-180 has removable drive trays for 3.5" magnetic drives and bolt-on slide rails for 5.25" opticals and accessory panels, enabling quick and easy access for maintenance and parts replacement.

Ahanix (www.ahanix.com/), maker of high-end High Definition TVs (HDTVs), offers several sleek and attractive cases for home theater and media center components. The Ahanix products run in the medium to high price range. Its D.Vine 5 case — what a great name! — features all aluminum construction and comes with a Vacuum Fluorescent Display (VFD), 300-watt ATX power supply, and two silent case fans.

SilverStone (www.silverstonetek.com), a major Taiwanese specialty case manufacturer, has product lines offering many entertainment-center-related aluminum case designs that natively provide excellent noise management while maintaining fair thermal properties. Their design characteristics also include mid- to low-profile heights, black and silver aluminum colors, and optional VFD read-outs, ideal for placement within an arena of shelf-kept entertainment equipment.

Also noteworthy is the thoughtful planning and careful consideration evident in the layout of SilverStone's LASCALA (LC) series lay-flat structures, which encompass a wide variety of designs. This particular line is well-suited to HTPC builds with low height requirements.

Although they are ideal cases for inclusion with any HTPC build, the SilverStone line carries quite a premium price tag. Base models sporting the bare minimum of features can easily go for $200 and up.

Table 1-1 provides a summary of case manufacturers.

Origen AE Technology (www.origenae.com), formerly Uneed International, is a leading manufacturer of high-end aluminum cases, specializing in HTPC enclosures encompassing a variety of designs and features. Most notable is the x15e all-aluminum case with touch-screen Vacuum Fluorescent Display (VFD) panel. The only downside to some of these units is that they are subject to inadequate ventilation issues, and all run at least $200 and up for basic models (the x15e costs $600 and up).

Fremont, California-based Casetronic (www.casetronic.com) designs and produces a variety of passive electronic components and specialty enclosures. Particularly worthy of mention is the Travla line of small form factor hobbyist enclosures fabricated entirely from aluminum. A unit such as the Travla C137 maintains the professional finish of a modern entertainment device, making it right at home on your television stand or bookshelf.

Table 1-1   Brief Summary of Case Manufacturers

Low-End	Mid-Range	High-End
Antec	Ahanix	Ahanix
Casetronic	Antec	SilverStone
	SilverStone	Origen

Motherboards

In terms of compatibility, Linux is mainly concerned with chipsets. Support relies on vendor cooperation so that Linux driver developers may properly implement hardware chipset support in the mainstream distribution channels. Motherboard chipsets are generally very well supported, so expect to find few if any obstacles in the path to a clean operating system installation. A few instances where problems may arise might occur when older Linux distributions are used on newer motherboards, or on motherboards using chipsets too new to find driver support in stable Linux releases.

The most significant decision is likely to be that of size: how big should the motherboard be? This should be a recurring consideration when picking and choosing MythTV components. Motherboard dimensions are governed by the overall space that the form factor makes available, or that the case chosen dictates. Those opting for small form factor components will find the most challenging experience when researching and pricing relevant parts as compared to builders who choose standard desktop PC components.

Advanced Technology Extended (ATX)

The most ubiquitous of all is the time-tested, industry standard Advanced Technology eXtended (ATX) form factor. As the oldest of all current motherboard types, the ATX design has experienced a rich history of evolution and enhancement. ATX is the de facto standard in motherboard design for the do-it-yourself consumer, and offers the most options in terms of on-board features and functions.

Setups requiring multiple tuner cards will most likely demand the use of this large layout. Lack of adequate airflow or sandwiching two tuner cards together is a quick shortcut to a system meltdown, however, so ventilation is an important concern when designing and building such a system. Optimal airflow may be achieved by placing cards in every other slot and introducing proper ventilation into the case design.

MicroATX (μATX)

Considered a smaller sibling to the original ATX form factor, microATX is popular among high-volume and low-volume desktop vendors alike owing to its smaller size (9.6" × 9.6") and relatively low cost. A smaller size enables the μATX to be shoehorned into a variety of small and mid-tower cases, some no bigger than VCR units or 8-bit Nintendo entertainment systems.

To achieve its mildly conservative dimensions, the μATX layout skimps on the number of socket types it provides (usually omitting on-board headers and extension cables for extended port availability). Small dimensions also leaves room only for a smaller number of PCI slots (commonly three instead of five) or cutting the number of Universal Serial Bus (USB) ports in half. This can pose design challenges for configurations that require multiple tuner cards along with add-in sound cards and other peripherals.

Specialty power supplies with smaller dimensions than typical ATX units are marketed solely for the μATX segment. These units generally maintain the same peak power output as the larger PSUs.

Mini-ITX

Among the newest of PC form factors, the mini-ITX layout is by far the smallest, measuring only 170 mm by 170 mm (approximately the width of ordinary printer paper). This form factor addresses a variety of needs for targeting embedded applications, most notably in the areas of low power consumption, low noise output, and minimal thermal signature (in fact, several early models lacked active CPU cooling up to the 1 GHz mark).

Developed by VIA technologies, the mini-ITX form factor has seen tremendous success in the hobbyist sector, primarily for home entertainment designs. Those tiny dimensions promise amazing potential in terms of the features thoughtfully included in such limited space, and in terms of creative case design and use. VIA markets a wide array of functionality neatly tucked into each ITX board, and some even sport on-board video processing with several types of video output ports provided.

Popular and creative cases for the mini-ITX board include gutted humidors, RC cars, vintage toasters, and even mock-ups of R2D2 (of Star Wars fame) and Bender the Robot (of Futurama sitcom fame). And this illustrates only a small part of the potential for new and clever uses for mini-ITX components.

A variety of low-profile components suited to the cramped environments of mini-ITX builds are available on the market. Everything from low-profile memory and processor heatsink/fan combinations to add-in cards and storage drives provide every means necessary to construct a functional mini-ITX DVR.

Processors

Standard-definition units emphasize lower demand on subsystem components, and therefore require less expensive parts to build and maintain. An AMD 3200+ or Intel P4 3.2 GHz core is pure overkill for anything but a high-definition build, so consider reallocating some of that expense toward a better tuner card or a PCI-based sound card. Higher clock speeds can contribute to higher bit rates for encoding audio or video, or enable higher-resolution capture and display, however, so buying cheap does have trade-offs.

Here are some key points of reference regarding CPUs in MythTV systems (taken from the MythTV Hardware page):

- A PIII/733 MHz system can encode one video stream using the MPEG-4 codec using 480 × 480 capture resolution. This does not permit watching live TV, but it does permit encoding video during capture, and then watching it later.

- One developer states that his AMD Athlon XP 1800+ system can *almost* encode two MPEG-4 video streams and watch one program simultaneously.

- A PIII/800 MHz system with 512 MB of RAM can encode one video stream using the RTjpeg codec with 480 × 480 capture resolution and play it back simultaneously, thereby permitting viewing of live TV.

- A dual Celeron/450 MHz can view a 480 × 480 MPEG-4/3300 Kbps file created on a different system with 30 percent CPU usage.

- A P4 2.4 GHz machine can encode two 3300 Kbps 480 × 480 MPEG-4 files and simultaneously serve content to a remote frontend.

AMD Semprons in their various socket types (Socket A/462, Socket 754) make an excellent economical choice for a basic MythTV box. They're inexpensive, provide high clock speeds, and are widely available. Selecting a Socket A/462-based motherboard is highly cost-effective. While the chipsets that accompany these boards are well supported under Linux, you should also expect fewer features and less power than motherboards with newer socket types would deliver. Socket 754 boards offer fairly recent technologies and newer features than socket 462 models, but they're old enough now that you should only expect them to deliver fair to mid-range capabilities.

The latest classes of chipsets and features are clearly present in Socket 939 motherboards for AMD processors, and LGA 775 for high-end Intel Pentium processors. All the latest development happens here, where bleeding-edge home entertainment features keep creeping into mainstream product lines offered by top-tier manufacturers. The top-of-the-line AMD and Intel processors that conform to sockets 939 and LGA 775, respectively, offer the highest clock cycles, best utilized in high-definition multi-user environments on MythTV systems.

While 64-bit computing offers little (if no) benefit to a DVR box, the nice thing about going with Linux and 64-bit processors is the freedom to compile kernel and system utility support in 32- or 64-bit modes. The performance advantage is only gained in applications specifically designed to take advantage of 64-bit registers and enhancements, which are few and far between on the desktop front. There is little evidence supporting the notion that 64-bit × 86 computing is inherently faster than 32-bit equivalents where such programmatic consideration is not involved. However, this problem will soon be academic, validating the forward-thinking choice of buying 64-bit now.

Memory

Installing copious onboard RAM will not necessarily benefit every individual MythTV build. For many applications, standard-definition television leaves memory in excess of 1 GB mostly unused. While there is certainly no harm in having maximum headroom, the added expense for unused memory might be better spent elsewhere on other system components.

Evidence of system performance in which all memory resources are completely consumed might indicate problems outside the hardware realm. For example, this might point to incorrect configuration settings, incompatible hardware, or inefficient usage. In fact, as long as you follow our basic recommendations you should be okay for memory as long as Linux and MythTV software doesn't go through too many major revisions in the meantime.

Unless your build is going to handle high-definition TV, 512 MB is sufficient for standard-definition TV (SDTV) playback. Be sure to choose memory that's suited to the Front-Side Bus (FSB) on your motherboard and your processor. For example, VIA C3/Eden mainboards sporting VIA's own CLE/266 Northbridge requires PC-133 Synchronous Dynamic RAM (SDRAM), a much older technology (though, perversely, more expensive) than the PC-3200 Double Data Rate RAM (DDR) used by current AMD chipset designs, or the PC-3200 DDR2 that most modern Intel chipsets demand.

Standard-definition systems can be equipped with a wide range of memory options — from budget-oriented Semprons and Celerons to mid-range Athlon and Pentium 4 cores. Such processors generally use Double Data Rate (DDR) SDRAM, which offers better performance than the older SDRAM technology. This translates into better overall responsiveness. DDR is available in a wide variety of capacities, from 256 MB up to 2 GB, with varying timing ratings, such as Column Address Select/Strobe (CAS) latency timing, that factor into part costs.

Memory timings determine how quickly memory cells may be loaded with fresh information, how quickly such information is refreshed and accessed, and how quickly the module can establish a ready state for the next operation. This impacts the rest of the input/output subsystem directly, much of which relies heavily on the current contents of main memory.

Standard memory timings for DDR modules usually sit somewhere around 3-5-5-8, a modest collection of values. High-performance DDR modules boast latency ratings of 2-3-2-6, and the absolute best is 2-2-2-5. DDR2 sports higher timing values, but the operation of DDR2 is entirely different from DDR. At any rate, low latency ratings for DDR2 are around 3-2-2-8, plus or minus a few points. DDR2 memory is currently used exclusively in recent Pentium 4 models, and does not affect systems with AMD processors.

While there's no rule that states low-latency parts will provide substantial performance gains, they are relevant for high-definition systems where high bandwidth, heavier encoding/decoding rates, and more data to handle puts more of a premium on system speeds. Your mileage will certainly vary.

TV/Capture Cards

Most of the underlying magic happens at the hardware level in the capture card (aka the *tuner card*, because of its ability to tune into specific channel frequencies). The capture card functions as a tuner to select among the different analog frequencies that make up television channels. A capture is then broken down from its native line-resolution format into a digital pixilated format that a modern computer can handle. To ensure best picture quality, this is one area where you shouldn't skimp on cost by buying bargain-bin hardware.

MythTV operates in two basic modes: software and hardware video encoding. Your choice of capture card influences this mode of operation directly, which may be classified according to what kind of encoding functionality the capture card can deliver. These two classes are called software encoding and hardware encoding.

Software encoding relies entirely on the CPU and underlying resources to process multimedia data. This offers the most cost-effective approach but also inflicts the heaviest performance penalty. Other system tasks will compete for available resources, all vying for slices of processor time to run alongside one another.

Software-based solutions usually occur on systems with motherboards that sport integrated video solutions or on video capture cards that lack vital Digital-to-Analog Converter (DAC) capabilities. For optimal performance, figure that one gigahertz in CPU clock speed (1 GHz) is required for each tuner or capture card that uses software MPEG-2 encoding.

Hardware-based solutions employ on-board processors to handle the heavy lifting for the analog conversion process instead of off-loading that burdensome task to the CPU itself. Spotty playback is indicative of an overtaxed processor, and is most apparent on systems that support multiple users or a multitude of system processes.

Therefore, our strongest recommendation is to make a proper video card selection. Better cards handle on-board MPEG-2 encoding and decoding (sometimes called *compression hardware*) functionality, freeing up system resources for the other tasks vital to regular system operation. Even TiVo and ReplayTV include hardware MPEG-2 encoders in their units; buying hardware with the right encoder chips is invariably worth the extra cost. A quality Hauppauge PVR-150 sells for around $70 or $80 in its retail packaging, and even less for the OEM version, which skimps on accessories and packaging. Likewise, the Hauppauge PVR-500 costs upwards of $150 online in its retail packaging. These are all excellent MPEG-2-based tuner cards, with software-based tuner cards starting around $40 for entry models.

Capture cards are available in a wide variety of designs. You choose from numerous internal and external models, from PCI add-in cards to USB and FireWire conversion units. But only a small number of these are known to work well both with Linux and MythTV itself. Several online resources name products that work well with MythTV. Thus, we urge you to consult the following resources to help you select a worthy tuner card:

- Red Hat Video4Linux Mailing List: `https://listman.redhat.com/mailman/listinfo/video4linux-list`

- Waikato Linux Users Group TV Tuner Cards: `www.wlug.org.nz/TvTunerCards`

- LinuxTV V4L Wiki survey of cards in use now: `www.linuxtv.org/v4lwiki/index.php/List_survey_of_cards_in_use_now`

Key Tuner and Capture Cards Considerations

Early TV tuner and capture cards had a miniscule 320 × 240 frame size, which offers relatively little picture element data. Contemporary cards can handle much higher resolutions — most commonly, 640 × 480 and 720 × 480. Regular coaxial television occurs at the highest resolution, 720 × 480, with higher-quality signals going well beyond. Modern capture cards should easily handle at least 720 × 480. Digital tuner cards receive a digitized signal in the form of binary MPEG-2 streams, obviating the need for on-board encoding, as the stream comes encoded right from the source.

However, not all cards truly support the 720 × 480 resolution size, and instead cheat by stretching a 640 × 480 image to match the larger size. Though largely historic, these less capable cards should be avoided, and the only real way to know whether you're getting a quality upscale or low-grade stretched image is to compare side-by-side captures of still frame high-definition video.

The following list shows known good capture cards compatible with V4L:

- Hauppauge Nova-T WinFast 2000 XP

- WinTV-PCI-FM model 619

- Plextor ConvertX PX-TV402U

- Hauppauge WinTV-DBX (model 401)

- LifeView FlyVideo 3000

- nVidia Ti4200

- pcHDTV HD-3000

- ADS Tech Instant TV PCI (PTV 350)

Direct Video Broadcast (DVB) Capture Cards

Cards adhering to a code of internationally accepted open standards for digital television are given the initials DVB — short for Direct Video Broadcasting. This set of standards is maintained by a well-represented consortium of industry representatives and is published by several European organizations. Variations of the specification are currently in use throughout Europe, Australia, Africa, South America, and several parts of Asia.

DVB is well supported under Linux and MythTV for those who may have the opportunity to work with European or other broadcasting equipment outside the United States at some point in their travels.

HDTV Tuner Card

Arguably the most commonly used interface for a high-definition picture is the Digital Video Interface (DVI) specification. This is because it enables the proper devices to realize the most enriching picture quality available. HDTV tuner cards are capable of resolution as high as 1920 × 1080i (the "i" represents interleave).

Modern tuner and graphics cards sport a few video ports on the backplane (commonly S-Video and DVI) and provide component and composite output to HDTV-ready and HDTV displays. In a concerted effort to reach an ever-widening array of video connector capability, many video card vendors offer several types of output connections in single blocky adapters that plug directly into the S-Video (or similar) socket.

Ensure that your HDTV tuner card and HDTV television are on the same page when it comes to wiring everything up.

Other Noteworthy TV Capture Cards

For high-definition setups, the pcHDTV HD-3000 offers the best available Linux experience. pcHDTV's founder and CEO, Jack Kelliher, is committed to the open-source initiative, particularly its role in the arena of television entertainment. Visit the vendor Web site at `www.pchdtv.com` for more information.

Astute readers will note that our favorite TV capture card, the Hauppauge WinTV-150MCE, is missing from the foregoing list. Despite its absence from that list, we've had no trouble with that card and the VL4 drivers (and have several such systems running right now, in fact). Visit the vendor Web site at `www.hauppauge.com` for more information about this and other Hauppauge TV capture cards available (the WinTV-500MCE has two built-in tuners, which some system builders may find attractive).

In addition to the thorough treatment given to MythTV on Fedora Core documented on Jarod Wilson's Web site (http://wilsonet.com/mythtv/), there is a collaborative write-up detailing the shared experiences MythTV users have with successful HDTV configuration. Happily, we have both Wilson and Matt Wright (of HTPCnews.com fame) aboard to walk us through the HDTV experience in later portions of this book.

HDTV is further explored in Chapters 3, 15, and 17.

FireWire and USB Capture Devices

Many MythTV users have reported success working with various FireWire- and USB-based capture card solutions. No coverage is provided here about the specific configurations and applications of such devices, but readers should be aware that these units can work.

Plextor's ConvertX PVR model PX-TV402U provides hardware capture and encoding for MPEG-1, MPEG-2, and MPEG-4 formats from real-time satellite, cable, or broadcast TV signals in an external USB 2.0 solution. ConvertX PVR device driver support under Linux is provided by Plextor via a special Linux Software Development Kit made available at www.plextor.com/english/support/LinuxSDK.htm.

Hauppauge's ever-popular WinTV-PVR-USB2 external capture device is reported to work well under Linux using the collaborative reverse-engineered driver support made available by Mike Isely. Along with the relevant driver code, Isley provides detailed information to get you up and running with the WinTV-PVR-USB2 (not to be confused with the WinTV-USB2, a less capable device), and found at www.isely.net/pvrusb2.html.

According to current information available on the MythTV.org Web site, the following devices have been proven problematic or otherwise unworkable under Linux:

- Hauppauge WinTV-D or -HD (no driver)
- Hauppauge WinTV-USB series
- Hauppauge WinTV-PVR-USB (model 602), or WinTV-PVR-PCI (model 880) cards (no driver — this is not the PVR-250/350 series of cards supported by the IvyTV driver)
- ATI All-in-Wonder series

Miscellaneous Graphics Processors

In a concerted effort to pack budget-oriented added value into low-cost motherboard solutions, manufacturers integrate video functionality directly into their feature sets. Owing to the poor performance integrated graphics typically deliver, we recommend that you use a dedicated hardware MPEG-2 encoder instead. Many leading vendors — including Intel (Intel Graphics Port, IGP), Silicon Integrated Systems (SiS), and ATI — presently develop discrete on-board video solutions for the consumer market.

VIA Technology, a leader in embedded technology hardware, produces the most desirable of all on-board processing solutions with its C3 Eden Core product line. Select models sport S-Video, Composite, and Component output ports right on the backplane along with onboard analog encoding capabilities. Such units are designed for use in set-top boxes and entertainment devices, and thus also work well with MythTV.

Audio Cards

When it comes to internal audio components, your options are clear-cut: on-board audio (integrated audio solutions) or off-board audio (in the form of PCI). Each has its strengths and weaknesses for a given application, but what matters most is your perception of ideal audio playback. The following sections lend insight into the underlying principles that might otherwise escape casual notice.

On-Board Discrete Audio Chips

Circuit board layout is as much art as it is science, and it merits special attention for audio purposes. Integrated sound solutions are generally based on the AC'97 codec (considered the industry standard) and are at the whim of the electronic pathways (called *traces*) that interconnect mainboard components. These traces emit varying ranges of electronic noise that can affect sound quality for poor circuit board layouts. Granted, only the most critical audiophiles will consciously notice the difference; most users will get by fine on standard fidelity output. Should you experience feedback during audio playback in the form of electronic hissing and popping, this would be the first possible cause.

On the upside, when going with on-board audio solutions, Creative Labs offers their Home Theater Connect DTS-610, a standalone bridge set inline between a PC and home entertainment system. This impressive little unit is capable of sampling audio streams with DTS quality compression, delivering a respectable 5.1 channel surround sound. This solution neatly sidesteps any potential conflict both with on-board circuit traces and substandard driver support under Linux.

PCI-Based Audio

For cheap and easy sound solutions, electronics manufacturer Chaintech provides fair quality sound at an affordable price with its AV-710 series PCI sound card. The AV-710 delivers 24-bit audio resolution with sampling rates up to 192 KHz and can output in digital optical (via SPDIF or tos-link).

The Chaintech USA daughter site is located at http://chaintechusa.com/.

Middle and high-fidelity audio solutions are provided by a relatively new line of PCI-based audio equipment by Creative Labs called Xi-Fi that targets the professional recorder and extreme gamer demographics.

Another Noteworthy Audio Card

DFI redefines the notion of integrating on-board audio by separating the audio chipset from the noisy circuitry in the form of an add-in card. This card, called the *Karajan module,* can deliver crisp 8-channel sound using the on-board Realtek ALC850 audio codec.

Users of the Realtek audio solutions have reported mixed results using the requisite Linux drivers, and recommend using the nVidia-based sound codec instead. Your mileage may vary.

Disk Drives

Storage is an important consideration in the design of any HTPC. Dealing with this subject matter means deciding how much capacity is needed, which file system to use, and understanding how stored files — particularly media files — will be accessed. You may know that a drive labeled "media-ready" has a spindle speed (rotational platter) of 7,200 RPM. It earns the media-ready designation because the drive's performance is adequate for the fairly low-latency requirements of high-resolution, real-time playback of multimedia data. Most modern 3.5" desktop drive offerings on the retail market are available only with 7,200 RPM spindles (suffice it to say, it's the most common rotational speed), but occasionally OEM versions are available at lower rotational speeds. The choice is clear: choose nothing less than 7,200 RPM, which is typical for most retail drives, and avoid the potential for undesirable artifacts in subsequent playback.

With that decision made, there's also the question of size: Standard MPEG-2, the de facto encoding format for distribution-quality streaming analog encoding and playback, can weigh in anywhere from 800 MB to 3 GB per hour, depending on the levels of compression elected. TV-quality content operates at a data rate of 1 Mb per second, which isn't asking much, but pushing higher resolutions places greater demand on the storage subsystem. This is most evident in terms of storage space requirements. You'd be surprised to know exactly how easy it is to fully saturate a seemingly gargantuan 300 GB drive using DVD data alone, without including additional image, audio, or TV recording files.

Size matters, but bigger drives also cost disproportionately more than smaller ones. While you can purchase 500 GB drives nowadays, you may be better off buying three 250 GB drives instead (which will cost less than a single 500 GB drive) even if you must also purchase a $40–$60 external USB 2.0 drive enclosure as well to accommodate the third drive. With storage densities increasing all the time, and storage needs growing even faster, we recommend building systems with no less than 300 GB of disk storage. We also assume you'll use one or more USB or FireWire attached drive enclosures to bump up storage for your MythTV system even further.

Motion pictures may not be the only content archived on those drive platters. As is commonly the case, picture files and audio files also consume substantial amounts of storage space. Assume that MP3 compressed audio requires about 1 MB per minute of playback time — a fair assessment — and that your music collection includes 200 CDs and another 200 individual songs. At 74 minutes per CD and 7 minutes per song, that's a total of 16,200 minutes, or 15.8 GB of space for your music. For smaller music collections, that's not bad; for larger music collections, only one 250 or 300 GB drive may not be big enough.

Table 1-2 provides estimated file format sizes according to an hour-long sampling for each type listed. This information should serve as a basis for your consumption needs when calculating the cost and capacity of storage drives.

Table 1-2   Estimated File Format Sizes per Hour of Footage

Quality	Per Hour	10 Files	100 Files	1000 Files
VCR/MPEG-4	700 MB	7 GB	70 GB	700 GB
RTJPEG	2 GB	20 GB	200 GB	2000 GB!
DVD/MPEG-2	2.5–5 GB	25–50 GB	250–500 GB	2500–5000 GB!
ATSC HDTV	7 GB	700 GB	7000 GB!	70000 GB!

These unusually large file sizes directly impact the overall performance of DVR units, so special attention is needed for those parts that bear the brunt of this burden. Drive storage is a primary component, as Direct Memory Access (DMA) leverages a straight line of communication with memory to quickly transfer data, without requiring processor intervention (until such time as said data needs to be interpreted or used in some fashion). DMA must be used to avoid jittery and choppy video playback. Because not all distributions enable DMA at boot time, ensure that both the BIOS and boot configuration settings explicitly enable DMA capability.

MythTV operates on any given number of files, the sizes of which vary, but any of which easily involves several gigabytes of information at a time. Most of this kind of material exceeds 4 GB, so particular attention must be paid to your choice of file system based on read/write/remove performance and maximum storage capacity.

According to the best available information, two specific file system formats are the best candidates when it comes to maintaining large data sets efficiently. Both are especially useful for DVR storage, as both provide a reliable, high-performance, fault-tolerant, and expandable framework for maintaining large data files. Characteristics related to the deletion or manipulation of large data sets are especially important.

- **Journaled File System (JFS)** — A mature, fault-tolerant design first implemented by IBM in early AIX versions that has seen over a decade of enterprise-level storage experience and expansion. According to benchmark information, JFS shows the best performance when deleting large files.

- **Extended File System (XFS)** — This also shares a rich and storied history in the enterprise storage arena and shows exceptional response when handling large data files. Not to be confused with the Linux native Extended File Systems (ext, ext2, ext3), XFS is a framework of its own, and provides online expansion (the file system dynamically grows), online defragmentation, and a real-time Input/Output (I/O) API for streaming time-sensitive hardware-based and software-based applications.

A Logical Volume Manager (LVM) offers greater flexibility in allocating and maintaining mass storage devices than conventional hard disk partitioning utilities provide. An LVM can concentrate separate partitions into a single expansive virtual partition that can be resized and moved. However, an LVM by itself is meaningless without a supportive file system format such as JFS or XFS.

While not every distribution will offer all (or even any) of the options during installation, Linux installations everywhere can still benefit from packaged-based additions after the disk drive is populated with viable system data. We suggest you use either JFS or XFS for your MythTV media files.

Parallel ATA Magnetic Disk Drives

Parallel ATA (PATA) is a geriatric standard in terms of technology, and has seen widespread use at both consumer- and enterprise-grade storage levels. PATA is by far the most common disk storage interface specification in use today, is available in a wide range of capacities, and works with most modern computer equipment.

The most distinctive aspect of PATA drives is the 40-conductor, 80-wire flat-ribbon cable used to connect the drive interface to the host controller. Use in small form factor systems makes ribbon cabling clearly impractical, where specialty rounded cables that provide better internal airflow management are normally used instead.

Perhaps the most important point about PATA drives is their impact on overall system performance. For each drive pair chained onto a single cable, the available bandwidth is effectively halved. PATA signaling is unidirectional, in pulses, and only a single drive may signal at any given time. These undesirable effects may be felt when storing a stream of high-definition data to a hard drive that's attached to the same cable as a DVD drive burning an image.

Serial ATA Magnetic Disk Drives

Serial ATA (SATA) signaling, conversely, provides a much cleaner method for dealing with bandwidth-intensive processing. SATA drives plug directly into a SATA port on the motherboard host controller, either directly linked to the Southbridge as part of a discrete chip solution, or as part of the Southbridge controller itself, as in the case of nForce4 and Intel Controller Hub 6/7 (ICH6, ICH7) series chipsets. SATA signaling occurs in a bidirectional, switch-arbitrated fashion (where quality of service influences prioritization of time-sensitive processing such as streaming live video) and offers a more efficient component interface.

While SATA disk drives show varying performance increases over PATA versions, a valid argument stands that SATA optical drives are not necessarily faster than their PATA counterparts. The choice in going with SATA is clear; raw performance is not the essential ingredient, but instead the more efficient utilization of system resources and better performance potential for fully loaded DVRs. Ostensibly, a pair of SATA optical drives will operate independently and create less interruption to other running tasks on the same machine, unlike mated parallel drives, which share a common (divided) resource. For MythTV units that will serve as on-demand back-up stations, SATA drives make the best choice.

Another unique feature about SATA drives is that true SATA drives (those not using parallel-to-serial bridge interfaces) support Native Command Queuing (NCQ), a shortest-path algorithm for multiple outstanding requests for data. Essentially, NCQ dynamically reorders pending requests for information in the most efficient sequence, so that the drive arm describes a single concentric circle around the disk platters, instead of randomly jumping from one location to another. Such jumping places excess strain on particularly active drives (such as with DVR boxes), so NCQ helps prolong the life span of a given drive by reducing normal wear and tear.

NCQ is a feature implemented in the drive and recognized by on-board chipsets that support the SATA 2.0 (SATA II) and SATA 2.5 specifications. Early adopters Seagate (Barracuda Series 7 and later) and Maxtor (Diamond Max 10 and later) drives implemented NCQ well before the SATA II specification was finalized. These particular drives also happen to be among the quietest on the market, with Seagate setting the trend for Fluid Dynamic Bearing drive acoustic dampening technology. Ensure smooth, reliable, near-silent operation by choosing a drive marked as having Fluid Dynamic Bearing, or FDB, on the retail packaging.

Optical Drives

Relatively little has changed in consumer-grade optical drive technology to the extent that Linux may give you significant problems when trying to establish a working relationship with the drive. Depending on which versions of kernel and supporting packages are used at the time of build, support may or may not be present for the latest drives. Such is the case with SATA DVD drives—not all distributions support SATA-based optical drives during the installation process, which is a compelling reason to keep a spare PATA DVD drive handy. PATA drive technologies have long been supported under Linux, and just about any parallel optical drive will work under Linux.

CD-ROM Optical Disc Drives

Compact Disc ROM (CD-ROM) technology hasn't changed much in the past few years, with minor incremental revisions to the core ATAPI specification and rotational spindle speeds. Overall, the underlying technology has remained consistent in its ability to read and write a variety of data to the optical CD-ROM media, and with fairly lasting results. However, CD-ROM inclusion within a DVR build seems a bit short-sighted and unnecessary because DVD-ROM drives are fully capable of reading and writing to both CDs and DVDs.

The ATAPI specification is well understood and widely supported under Linux. Very few exceptions arise with regard to drive compatibility, short of manufacturer-specific implementations that clearly limit compatibility by their very use (overburn technologies, for example, that allow for writing more data to disc than is apparently available). Any functional CD-ROM drive should work fine and be properly identified under Linux.

DVD-ROM Optical Disc Drives

Current Digital Video Disc (DVD) drives offer a wealth of options in the areas of aesthetics, features, and media compatibility. Dual-Layer (DL) DVD burners are becoming more apparent in the marketplace, alongside the readily available single-layer DVD plus/minus R/W drives.

Most DVD offerings are available as PATA drives, while a few vendors offer select models with SATA support (such as Plextor's 712-A PATA and 712-SA SATA optical drives). Table 1-3 lists DVD disc media types and their estimated on-disc sizes for the most common formats.

When searching the marketplace for a suitable optical drive, seek out those products with the most suitable acoustic and vibration characteristics. Unnecessary noise during drive spin-up and unsteady disc rotation are the hallmarks of cheap drives. With decent and fairly quiet drives available for between $70 and $100 (SATA) or $40 and $60 (PATA), there's no reason to use cheaper but noisier drives. Savings of $20 or $30 won't make up for the added noise.

Table 1-3   DVD Disc Media Types and Features

Format	Sides	Layers	Capacity
DVD-5	Single	Single	4.7 GB
DVD-9	Single	Double	8.5 GB
DVD-10	Double	Single	9.4 GB
DVD-14	Double	Double	13.3 GB
DVD-18	Double	Double	17.1 GB

Apart from slot-load versus tray-load mechanisms, the major distinction among optical drive technologies is form factor. Common dimensions measure anywhere from $146 \times 41.2 \times 177.5$ mm and up for a modern desktop optical drive. Unusual and creative uses come from the laptop world, where slim-line drives reign supreme and stand a mere 12 mm (not quite half of an inch) high and easily adapt to most desktops with the appropriate backplane converter (44 pin to 40 pin IDE). However, these drives carry a premium for their small size.

For completeness, some unconventional methods, requiring expertise to set up and operate, are noted in the following sidebar.

Power Supply Units

The system Power Supply Unit (PSU) is perhaps the most casually overlooked and easily underestimated component consideration made during common consumer decisions. We pay special attention to the PSU for several key reasons, including efficient thermal design, economy of sound, and optimal airflow management. PSUs are manufactured to a variety of specifications, the most common of which are the ATX and micro-ATX form factors.

We can make some general approximations about the power consumption requirements for a given component based on its power ratings listed on the product label. On an optical drive, this appears topside, where the required FCC (in the United States) compliance tested seal of approval appears. A Mitsumi CD-ROM optical drive manufactured in August of 2000 states VDC ratings of 0.8 Amps at 5 Volts and 2.0 A at 12 V. By multiplying amps and volts and then adding the respective values of both the 5 and 12 V rails, we can determine the maximum power consumption by this device (in watts), which is 28 — about average for an optical device.

Consider this an operational consumption requirement — that is, the power drawn necessarily under load. There is also a peak efficiency rating on most PSUs that determines the maximal amount of current that can be overdrawn by several components at once during the initial power-up phase. When a computer boots up, each spindle-based device promptly fires up its engines and begins a ready state to be interrogated by the BIOS and subsequent operating system components. During this period, a device will use twice its rated power consumption when initializing the rotational pieces.

Depending upon CPU clock speed and core features, the hottest running component in a DVR box will draw anywhere from 65 to 130 watts at most. Add-in cards on the PCI bus draw on the steady 3.3 to 5 volt signaling, and the tuner cards mostly target this connection interface. In addition, expect the tuner cards to run quite hot, as they rely on mostly passively cooled aluminum shield designs enclosing the encoder chip.

Ideally, for economy of sound and power, the power supply should be a "smart" consumer by selectively throttling its main fan and auxiliary fan as load increases. Leading PSU manufacturers such as Seasonic, Antec, and OCZ design thermally sound, highly efficient units that adapt well to the ever-changing demands of a dynamic environment.

For suggestions, see the SilentPC Power Supply Fundamentals and Recommendations at `www.silentpcreview.com/article28-page1.html`.

Storage Solutions for the Intrepid

RAID Technology

Redundant Array of Independent Disks (RAID) provides certain optional features that can improve performance for high-demand audio and video processing. RAID functionality is provided either as an add-in card or as an optional integrated motherboard feature. Only specifically marked motherboard packages are capable of RAID, and these packages usually carry a premium. The intrepid builder who places the utmost emphasis on pure performance should consider RAID performance benefits for inclusion in his or her build.

RAID comes in a variety of levels and configurations, most of which are beyond the scope of this book. Only the applicable variations earn mention herein:

- RAID-0 (striping) — Requires at minimum two drives; splits data in half (parts A and B), and stores one half (A) on one drive, and the other half (B) on the second drive. Once accessed, the data is effectively pulled from two drives in shorter time than a single drive. This offers the best performance for high-density storage applications and is commonly used in industrial-grade digital video production rigs to store and maintain raw footage.

- RAID-1 (mirroring) — Requires at minimum two drives; copies data twice, to two or more drives, offering the best reliability at the cost of performance. This method is of little use to most users, finding purpose only for prolonged and verified archival reasons.

- RAID-10 (mirror/stripe) — Often also interchanged with RAID-10, RAID-0+1, or RAID-1+0, though each is implemented differently; basically, the reliability of mirroring with the blazing fast access times of striping.

Gigabyte i-RAM: Solid-State DDR Storage

Solid-state storage devices such as Gigabyte's i-RAM PCI add-in card utilizes four DDR sockets capable of supporting up to 8 GB of 200 MHz RAM. Gigabyte's technology merges the speed of dynamic memory with the persistence of solid-state disk drives. What this means for the intrepid DVR builder is an ultimately silent playback unit with an ultra-responsive storage repository for the host operating system and the entirety of the MythTV code base and packages.

Other Useful Peripherals

Remote controls are bundled with some capture cards but not with others, as is the case with the OEM Hauppauge PVR-150, and one reason for its lower cost than the 350 and 500 series. However, these bundled remotes often skimp on features and provide only the functionality a manufacturer is willing to invest in, so you may want to purchase a remote control separately. The following sections provide you with need-to-know information regarding the operation of remote controls in the context of a MythTV DVR.

Remote Controls

Bundled remotes included with most capture card retail packages leave much to be desired. Most general users will get by fine with the rather lackluster features present on bundled remotes — they're not entirely useless, of course — but for the power user, they just won't have any appeal.

SnapStream's Firefly remote and paired USB receiver are entirely Radio Frequency (RF) based, meaning greater freedom of range and motion (note the occasionally necessary stretching of arms required for negotiating weakling Infrared Data Association, or IrDA, signals around solid objects). Everything from functionality to ergonomic design is well considered in the construction of the Firefly. It contains plenty of programmable buttons and integrates well with MythTV using the Linux IrDA Remote Control Daemon (lircd). Plus, the well-balanced design provides smooth handling and superior grip to conventional blocky shapes that disregard hand contour and formation.

The Firefly is very affordable and can be found for around $50. For more information, visit the SnapStream Firefly Product Page at www.snapstream.com/products/firefly/.

Logitech offers a pretty potent package in its Harmony 680 series of USB-based superior remote controls. The 680 is pretty advanced: It's a programmable remote control capable of downloading configuration settings for various AV components — all with a simple visit to the vendor Web page and quick setup of the applicable profile.

The Harmony 680 is encased in a durable dark-gray plastic enclosure sporting a backlit keypad and LCD read-out. As an ultimate example of following the convergent technology ideology, Logitech does an excellent job of freeing the hapless end-user from a multitude of mutually independent remote controls. According to the manufacturer's suggested retail price, the Harmony 680 carries a hefty price tag of $199, but you may be able to find it for as little as $120.

For more information, visit the Logitech Harmony 680 product page: www.logitech.com/index.cfm/products/detailsharmony/US/EN,CRID=2084,CONTENTID=9568

Jarod Wilson, the very same maintainer of the ultimate MythTV How-To and a major contributor to this text, also offers useful pointers for remote control set-ups. Check out the following sites:

- Linux and LIRC:
  http://wilsonet.com/mythtv/#lirc

- Remote Controls and MythTV:
  http://wilsonet.com/mythtv/remotes.php

SIP Phones and Videophones

Users of phone and videophone equipment benefit from telecommunications integration via the standard SIP protocol courtesy of the MythPhone plug-in. MythPhone is a core component of the MythTV plug-ins package and thus requires minimal setup time. Interested readers are advised to consult the release documentation and distribution changelogs for information about the latest and greatest features supported. Find more info at the following sites:

- MythTV MythPhone plug-in home page:
  www.zen13655.zen.co.uk/mythphone.html

- MythTV MythPhone User Guide and How-To:
  www.zen13655.zen.co.uk/mythphone-howto.html

Suggested Linux Distributions

Throughout this book, the reader is treated to a comprehensive hands-on approach to building a Linux-based DVR from scratch, starting with a Fedora Core base installation and importing the appropriate packages and package dependencies. Fedora Core has been chosen for its general ease of installation and ease of use, and its reliable and consistent professional-grade quality. While initial portions of this book were written for Fedora Core 4, the techniques will translate to Fedora Core 5, but you should be aware of any subtleties regarding placement of utilities (such as the terminal application, which appears in System Tools on the taskbar in FC4, and Accessories in FC5).

While this book maintains strict adherence to the Fedora Core installation, configuration, and maintenance procedures, the reader is at liberty to choose among any of the readily available Linux distributions. Each distribution brings with it unique quirks and obstacles, so expect to see quite a bit of variance among other installation processes.

Table 1-4 is not meant to be exhaustive, merely a summary of distributions showing general popularity within the Linux PVR/DVR community.

Table 1-4   Suggested Linux Distributions for MythTV

Fedora Core Linux with MythTV Resources	
Fedora Core Linux Web Site	http://fedora.redhat.com
Fedora Myth(TV)ology	www.wilsonet.com/mythtv/
Gentoo Linux MythTV Resources	
Official Gentoo Linux Web site	www.gentoo.org
Official Gentoo MythTV Install Guide	http://dev.gentoo.org/~cardoe/mythtv/
Gentoo How-To Setup MythTV wiki	http://gentoo-wiki.com/HOWTO_Setup_MythTV
Mandrake Linux MythTV Resources	
Mandriva (formerly Mandrake) Linux Web Site	www.mandriva.com/
Maiku's Setting up MythTV under Mandrake 10.1 Guide	www.byopvr.com/Sections+index-req-viewarticle-artid-13-page-1.html
Thac's Mandrake 10.1 MythTV RPMs	www.mde.djura.org/10.1/RPMS/
SuSE Linux MythTV Resources	
Novell SuSE Linux Web Site	www.novell.com/linux/suse/
OpenSuSE 10.1 Distribution Site	www.opensuse.org/Welcome_to_openSUSE.org
MythTV Custom Builds	
KnoppMyth Web Site	www.mysettopbox.tv/knoppmyth.html
KnoppMyth Forums	www.mysettopbox.tv/phpBB2/

Getting Help from the MythTV Community

The MythTV community is a growing body consisting of tens of thousands of users from around the world, each contributing his or her own perspective and unique experiences. Parts of this community are represented by collaborative HOW-TOs, and other parts via online forums in which users can interact to resolve issues or explain specific configurations. The MythTV Forum at www.mythtvtalk.com/forum/is a main entry point for the MythTV community.

The following resources should provide a good jumping off point for the MythTV audience. Certainly no single resource has it all, so we provide several listings for the more popular areas of MythTV information.

Start with a Search Engine

Probably the best and first resort for quick problem resolution and troubleshooting methods is your preferred search engine. The Internet contains a wealth of cached user experiences detailing various symptomatic problems and resolutions encountered during individual MythTV builds. Many installation issues are commonly shared, and therefore abundantly documented. More obscure configuration or compilation problems may warrant further investigation by experienced forum moderators or the developers themselves, depending on the nature of the problem.

Before making a post in any forum, search for information specific to your condition. Include relevant portions of error messages produced either in consoles, message boxes, or log files. Google does an excellent job of ferreting out relevant information based on a precisely structured query with the appropriate descriptive terminology. Your search query results are likely to direct you to forums and message boards to pinpoint a post relevant to your scenario. The Linux community is generally very helpful, but your experience relies heavily on your approach; submitting obvious or known-and-resolved problems without first checking whether the fix has already been posted is frowned upon, and such requests for help have the potential to be met with rejection.

Mailing lists also provide a treasure trove of answers, which again depends on how well you structure your query. Searching directly within a specific page helps quickly locate key terms and makes more efficient use of time in weeding out helpful information from useless detail. Developer communications happen here, detailing the development process, occasionally information regarding fixes and workarounds to known and suspected problems.

User Resources

User resources are for the core audience — the user base of MythTV. Answers to common and popular questions are found here, as well as many pointers to resources further describing unique scenarios from MythTV users around the world. To obtain the most current and accurate information available regarding the configuration and operation of MythTV, check the following sites:

- MythTV Installation and Usage
  www.mythtv.org/modules.php?name=MythInstall
- MythTV User Mailing List
  www.mythtv.org/mailman/listinfo/mythtv-users
- MythTV User Mailing List Archive
  www.gossamer-threads.com/lixsts/mythtv/users/
- MythTV Home Page
  www.mythtv.org/

- MythTV HOW-TO Guide
  http://wilsonet.com/mythtv/

- Linux WiFi Compatibility List
  www.linux-wlan.org/docs/wlan_adapters.html.gz

- MythTV HOW-TO Guide
  http://linux-wless.passys.nl/

Resources for Developers

Developer resources are channels open to discussion regarding the programmatic aspect of MythTV. As such, these resources follow strict adherence to development-related subjects, and in some cases explicitly state that off-topic material will be promptly disregarded. The following links refer to points of interest regarding code-related inquiries:

MythTV Developer Mailing List
http://mythtv.org/cgi-bin/mailman/listinfo/mythtv-dev

IRC
irc.freenode.net #mythtv, #mythtv-users

Bug Tracking
http://cvs.mythtv.org/trac

Final Thoughts

MythTV truly is a departure from garden-variety video recording appliances that often represent only a small subset of the functionality present in the MythTV framework. Its robust client/server architecture, flexible configuration scheme, and extensive plug-in framework give you the ultimate freedom of choice. MythTV is unbeatable in terms of overall features, capability, and functionality, especially for the price — free. In the following chapters, we demonstrate how to obtain and install MythTV for existing Linux distributions (Chapter 2), walk you through setting up sound and picture (Chapter 3), and then, in subsequent chapters, show you how to configure a wide variety of software and hardware components to enhance your MythTV experience.

Fundamental Linux Concepts for MythTV

chapter

2

in this chapter

☑ Basic system requirements

☑ Prepping for installation

☑ Working with program guides

☑ Initial tweaking and tuning of MythTV

This chapter assumes the reader possesses a fairly intimate knowledge of the inner workings of modern desktop computers. That said, our emphasis is on providing accurate and useful information so that even inexperienced builders may follow along with ease. Prior experience with Linux and the Linux console terminal (also called the *command line*) is helpful, but not mandatory.

In this chapter, we delve into the most complex portion of dealing with Linux and the peculiar manner in which it operates. This initial stage — the build-up of a MythTV system — is likely to be a sticking point for those users whose background is exclusively Windows-based. Linux is still very much tied into the console (also called the *command line interface*, or *CLI*), and this is where much power and capability may be leveraged. Windows users are not as attuned to the command line (although many have used it as a matter of course) and should therefore devote special care and attention to detail (and keystrokes) when attempting the following procedures.

Although Chapter 4 covers Fedora Core and MythTV installation, this chapter helps you understand many of the caveats surrounding the programs and their installation, and how to obtain the software. You also get a heads-up regarding some important post-installation considerations.

A Few Essential Linux Conventions

For those uninitiated in the Linux realm, many of Linux's workings can create confusion. Entire volumes have been dedicated to introducing beginners to working with Linux, so our book covers only those aspects most relevant to MythTV. Readers who require more information to get started are advised to consult supplementary online documentation and print publications for an introduction to the Linux operating system. The Linux

Documentation Project (TLDP) is a great entry point for your journey into Linux, with many excellent in-depth how-to guides covering a broad range of configurations.

For a jump-start with the Linux operating system itself, check out the Introduction to Linux currently maintained at `http://tldp.org/LDP/intro-linux/html/index.html`.

In Linux, there is no ubiquitous `C:\>` prompt. Linux has several available console *shells*, and distinguishes among a broad range of user privileges. This is most evident in the appearance of terminal window output. Administrator-level access is indicated by a hash mark (#) under bash and sh where line input is expected. Everything below administrator level (also known as `root`, from the `root` account) is indicated by a dollar symbol ($). This book relies heavily on both the `bash` and `sh` shells because they are by far the most common and widely used by new and old Linux users alike.

Owing to the intrinsic properties of Linux binary paths and shared user environments, we strongly advise use of absolute path names to promote proper usage habits from the get-go. For example, executing `uname -a` and `/bin/uname -a` effect the same results, but the second example ensures that the correct binary is called instead of one located in another portion of the directory tree. While it is generally safe and more convenient to invoke programs without using absolute path names, security implications may arise in unsanitary multi-user environments. Because security isn't a significant aspect of our MythTV coverage, no such discussion is provided.

In addition, as a matter of best practice, we urge ultra-conservative use of the administrator-level account, `root`. Access to this account gives the user access to everything within the system, including the capability to influence software and hardware behaviors normally reserved only for system operators. For that reason, this chapter demonstrates use of `su` (substitute user) and `sudo` (a portmanteau of the words *super-user*— the root account — and *do*— as in perform), an application that applies the principle of least privilege while maintaining restrictive access to privileged processes for regular account holders. Using either of these is not mandatory in Linux, but helps form proper Linux usage habits.

Case Counts!

When working with Linux, particularly on the command line (or console, or terminal — whatever you want to call it), keep in mind that Linux exhibits case sensitivity. Combining uppercase and lowercase letters in the same filename produces separate files. For example, `FILENAME`, `FiLeNaMe`, and `filename` are three distinct files under Linux.

Naming conventions for Linux packages may contain mixed case, while the actual utilities themselves may conform to all lowercase lettering. Do not be fooled by this.

Software Solutions for Compiling MythTV

In computer science, compiling is the simple act of translating high-level textual languages into symbolic machine code form for consumption by the target processor. This means building applications from raw code fragments. As a newcomer to Linux you should initially be concerned with the package management system to make the most effective use of your time. Leave the compiler alone until you gain sufficient experience with the operating system environment, but don't be discouraged from giving it a try. Oftentimes, a README or INSTALL file appears in the main directory of a source archive you extract into a directory, giving you directions on how to use the compiler to build the applications.

First and foremost, to build your MythTV system you need a working Linux installation. This can be acquired a variety of ways: through any number of distributors via FTP or HTTP package servers, or from CVS (concurrent versions system) and SVN (subversion control system) repositories.

Several options are available to ready a workable MythTV system, but each differs in its initial approach and is particular to a specific Linux distribution. A modern SUSE distribution employs yast as an integral package management solution, whereas Fedora Core relies on yum, and Debian uses apt. All of these may be used to install a live, fully functional system straight onto a hard disk (or compact Flash, Ramdisk, and so on).

Other solutions exist in the form of read-only CD-ROM images that decompress a kernel into RAM and operate mostly from memory. These solutions are ideal for preparing quick and simple system solutions from existing desktop hardware by custom-fitting the MythTV framework into a streamlined Linux distribution, such as Knoppix.

Of the many possible methods for preparing a working MythTV system, we cover three:

- **CD-ROM images** — CD-ROM images are obtained from the distributor site of choice and made available via either FTP or HTTP. Where applicable, DVD ISO images may also be available (this means the media is bootable and can handle installation to a PC with no operating system already installed).

- **Source packages** — Compiling from source code offers fine-grained functionality and code optimizations not available in pre-compiled packages. Casual and power Linux users alike should be well aware of the benefits of tailoring source code into binaries optimized for local hardware.

  Compiling MythTV from raw source code requires an established C/C++ development environment, including a recent compiler or compiler toolchain suite in working condition, a recent version of automake utilities, and requisite header files for shared libraries. Current mainstream Linux full installation distributions carry most or all of the required components to flesh out a usable development environment during the initial installation phase. Stripped-down variation installation images — so-called minimal install boot images — provide the barest ingredients essential for proper Linux installation, and little else. These setups require post-install upgrades from either the distribution vendor package repository or some third-party site.

■ **Pre-compiled packages** — Packaged deliverables are provided as Red Hat Package Manager (RPM) archives. The second best online resource (apart from the distributor site) for locating such packages is at `http://rpm.pbone.net`, which supports search options, including platform and version specifics, package provisions and requirements, and more.

Using precompiled MythTV packages for your specific hardware arrangement is the easiest, quickest, and most effective means to establish prerequisite and additional software applications. You encounter none of the inevitable missing dependency entanglements and exert minimal effort by leveraging the package manager for your flavor of choice. The MythTV framework has expanded considerably since earlier revisions — there are more variables to consider — so it is recommended that you utilize any native package management facilities at your disposal.

Clearly, pre-compiled packages offer an advantage to the compilation process and are strongly recommended to all first-time or novice users of Linux. (Linux aficionados or experts generally do what they like anyway, so we won't dispense too much advice that targets them directly.)

Obtaining Fedora Core or KnoppMyth

We recommend using the Fedora Core distribution of Linux, which is proven to work exceedingly well with MythTV. For that reason, this book targets Fedora Core installation procedures alongside KnoppMyth as its primary focus, but that in no way limits your options when it comes to the many other Linux distributions readily available (but you won't have the benefit of the step-by-step details you'll find in this book for those two primary targets).

The latest version of Fedora Core is available as a free download at `http://fedora.redhat.com/Download/`.

Briefly summarized, KnoppMyth is the CD-based Knoppix image with MythTV pre-installed but not preconfigured (you will still need to set up backend and frontend parameters). This method trivializes the installation process and dramatically reduces your overall setup time — just pop in the disk, boot it up, and MythTV will be delivered to your hard drive in a matter of minutes. You have the option of running the KnoppMyth CD as a frontend client, but KnoppMyth itself must be installed on your hard drive for backend services.

For the latest in KnoppMyth releases, check out the developer Web site at `http://mysettopbox.tv/knoppmyth.html`. Interested readers are also advised to browse the link to the unofficial KnoppMyth wiki located at `www.knoppmythwiki.org/`.

We assume readers will determine an appropriate means for obtaining and installing a base Linux distribution based on the resources available. Readers who lack high-speed connections may obtain Linux through other means, such as print media, which often contains CD-ROM or DVD-ROM images for current Linux distributions.

Cross-Reference A full version of Fedora Core 5 comes on DVD and CDs with the *Fedora 5 and Red Hat Enterprise Linux 4 Bible* by Christopher Negus (Wiley, 2006).

Modifying /etc/ld.so.conf for MythTV

In earlier versions of Linux, you will find some discrepancies across each distribution regarding how it views and shares library code among the installed applications. If you happen to be working from a fresh install using a current Fedora image, skip this section because the package manager will satisfy all of your software requirements.

MythTV departs from standard practice in using a local library as part of its runtime environment. Normally, the dynamic linker/loaders found on every Linux system are named ld.so and ld-linux.so*, and they typically use global shared libraries. Both of these linker/loaders are responsible for the runtime management of shared library code segment locations and content. The ld.so object acquires configuration information from /etc/ld.so.cache, which in turn is built by the ldconfig binary. MythTV tucks portions of its shared library functionality away in /usr/local/lib. Therefore, you must add this path to the linker cache so that the runtime manager knows to include this directory when resolving shared library function calls.

The following command sequence illustrates this process:

```
$ /bin/su -
Password:
# /bin/echo /usr/local/lib >> /etc/ld.so.conf
# /sbin/ldconfig
# exit
```

Executing the preceding commands in the order shown establishes a workable shared library environment for both Linux and MythTV.

Environment Variable Requirements for MythTV

Environment variables represent configuration values that help drive the runtime behavior of Linux (and MythTV) as it goes about running programs and linking them to the hardware and software components of a specific installation (such as your PC). Managing environment variables properly is a key ingredient in creating a workable, predictable Linux system.

Setting Environment Variables in Fedora Core

The following environment variable exists purely for convenience, and does not affect the daily operation of MythTV or the underlying operating system. Setting this variable helps facilitate tailoring a custom build specific to the local kernel version (as documented in the Fedora MythTV How-To):

```
# /bin/echo "export KVER=\`uname -r\`" >> /etc/profile.d/kver.h
```

Note   Back-ticks (not single-quotes) are escaped by a backslash between the double-quotes. Escaping is necessary because the shell won't evaluate escaped input and can pass that input unaltered to the uname utility.

Although the purpose of this variable is not immediately obvious, it will become apparent later when you configure software specific to your Linux kernel version. The preceding variable is populated with a string that identifies the revision level of your running kernel, which you will then utilize to identify the appropriate packages for your needs.

Convenience Variables for Source Code Compiles

Concurrent Versions System (CVS) and Subversion (SVN) implement formalized methods for auditing and controlling software revisions — also known as *version control systems*. They're responsible for managing multiple versions of a single set of source code elements. As far as MythTV is concerned, this approach applies to the development of the latest source code archives for applications you will soon install.

Both CVS and SVN make numerous environment variables available for your convenience when checking CVS development servers for the most recent application code. We cover only a small subset of CVS capability here, both for brevity's sake and to avoid extraneous details — our goal is to explain just enough to get you going with MythTV. Here's an example:

```
$ export CVSPATH="/var/lib/mythcvs"
$ export CVSROOT=":pserver:mythtv@cvs.mythtv.org:${CVSPATH}"
$ /usr/bin/cvs login
Password: mythtv
$ /usr/bin/cvs checkout -r release-0-18
$ cd mythtv && ./configure && /usr/bin/make all
$ /usr/bin/sudo make install
Password:
```

Executing the preceding sequence of commands achieves the following (described in context):

1. Creates (export) a local convenience variable named CVSPATH (not CVS-specific) that contains the MythTV directory as it appears on the CVS server.

2. Creates (export) a local convenience variable named CVSROOT (very CVS-specific) that contains the MythTV server address and the MythTV code directory. The actual line entry resolves to :pserver:mythtv@cvs.mythtv.org:/var/lib/mythcvs because the final element in the second entry references a variable set in the first entry.

3. Using the CVS binary, log into the previously specified CVS server using the public password mythtv.

4. Once logged in (you will be dropped back to the original shell prompt), poll the server (checkout) for the latest source code revision (in this case, that's release-0-18).

5. Change into the newly created local directory called mythtv (created in the current path), configure the source code using the packaged configuration script, and then use the make utility to build everything for the compiler.

6. Elevate privileges from mere-mortal to super-user (sudo) for the duration of the code compilation phase.

A less involved process for interacting with CVS and SVN repositories is included elsewhere in this chapter, and accompanies our instructions for package manager-based installations. We leave the steps involved in implementing each of the MythTV packages and its supporting libraries as an exercise for the reader, but provide the information you'll need to get going with MythTV.

Compiler Optimization Flags and Variables

Additional GCC optimization flags are available to the user during the compilation phase that tailors code local to the host hardware. Not all of these flags work on every machine, so expect some variance in your experiences when compiling various source code components for MythTV.

Consider these items to be power user options, and therefore purely optional (but interesting nonetheless).

Table 2-1 illustrates a few of the compiler flags that influence runtime operation. You are not required to use any of these, as most packages are configured with their own specific compiler flags.

Table 2-1   Gnu Compiler Optimization Flags

Compiler Flag	Brief Description
-fthread-jumps	Perform branch instruction jump-ahead optimizations.
-fcse-follow-jumps	Scan through jump instructions when the target is not reached.
-fcse-skip-blocks	Follow jumps that conditionally skip over blocks.
-frerun-cse-after-loop	Run the loop optimizer twice for better effect.
-fexpensive-optimizations	Perform a number of optimizations that are relatively expensive.
-ffast-math	Define a preprocessor directive for faster math calculations.
-fPIC	Emit position-independent code for speedier execution.
-fomit-frame-pointer	Perform stack-based optimizations.
-fstrength-reduce	Perform loop and iteration variable optimizations.
-funroll-loops	Unroll loops for speedier execution.
-finline-functions	Integrate simple functions into the caller.

For a detailed explanation of what each of these flags tells the compiler to do, consult the on-disk manual reference pages (where available) or information pages by entering either of the following commands:

```
$ /usr/bin/man gcc
$ /usr/bin/info gcc
```

Users of 64-bit processors who want to utilize the full potential of their chips are also advised to include the following flag:

```
-m64
```

This generates code for 64-bit environments. Flagging this option will set int to 32 bits, and long and pointer to 64 bits. The directives

```
-march=i586
-march=i686
```

generate code for Intel 586 and 686 (fifth and sixth) generation architectures, which includes most relatively recent x86 CPUs, including those from AMD, Cyrix, and other third parties, as well as Intel Pentium processors. When in doubt, do some research on the Web to determine whether you can associate your CPU with a specific x86 processor generation. In fact, chips newer than 2002 are likely to classify as 786, which means you can safely select 686 without incurring any dangers thereby.

Use any of these flags in combination at compile time during the initial configuration script process (where applicable) for individual compilations or to define well-known compiler environment variables for global optimization.

Executing the line

```
$ ./configure CFLAGS="-fPIC -funroll-loops --march=i686"
```

produces an individual local code optimization, whereas the entry

```
$ export CFLAGS="-m64 -march=i686"
$ ./configure && make
```

produces global code optimizations (for the duration of the entire terminal session).

These environment variables will be cleared once you exit the console unless you specifically add an export statement somewhere in your shell profile (most likely .profile in your home directory).

Pre-Installation Tasks

You should only perform the following actions on existing systems, as they are unnecessary for package manager installations. This is another valid argument for the ease and efficiency of using pre-built software versus rolling your own — why mess with any of this stuff if you don't have to?

Ensure that your computer is set to boot from CD-ROM first so that the installation media is initialized before launching into the operating system. Most common desktop BIOSs require pressing the Delete or function keys during initial boot-up to access configuration settings. Often this is advertised during the memory count check, and creates a small window of opportunity to access a setup program wherein you can inspect (and if necessary, alter) BIOS configuration settings.

Generally speaking, we advise you to work with the latest kernel and/or distribution of choice available. Our reasons for this advice are many. Newer kernels and distribution sources address and resolve several key functional shortcomings, insecure programming constructs, demonstrably problematic code bugs, and previously unsupported hardware drivers. Therefore, to ensure optimal build time and minimize potential hang-ups, work with the most current applicable sources and packages whenever possible.

Throughout this book, we give preferential treatment to the Fedora Core, simply because it offers the best possible experience when building a MythTV system from scratch. Fedora offers one of the better Linux package managers available, and goes a long way toward streamlining the installation and upgrade process, especially with regard to how it handles new kernels. Fedora's package manager will gladly implement a new kernel (either freshly compiled or as part of a pre-compiled package) and begin using it right away upon the next reboot. This is a much needed departure from the tedium found in similar package management solutions from competing Linux distributors, most of which require a fair amount of user interaction before readying a new kernel for use.

The latest version of Fedora Core is available at `http://fedora.redhat.com/download/mirrors.html`.

Applying the ISO image (or image set) to a bootable medium is left as an exercise for the reader. Those who need step-by-step instructions can find them on the Web; one good tutorial is available from `www.redhat.com/docs/manuals/linux/RHL-9-Manual/getting-started-guide/s1-disks-cdrw.html`.

Fedora/Red Hat Configuration Considerations

Although Chapter 4 walks you step by step through Fedora Core installation, you need to make some decisions and get a game plan together before starting the installation. This section helps you navigate that process.

Red Hat has gone to great lengths to streamline its installation process — to the point where it rivals Windows' ease of use. Whether installing from multi-part CD-ROM images or a single DVD ROM image, the general setup procedure remains the same.

Before installing Linux, determine which file system(s) you want to use and the general layout for each storage volume. This comes into play during the Fedora Core installation process when you are prompted to partition the disk for Linux.

During installation, when you are prompted to install from a series of profiles, choose Custom Install. Doing so enables fine-grained package selection for a custom-designed build. Then you will be asked whether to automatically or manually partition the first initialized drive using Disk Druid, a Linux partition management tool. Each custom build has its own unique set of requirements, so your partition scheme and file system format will vary according to need.

By default, the Fedora Core installer will specify EXT3 as the file system for the first identified disk drive. In Chapter 1, we explained that either JFS or XFS is better suited to storing large data sets such as video footage and music files. The EXT3 format is fine for the root and boot partitions but we recommend using a separate JFS or XFS partition to store MythTV data.

Installing grub (a Linux boot manager) to disk allows for the management of multiple operating system partitions on the same or a series of volumes. Unless you have a boot manager already, choose to install grub to disk. Configuration of the network device depends entirely on your network setup — whether your DVR is directly exposed to the Internet or part of a greater topology of clients and gateway devices.

This decision is also related to the subsequent step, installation of a firewall. While not entirely necessary for a DVR (unless directly exposed to the Internet — a truly bad idea), if you choose to enable one, then be sure to permit Secure Shell (SSH) access and Web-based traffic at minimum. SSH access allows for remote administration over secure channels, while the Web server functionality is integral to the daily operation of MythTV.

Finally, you will set the local time zone, establish an administrator password, and then be presented with a list of packages and subpackages from which to select for installation. Although the KDE desktop environment is recommended for all around compatibility with MythTV, GNOME reportedly works quite well and is an equally good alternative window manager. These are the two window managers of choice for use with MythTV and remain the only two we recommend for first-time users of Linux for this purpose.

Among the remaining selections, you may choose to install MySQL now or build from source code and packages afterward. If you plan on using the MythWeb plug-in, you should select the Web server packages at this time. Recommended, but not required, for compilation of source code are the development tools — in particular, GCC and the automake utilities.

Fedora's installer will then begin the process of installing Linux to your chosen hard drive. How long this process takes depends on a few variables, including the hardware in question, the method of install (remote or local), and the number of packages selected.

Once this finishes, you may proceed with the segment on creating the MythTV program database.

Disabling SELinux Post-Installation

In addition to tackling numerous post-installation tasks, Fedora Core must give special consideration to the Security-Enhanced Linux (SELinux) role-based policy extensions. (Comprehensive coverage of SELinux is not provided in this book.) Be aware that its mere presence and activity on the system can impede proper operation of MythTV. For example, communications between a MythWeb plug-in to a backend server are prohibited by the default SELinux extensions. We could go on about similar issues ad nauseum, but instead provide pointed advice in Chapter 4.

Fedora Core and Yellowdog Updater, Modified

Updates handled via Fedora's adopted package manager yum (short for Yellowdog Updater, Modified) install the latest available kernel. yum configures all relevant underpinnings transparently and conveniently for the end-user, streamlining the entire installation process and handling all the dirty details behind the scenes. Newcomers to the Linux realm (especially those users most accustomed to Windows) will find yum and similar package management utilities a very pleasant departure from the typically cryptic and off-putting textual installation methods common to older distributions.

Third-party repositories should be introduced to yum at this stage to avoid any potential conflict later during the upgrade process (the following section of the chapter explains how to do this).

An excellent third-party repository — especially for MythTV purposes — that coordinates with several other major third-party repositories is maintained online by Axel Thimm at http://atrpms.net.

Of special interest is the Fedora Core 5 node situated at http://atrpms.net/dist/fc5/ and multimedia at http://atrpms.net/topic/multimedia/, both of which contain a variety of available MythTV packages necessary for a functional build (32-bit versions: mythtv, mythmkmovie, mythplugins, mythstream; 64-bit versions: mythtv-x86_64, mythplugins-x86_64).

A quick jump-start procedure taken from the Fedora MythTV How-To is in order to quickly add these two repositories to your yum file so yum will search for packages there:

```
# cd /etc/yum.repos.d/
# /usr/bin/wget http://wilsonet.com/mythtv/atrpms.repo
# /usr/bin/wget http://wilsonet.com/mythtv/freshrpms.repo
```

Jarod Wilson makes a very important observation in his authoritative Fedora MythTV How-To regarding the Fedora Core/Red Hat package management system:

> *WARNING:* Do NOT attempt any other rpm activity while the upgrade is in progress. Performing multiple exclusive rpm operations at the same time can lead to very bad things happening (rpm database inconsistencies, race conditions, completely hosed database, etc.). After the big upgrade, you MAY get an error about being unable to open the rpm database (this used to happen to me w/RHL9, but hasn't ever with FC). If you do encounter this error, try the following:
>
> ```
> # /bin/rm -f /var/lib/rpm/__db*
> ```
>
> ```
> # /bin/fm -f /var/lib/rpm/
> ```
>
> Corrections made in this manner are thorough and can run for great lengths of time especially on particularly outdated distributions and packages, or machines working with conservative system specifications.

On a 2.2 GHz AMD Athlon 64 processor with 1 GB of DDR400 RAM, the aforementioned process was timed with the following results:

```
# /usr/bin/time $(/usr/bin/rpmdb -vv --rebuilddb 2>&1 >/dev/null)&
real    0m46.769s
user    0m20.301s
sys     0m3.084s
```

Packages are made publicly available in a variety of formats and compression schemes. This text primarily deals with gzip compressed archives (suffixed by .gz) and bzip2 compressed files (ending in .bz or .bz2). Such archives are unfurled with their complementary decompression utilities, gunzip and bunzip2, respectively.

For a complete walkthrough of the entire Fedora Core installation process, readers are advised to consult the following documentation provided by the Fedora Project:

`http://fedora.redhat.com/docs/fedora-install-guide-en/fc5/`

The next course of action is to obtain and install MythTV source code as described in the next section. Although building MythTV from source is more time consuming than using the prepackaged version, you do have the flexibility to control what is compiled into MythTV and how (if you are so inclined).

Downloading and Compiling MythTV: The Pre-Packaged Version

MythTV and the entirety of its prerequisite and supporting codebase (in the form of add-in modules and theme collections) comes conveniently pre-packaged for your convenience courtesy of Axel Thimm on his Web site, `http://ATrpms.net/topic/multimedia`. It is advisable to use this resource to your advantage, especially for first-time builders. This way, all the dirty work involved in resolving hidden dependencies and coordinating all appropriate header files and shared libraries is already handled.

This section provides a brief summary of the instructions for installing and operating ATrpms. You can obtain more detailed instructions directly from the ATrpms Web site at `http://atrpms.net/install.html`.

First, import the ATrpms PGP signature key found at the following address:

`http://atrpms.net/RPM-GPG-KEY.atrpms`

These keys are vital to ensuring the integrity and authenticity of any files you obtain through the ATrpms repository and are used for the commands that follow shortly. There are two ways to implement this key for use with ATrpms. Recent versions of the Red Hat Package Manager utility (`rpm`) work with the following single-line command:

```
$ /usr/bin/rpm --import http://ATrpms.net/RPM-GPG-KEY.atrpms
```

Older versions may not work this way, and must instead use a second intermediary step:

```
$ /usr/bin/wget http://ATrpms.net/RPM-GPG-KEY.atrpms
$ /usr/bin/rpm --import RPM-GPG.KEY.atrpms
```

By following one of these paths, you are at liberty to manually download each of the RPMs necessary for your MythTV build (which can be tedious and error-prone), or to force the native package manager to do all the heavy lifting for you instead (depending upon the distribution, this may mean using `smart`, `apt`, `yum`, or `up2date`).

Sample configuration files for some common package management utilities are shown in the following code, as they appear in the ATrpms install guide (all are specific to Fedora Core 5).

From the `/etc/smart/channels/smart.channel` file:

```
#
# atrpms
# Fedora Core 4 - i386 - ATrpms
#
[atrpms]
name=Fedora Core 4 - i386 - ATrpms
baseurl=http://dl.atrpms.net/fc5-i386/atrpms
components=stable
type=apt-rpm
```

From the `/etc/apt/sources.list` file:

```
#
# atrpms
# Fedora Core 5 - i386 - ATrpms
#
rpm http://dl.atrpms.net fc5-i386/atrpms stable
```

From the `/etc/yum.conf` file:

```
[atrpms]
name=Fedora Core $releasever - $basearch - ATrpms
baseurl=http://dl.atrpms.net/fc$releasever-$basearch/atrpms/stable
```

From the `/etc/sysconfig/rhn/sources` file:

```
#
# atrpms
# Fedora Core 4 - i386 - ATrpms
apt atrpms http://dl.atrpms.net fc5-i386/atrpms stable
```

Additionally, MythTV provides 64-bit packages for users who want to leverage the full potential of the latest AMD and Intel CPUs. You must take special care to ensure that all requisite packages are 64-bit editions (usually indicated by an `x86_64` suffix that replaces an `i386` suffix).

After you enter one of the previous sets of commands (or whatever set is appropriate for your specific situation), your local package manager is ready to begin obtaining and installing pre-compiled packages from third-party repositories. Subsequent to these actions you should then continue to the next section, which offers an excellent font library to work from that makes all the difference for MythTV. You may also want MP3 support in your MythTV box, and due to copyright restrictions, the MP3 library is not shipped with Fedora by default; you will have to build and install the LAME MP3 library (or similar), which we demonstrate for you next.

Building True Type Fonts (libttf)

The FreeType 2 library of fonts is a requirement for MythTV installation as of the current version (0.18.1). FreeType 2 is a software library used to implement a lightweight and efficient font engine capable of rasterizing characters into bitmaps, and it plays host to a variety of font-related runtime operations. It is used for everything from graphics libraries and display drivers to font conversion and text image-generation tools.

This library is made available for public consumption through the FreeType Project (www.freetype.org/) under both the BSD-Like FreeType and GPL licenses.

The source code is available in various file formats:

- JPEG—www.ijg.org/files/jpegsrc.v6b.tar.gz
- TIFF—ftp://ftp.remotesensing.org/pub/libtiff/tiff-v3.6.1.tar.gz
- LibPNG—http://prdownloads.sourceforge.net/libpng/libpng-1.2.8.tar.gz?download
- zlib compression library—www.zlib.net/zlib-1.2.3.tar.gz

Existence of these library dependencies can be verified using the following commands:

```
# /usr/bin/rpm -q -a | /usr/bin/grep "gd|libjpeg|libtiff"
# /usr/bin/rpm -q -a | /usr/bin/grep "libpng|freetype|zlib"
```

The following section describes how to manually install the FreeType 2 font engine library.

Installing FreeType 2 by Package

The next sequence of commands not only illustrates how to use a package manager to get things done in Linux, it also shows how simple it can be to use such a tool to install packages and resolve conflicts.

For Fedora Core users, execute the following:

```
$ /usr/bin/su -
Password:
# /usr/bin/yum -y install freetype freetype-devel
```

For KnoppMyth and Debian installations using apt-get, issue the following commands:

```
$ /usr/bin/su -
Password:
# /usr/bin/apt-get install freetype freetype-devel
```

Building FreeType 2 from Source Archive

Once the aforementioned dependencies are resolved, you will be permitted to build the requisite codebase for the FreeType 2 API. The following instructions complete this process:

```
$ /usr/bin/tar -zxf freetype-2.1.10.tar.gz
$ cd freetype-2.1.10
$ ./configure --prefix=/usr --enable-shared --enable-static
$ /usr/bin/make
# /usr/bin/sudo /usr/bin/make Install
```

For any outstanding library dependencies, each package must be obtained individually and then compiled until the FreeType library can be constructed. Once that library is complete, you are ready to move on to building the libmp3lame library.

Building LAME (libmp3lame)

The LAME acronym is recursive and expands to "LAME is not an MP3 Encoder" (following the lead of the open-source initiative GNU, which stands for "GNU's Not UNIX"). LAME is an open-source MPEG-1, MPEG-2, and MPEG-2.5 (audio layer 3) encoder that produces high-quality bitrate samples (128 kbit/s or better), and is publicly available, free of charge, under the GNU Lesser General Public License (LGPL).

LAME offers a multitude of command-line flag optimizations specific to the audio sample quality of the underlying sound-card device or audio chipset in use. LAME can encode audio in Average Bit Rate (ABR), Constant Bit Rate (CBR), and Variable Bit Rate (VBR) formats, although VBR is the preferred method of choice for space-conscious storage. In addition to MP3, VBR methods for encoding Advanced Audio Encoding (AAC), Windows Media Audio (WMA), and Ogg Vorbis audio file formats also exist, which allocate more storage space to complex audio segments while making conservative allocations for everything else.

Existing installations can verify the presence of LAME with the following commands:

```
# /bin/ls -l /usr/local/lib | /usr/bin/grep lame
# /usr/bin/which lame
```

Unless you intend to build the application from scratch, you may proceed to the section on building the Qt library and binary packages.

Installing LAME by Package

Installing the LAME MP3 encoder library couldn't be more straightforward. Using the Fedora Core preferred method of choice goes like this:

```
# /usr/bin/yum -y install lame lame-devel
```

Conversely, Red Hat–based installations that lack the Yellowdog Updater, Modified can use the old standard rpm utility:

```
# /usr/bin/rpm -ivh lame-*
```

Finally, KnoppMyth or Debian-derived distributions can use the native Debian package manager, apt-get, to acquire an MP3 library:

```
# /usr/bin/apt-get install lame lame-devel
```

Any of those command sequences should install LAME from the Linux distributor site.

Building LAME from Source Code

Fetch the latest source archive from the SourceForge code repository:

```
http://lame.sourceforge.net
```

The most current (non-beta) version as of this writing is lame-3.96.tar.gz (dated July 1, 2004), and currently lame-3.97b2.tar.gz is available in beta form. Either is suitable for MythTV.

The following URL leads you directly to the SourceForge download mirror browser:

`http://prdownloads.sourceforge.net/lame/lame-3.96.tar.gz`

Following are the contents of `lame-3.96.1-0.1vn.4.4.i386.rpm`:

```
/usr/bin/lame
/usr/bin/mp3rtp
/usr/lib/libmp3lame.so.0
/usr/lib/libmp3lame.so.0.0.0
/usr/share/doc/lame-3.96.1
/usr/share/doc/lame-3.96.1/COPYING
/usr/share/doc/lame-3.96.1/ChangeLog
/usr/share/doc/lame-3.96.1/LICENSE
/usr/share/doc/lame-3.96.1/README
/usr/share/doc/lame-3.96.1/TODO
/usr/share/doc/lame-3.96.1/USAGE
/usr/share/doc/lame-3.96.1/basic.html
/usr/share/doc/lame-3.96.1/contributors.html
/usr/share/doc/lame-3.96.1/examples.html
/usr/share/doc/lame-3.96.1/history.html
/usr/share/doc/lame-3.96.1/id3.html
/usr/share/doc/lame-3.96.1/index.html
/usr/share/doc/lame-3.96.1/lame.css
/usr/share/doc/lame-3.96.1/modes.html
/usr/share/doc/lame-3.96.1/node6.html
/usr/share/doc/lame-3.96.1/presets.html
/usr/share/doc/lame-3.96.1/switchs.html
/usr/share/man/man1/lame.1.gz
```

Compile and install LAME from source with the following command sequence:

```
$ /bin/tar -zxf lame-3.96.1.tar.gz
$ cd lame-3.96.1
$ ./configure  --disable-static --disable-frontend
$ /usr/bin/make
$ /usr/bin/sudo /usr/bin/make install
```

Barring any fatal errors emitted from the compiler during compilation, the preceding list of commands builds and rolls out the LAME MP3 encoder library.

Building Qt Libraries and Binaries

The Qt Class Library is a large Application Programming Interface (API) composed of C++ classes that encapsulate the range of functionality necessary for end-to-end application development. Portions of that framework include Graphical User Interface (GUI) API calls, database and network programming, internationalization, and other important functions.

Proper installation of the Qt Class Library is essential to proper operation of MythTV. The Qt library is available from `http://atrpms.net` for the `yum` package management system using the previously cited ATrpms configuration.

We advise you to use the package manager designed for your chosen distribution for ease and efficiency. However, this may not always be feasible for various reasons. A given package may not appear in a particular distribution, so the only option then becomes third-party packages (in the form of RPMs) to handle locally through your update manager (instead of querying online repositories) or generated from compiling from raw source code.

Your first order of business must be to verify whether or not the Qt libraries are present and identified by the system. A quick check of the $PATH and $QTDIR environment variables can be informative:

```
$ /bin/echo $QTDIR
/usr/lib/Qt-3.3
$ /bin/echo $PATH
/usr/local/bin:/usr/bin:/bin:/usr/lib/qt3/bin
```

The $QTDIR environment variable points to the location of the Qt libraries, which the compiler suite inspects when building packages that require Qt. As shown, the Qt directory path variable is already set. The $PATH environment variable appears beneath it. This entry shows a brief list of paths to traverse (literally from left to right) when searching for executables. While your $PATH will certainly vary, what's important is that it contains an entry for /usr/lib/qt3/bin (or wherever your Qt library binaries reside).

Next, to verify that qmake, Qt's own specialized version of the make utility, is also present, try the following command:

```
$ /usr/bin/which qmake
/usr/bin/qmake
```

Next follows a series of commands that create a shell script named mythtv.sh within the /etc/profile.d directory. This script establishes the Qt variable dependencies necessary for the proper operation of all applications that use Qt libraries. Create this file by hand only if the preceding entries are not set or do not make mention of the Qt directory:

```
# /bin/cat > /etc/profile.d/mythtv.sh <<_EOF_
#!/bin/sh
export QTDIR=/usr/lib/qt3
export PATH=${PATH}:/usr/lib/qt3/bin
_EOF_
# /bin/chmod a+x /etc/profile.d/mythtv.sh
```

Installing the Qt Library by Package

When implementing the Qt libraries through the Fedora Core package manager during post-installation tasks, be sure to include the qt-MySQL portion (required for use with MythTV and MySQL):

```
# /usr/bin/yum -y install qt-devel qt-MySQL
```

This library is not implicitly required for the Qt framework and will not be installed by default.

Fedora's package manager will then fetch the current development libraries in addition to the MySQL Qt library and resolve any unmet dependencies for both.

Building the Qt Library from Source

Compiling Qt can take a while to finish because it chunks through the entire library API, not all of which is entirely necessary for a MythTV system. For this reason, users with especially conservative system component specifications may want to use a variety of compile-time flags to help compress the build:

```
$ ./configure -no-style-cde -no-style-motif -no-style-mac \
  -no-style-motif -no-style-motifplus -no-style-platinum \
  -no-style-sgi -no-ipv6 -thread -qt-imgfmt-png \
  -qt-imgfmt-jpeg -no-imgfmt-img -no-tablet \
  -system-zlib -fast -qt-sql-mysql \
  -I/usr/include/mysql \
  -I/usr/lib/mysql
```

Note   Line breaks are indicated by backslashes. For Linux, this informs the user shell that long lines of text wrap around to the next line, so they may be properly parsed inside the Linux command-line utilities.

Once you've agreed to the obligatory GPL user license agreement, the pre-compile configuration utility handles all the dirty work to ready Qt libraries for use on your hardware. Following that, make a simple modification so that Qt will compile cleanly and correctly with MySQL:

```
$ /bin/echo 'QMAKE_FLAGS_SHLIB += -single_module' >> src/qt.pro
$ /usr/bin/make sub-src
```

The preceding flags primarily turn off specific Qt features, such as compiling in library requirements for various optional components such as the Qt style libraries. As an example, we turn off CDE, Compact, Mac, Motif, Motif-Plus, Platinum, and SGI styles, disable Internet Protocol version 6, and link against the MySQL library. It is not required that all (or any) of these flags be used in combination; we merely illustrate the fine-grained control you have when compiling application software under Linux, and how compile-time options influence compile-time execution. Your mileage will certainly vary.

To see a list of all currently supported compile-time options, invoke `configure` with the following parameter:

```
$ ./configure --help
```

Each set of `./configure` options is unique to the application software being compiled. Be aware that the configuration script makes a best-effort attempt to pull in all the necessary information to achieve successful compilation so that little (if any) user interaction (including use of flags) is only seldom needed.

Working with Program Guides: XMLTV and Zap2It.com DataDirect

In Chapter 3, we provide information about how to configure your MythTV backend to use Zap2It services for obtaining program guide listings. If you are working from an existing installation, you are required to complete these tasks to fulfill the requirements for using the Zap2It/DataDirect services.

Installing XMLTV by Package

ATrpms packages for Fedora Core and MythTV are available at `http://atrpms.net/dist/fc5/xmltv/`.

Currently there are five XMLTV package dependencies (in order of appearance):

- xmltv-gui-0.5.42-65.rhfc5.at.noarch.rpm
- xmltv-grabbers-0.5.42-65.rhfc5.at.noarch.rpm
- xmltv-0.5.42-65.rhfc5.at.noarch.rpm
- perl-XMLTV-0.5.42-65.rhfc5.at.noarch.rpm
- xmltv-0.5.42-65.rhfc5.at.src.rpm

The sixth and final file is a specification file for use internally with the package management system when configuring the XMLTV package. Installation of the preceding items is straight-forward, using the following command:

```
# /usr/bin/rpm -Uvh xmltv* perl*
```

That's it, you're done. Proceed to the next section on building MythTV.

Building XMLTV from Source

XMLTV is a suite of television program guide management applications based on the Extensible Markup Language (XML) format, as the name implies.

XMLTV software for use with MythTV is available at `http://xmltv.sourceforge.net/`.

A checkout (CVS) version of the XMLTV software package is available from `http://sourceforge.net/project/showfiles.php?group_id=39046`.

Two packages are contained at this address: The first is the `xmltv` base package, and the other is a series of prerequisites for getting the `xmltv` application up and running.

The following code example demonstrates how you can obtain current source code from the XMLTV CVS server at SourceForge:

```
$ export CVSROOT=":pserver:anonymous@cvs.sourceforge.net:"
$ /usr/bin/cvs -d ${CVSROOT}/cvsroot/xmltv login
$ /usr/bin/cvs -z3 -d ${CVSROOT}/cvsroot/xmltv
```

First, you create the CVSROOT environment variable (for your own convenience in the following commands), and then log into the CVS server on the second line. Next, request the current software suite from SourceForge; your current directory will become populated with an xmltv path with all the requisite files. Finally, create and invoke the script that will make this package and install it:

```
$ /usr/bin/perl Makefile.PL
$ /usr/bin/make
$ /usr/bin/sudo /usr/bin/make install
```

Requisite PERL modules are listed in the README file contained with XMLTV source packages. Each of these dependencies must be resolved through the use of a PERL-oriented service called CPAN — the Comprehensive Perl Archive Network. CPAN is the canonical gateway for PERL code and modules and is made available to any Linux distribution with the PERL development package.

Begin using the CPAN service through invocation of the /usr/bin/perl binary, and begin installing the requirements as listed in the XMLTV README file. An example session follows, demonstrating the use of CPAN to resolve PERL dependencies:

```
# /usr/bin/perl -MCPAN -e shell
cpan> install Bundle::CPAN
cpan> reload cpan
cpan> install XML::Parser
cpan> install XML::Twig
```

As of this writing, the most current version of XMLTV has at minimum the following PERL dependencies:

```
LWP 5.65
XML::Parser 2.34
XML::Twig 3.10
XML::Writer 0.4.6
Date::Manip 5.42a
Memoize (included with PERL 5.8 and later)
Storable (included with PERL 5.8 and later)
```

At this time you may be asked to install additional modules or other dependencies. Once this completes, you are ready to move ahead.

Building MythTV

Acquiring the necessary source files and packages for a fully functional MythTV build can be handled in a number of ways, as described previously. Because you have acquired and built all the foundational material, all that is left is to build MythTV.

Installing MythTV by Package

Here again the ease and efficiency in the package manager method of getting things done is evident in this single-line command:

```
# /usr/bin/yum -y install mythtv-suite
```

Execution of this single entry results in the entire installation of MythTV packages and dependencies (altogether totaling nearly 100 files!).

Building MythTV from Source

The following instructions are used to unfurl an archive created by the `bzip` utility:

```
$ /bin/tar -xjf mythtv-0.18.1.tar.bz2
$ cd mythtv-0.18.1
$ ./configure
$ /usr/bin/make
$ /usr/bin/sudo /usr/bin/make install
```

Notice that the preceding is specific to archives created by `bzip` (though universal to all distributions). The archive utility `tar` is called with the `-j` flag to decompress the `.bz2` format. Had the preceding archive instead ended in `.tgz` or `.gz`, indicating a `gzip` compressed archive, the first command from the preceding series would be changed as follows:

```
$ /bin/tar -xzf mythtv-0.18.1.tar.bz2
```

In this case, the `z` flag is used to decompress the archive.

Building MythTV through SVN Repository

The following instructions are used to obtain the latest development code through the Subversion revision control system (distribution-independent):

```
$ /bin/mkdir mythtv
$ cd mythtv
$ /usr/bin/svn co http://svn.mythtv.org/svn/trunk/mythtv
$ /usr/bin/svn co http://svn.mythtv.org/svn/trunk/mythplugins
$ /usr/bin/svn co http://svn.mythtv.org/svn/trunk/myththemes
$ /usr/bin/sudo ./configure
$ /usr/qt3/bin/qmake mythtv.pro
$ /usr/bin/make
$ /usr/bin/sudo /usr/bin/make install
```

Successful execution of the preceding commands will fetch the latest development source from the distributor Web site and then build the requisite application files for MythTV.

Building MythTV through CVS Repository

The following instructions are used to obtain the latest development code through the Concurrent Versions System:

```
$ /bin/mkdir mythtv
$ cd mythtv
$ export CVSROOT=":pserver:mythtv@cvs.mythtv.org:"
$ /usr/bin/cvs -d ${CVSROOT}/var/lib/mythcvs
$ /usr/bin/cvs -z6 -d $CVSROOT
$ /usr/bin/sudo ./configure
$ /usr/qt3/bin/qmake mythtv.pro
$ /usr/bin/make
$ /usr/bin/sudo /usr/bin/make install
```

Successful execution of the preceding commands will fetch the latest development source from the distributor Web site and then build the requisite application files for MythTV.

Installing MythTV from Source Code

Completion of either a CVS or SVN checkout and subsequent compilation requires one final step before going live, and that is to introduce the MythTV scripts into the fray of Fedora initialization scripts.

This set of commands shows you how:

```
$ cd contrib./
$ su
```

Change your current directory position to the contribution path, and then switch to the root user account. Enter the root password when you are prompted to do so.

```
# /bin/chmod a+x etc.rc.d.init.d.mythbackend
# /bin/cp etc.rc.d.init.d.mythbackend /etc/rc.d/init.d/mythbackend
# /bin/cp etc.sysconfig.mythbackend /etc/sysconfig/mythbackend
# /sbin/chkconfig mythbackend on
```

Make the example start-up script executable, and relocate that script into your MythTV configuration directory (called /etc). The second command uses the Linux copy command to rename and relocate this file at the same time. Replace only those periods between words that appear in the preceding code — Windows users will notice the unusual naming convention for a directory component, but this is valid in the case of rc.d and init.d. Next, copy your system configuration file into place and specify that the backend process is to persist across reboots.

That's all there is to it. Your MythTV build is almost ready for prime-time television.

Working with Pre-Compiled Versions of KnoppMyth and Fedora

Perhaps the ultimate solution when building your own MythTV system involves using an existing Linux installation, which clearly eliminates most of the initial work involved. MythTV may be easily implemented as a series of add-on packages to an existing Linux installation by going through the proper channels — usually meaning directly from the distributor. However, there is greater potential for conflict among updated packages coupled with the kiss of death — that is, *deprecation*, or the inevitable end-of-life label branded on packages slated for removal.

Conversely, third-party repositories can help you establish a given package quickly, by covering all related dependencies in a single package, or group of interrelated packages. These work equally well in lieu of official releases from the main distribution channels. Furthermore, any package marked as obsolescent by the main top-level distributor (such as Fedora/Red Hat) may remain valid and actively developed in the public domain. Software does not become useless just because an application is replaced by the point-of-view (distributor-specific) application of the month.

The distinction made here is that you can custom configure, compile, and install MythTV from source code or just pull down pre-compiled packages from your distributor's Web site (where they are available). Your level of comfort and desire to understand the inner workings of Linux will determine how involved you want to get in this process. We provide you with the information to get it done.

Getting Fedora Core Up to Date

Easily the most time-consuming phase during your MythTV build process is the initial update procedure, so plan for this process to carry on during a period of downtime. One way to do this would be to schedule the system-wide update utility to run at night, after you're done for the day. Fedora Core harnesses tremendous power in its package manager, yum. The nice thing about yum is that it resolves library dependencies transparently on the user's behalf:

```
# /usr/bin/yum -y update
# /usr/sbin/reboot
```

Current packages are essential to ensuring a smooth MythTV build. We advise you to update whichever distribution you choose by going through proper channels. Ideally, a proper channel is the distributor site, but in the interests of stability only known, good (meaning thoroughly field-tested) packages ever make it into a stable distribution repository. Whether you are working with a fresh or existing Linux installation, you should still update any applicable software to attain the highest level of functionality and compatibility.

Getting KnoppMyth Up to Date

Another nice thing KnoppMyth has going for it (apart from its quick time-to-use) is that all (or most) of its dependencies are taken care of well before an ISO image is ever created. The developers have gone through all the trouble of resolving dependency issues and implementing the MythTV package to the point where you literally just boot and install KnoppMyth.

KnoppMyth is pre-loaded with the IVTV driver stack that supports the ever-popular Hauppauge PCI-based capture cards (PVR-150, PVR-150MCE, PVR-250, PVR-350, and the PVR-500 series). Probably the one activity you will find yourself undertaking is applying post-installation maintenance updates for incremental code fixes and enhancements from time to time — if you're at all concerned about running the most current packages. A bit of post-installation tweaking and tuning is all that follows after the KnoppMyth method before you find yourself up and running with a Linux-based MythTV system.

The MythTV Program Database

Creating and maintaining the MythTV program database is the responsibility of the master backend server — whether it operates with one or more slave backend machines or exists as a single standalone device. The MythTV database need not be duplicated elsewhere, for the master backend server will inform any slave backend machines about program guide information.

The database management system for MythTV is MySQL.

Working with MySQL

MySQL holds a good market share of installations across a variety of platforms — from BSD to Windows. It's a formidable Structured Query Language (SQL) Database Management System (DBMS), and is available under the terms of the GNU GPL.

Common MythTV configurations maintain a MySQL database locally on the one and only MythTV system in the picture. Distributed implementations that employ multiple slave backends do not require local copies of the database on each machine.

The following commands enable MySQL to show up across system reboots, with the second command enabling MySQL to be active on the local machine:

```
$ su -
# /sbin/chkconfig mysqld on
# /sbin/service mysqld start
```

These commands will come in handy later, especially in Chapter 6, when we discuss how to fill out the program database using MySQL and XMLTV listings from Tribune Media Services.

Creating the MythTV Program Database

To make MythTV useful in any way, you must first establish a MythTV-specific database entry; otherwise, MySQL will not understand what MythTV wants or needs to know. The following command configures MySQL with a generic MythTV database template:

```
$ /usr/bin/mysql -u root < /usr/share/mythtv/database/mc.sql
```

Next, configure MySQL so that it cooperates nicely with MythTV's database application without throwing errors. To illustrate, one error produced by MySQL occurs when a user has insufficient privileges to modify global tables, which may be remedied as follows:

```
$ /usr/bin/mysql -u root mytconverg
mysql> GRANT ALL ON mythconverg.* TO mythtv@"localhost" identified
by \ "mythtv";
mysql> flush privileges;
```

Or for a more restrictive (and thus safer in multi-user environments) alternative:

```
$ mysql> GRANT ALL ON mythconverg.* TO mythtv@"192.168.1.%"
identified by "mythtv";
mysql> flush privileges;
```

With the preceding code, access to the MythTV database is restricted only to hosts resident on the local network. Chapter 6 explains how to set up a regularly scheduled batch job to maintain the program guide listings, occasionally polling relevant servers for updated information so that no user interaction is required.

Final Thoughts

From the instructions in this chapter, you should now have most of the software you'll need to begin the MythTV build process on an existing Linux installation — primarily on Fedora Core 5. Any previous Linux experience you have will provide you with fewer potential hang-ups than an inexperienced user, but you are advised to create a new installation because it is much cleaner and less error-prone than implementing these details by hand. Chapter 4 provides coverage for installing a clean image of Fedora on your MythTV hardware if you prefer to sidestep these avoidable complications altogether.

The following chapters cover an array of interrelated subjects that address fine-tuning the operational aspects and behavioral controls of MythTV. Co-authors Jarod Wilson and Matt Wright tackle advanced topics for eking out a little more performance from your DVR build by exposing the mystery behind MythTV operation. In addition to the thorough treatment provided for building a functional DVR solution fashioned from Linux and MythTV, they lend their expertise and insight to several areas — ranging from optimal handling of high-definition audio and video playback to interacting with external entertainment gear.

Chapter 3 covers key aspects of sound and picture, from standard-fare to high-definition playback. We discuss the selection of and settings for requisite sound drivers, mixers, and multichannel sound, and explain how to deal with optical audio. After that, you will learn how to work with SDTV and HDTV components, and how to optimize playback quality.

To kick off Part II, Chapter 4 walks through initial setup and fleshes out a proper working environment for MythTV under Linux. This is where the book becomes truly hands-on, as we cover both software and hardware aspects of a MythTV system build. Chapter 5 goes on to explain remote control selections particularly well-suited for use with Linux and suitable for MythTV.

Following the initial build-up, Chapter 6 primarily deals with post-installation tasks to ready a MythTV system for use with a live television feed. Configuration of both master and slave backend systems is described, along with their mutually dependent database utility and a special note about DataDirect usage.

The MythTV frontend is explored further in Chapter 7. This is the window into your MythTV system, and provides onscreen access to control panel functionality that governs MythTV look, feel, and behavior. General and appearance controls are examined, in addition to program guide and playback and recording controls.

In Chapter 8 we dig deeper into the mysteries of MythTV and describe keyboard commands, how to create and implement themes, and explain how to work with both DirecTV and DishTV input streams. Special treatment is provided for advanced options such as shutdown and wake-up commands, scheduling recordings under MythTV, and working with multiple tuner cards — a must for anyone who wants to record and watch separate programs simultaneously.

In Part III, MythTV's modular plug-in framework is discussed at length. We define what a plug-in does, describe a list of plug-ins currently found with MythTV, and plug-ins not part of the core package, and then focus specifically on each plug-in and what each can do to enhance your MythTV experience.

Power users are treated to advanced topics on MythTV usage encompassing a variety of tips and tweaks in Part IV: Advanced MythTV Hacks. Chapter 15 breaks down the various aspects of the MythTV aesthetic, providing information about how you can fine-tune those little details that can make all the difference. You will learn how to add DVD menu support to MythTV, widescreen HDTV tweaks, how to handle raw digital streams to external decoder devices, along with various other hacks.

Chapter 16 is dedicated to performance issues when operating MythTV. From runtime privileges to maximizing throughput, we illustrate how to fine-tune the most important aspects for optimal playback. Chapter 17 deals with extending the functionality of your MythTV DVR environment through advanced topics related to importing and exporting file formats and controlling external devices through MythTV. Finally, Chapter 18 is devoted to troubleshooting.

We hope you enjoy the fruits of your labor just as much as we have in the collectively rewarding experience it took to make this book what it is.

MythTV Sound and Picture

I n this chapter, you explore the ins and outs of installing, configuring, and using sound and video sources inside MythTV. Our goal here is to help you understand what hardware components and software elements you need to make these key aspects of MythTV work, and how to make the most of their use. Along the way, you'll learn how to select the right kinds of hardware and what's involved in making things work.

Much of the magic that happens behind the scenes of MythTV occurs here with sights and sounds. MythTV usually provides a great out-of-the-box experience, which you can further improve by taking advantage of any special properties your sound or video cards may have. For example, high-definition audio can be played through optical or coaxial connections between your MythTV box and other electronics for an enriched audio experience. HDTV via Digital Video Broadcasting (DVB) playback is a relatively simple matter for you to set up, provided you possess the appropriate inputs on your television. This chapter also describes how to interact with the Zap2It DataDirect services for obtaining channel guide listings relevant to your subscription and region. Your journey through this chapter begins with configuring the sound aspect of your MythTV setup.

Sound and MythTV

MythTV is built upon the Advanced Linux Sound Architecture (ALSA) sound libraries. In Linux, multiple sound libraries may be used by a program to communicate with soundcard hardware. ALSA is the newest and most advanced. The Open Sound System (OSS) is the older foundation, now considered defunct by most of the Linux community.

Selecting and Setting Up a Sound Driver

The ASLA libraries needed for MythTV are installed by default with nearly all modern Linux distributions. Included with the ASLA package is a series of kernel module drivers for most common soundcards and on-board motherboard audio. You can check whether your sound card is supported by using the ALSA Sound Card Matrix, available at www.alsa-project.org/alsa-doc/.

The good news is that almost all on-board sound chips use the intel8x0 driver; it's a pretty safe bet when in doubt. If you have a newer motherboard with Intel HD audio on-board, then you'll use the hda-intel module. In addition, nearly all of the Creative family of sound cards is supported. The ALSA Sound Card Matrix will tell you which module to use if you find that you need to manually configure your sound.

Configuring Sound Settings

Many modern Linux distributions have an auto-detection setup for the sound card; if your system detects your card correctly, you should be ready to go.

Should you need to set up your sound card, a handy utility called alsaconf may or may not be included in your Linux distribution. If your installation does not already include this utility, grab it from the ALSA FTP site at www.alsa-project.org/alsa/ftp/driver/alsaconf/.

This handy tool will try to detect which Linux distribution and sound card (or circuitry) you are using, and then generate the appropriate module configuration statements for modprobe .conf or modules.conf, depending on how your distribution is set up.

Setting Up the Mixer

Most distributions include a nice mixer application for use within X-Windows. These vary by X-Window manager and distribution. The popular GNOME interface includes the straightforward mixer shown in Figure 3-1.

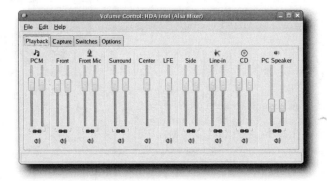

FIGURE 3-1: The GNOME mixer

If you cannot find your X-Windows mixer, there's also a text mode mixer available for you to use that should give you access to every volume setting you might ever want or need. The mixer is called alsamixer. Use the up and down arrows to raise or lower the volume of a selected channel; use the left and right arrows to make a selection; and use the M key to mute the current selection. You can see the Mic setting is muted in the example shown in Figure 3-2.

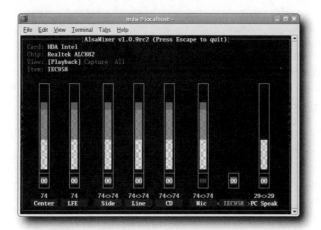

FIGURE 3-2: ALSAMixer (notice the MM, for muted, in the Mic column)

Multi-Channel Sound

Generally multi-channel analog sound is painless. Check the mixer to ensure that all surround channels are not muted and that all channel volumes are properly set.

S/PDIF Outputs

Enabling S/PDIF (Sony/Philips Digital Interface, a standard digital audio file format) output is normally as simple as unmuting IEC-958 playback in the mixer. (Note that S/PDIF is sometimes written SPDIF.) S/PDIF permits transfer of digital audio signals from one device to another without requiring conversion to analog, and thus retains maximum signal quality throughout the transfer.

Tip

In the ALSA materials you will also see S/PDIF output called IEC-60958; in `alsamixer` it is simply called IEC-958.

If you get stuck, you can find a lot of advanced information on making digital audio output work manually with ALSA at `www.mythtv.info` in their Digital Sound How-To (`www.mythtv.info/moin.cgi/DigitalSoundHowTo`).

Testing It All Out

To test things at a basic level, open a Terminal session and change the working directory to `/usr/share/sounds`. There you will find all sorts of sound clips that the system uses, along with various tools for X-Windows. Pick one that seems appropriate (`Startup3.wav`, for example) and then try playing it with the `aplay` command-line tool. Issue the command `aplay Startup3.wav` and see how it sounds — or whether you get sound at all. You may need to open the mixer and set the levels the way you want them to sound.

There are many more ways you can tweak your MythTV audio setup. See Chapter 15 for some useful suggestions.

MythTV Audio Setup

Once you have determined that your audio is working using the standard tools, run `mythtv-setup` and verify that `/dev/dsp0` is set for sound output. This is the default audio processor, and it should work for the vast majority of configurations.

Capturing TV with MythTV

A TV *capture card*, also called a TV *tuner card*, is a device that receives TV signals and converts them into a digital format your PC can understand and use. MythTV works with just about any TV capture device for which drivers made for the Video4Linux (V4L) application program interface are available. Digital TV devices, including both European DVB and North American ATSC standards, are supported within the Linux DVB subsystem. As of this writing, the DVB group is working with the V4L group to unify analog and digital TV subsystems into one single general-purpose subsystem.

Understanding Some Basic TV Terminology

Software Encoding Versus Hardware Encoding for Analog Capture

A typical inexpensive standard TV capture card enables your system's processor to do the heavy lifting when it comes to recording a TV signal using some digital video format that your PC understands; relying on the processor for this task is referred to as *software encoding*. More advanced TV cards can record directly to MPEG2 (the same digital video standard that DVDs use) using on-board hardware (*hardware encoding*), leaving your processor free to handle other tasks. Thanks to on-board MPEG encoding, it's possible for a MythTV system to incorporate multiple TV tuners so they can record two or more programs at the same time. With two tuners installed, you can record one program while watching another, or record two programs at the same time while you're off doing something else.

Digital TV (HDTV) Capture Versus Analog Capture

Most local broadcasters in the United States now offer digital transmissions in addition to standard analog feeds. These broadcasts consist of digital data streams sent over the air. Because they are digital, image quality can be many times better than analog, and reception is not subject to snow, static, or degradation from weak broadcast signals. Because HDTV is already digital, no encoding is needed, and a PC can understand these digital transmissions without additional processing effort. An HDTV tuner simply finds the right frequency and starts pulling a data stream down to your PC for display (and possibly recording to a hard drive). As you might imagine, recording HDTV requires very little CPU resources. However, thanks to the large jump in resolution compared to standard TV, playing back or watching live HDTV still requires quite a bit more CPU resources. A modern graphics card that offers MPEG2 acceleration can unburden your CPU quite a bit.

 Cross-Reference For more information on graphics cards and their associated drivers, consult Chapter 4.

Finding and Configuring TV Drivers

Modern kernels include the basic V4L modules that support most common software encoding TV tuner/capture chips, such as the Brooktree BT878, the Conexant CX23880, and the Philips SAA7134. Support for the Hauppauge PVR family of hardware MPEG2 encoding cards and a small group of their clones comes from a different V4L-compatible project known as IVTV.

The Plextor ConvertX TV402U and M402U are external USB 2.0 devices that can hardware encode analog video into MPEG2 or MPEG4. Proprietary drivers are available directly from the capture chip's manufacturer. The Plextor devices utilize chips from a company called WIS Technologies; drivers are available at its open-source software site: `http://oss.wischip .com/`. Currently MythTV only exposes MPEG4 encoding support.

For HDTV tuners, all necessary drivers are built into kernel versions 2.6.13 and later, and more new devices are added to each new version. It's a good idea to update to the latest stable kernel to make sure you get the best HDTV support possible.

Table 3-1 lists Web sites and links to additional information and resources for TV cards.

Table 3-1   TV Card Links

Site Name	URL and Comments
Video4Linux Wiki	http://linuxtv.org/v4lwiki/index.php/Main_Page This is the wiki for the Video4Linux project. It provides more information than you'll ever need about the various drivers and configuration settings for various supported TV cards.
LinuxTV.org DVB Wiki	http://www.linuxtv.org/wiki/index.php/Main_Page This is the sister project to Video4Linux for digital TV cards. It has a cornucopia of information about DVB cards.

Continued

Table 3-1 *(continued)*

Site Name	URL and Comments
IVTV Project Wiki	http://ivtvdriver.org/index.php/Main_Page This wiki for the IVTV project contains everything you need to know to get started with a Hauppauge PVR card, including links to downloads and common troubleshooting methods.
Plextor ConvertX PVR – Gentoo Linux Wiki	http://gentoo-wiki.com/HARDWARE_go7007 While this wiki is made for the Gentoo distribution, it contains a wealth of knowledge about making the Plextor ConvertX work and it can be adapted to any distribution.

Software Encoding TV Cards

Support for most of the software encoding TV cards is included in the Video4Linux system, part of all modern Linux distributions. Generally, all you need to do is simply install the card and power up your system. Linux will detect the new device, and normally it gets auto-detection of specific variations right.

IVTV Supported TV Cards

Using a Hauppauge PVR card requires slightly more effort because the needed modules are not included in typical distributions. Obtaining the modules is generally as simple as using your preferred updater, such as yum in Fedora Core. Chapters 2 and 4 include information on using yum.

Tip

If you install more than one IVTV-supported TV capture card in a MythTV system, or if you use a dual-tuner card such as the Hauppauge PVR-500MCE, then you'll need a second `alias char-major-81-x` entry for each individual capture device in your module's configuration:

```
alias char-major-81 videodev
alias char-major-81-0 ivtv
alias char-major-81-1 ivtv
```

Plextor ConvertX Family

Unlike other options presented here, Plextor support comes directly from the vendor and is only available for download in the form of source files that you must compile yourself. Instructions for doing this are included in the README file that's bundled with the download inside the compressed archive file in which it resides. Once compiled and installed, hook up the ConvertX device and then reboot your PC. After rebooting, Linux should automatically detect the ConvertX device.

High Definition Digital TV Cards

The list of working HDTV tuners for MythTV grows almost daily. Right now, that list includes some popular options from the Windows world, such as the DVICO Fusion 5 Gold and Lite, and the AVerMedia AVerTVHD A180. Also available are two series of HDTV tuners made only for Linux: the older air2pc family (now discontinued, but often found for sale on auction sites fairly easily), and the pcHDTV HD-3000, which is actively sold and supported today.

If you want a truly plug-and-play affair, go with the pcHDTV, but be prepared to pay a premium price because it is a custom-made card that is only supported under Linux. That said, the Fusion 5 series and AVerMedia A180 have been supported for a good while now, and should be nearly as easy to get working as the pcHDTV card. For more information on this device, visit the pcHDTV Web site at www.pchdtv.com.

As they support software encoding TV cards, modern Linux kernels also include the DVB system. Generally, all you need to do is install the card and power up your MythTV system. Linux will detect the new device, and it generally auto-detects specific variations correctly.

Setting Up Guide Listings

Guide listings for the United States are easy to obtain and have the same depth of information as commercial PVR solutions. As mentioned in Chapter 2, the nice folks at Tribune Media (owners of the Zap2it website) who provide TV guide data to most PC PVR solutions, as well as TiVo and more, have graciously allowed those who use free and open-source HTPC applications — such as MythTV — access to their guide listings. To get the guide setup you'll need to register with Zap2it Labs at http://labs.zap2it.com.

When you register, you'll be asked to take a short survey. You must also take a new survey in three months to keep your listings subscription active, but this is a small price to pay for free detailed guide data. You will also be asked for a Certificate Code to let Zap2it know you are using a legitimate freeware/open-source application. This code is not something Zap2it would like shared, and that code can be revoked or changed should something happen. Zap2it requests that the code only be shared in an application's official documentation. Thus, rather than repeat it in this book, we can tell you that the code may be found on the MythTV Web site: www.mythtv.org/docs/mythtv-HOWTO-5.html#ss5.3.

Go through the options and choose the right provider and channel packages for your TV card. If you have more than one lineup, such as analog cable, plus over-the-air HDTV, you must go back and set up any additional channel lineups you wish to add.

Importing Zap2it Data into MythTV

Next, run mythtv-setup and choose option 3 (Video sources). Create a new source and give it a descriptive name so you can distinguish it among various sources. For the XMLTV listings grabber, choose North America (Data Direct). Fill in the User ID and Password fields with the login you made for the Zap2it Labs Web site and then select Retrieve Lineups. You may choose between your channel lineups if you made more than one in the Data Direct Lineup field. Leave Channel frequency table at default. Click Finish to retain your settings. Figure 3-3 shows the completed Video source setup screen.

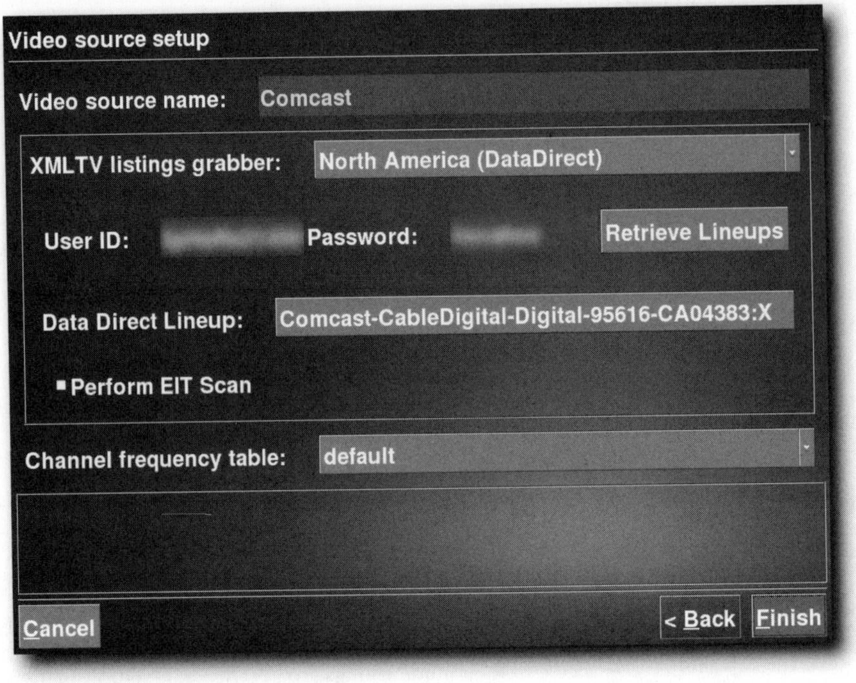

Video source setup

Video source name: Comcast

XMLTV listings grabber: North America (DataDirect)

User ID: ███████   Password: ███████   Retrieve Lineups

Data Direct Lineup: Comcast-CableDigital-Digital-95616-CA04383:X

■ Perform EIT Scan

Channel frequency table: default

Cancel   < Back   Finish

FIGURE 3-3: The Video source setup screen

Completing the TV Capture Setup

Configuring your standard-fare analog capture card is a relatively simple affair and — barring any errors in configuration or operation — you can have live television streaming into your home via MythTV in a matter of minutes. We provide you with basic examples for setting up standard definition television capture cards in both hardware (integrated) and software encoders, configuring digital television capture cards, and using the Zap2It DataDirect service for getting the latest program guide listings for your broadcast region.

Working with a Standard Definition TV Card with a Hardware Encoder

When it comes to handling coaxial cable feeds within a purely Linux context, Hauppauge manufactures superior internal components with excellent driver support and feature set. If you prefer the luxury of external video capture solutions, Plextor ConvertX USB units can be used in lieu of internal counterparts (configuration for this is provided below). Whether you are working with a software- or hardware-based encoder, we provide you with the basic details for setting up your capture device, starting with the popular Hauppage PVR-x50 series:

■ **Hauppauge PVR-250, PVR-150, and so on** — When you run `mythtv-setup`, choosing the second option (Capture Cards) presents you with an option to choose the card type. For an IVTV-supported card, you must choose MPEG-2 Encoder Card (PVR-x50, PVR-500), as shown in Figure 3-4.

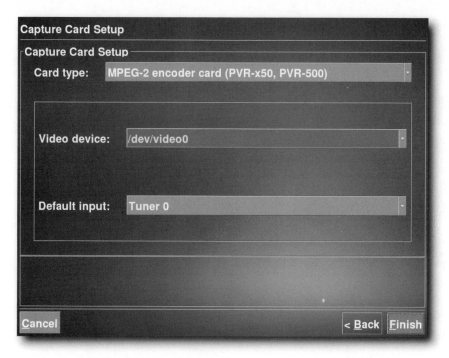

Figure 3-4: Hauppauge Capture Card setup

 Tip

If you have multiple standard-definition TV cards, the first device should be /dev/video0, the second would be /dev/video1, and so forth.

■ **Plextor ConvertX 402U family** — Run myth-setup and add a capture card (option 2 on the main screen); the proper device is called USB MPEG-4 Encoder (Plextor ConvertX, etc). You will need to change the audio device to /dev/dsp1 to record sound. After completing mythtv-setup, you must go into the MythTV frontend and customize recording profiles. Access the frontend, select Utilities/Setup → Setup → TV Settings → Recording Profiles. Choose USB MPEG-4 Encoder (Plextor ConvertX, etc).

To record TV properly, you need to adjust the ConvertX (see Figure 3-5) width to 640, but the default height of 480 is fine. A lower recording quality of 320 × 240 is also valid, and useful for archiving to CD. Go through each of the listed recording qualities, which are ordinarily Default, Live TV, High Quality, and Low Quality. The first screen enables you to rename the profile. Skip this and move to the second screen, and edit the width to 640. Skip the third screen, and on the final screen, Audio, set the value to Uncompressed. Now go back and make these changes to all of the listed recording qualities.

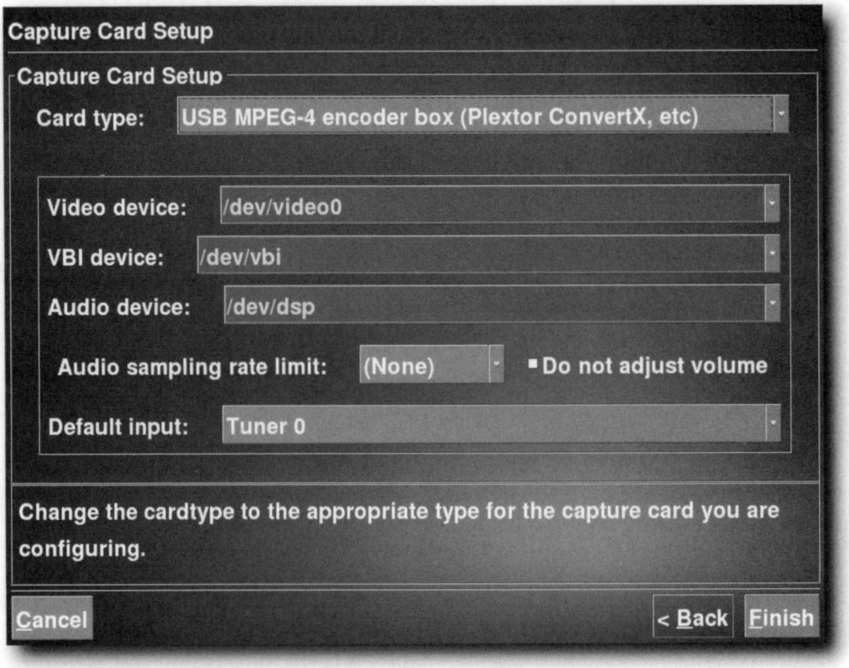

Capture Card Setup

Capture Card Setup

Card type: USB MPEG-4 encoder box (Plextor ConvertX, etc)

Video device: /dev/video0

VBI device: /dev/vbi

Audio device: /dev/dsp

Audio sampling rate limit: (None)   ▪ Do not adjust volume

Default input: Tuner 0

Change the cardtype to the appropriate type for the capture card you are configuring.

Cancel   < Back   Finish

FIGURE 3-5: Plextor ConvertX 402U setup

Working with a Standard Definition TV Card with Software Encoding

This broad range of TV capture cards is encapsulated under one card type simply called *Standard V4L capture card*. Figure 3-6 shows you the V4L setup screen. There isn't much more you'll need to do here for configuration. This class of TV capture cards relies on your CPU to do the work. Depending on your system's processor speed, you may need to adjust the Recording Profiles in the MythTV frontend to use a somewhat lower resolution such as 480 × 480, 320 × 480, or 352 × 240 to capture stable recordings without dropped frames. The steps to do this are outlined in the preceding section under the Plextor ConvertX devices bullet.

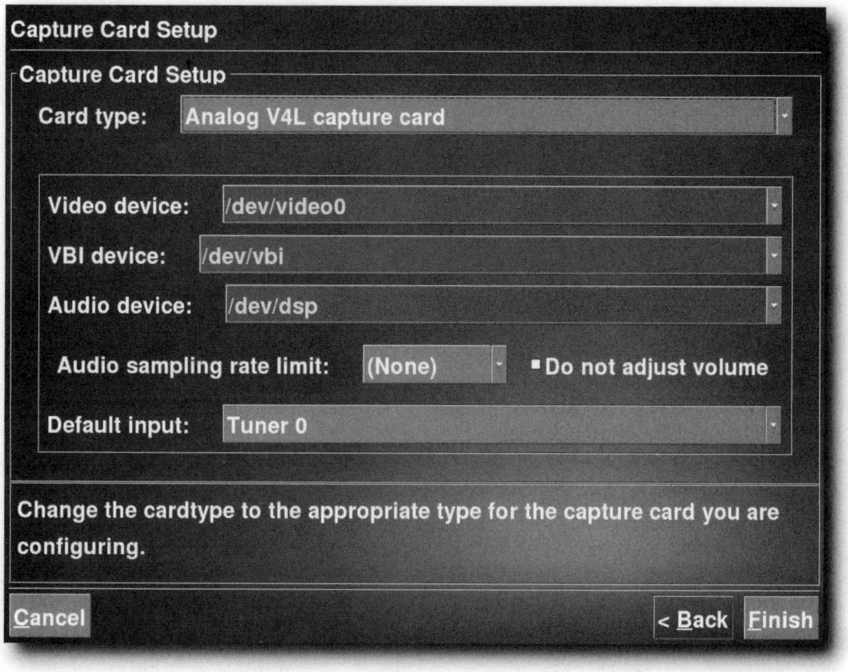

FIGURE 3-6: Analog V4L Capture Card setup

Working with a High-Definition TV Card

Just as with standard-definition cards, with a high-definition TV card in mythtv-setup, choose
the second option (Capture Cards). When you add a new card you must choose DVB; information about your HDTV card should appear under Card Name where Card Type should be
ATSC. Please note that Card Name may not be the actual brand and model number for your
HDTV tuner; it may instead simply name the vendor of the HDTV receiving chip your
HDTV tuner uses, as shown in Figure 3-7. The nice thing here is that there isn't really anything else to do, so click Finish to move on!

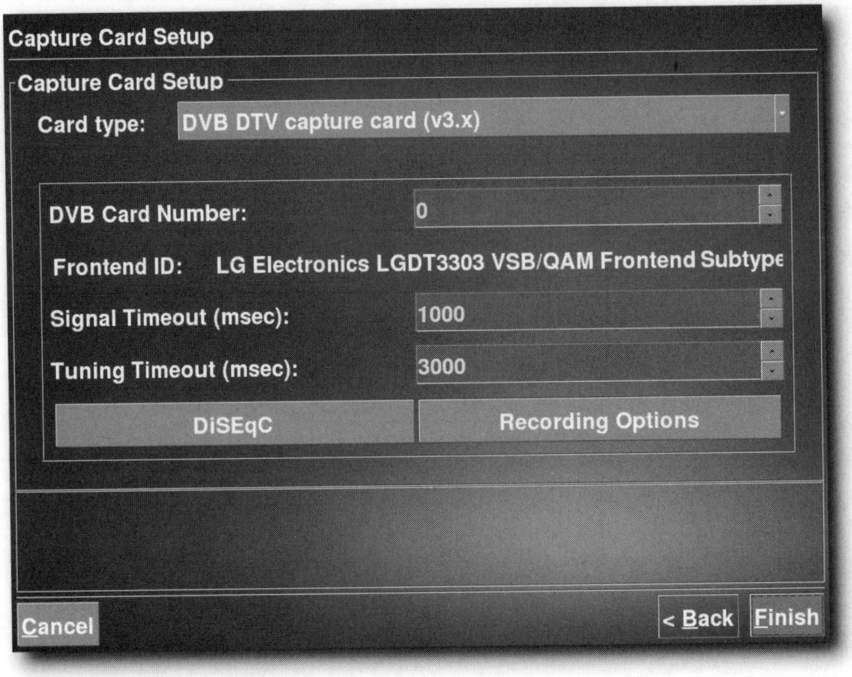

Capture Card Setup

Capture Card Setup

Card type: DVB DTV capture card (v3.x)

DVB Card Number: 0

Frontend ID: LG Electronics LGDT3303 VSB/QAM Frontend Subtype

Signal Timeout (msec):   1000

Tuning Timeout (msec):   3000

DiSEqC   Recording Options

Cancel   < Back Finish

FIGURE 3-7: HDTV tuner setup

Associating Channels with TV Cards

By now, you have built a channel listings setup from Zap2it, and MythTV knows what kind of TV capture cards you have. Next, you must link those listings to a TV card. In the main menu of the MythTV Setup, choose option number four (Input connections). As shown in Figure 3-8, you'll be presented with all possible inputs for each capture card. Selecting one enables you to choose which channel lineup to use as its input.

Note   You must enter a valid *Starting channel* to enable MythTV to initialize properly. This is especially important for HDTV: Without a proper digital channel to use as a starting point, the HDTV tuner fails to initialize correctly.

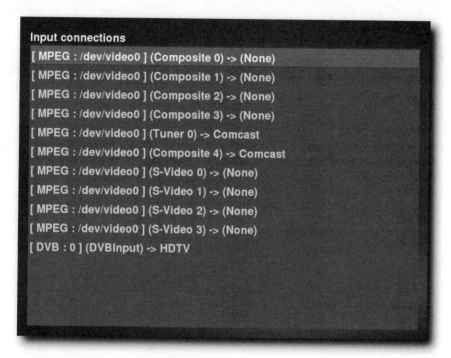

FIGURE 3-8: The Input connections screen

Finishing Up and Enjoying TV

When you are done associating channel lineups with TV cards, return to the main menu and press Escape to return to the command line. MythTV Setup will remind you to run mythfilldatabase. This is a critical step: It synchronizes the MythTV database with your new settings and starts the download and import of your first batch of program guide listings.

Once mythfilldatabase finishes, start the MythTV frontend by either choosing it from your window manager's program menu or starting it manually using the mythfrontend command. Now you're ready to enjoy your new digital video recorder!

Table 3-2 shows the basic core commands you'll need to get you through your first MythTV experience.

Table 3-2   Core MythTV Commands

Key	Command
Number pad 0-9	Enter the corresponding digit for channel changes
p	Pause live TV or currently playing recording
c	Change input on the selected TV tuner
y	Switch between capture cards when multiple cards are defined
T	Toggle closed caption support
[,]	Decrease or increase volume
	or [F9]	Mute
[ESC]	Quit TV

Tip   There are many more keys and key combinations, depending on the tasks you wish to tackle. For a complete list of keys and key combinations, consult section 11.1 of the official MythTV HOW-TO at www.mythtv.org/docs/mythtv-HOWTO-11.html.

Final Thoughts

From the information provided in this chapter you should be able to properly establish your video card within the MythTV setup interface. Extra options are visible only where specific parameters apply to a select card or series of cards such as those made available to the Hauppauge PVR-350 series (you can find details for this in Chapter 7).

The MythTV suite continues to evolve and take on additional properties to further enhance your viewing and listening experience. From analog to digital, standard definition to high definition, MythTV can handle any resolution of media you throw its way. If you have access to the Internet, check the Daily Use guide online at http://mythtv.org/wiki/index.php/User_Manual:Daily_Use.

The Daily Use guide is a work in progress that is already brimming with useful information about how to apply the features of your MythTV audio and video devices. More important, you have Chapter 5 to read for establishing remote control for your frontend device, and Chapter 7 helps you tie it all together.

Installing and Configuring MythTV

O nce you've put together a PC on which to run MythTV, and gathered all the pieces and parts necessary to install MythTV, the real fun begins. That's when you'll install some stable (and, it is hoped, recommended) version of Linux, and then pile on the MythTV elements and supporting software until you've got a working installation. Finally, you must complete MythTV setup, after which you'll want to start tweaking all kinds of essential functions.

Chapter 4 deals with installing MythTV. Perforce, that means starting by installing Linux (we recommend Red Hat Fedora or KnoppMyth in particular), and then working through the steps involved in installing the three primary MythTV distribution packages. You'll also set up a TV capture card, MySQL, and various other ingredients essential to waking up MythTV and making it work.

Chapter 5 deals with the couch potato's best friend: the remote control that's such a key part of any modern multimedia or entertainment system. After we review your remote control options and recommend some specific makes and models, you'll learn how to install the necessary infrared signaling support to enable your remote to talk to your MythTV system, and get that remote up and running.

Chapter 6 digs into the mysteries and magic inherent in MythTV configuration. You'll learn about master and slave backends and how to configure them, how to set up and use your TV program guide, and how to work with channel icons and TV programming.

Chapter 7 digs into the software module known as `mythfrontend`, the onscreen display for MythTV that serves as its user interface. You'll get an overview of its many capabilities before diving into its general controls, managing its appearance, establishing program guide controls, and working with recording and playback controls.

Chapter 8 deals with what some consider to be the heart and soul of MythTV: working with its many and varied television capabilities. You'll learn about keyboard commands and onscreen themes, as well as adding DirectTV and/or DishTV to your television lineup. You'll also learn how to work with external tuners or set-top boxes, and about scheduling and recording TV programs.

By the time you finish this part of the book, you'll have learned the basics involved in creating a rudimentary MythTV system. Though your work is far from complete at this point, you'll still be able to sit down with a beverage and watch the evening news (or perhaps "Beauty and the Geek").

Downloading, Installing, and Configuring Linux for MythTV

This chapter builds on the introductory Linux installation procedures described in Chapter 3, which assume an existing Linux installation. For your benefit, this chapter describes the procedures necessary to lay a workable Linux foundation upon which you can erect a "mythical convergence box." Two approaches, one with KnoppMyth and one with Fedora Core, are described in order of relative ease and simplicity in setting up and configuring a proper Linux installation, but either one should be suitable for your purposes.

A wealth of storage options, connections, and formats is available owing to the widely supported Linux and UNIX versions of file system types, which extends to Windows varieties as well (FAT and NTFS). Concepts of dynamic and expandable storage solutions are covered, followed by specific recommendations for MythTV use.

Nowhere is the build process more exciting (and increasingly more involved) than when modifying the platform underlying MythTV's entertainment framework. You don't have to be a Linux expert to customize Linux and MythTV to your specifications — you just have to follow their guidance!

To make more efficient use of your time and avoid unnecessary flipping of pages, some of the information produced here repeats information from Chapters 1 and 2. Detailed explanations of fundamental concepts are included to guide you through a first-time build, with references to more complex or specialized methods to get better hack value out of MythTV.

Pre-Installation Preparation

You will need a computer with a connection to the Internet, a working CD or DVD disc burner, and a weekend clear and free of entanglements (because Linux setup time is considerably more protracted than plug-and-play). Completion time for a MythTV build varies based on your experience with the hardware and software involved, and how quickly you can troubleshoot and resolve installation issues as they come up. Total build time also depends on where and how you obtain installation images. (You may want to background this task during the week just to free up extra time during your installation weekend.)

Throughout this book, the MythTV transformation operates on the assumption that the underlying hardware uses the Intel/x86 instruction base — more commonly known by make and model, such as Intel Pentium 4 or Advanced Micro Devices (AMD) K8 — which happen to be the dominant desktop processors. As a result, all material here is specific to the Linux platform on x86 chips; no other architectures are covered. If you follow along with a processor of a different kind, you will definitely notice differences in configuration details, and possibly even in the operation of software and hardware. Your mileage will most certainly vary.

In each of the following two installation procedures, you need to enable your CD or DVD drive as the preferred boot device, and you may also give it first priority — depending on how you cabled your drives and in what order the BIOS recognizes them. In addition, before doing anything further, make note of which drive entry you intend to dedicate for Linux use if your PC is home to multiple disk drives. There's no sense in clobbering a perfectly good, usable partition or disk unintentionally or because you are unsure of the order or entry for the target drive. Most notably, using the KnoppMyth auto-installer requires that you destroy all existing content on your target disk before you can proceed with its installation.

Read through the information contained in this section especially carefully if you are a newcomer to Linux file systems. Unlike Windows, Linux provides you with an array of file system options, each with its own unique set of strengths, weaknesses, and particularly useful features for MythTV.

Because the following information is generic with regard to Linux, it appears before the individual sections on installing from a KnoppMyth or Fedora Core ISO image.

Storage Considerations

By now, you should have at least a vague idea about how much storage you want to dedicate to your MythTV installation (if not, refer to the discussion of disk drives in Chapter 1). You need this information to create partitions for Linux — most importantly, for MythTV audio and video storage — and the partitioning choices you make are crucial. While you can resize partitions to some extent (with varying degrees of success) after the fact, it's most effective to properly partition storage from the get-go. One quick solution for this need involves using external storage devices in their various forms — external USB, FireWire, or SATA drives, to name a few — which are great for plug-and-play capability, and provide instant extensibility that is quite portable.

Furthermore, you must also choose appropriate file system formats for each applicable disk partition. Each format choice depends on the data types it must accommodate, so this requires a bit of calculation on your part. Several storage concepts are introduced during the course of this discussion, including information about journaling file systems.

The Dynamic Storage Concept

Any self-respecting geek (and even a periodic system upgrader) prides himself or herself on hardware acquired over the years, which usually means hanging onto precious relics of computing history. Chances are good such geeks — which could be you — have a variety of unused disk drives hoarded away for some as yet unfulfilled dream project. Why not fulfill that dream? Using clever logical volume management, you can "glue" multiple physical drives into contiguous storage spaces.

Just a Bunch of Drives (JBoD) is considered to be part of the RAID family of storage concepts, but it possesses none of RAID's speed or reliability. Instead, JBoD excels at one thing: creating monolithic storage space out of multiple disk drives (much like RAID). This process is known to the technical crowd as *concatenation* or *spanning*, but all you need to know is that it involves linking together a variety of 8, 15, 20, or 80 GB (or an array of any size) drives into a single storage volume for your MythTV recordings. JBoD is provided by way of some on-board discrete RAID solutions — known as *fakeraid* because they do not represent true RAID card functionality — by both Northbridge chipset makers (such as nForce4) and secondary disk driver chips (such as Silicon Image SiI3112, SiI3114, or SiI3114-2 chips).

JBoD offers the added advantage of offloading volume management tasks to an integrated chipset solution, and frees the host operating system and processor from handling that task. Where JBoD may be inappropriate or unavailable, software solutions can emulate the same behavior — including the ever-popular Linux Volume Manager (LVM).

Using LVM affords additional capability not available for plain vanilla JBoD configurations, including the capability to resize online Logical Volumes (LVs) — the mechanism responsible for grouping Physical Volumes (PVs, aka component disk drives) together — and Volume Groups (responsible for grouping LVs and PVs into single storage units). This means you can add more storage later, and begin with only a modest amount for now. Furthermore, the Linux LVM implementation can also apply RAID0 striping to its LVs — and you can implement the Linux software RAID driver to create mirrors of your PVs for added reliability.

Using LVM with MythTV is covered in the definitive MythTV HOW-TO Guide online: http://mythtv.org/docs/mythtv-HOWTO-24.html#ss24.1.

Here's a brief synopsis of the steps involved for setting up LVM:

1. Use a disk partitioning utility to create and label a partition as LVM.

2. Create the physical volume from the raw partitions.

3. Create the volume group out of the physical volume.

4. Create the logical volume.

5. Format the logical volume using a specific format type.

From that same HOW-TO guide, the following command sequence illustrates LVM usage:

```
# fdisk /dev/hda
...
Command (m for help): t
Partition number (1-6): 5
Hex code (type L to list code): 8e

Command (m for help): w
```

The first command creates a new Linux partition type using the native disk editing utility fdisk, which completes the first setup of the previous sequence summary. Using the next two commands you then create the physical volume and a volume group for MythTV:

```
# pvcreate /dev/hda5
# vgcreate VGforMyth -s 64m /dev/hda5
```

The following sequence of commands demonstrates how you can create a logical volume group for video storage and format the new volume as ReiserFS (although this could easily be replaced with EXT3 or any format you prefer):

```
# lvcreate --name video --size 5G VGforMyth
# mkreiserfs /dev/VGforMyth/video
# mount /dev/VGforMyth/video /var/video
```

Here's another sequence that shows how to create a 3 GB partition for music:

```
# lvcreate --name music --size 3G VGforMyth
# mkreiserfs /dev/VGforMyth/music
# mount /dev/VGforMyth/music /var/music
```

Later, you may add more drive space, first by using the pvcreate command on the new drive entry, and then by using vgextend to add the new physical volume to the volume group. Don't feel bad if you fall a little short on disk capacity during the parts round-up for your MythTV box—now you have a justifiable reason to put off adding more storage space. It's just too easy for you to expand at will using LVM!

Other options abound; you just have to find them. Following the Logical Volume Manager example configuration from the same HOW-TO guide, there's a short discussion on Advanced Partition Formatting (item 24.2, at http://mythtv.org/docs/mythtv-HOWTO.html#toc24.2). Please give this material a quick read-through if the concepts of Linux storage formats remain foreign or off-putting to you.

The Journaling File System Concept

A *journaling file system* is one that maintains a journal of outstanding data pending disk write operations. Should the system become unstable or a power failure occur, this data will be left in an indeterminate state. Under normal file system operation, the recovery process consists of mounting and walking the entire length of the disk's data structures, which would be horrendously slow for the large data sets stored by MythTV. In a journaling file system, an interruption of service results in the system having to reread only the latest journal entries to restore a consistent state. The recovery time is much quicker using this method.

Advanced Storage Concepts

According to lead author Jarod Wilson in his MythTV guide, it's ill-advised to use RAID, LVM, and XFS in combination because of known stability issues with stock Fedora kernels. Moreover, such implementations are best left in expert hands, as they do require some experience to configure properly. In fact, configuring those kinds of logical storage solutions varies widely case by case (and depends in part on whether or not you use integrated hardware RAID functionality or software applications) and is therefore beyond the scope of this book. This information is purely for your enlightenment, and a goad to those who may be interested in exploring the endless possibilities for handling the dynamic storage demands that Linux affords.

Based on a variety of benchmarking and analysis reports from around the Web (most notably extensive work from Justin Piszcz for LinuxGazette in Benchmarking Filesystems Part II, http://linuxgazette.net/122/TWDT.html#piszcz) XFS, JFS, and ReiserFS (particularly version 3) are top candidates when it comes to handling large files.

During a copy procedure utilizing a 1 GB test sample, JFS and XFS shine as top performers, with ReiserFS (particularly version 3) trailing behind, while EXT2 barely edges out EXT3 in this same category. Notably, ReiserFSv4 performs poorly, coming in well behind the next best format — EXT3. Copy procedures on the same 1 GB sample illustrate another story, showing ReiserFSv4 to be a strong leader, followed closely by XFS, and then JFS. EXT versions 2 and 3 perform equally well, and ReiserFSv3 fumbles its way to dead last.

Confirming Wilson's original suggestions, Piszcz goes on to recommend XFS as the file system of choice for performance and scalability. JFS shows marked improvement from earlier testing conducted in a previous article by the same author, indicating a strong alternative. ReiserFS versions 3 and 4 do not show promise as top contenders in the arena of high-volume storage solutions.

Wilson also goes on to recommend a generic partition scheme that is further broken out into a formulaic method that works for a variety of configurations. He also advises dedicating one disk entirely to Linux and MythTV for simplicity's sake — dual boot setups are quite common, but can complicate this phase of the build unnecessarily. The Linux Documentation Project at www.tldp.org, listed in Appendix A, is a clearinghouse for a fantastic variety of definitive HOW-TO articles and project guides, among them a Linux and Windows HOW-TO.

The Partitioning Scheme

Conventional wisdom dictates that swap space be allocated in proportion to the amount of memory on a given system. However, this can grow unreasonably large despite the decreasing cost of memory chips and increasing demand for computing resources. As a consequence, an 8 GB swap turns out to be both cumbersome and inefficient. Ideally, you want to swap as little information from memory to disk as possible — otherwise, performance suffers, which may point to inefficiency issues elsewhere in a system. About 512 MB is adequate, and 1 to 2 GB is okay on the high end (though, as with other resources, more is better when it comes to handling HDTV).

The boot partition is reserved for configuration data necessary to get the Linux kernel bootstrapped and in working order. Keeping this partition isolated from others makes for a clean and easy recovery process (and is a best-practice habit for experienced users). How much space you allocate for the video (and optional audio) partition depends on your daily use and recording habits. Table 4-1 presents a slightly modified version of information from the Fedora MythTV HOW-TO.

Table 4-1 Linux Partition Guidelines for MythTV

Partition	Mount Point	Size	Format
/dev/hda1	/boot	50–100 MB	Ext3
/dev/hda2	swap	Equal to RAM	Swap
/dev/hda3	/	8–12 GB	Ext3
/dev/hda4	/video	Capture storage (a portion or the full remainder disk space)	JFS
/dev/hda5	/audio	Optional. Audio storage (ration according to the above choice)	JFS

Please note the peculiar naming convention that Linux uses to label raw drive partitions — it is consistent throughout, and is used later when mounting or unmounting drive images. Each partition name begins with the universal device entry, /dev, and is assigned a drive letter-letter-number combination according to its IDE channel position.

For example, the first drive on IDE channel 0 appears simply as /dev/hda, with its first and second partitions at /dev/hda1 and /dev/hda2, respectively. Later, you may interrogate the drive's partition table by pointing the native Linux fdisk utility at /dev/hda, which in turn shows partitions hda1 and hda2 (and any others you may have created). As described in Chapter 2, you may use fdisk -l on the command line to reveal all attached drives that the operating system recognizes, including removable media.

Further File System Hacks

Still other arrangements are possible, such as importing from Samba shares, or using the Network File System (NFS) from a central master backend server (subsection 23.10 of the MythTV HOW-TO). On the flip side, Windows can serve as a frontend for a MythTV backend server (using plug-ins covered in Chapter 14), an option of potential interest to some.

You might also like the additional features provided by using the Filesystem in Userspace (FUSE) API, which operates as a mezzanine layer for more interesting file system formats. A few of the projects based on the FUSE framework include the following:

- **CDDFS** — Another compact disc file system; this one uses libparanoia to mount audio media (http://castet.matthieu.free.fr/cddfs/)

- **djmount** — An audio-video solution for mounting multimedia content Universal Plug-and-Play (UPnP) devices (http://djmount.sourceforge.net/)

- **MediaDatabase** — An offline media content database storage solution for managing compact disc music collections (`http://mediadatabase.sourceforge.net/`)

- **Captive NTFS** — A file system layer providing transparent write support for the NTFS format (`www.jankratochvil.net/project/captive/`)

- **ntfsmount** — A more feature-rich option than the kernel driver variant, ntfsmount provides limited support to creation and deletion options to NTFS volumes (`http://linux-ntfs.org/`).

- **SMBNetFS** — A file system layer for remotely mounting Samba shares, much like Microsoft Windows' own Network Neighborhood (`http://smbnetfs.airm.net/`)

These are just a few of the growing number of projects that utilize FUSE. Other interesting titles include Lkarmafs, which provides access to Roxio Karma digital MP3 players; FUSEPod, a virtual file system for interacting with iPods; the Bluetooth File System, to map basic Bluetooth file system functionality; and the compFUSEd and FuseCompress projects, both of which provide transparent data compression at the file system layer. All seem promising for inclusion with some MythTV project builds.

Check the FUSE project page for current implementations: `http://fuse.sourceforge.net/wiki/index.php/FileSystems`.

Each of these illustrates just how powerful MythTV really is, and exactly how it lives up to the idea of convergence technology. Next, you get a chance to walk through a general installation procedure for Linux, where all the magic begins.

Installation the KnoppMyth Way

KnoppMyth attempts to trivialize the MythTV installation process by using a popular bootable ISO distribution called Knoppix. KnoppMyth specifically targets newcomers to Linux and MythTV, but anyone may use KnoppMyth for quick deployment of MythTV frontend systems or demonstration units.

Though KnoppMyth offers an expert configuration option for the installation process, it does not provide the level of granularity and breadth of package selection that you'll find in Fedora Core. Using the expert option essentially means loading modules by hand and answering a series of questions that automatic hardware probing resolves transparently. However, the KnoppMyth installation base is incredibly small (623 MB, a single CD image) compared to the Fedora Core distribution (a four disc set at 600-plus megabytes per disk, or a larger single DVD image). If you happen to be familiar with the unattended install feature for specially configured Windows installations, you'll feel right at home using KnoppMyth.

You can get your feet wet with a dip into these shallow waters and then later dive into the deep end with Fedora when you feel more ambitious. However, there are subtle differences in how the same actions are performed across these two distributions, so you should only expect the MythTV package itself to be consistent in deployment.

The official home for KnoppMyth is `http://mysettopbox.tv`. It also lists mirror links to ISO downloads. As of this writing, KnoppMyth is at revision R5A30-2, dated January 2006.

Pre-Boot KnoppMyth Options

You will be presented with an initial (pre-boot) window upon loading KnoppMyth into system memory from a fresh start. In this window you are provided several additional options that allow you to modify the way Knoppix (the underlying OS) boots. You may activate help screens at any time during this phase for more information about the parameters that you may pass to the initial boot loader before the installation process even begins. The following paragraphs detail some of these properties about the KnoppMyth boot loader.

Optical Serial ATA Installation Pitfalls

Before booting the KnoppMyth ISO installer you should be aware that installing from a SATA CD/DVD drive can be problematic. Alas, the current release, R5A30-2, produces the following output when run from a SATA DVD-ROM:

```
[ INITIAL TEXT OMMITTED FOR BREVITY ]

...

Enabling dma acceleration for: hdb

Can't find KNOPPIX filesystem, sorry.

Dropping you to a (very limited) shell.

Press reset button to quit.


Additional built-in commands available:

      cat        mount      umount

      insmod     rmmod      lsmod


knoppix#
```

Even for an experienced Linux integrator, this is a cripplingly limited command set, and you can do nothing useful with these commands alone. Should you find yourself in this situation, there are some quick workarounds. If you already have a Parallel ATA (PATA) CD/DVD optical drive, use that instead during the build phase, and then reintroduce the SATA drive once the system is established. Another option using the installer is described later in this chapter, in a section that deals with manual installation.

F2 Help Screen

Press the F2 key once to bring up a few additional boot-time options. The main window title appears with the following text: KnoppMyth Boot Options (Back to main with F1). The following options are available during pre-installation:

- `knoppmyth` — Load the standard 2.6 kernel version of KnoppMyth
- `tv` — Boot directly into 800 × 600 mode, for setup with a television
- `dragon` — For use with Dragon (commercial set-top box) from mythic.tv
- `memtest` — Memory integrity instrumentation
- `expert` — Interactive setup (expert mode)
- `expert26` — Interactive setup with experimental 2.6 kernel
- `fb1280x1024`, `fb1024x768`, or `fb800x600` — Framebuffer mode for notebooks
- `failsafe` — Turn off automatic hardware detection for nearly everything

The `knoppmyth` keyword takes additional parameters, some of which are described in the next section. A full listing of cheat codes appears online (and on disk, after installation) in a file named `knoppix-cheatcodes.txt`. The content of that file is too long to include verbatim, so it does not make an appearance here.

F3 Help Screen

Press the F3 key to bring up yet another window of hidden menu options. You will see a window titled "KnoppMyth CHEATCODES (F1 for main page)." In this window the following options are available:

```
knoppmyth lang=us|cs|da|de|es|fr|it|nl|pl|sk|...
knoppmyth desktop=icewm|kde|wmaker|twm|xfce
knoppmyth screen=1280x1024 depth=24
knoppmyth nodma
knoppmyth vsync=85 hsync=78
knoppmyth 2
knoppmyth myconfig=scan home=/dev/sda1
knoppmyth no{scsi,pcmcia,usb,agp,swap,apm,apic,mce,dde}
knoppmyth blind brltty=typ,port,tbl
failsafe
expert
```

The preceding entries require some explanation. For your benefit, a line-by-line dissection of that information follows:

- `knoppmyth lang` — This is a language specification option. It appears now, but you can also change this later while performing post-installation configuration tasks.
- `knoppmyth desktop` — The desktop option offers a choice of window managers. By default, KnoppMyth uses fluxbox unless configured to use one of the other entries shown. We encourage you to try them all out and discover which one is right for you.

- `knoppmyth screen=1280x1024 depth=24` — This option specifies screen resolution and bit depth settings. You may prefer to run natively at 1024 × 768 and a color depth of 24 bits, or perhaps even lower (if you must configure through a television set, you can also do that here).

- `knoppmyth nodma` — The `nodma` setting turns off direct memory access (DMA) for drives that do not support this feature. If you're not sure what this does, leave it alone — it actually helps performance when it's enabled on drives that support this feature, and hardware detection usually gets this right.

- `knoppmyth vsync=85 hsync=78` — The `vsync` and `hsync` settings correspond to vertical and horizontal synchronization, respectively, and enable you to fine-tune monitor settings. Use these with caution, because the wrong settings can be potentially harmful, both to you (by provoking excessive eyestrain) and to the monitor (by causing it to run at incorrect frequencies).

- `knoppmyth 2` — This option sets KnoppMyth to run-level 2 (text mode) — for experienced users only. Use this to troubleshoot a dysfunctional installation or hardware problems (primarily, those that are video card or monitor related). Certain high-level functionality (such as access to GUI utilities) is prohibited due to the limited operational capabilities of this run level. Normally, once it's completely installed, KnoppMyth operates at run-level 5 (graphical mode), which presents and enables all of MythTV's normal graphical user interface. At the outset, character mode is the only thing that makes sense because you have to configure your display, your inputs and outputs, and so forth before KnoppMyth knows how to behave.

- `knoppmyth myconfig=scan home=/dev/sda1` — According to the cheat sheet, you may direct the installer to look in one of several places for a configuration file. Use `floppyconfig` if you want the installer to look for `knoppix.sh` on a floppy disk; `myconf=/dev/sda1` to find one on a removable medium or a SATA drive; or `myconf=scan` or `config=scan` to find `knoppix.sh` automatically.

- `knoppmyth no{scsi,pcmcia,usb,agp,swap,apm,apic,mce,dde}` — This directive turns off detection of certain hardware during the installation process. You really have no reason to use this unless you suspect some problem with your hardware and want to narrow the options down to potential culprits. There are valid reasons to disable some of these during installation, but you need a specific reason to do so (which also implies you already know what you're doing). The braces ({}) around the comma-separated fields are particularly noteworthy: Don't type the command literally as it appears — braces signal that options may be grouped, with each option separated by a comma. Use `knoppmyth noscsi, nopcmcia` to turn off scanning for SCSI and PCMCIA devices, for example.

- `knoppmyth blind brltty=typ,port,tbl` — This parameter starts a Braille terminal and the parameters for setting the Braille device.

- `failsafe` — Boot with (almost) no hardware detection. Use this option only when you suspect some hardware component may be faulty. By going through each option by hand, you can (hopefully) discover the culprit.

- **expert** — Open up an interactive text-driven session (for experts). Use this if you are interested in observing how the pre-installation process works, one step at a time. In addition to the series of questions you answer to enable or disable hardware, the following modules are made available for you to load:

```
BusLogic.o              NCR53c406a.o
a100u2w_CAUTION.o       aic7xxx_CAUTION.o
dtc.o                   eata.o
ehci-hcd.o              fdomain.o
gdth.o                  ieee1394.o
megaraid_CAUTION.o      ehci1394.o
pas16.o                 psi240i.o
sbp2.o                  t128.o
tmscsim.o               u74-34f.o
ultrastor.o             usb-ohci.o
usb-storage.o           usb-uhci.o
usbcore.o               wd-7000.o
```

At the boot prompt you may specify any combination of the preceding parameters, along with their additional subparameters. For generic installations, no arguments are required; just press the Enter key at the prompt and the process begins. Example commands follow:

```
boot: expert26 knoppmyth screen=1024x768 depth=24 desktop=kde
boot: knoppmyth lang=us desktop=icewm
```

Following this, the post-boot installation process kicks off, and begins another round of Q and A before finally dropping you onto the KnoppMyth desktop.

Post-Boot KnoppMyth Options

Upon entering the after-boot installation screen, you are presented with the following options to configure KnoppMyth:

- **Frontend** — Use CD as a frontend for an existing backend
- **Auto-Install** — Automatic installation of KnoppMyth (with prompts)
- **Auto-Upgrade** — Automatically upgrade older version of KnoppMyth
- **Manual Installation** — Custom profile, expert mode
- **Reboot** — Reboot the machine
- **Quit** — Quit the installation process

Explanations for each of the preceding modes of operation and one additional operation (creating a backend server) appear in the following sections, starting with the missing backend operation.

Backend Operation

According to the KnoppMyth Pamphlet, the definitive guide on KnoppMyth installation and operation (`http://mysettopbox.tv/doc.html`), KnoppMyth can be set to run as a backend server (for use with the next option, the frontend client) with a few special preparations. The KnoppMyth Pamphlet instructs you to implement the following changes:

> MySQL must be configured to accept connections (by default, this authenticates only for the default MythTV user). The configuration script is located in the system-wide configuration directory and is named `/etc/mysql/my.cnf`. Open this file with the editor of your choice (Kedit is readily available within the KDE application bar) and find the following line entry:

> `skip-networking`

> And comment-out this line by inserting a hash '#' symbol:

> `#skip-networking`

> Then save the file, and close it.

> The MySQL daemon must be restarted for the changes to take effect, and you can do this by issuing the following command in a console window:

> `# /etc/init.d/mysql restart`

> Finally, as the MythTV user, reconfigure MythTV by invoking the mythtv-setup configuration utility. On the first screen, change both line entries with the IP address corresponding to localhost (127.0.0.1) to that of your MythTV backend server.

That concludes the changes necessary to establish a backend server using KnoppMyth.

Frontend Operation

Frontend configuration is straightforward; its prompts walk you through each step of its pre-installation process. You must have a working MythTV backend system already established (using the preceding instructions) for this to work, and set this frontend installation to feed from that backend server.

The pre-installation configuration process follows:

1. **KnoppMyth Timezone** — The installer will automatically detect the current time-zone settings and default to these, unless you specify any changes.

2. **Configure KnoppMyth Database** — This is where you specify the database access settings. The following options are made available here, shown with their defaults:

```
DBHostName=localhost
DBUserName=mythtv
DBPassword=mythtv
DBName=mythconverg
LocalHostName=mythfe1
```

3. **Use DHCP Broadcast** — Specify whether your network configuration requires DHCP lease assignments. Your connection to the Internet (or internal network) will determine whether or not this is necessary for your operation.

4. **Set IP Address for First Active Interface** — The installer will make a best-effort attempt to identify the first active network interface, and report its name (usually eth0) at this time. The default IP address is 192.168.0.1, but you are free to change this to better suit your needs.

5. **Set Network Mask for Network Interface** — For most applications, this value will be the default 255.255.255.0, and you only need to edit this if the previous line changes to reflect a larger class of address spaces. Chances are good you'll know if this applies to you.

6. **Set Network Broadcast Address** — Specify the broadcast address for receiving network-wide messages on your network interface.

7. **Set Default Gateway Address** — Your gateway address corresponds to the machine serving as the entry and exit point into and out of your network. This could be your router or a dedicated server box, for example. Specify that device address here.

8. **Set Default Name Servers** — On the off chance that you connected your MythTV box to the Internet already, this entry will be filled with the relevant primary and secondary servers for resolving host names. Otherwise, you will have to know these addresses in advance — guessing at them is not an option. DNS addresses are separated by a single space, and can contain multiple entries.

At this point, the KnoppMyth installer will effect a few of the settings specified above. Once this is done, a graphical interface presents you with a new series of configuration options:

1. **Select Preferred Language** — This setting defaults to English. You may specify any language you prefer, but this book focuses only on English language deployment.

2. **Database Configuration (1/2)** — This window presents you with the same options that appear in the list entry titled Configure KnoppMyth Database. Use the up and down arrow keys to navigate the interface if your mouse is nonfunctional at this time.

3. **Database Configuration (2/2)** — The Use Custom Identifier option will already be enabled. You may uncheck this box if you prefer not to identify your MythTV box by name (default: mythfe1). Another option, Use Wake-on-LAN, is present for remotely waking up the MythTV backend server, if it is configured accordingly. Use the up and down arrow keys to navigate the interface if your mouse is nonfunctional at this time.

Automatic Installation

The automated installation procedure is the most efficient way to establish a working MythTV stand-alone system. You will be prompted to specify a handful of settings in preparation for the pre-build phase:

1. **Set KnoppMyth Timezone** — As earlier, the installer will automatically detect current local settings, and prompt you to change them if necessary.

2. **A Warning About Installation** — You won't make any configuration changes here; the only change that will occur is when you agree to blow away the contents of the current drive. The warning message has this to tell you:

```
Initialization of KnoppMyth-Installation

WARNING:  Danger, Will Robinson!

This script will auto-install KnoppMyth to disk.
Note: this version is still an early
version and is under heavy development.

The authors take no responsibility
for data loss or hardware damage

Agree?
```

3. **Creating KnoppMyth Configuration Step (1/5)** — Input your whole name; at least, that's what the installer expects of you. This does not literally need to be your real name — it can be the nickname of the machine or a deliberately bogus entry, like Knoppix Myth.

4. **Creating KnoppMyth Configuration Step (2/5)** — Input your username (not mythtv!). This must be an alternate username (default: knmyth) that you intend to use separate from the main mythtv account (which will be established behind the scenes by the installer).

5. **Creating KnoppMyth Configuration Step (3/5)** — Input your user password, for the name listed in the previous step. You will be prompted to repeat this again for accuracy.

6. **Creating KnoppMyth Configuration Step (4/5)** — Input your administration password. The administrator account is built-in like the mythtv account, and is called root.

7. **Creating KnoppMyth Configuration Step (5/5)** — Input your preferred host name. This is the name you wish to call your MythTV box internally (for local references, unless you specifically establish an Internet-facing setup).

You are given an opportunity to review all current settings before they are committed to an on-disk installation. Now's the time to change any parameters that may be incorrect. This "last chance" screen appears and shows text similar to the following:

```
Name-Options:
  Your name is: Knoppix Myth
  Your chosen username is: knmyth
  Your hostname is: mythtv
Services-Options:
```

```
   Following services will be started, after each system
bootup: #modified
System-Options:
   The installed system will be a debian type system.

Several of these options can only be changed in the configuration
file //.knofig. The installation will now be started. The author
gives no warranty for any damage caused by this script.

Do you want to proceed with these parameters?
```

Note Debian is a particular top-level distribution of Linux upon which Knoppix (the basis for KnoppMyth) is based. Knoppix is a specialty distribution tailored to operate Linux purely from memory resources (as opposed to a hard drive) on what is called a *ramdisk filesystem*. KnoppMyth takes Knoppix in another direction by tailoring the CD-based image for MythTV usage.

Once you choose to continue the installation process, your first disk drive is pre-formatted to include four primary entries: the root partition (/), a swap partition (swap), a /cache partition to buffer live television feeds, and a /myth partition for everything else. After one final warning (and a final chance to back up your data) the KnoppMyth installation process begins:

```
### WARNING: Destruction WILL occur. ###
     This process will overwrite ALL of hda. If you have data
          on hda, you MUST back it up before continuing
               or you WILL lose ALL of that data.
```

Completion time depends entirely upon the hardware choices you make for your MythTV build. Expect a modern processor to finish anywhere from 15–25 minutes from this point in the installation, and approximately 30–40 minutes (possibly more) for older processors or especially conservative configurations. After it's finished, KnoppMyth informs you that it has completed all pre-boot installation tasks, and asks you to reboot the machine. Remove the CD/DVD installer disk from the tray before you reboot your machine.

Automatic Upgrade

This option upgrades an existing (and presumably older) version of KnoppMyth to whatever the current version may be (as of this writing, that's R5A30-2). Most of these configuration steps resemble those in the Automatic Installation procedure just recounted, and are therefore not reproduced here.

Once installation finalizes, you are delivered to the specified KnoppMyth GUI and presented with a console window that walks you through reconfiguring MythTV. Those options appear later in this chapter, under the "KnoppMyth Post-Installation Tasks" heading.

Once you're on the KnoppMyth desktop, you can issue the following command on any console to update your system:

```
# apt-get update
```

You may have to answer yes to questions apt-get asks you for the installation to complete successfully.

Manual Installation

This part of the process takes you through configuration settings with only minimal prompting from the installer. Clearly, this option is intended for experienced users, and you should only need to install in this manner if you use a SATA drive (as the default installation only looks for a PATA drive). The difference here is that you will install to a SATA disk drive, not read from an optical SATA drive (as mentioned earlier in the chapter, this can be problematic). A workaround is described shortly.

Given a new, completely empty storage volume, you are offered only two options: partition and quit. You must partition the first drive identified by the partitioning utility cfdisk and ensure that it's marked active (bootable). Write your new partition table to disk, and then quit the editor.

Use the three-key combination CTRL+ALT+F2 to select another working terminal window, and issue the following command sequence (as directed by the KnoppMyth Pamphlet):

```
knoppix# mkswap /dev/xda2 && swapon /dev/xda2
```

For novice users unfamiliar with the preceding commands, the following explanation may be helpful; experienced users can skip ahead. The first command creates swap space, a temporary holding cell responsible for handling overflow from memory. The second command tells the host operating system to make the specified partition into an active swap cache.

Now you can format the partitions however you see fit. Although the KnoppMyth Pamphlet suggests using EXT2 and EXT3, you could select a more responsive file system type as we recommended earlier in this chapter. For your benefit, the original commands from that pamphlet appear next:

```
# mke2fs -O sparse_super -m0 -i8000000 -L cache -M /cache /dev/hda3
# mke2fs -j -O sparse_super -m0 -i8000000 -L myth -M /myth /dev/hda4
```

The KnoppMyth Pamphlet also states that the preceding command sequence yields a performance increase for the ring buffer on /dev/hda3 and implements a journaling file system on /dev/hda4, which is a common recommendation.

After you are finished, hold down CTRL+ALT+F1 to return focus back to the original installation window.

On a system where the installer identifies an existing partition table, the following six options are made available:

```
1) Configure Installation
2) Start Installation
3) Partition
4) Load Config
5) Save Config
6) Quit
```

You may use an existing configuration at this time, provided you either created one from a previous installation or borrowed one from an online example. Manual drive partitioning is also allowed here, as is creating a new configuration and then starting it. Otherwise, if the installer cannot immediately identify your drive (as is commonly the case with Serial ATA and other exotic drive interfaces) or partition table, then you will only be given the option to partition or quit.

The first step involves creating a KnoppMyth configuration — that is, a layout for the file system. Steps two through six are exactly like the series of prompts described in Creating KnoppMyth Configuration Steps one through five, discussed earlier under the "Automatic Installation" heading. A seventh and final option enables you to specify where LILO, the Linux boot-loader, should reside.

Installation using SATA-based drives is enabled here. According to the KnoppMyth Pamphlet, SATA users should select option 4) Load Config, and choose /KNOPPIX/knoppmyth-sata. This should resolve any issues related to hidden or inaccessible SATA storage drives.

Verify the current configuration data and then allow the KnoppMyth installer to go to work.

KnoppMyth Post-Installation Tasks

A lengthy runtime configuration routine executes before delivering you to the KnoppMyth desktop. Following the successful completion of the prior pre-installation process, you are presented with one last series of prompts before being turned over to the MythTV setup utility. A prompt that contains the line Please provide the root password: in a console window means you have arrived safely. Type the administrator password you specified earlier during the pre-installation process.

Next comes a series of questions, another round of time zone and date settings, and a last request for an IP address. Then the software performs some automated configuration tasks before stopping to ask you to enable a BootSplash screen. That text is reproduced here, verbatim:

```
BootSplash
If you wish to add BootSplash, please answer the following
question.

Note: BootSplash uses the framebuffer, if you have a video card w/
an nVidia based chipset, the virtual console won't appear
correctly. Certain devices (VGA to component adapters), may not
display the splash at all. If you have an issue, you can change
vga=788 to vga=normal in /etc/lilo.conf after which, you should
run lilo -v.
```

In case you're wondering, BootSplash is a KnoppMyth image that displays at boot-time. It shows a simulated plasma display accompanied by a welcome message — nothing fancy, but mildly interesting to watch. After that, you may select from a list of the most commonly used remote controls by make (41 entries in total) and model for use with the Linux Infra-Red Control daemon (LIRCd).

Services are configured next, including LIRCd (for remote control) and the Network Time Protocol (NTP) to keep system time accurate. After that, you're prompted to set a password for MythWeb access, which applies to files you create for the HTTP server to access.

Next, you must select either the default i586 drivers or the i686 version before proceeding with a few more runtime services configuration tasks. The i586 class of processors encompasses a variety of makes and models, including Pentium-class processors, AMD K6 series, and VIA C3/Eden cores. Use i686 if your processor is a Pentium Pro or better, or Athlon/Duron series AMD or better.

Note If your video adapter uses an nVidia chipset that supports XvMC, the KnoppMyth Pamphlet advises against selecting XvMC at this time. Prior to invoking the MythTV setup application, KnoppMyth will load the appropriate packages for nVidia-XvMC compatibility.

The MythTV setup utility appears next. This process is described in detail later in this chapter. The auto-installer kicks in once again, to configure the MythWeather plug-in locale before prompting you for a zip code or non-use locale (to obtain program listings). A few more services are configured (and some reconfigured) before you are presented with the MythTV frontend. Operation of the `mythfrontend` application is described later, following the Fedora Core instructions that appear in the next section.

In addition, the KnoppMyth Pamphlet recommends installing the nVidia chipset drivers after the `mythfrontend` has started, so you will return to this point later. Commands described in the KnoppMyth Pamphlet are reproduced here:

```
<CTRL><ALT><F1>
log in as root.
install-nv<TAB><TAB> (you have two options)
This will install the drivers and restart GDM.
```

Note If your system includes an nForce/nVidia-based chipset, the following additional entry to /etc/X11/XF86Config-4 is required, as per the KnoppMyth Pamphlet's instructions:
`Option "ConnectedMonitor" "TV"`

A sample nVidia configuration file appears in the `/etc/X11` directory in a KnoppMyth installation. More configuration options are available, and you can read the complete listing in a document provided by the vendor. The Linux version, current as of this writing, is 1.0-8178, and the `README.txt` file that documents these details resides here:

```
ftp://download.nvidia.com/XFree86/Linux-x86/1.0-8178/README/
README.txt
```

KnoppMyth Post-Installation Tips

As mentioned in the KnoppMyth Pamphlet, the wrong horizontal and vertical sync settings in `/etc/X11/XF86Config-4` can be harmful to the television. Therefore, you should ensure that the settings are as follows:

```
HorizSync "30 - 50"
VertRefresh "60"
```

The previous settings for horizontal and vertical synchronization are taken from an automatically generated configuration file; you should define these parameters (with or without quotes and hyphenated ranges) according to your particular monitor. Finally, the Pamphlet goes on to say this:

> If you have your box hooked up to a TV and, when it boots, you see a message saying `Press <RETURN> to see modes......` You'll need to edit your `lilo.conf`. At the top, it should say `vga=<XXX>`; change it to `vga=normal`. Don't forget to `lilo -v` when you are done.

Should you find this information pertinent and useful, be sure to give Cecil and Dale (the original authors of the R5 Pamphlet of KnoppMyth) a big thank-you. They deserve kudos for figuring all this out!

Installation the Fedora Core Way

Red Hat has gone to great lengths to streamline its installation process, to the point where it rivals Microsoft Windows' ease of use. Whether installing from multi-part CD-ROM images or a single DVD-ROM image, the general setup procedure remains the same.

Based on the storage decisions you made earlier, you will configure the Fedora Core installer as it guides you through installation. Before you boot the CD/DVD installation media, you must flag the appropriate parameters at the `boot:` prompt. For instance, the Fedora MythTV guide suggests you try the following command if you intend to use JFS as your main file system format:

```
boot: linux jfs
```

You may also use `linux xfs` or `linux reiserfs` if you prefer. The reason you must specify these at boot time is because the Fedora Core installer does not otherwise permit you to choose these formats. Fedora is partial to the EXT family of file systems, as Red Hat itself extensively developed and thoroughly battle-tested both versions 2 and 3. As such, these are the primary options that appear by default during installation.

Initial Installation Steps

The steps outlined in this section take you through the screens of a Fedora Core installation. The following two sections describe the choice of packages in Fedora Core and walk you through the First Boot setup process.

1. **Check Install Media** — The first option the Fedora Core installer gives you is to test the CD/DVD media for flaws. Basically, the installer checksums and verifies itself to make sure file integrity is preserved. Otherwise, you might experience inexplicable problems later during installation, which is likely to result in a partially installed, nonfunctional system. As a matter of general principle, you should give this a go the first time through. This way, you can be sure that you have a viable image to begin with, and any complications that may arise later won't necessarily result from a poor burn or defective media.

2. **Identifying Your Locale** — Next, the Fedora Core/Red Hat installer (Anaconda) kicks into gear, automatically detecting the video card, monitor, and mouse. Unless your display subsystem is misidentified (or not at all identified) by the installer, it then cranks over into graphics mode. Otherwise, you must use a text-based installer, which provides identical functionality in character mode.

   At this point, you can read the release notes by selecting the appropriately labeled button, or click Next to proceed past this welcome screen to the language selection screen. Next, you must specify a keyboard layout based on your language preferences.

   a. **Language Selection** — Choose your native tongue; here, we assume English, but this can be anything you are comfortable using.

   b. **Keyboard Configuration** — Depending on the preceding setting, you must define keyboard mappings for your language of choice. Here again, we assume English is your primary language.

3. **Choosing an Installation Type** — Anaconda will initially search for an existing Fedora Core installation to upgrade before proceeding with the installation. When Anaconda has finished searching, choose the Custom Install radio button. You may upgrade an existing Fedora Core installation using a more recent version of the installation image, but the instructions provided here only cover the process for new installations.

4. **Disk Partitioning** — You will need to whittle down the package selection to a minimum to leverage more space for video archives, but first you must apply whatever partitioning scheme you designed earlier to meet your needs. Inside the disk partitioning setup screen, shown in Figure 4-1, select Create custom layout. (In older versions of Fedora Core, the option is called Manual partition with Disk Druid.) You must supply some direction here, because the automatic installer won't do that for you.

5. **Boot Loader** — Once you've diced up the disk platters and applied your preferred file system formats, you must decide where to locate GRUB, if not in the default location on /dev/hda. Figure 4-2 shows the boot loader options screen. Installing GRUB (a Linux boot manager) to disk enables you to manage multiple operating system partitions on the same drive, or a series of drives. Unless you already have a boot manager installed, you should elect to install GRUB to disk (this clobbers any existing boot loader, especially the Windows version).

6. **Network Configuration** — When you come to the Network Devices selection screen, shown in Figure 4-3, you must decide how to address this machine — if at all. Are you building a stand-alone unit, capable of serving itself, or is this a client that feeds from a backend server that harvests all program data?

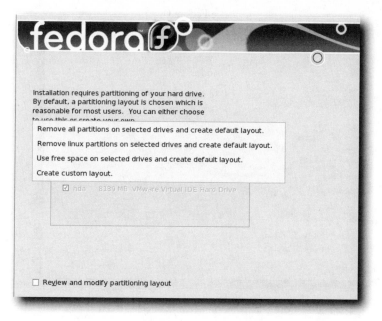

FIGURE 4-1: Fedora Core 5 installation disk partitioning screen options

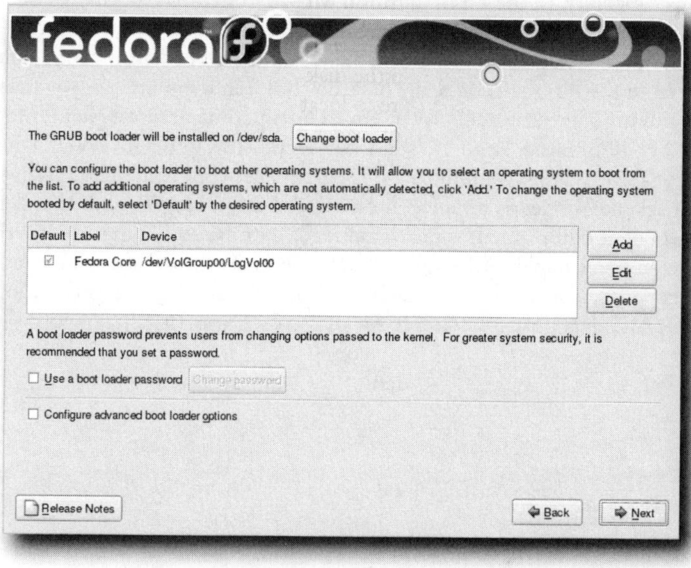

FIGURE 4-2: Fedora Core 5 installation boot loader options screen

FIGURE 4-3: Fedora Core 5 installation network device screen

7. **Security Configuration** — Here's an important point to note at this point during the installation process: For simplicity's sake, we advise you to disable both the firewall and SELinux capability. In the Firewall screen, shown in Figure 4-4, change the Firewall drop-down list entry to Disabled. In the SELinux screen, shown in Figure 4-5, use the SELinux Setting drop-down list to disable SELinux. Of course, if your MythTV box is connected to the Internet, you really have no choice in the matter — you must use a firewall. Should you need firewall protection, at least permit Secure SHell (SSH) and HTTP/HTTPS traffic. Jarod Wilson recommends this in his HOW-TO guide as a precaution against creating communications barriers between secondary systems and their master backends — clearly a subject for advanced users. He also adds that default SELinux policy enforcement is problematic for both ReiserFS and MythWeb (which cannot communicate with MySQL). Unless you know how to establish a proper SELinux policy, it's safe just to abide by Wilson and disable it altogether. To learn how to disable SELinux post-installation, see the "Post-Linux Installation Tasks" section.

FIGURE 4-4: Fedora offers various firewall settings during the install process.

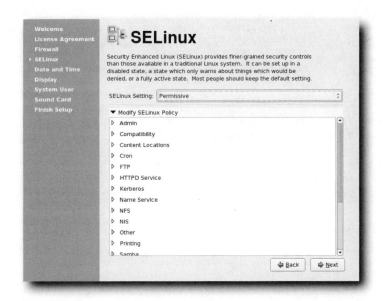

FIGURE 4-5: Disable SELinux during installation to prevent problems with MythTV.

8. **Time Zone Selection** — On the next screen, Anaconda prompts you to identify your time zone. To navigate the list box of locale entries, use the up and down arrow keys. On some displays, the window is too small to use with the scrollbar — options whiz by entirely too quickly. The arrow keys permit you to move one entry at a time and offer better control and selection ability.

9. **Set Root Password** — On this screen, you must specify an administrator password, which you will actually use separately (and repeatedly) throughout setup and configuration of Linux and MythTV. That said, make it something you can recall and reproduce easily on the keyboard. Though this goes against the notion of a strong security model — even a well-developed cryptographic implementation does nothing for poor password selection — you can always reset the password when the installation process is completed. To make things simple, we recommend picking something easy and memorable, if only for temporary use during installation.

The next section addresses the package selection step of the Fedora Core install.

Package Selection

Don't be hesitant about selecting packages for removal, especially when it comes to conserving disk space. You can always put things back later, and it certainly makes more sense to begin with a minimal base Linux installation, and then build your environment once the install is finished and working properly.

For every selection you make, an icon labeled "details" offers information about the packages available in any given category. You may then pick among them individually, enabling and disabling options as you see fit. The package recommendations that follow are based on the assumption that you are building a dedicated MythTV box. If you intend to do more with your MythTV box, then you may disregard the minimalist approach to software installation described here.

Desktops

The Desktops packages include the essential X Window system, along with the choice of the GNOME and KDE desktop environments:

- **X Window System** — You will absolutely need the X Window System for MythTV. This package represents the foundation for building graphical user interfaces and desktop environments under Linux. From this category, you may safely remove the following packages:

  - authconfig-gtk
  - krb5-auth-dialog
  - linuxwacom
  - openssh-askpass
  - openssh-askpass-ssl
  - synaptics

These are not vital to MythTV's operation. The installer provides brief descriptions of each package so you can confirm this for yourself if you'd like.

- **GNOME Desktop Environment** — Many window managers are available and many work well with MythTV. GNOME is among the more popular full-fledged desktop environments, alongside KDE. You may use GNOME and any of its applications at your discretion, but this book is written around KDE (as the original MythTV maintainer suggests).

- **K Desktop Environment** — Examples used later in this book are built around the KDE interface. You may use any other graphical user interface you like, but detailed command sequences will be quite different. Unless you're already familiar with Linux and MythTV, you should select and use KDE initially so you can follow along with our MythTV setup before you explore other GUIs.

Applications

- **Editors** — Choose your favorite editor(s). For novice users, `nano`, `pico`, or `joe` are recommended; experienced users usually enjoy `vi` (or its many variants — `vim` and `vim-enhanced`) or `emacs` because of their advanced functionality.

- **Engineering and Scientific** — You won't need any of this for MythTV, but you may select this package for your personal use (after all, your PC remains a capable desktop machine beneath the veneer of the MythTV `frontend` interface).

- **Graphical Internet** — This category encompasses a variety of applications for online communication, which you may or may not need. The following items are otherwise safe to remove:

  - evolution

  - evolution-webcal

  - gaim

  - gnomemeeting

  - xchat

You won't free up much space by doing this, but you will clean up a bit of clutter on your application taskbar.

- **Text-based Internet** — These utilities make great fallbacks to their corresponding graphical utilities (browsers, news readers) but are not essential to MythTV.

- **Office/Productivity** — This category of applications is optional. Selections consist of office suites, Portable Document Format (PDF) viewers, and others.

- **Sound and Video** — You want this category to be checked, and several items in this category may be suitable for inclusion with your build. The following items are of particular interest:

  - **k3b** — A simple GUI for CD and DVD image burning

  - **xcdroast** — A flexible, intuitive CD-burning application

- **Authoring and Publishing** — This category includes many applications for converting from DocBook format to HTML, PDF, PostScript (PS), or text files. Translation: Unless you already work with DocBook, you won't need this.

- **Graphics** — This contains a variety of applications for manipulating and scanning images. You might find some use for these applications, but they're otherwise safe to omit.

- **Games and Entertainment** — Because MythGame comes with its own set of libraries and dependencies, you can leave this unchecked. Once MythTV is fully installed, it can handle gaming functionality through the `frontend` interface.

Servers

- **Server Configuration Tools** — You may find some useful tools here if you intend to operate MythTV in a remotely controllable networked environment. Otherwise, you may leave this unchecked.

- **Web Server** — Part of the MythTV frontend operation (MythWeb) relies on a functional HTTP server to serve up backend content. You absolutely need this for MythWeb to work.

- **Mail Server** — This category is entirely unnecessary, so you are safe to uncheck it.

- **Windows File Server** — If Windows machines are network accessible to your MythTV box, additional storage opportunities can be realized by selecting this category. Several plug-ins and additional software suites provide great functionality for copying media from remote Windows systems, or using those systems for frontend playback.

- **FTP Server** — This category is entirely unnecessary, so it's safe to uncheck it.

- **PostgreSQL Database** — Choose this only if you expect to use PostgreSQL-specific applications; MythTV is concerned only with the MySQL database. Thus, you may safely leave this unchecked.

- **MySQL Database** — Definitely choose this option; MythTV depends on it! MySQL acts as a storehouse for program guide listings, and plays a major role in delivering back-end services. Click the Details tab and scroll down to find `mysql-server`; make sure it is selected.

- **News Servers** — This category is entirely unnecessary, so you are safe to uncheck it.

- **Network Servers** — This category provides additional network services that are optional for MythTV purposes. Although nothing in this category is strongly required, you may find these additions useful in your existing network context.

- **Legacy Network Servers** — This category is entirely unnecessary, so you are safe to uncheck it.

Development

- **Development Tools** — You should probably go ahead and enable this, even if you don't expect to compile anything. There's no harm in having a compiler and interpreter around and not using them, but adding them in later when you need them can be more hassle than it's worth. The default selection is fine, should you choose to include them.

- **X Software Development** — This is entirely optional; use only if you intend to compile X Windows applications.

- **GNOME Software Development** — This is entirely optional; use only if you intend to compile GNOME applications.

- **KDE Software Development** — This is entirely optional; use only if you intend to compile KDE applications.

- **Legacy Software Development** — This category is entirely unnecessary, so you are safe to uncheck it.

- **Java Development** — This category is entirely unnecessary, so you are safe to uncheck it.

- **Eclipse** — This category is entirely unnecessary, so you are safe to uncheck it.

- **Language Support** — Unless you selected a native language other than English, or need multi-language support, you may safely uncheck this option.

System

- **Administration Tools** — This category is optional, but contains a handful of useful graphical utilities for administering MythTV. A few of the select applications are as follows:

  - system-config-keyboard

  - system-config-language

  - system-config-lvm

  - system-config-network

  - system-config-soundcard

  The Details tab of the Anaconda installer interface will provide details about any or all of these items if needed.

- **System Tools** — Another collection of client applications, the System Tools category provides support for connecting to SMB shares and monitoring network traffic. You won't need these, but you may find them useful.

Miscellaneous

- **Printing Support** — Unless you have reason to print from your "mythical convergence box" — and indeed, there can be both practical and creative reasons — then you may deselect this category in whole.

Note   Gone in Fedora Core 5 are the categories for Everything and Minimal installation profiles. However, you will still be given the opportunity to selectively install packages on a case-by-case basis. These options appear during the Fedora Core 4 installation process and appear here for completeness in case you are working with version 4.

Everything and Minimal

Last in this list are the Everything and Minimal package profiles. As each name implies, the respective profile adds or removes packages accordingly. These two groups are exclusive to any other group options (personal desktop, workstation, server, or custom) and invalidate all current selections. Use the Minimal profile for very small footprint machines with precious little on-board storage to spare, but beware: No other options are available once the Minimal profile is selected. Any additional packages you might want must be added after installation.

Once you make your final package selections and click through the next two installer dialogs titled Additional Language Support and About to Install (the second, and last, dialog tells you where installation logs reside), Anaconda begins its routine. Afterward, it asks you to reboot (at which time you should remove the installation media) and proceed to the next segment.

First Boot Setup

The following steps lead you through the screens for the First Boot setup:

1. **Welcome** — When the Fedora Core installation process resumes, you are presented with a Welcome screen. Click Next to continue.

2. **License Agreement** — Click Agree to accept the license terms.

3. **Date and Time** — At this screen, click the tab labeled Enable Network Time Protocol to enable NTP. You don't have to know the NTP server that's closest to you — the installer makes a best guess attempt on your behalf. Later, you may check your nearest time server online and replace the initial selection if necessary.

4. **Display** — Next comes your chance to set default MythTV display settings — this depends on the resolution of the display unit for which you configure (and/or use) MythTV. You can always change this later using any of the GUI display utilities if you must. Then, click through to the next dialog.

5. **System User** — Fedora needs a MythTV user, and this is where you create one. Because most applications are written with the username `mythtv` in mind, it's wise to stick with that cognomen. You may, however, choose whatever you like.

6. **Sound Card** — Anaconda will try (and occasionally fail) to detect your sound card. At this stage, Anaconda also permits you to test sound settings, so have a pair of head-phones or speakers nearby to plug into your computer's audio jack(s). Click the button to hear a short audio sample of someone playing the guitar (see the "Audio Setup" section later in this chapter for more information).

7. **Additional CDs** — If you have additional packages on CD, you can install them here now. Otherwise, you can handle software additions and upgrades using the native Fedora package manager.

Post-Linux Installation Tasks

You are done with the initial portion of the Fedora Core installation. The following sections cover a few essential post-installation tasks.

Disabling SELinux

Because SELinux can impede proper operation of MythTV, spare yourself the headache now and disable SELinux functionality if you didn't do so during Fedora Core installation. While this advice may be questionable from a security standpoint, there is little reason to dig into SELinux when building a MythTV system.

There are a few post-install methods for disabling SELinux, to prevent potential problems down the line. For starters, you can temporarily disable SELinux as follows:

```
# getenforce
Enforcing
# setenforce 0
# getenforce
Permissive
```

Reporting the `Permissive` state is highly desirable for ease of use and proper MythTV operation. This change takes effect immediately, and does not require a reboot.

In addition, the following utility also reports SELinux status from a root prompt:

```
# /usr/sbin/sestatus -v
SELinux status:              disabled
```

To permanently disable SELinux, edit the `/etc/selinux/config` file with your editor of choice, changing this entry

```
SELINUX=enforcing
```

to read

```
SELINUX=disabled
```

Here is a symbolic link to the original copy:

```
/etc/sysconfig/selinux
```

This change will take effect upon the next reboot, and remain permanent until either the configuration file is restored to its original state or the `selinux=0` directive is given at boot time (boot parameters override system configuration file settings).

During the Fedora Core installation process — whether by disk or download — the installer provides an option to toggle SELinux on or off (it's on by default). Should you happen to work from an existing installation of Fedora Core and experience problems in persisting SELinux settings across reboots, there is a second place to look. Buried in the relatively untrodden directory path `/boot/grub` there resides a boot loader configuration file named `grub.conf`. SELinux is implemented from the bootstrap procedure all the way through to the operating system, and this is where it all begins.

The following code shows example grub.conf entries indicating SELinux extensions:

```
# grub.conf generated by anaconda

[...TEXT OMMITTED FOR BREVITY...]

title Fedora Core (2.6.15-1.2054_FC5) SELinux Enforced Mode
  root (hd0,0)
 measure (hd0,0)/etc/security/selinux/policy.17 9
  kernel /boot/vmlinuz-2.6.15-1.2054_FC5 ro root=LABEL=/
    enforcing=1 rhgb quiet 3
  initrd /boot/initrd-2.6.15-1.2054_FC5.img
```

The text that appears in boldface shows SELinux engagement during the boot process. To fix this, you can create a new grub entry or simply edit the existing one in place. Any changes made to SELinux policies already in effect on a live system will require a reboot to take effect.

System Updating

Following the Fedora install, you should perform a general system update to establish consistency with the latest release. Fedora uses a mature and capable package manager called yum for this task (refer to Chapter 2 for more details on using yum). You can also use yumex, a frontend for yum, to perform the update — see the related sidebar.

To run the update, issue this command inside a super-user terminal window:

```
# yum -y update
```

Expect this process to take a while, even if you have the best resources available — the update process is very thorough and can encompass a wide variety of applications even for the latest installer images.

Using yumex

The yum package manager uses a frontend called yumex. You don't need yumex but it is convenient, and is much more user-friendly (especially if you don't care for command-line utilities). You can obtain yumex by issuing the following command in a console window:

```
# yum -y install yumex
```

If you are new to Fedora and don't know where to find a console window, click the little red fedora (hat icon) on the toolbar, locate the System Tools entry, and expand it to find the Terminal Program – Super User Mode application (if you're logged in as any other user). You are then prompted for the administrator password, after which you may use the terminal with full administrative privileges.

You will find yumex (labeled 3) on the taskbar under System Tools. Fire up this application and click the Install tab (be patient, it can take a while to initialize) and browse for the desired entries in the list inside the main window. Here's a hint: You can home in on a specific package by typing its name into the search bar and clicking the Search button. This filters out all irrelevant packages, and gives you license to enable all the packages you need in one go.

Configuring Third-Party Repositories

You should now turn back to the "Fedora Core and Yellowdog Updater, Modified (YUM)" section of Chapter 2 to review the specifics about independent package repositories for Fedora installations. Not only do these repositories provide you with applications and suites excluded from the official distribution (owing to licensing restrictions or the experimental nature of some drivers), they are often the only means of acquiring the properly pre-compiled and pre-configured software you need for MythTV.

Obtaining and Installing Video Card Drivers

Historically, nVidia has offered strong driver support for Linux, both for its graphics and Northbridge (and now, pure Southbridge nForce4 and later versions) chipsets. ATI has largely ignored the Linux community, and so far only hit-or-miss performance can be expected from many of their cards. ATI is proactive about support for Windows machines — but only time will tell if they decide to do likewise for Linux.

Thus, a primary advantage of nVidia graphics chips and Linux is they just work. So far, nVidia has demonstrated genuine interest in the Linux community and has been supportive of its needs.

To obtain and install the driver, follow these steps:

1. Create a backup of your original X11 configuration file:

```
# mv /etc/X11/xorg.conf /etc/X11/xorg.conf.orig
# cp /etc/X11/xorg.conf.nvidia /etc/X11/xorg.conf
```

2. Obtain a specified version (currently 1.0-8178):

```
# export KVER=`uname -r`
# yum -y install nvidia-graphics8178-kmdl-$KVER
# yum -y install nvidia-graphics8178
```

3. Optionally, grab the libraries and devices:

```
# yum -y install nvidia-graphics8178-devices
# yum -y install nvidia-graphics8178-libs
```

4. You may then toggle between driver revisions if one set creates problems that another resolves, assuming you have more than one version handy:

```
# init 2
# nvidia-graphics-switch 7676
# init 5
```

Here's an example configuration for an nVidia GeForce MX outputting NTSC through S-Video, as shown in the Fedora guide:

```
Section "Device"
    Identifier   "Videocard0"
    Driver       "nvidia"
    VendorName   "Chaintech"
```

```
        BoardName      "nVidia GeForce 4 MX 440"
        Option         "TVStandard" "NTSC-M"
        Option         "TVOutFormat" "SVIDEO"
    EndSection
```

5. For configurations that use a display attached through an audio/video switchbox, or setups in which display properties are not detected automatically, you may add this option:

```
    Option         "ConnectedMonitor" "TV"
```

Troubleshooting advice appears in Chapter 18, should you need it. Fortunately for you, most issues will be handled transparently by the time you arrive at the desktop for the first time.

Audio Setup

In earlier revisions, the native KDE sound daemon (aRts) reportedly did not work well with MythTV, but stabilized later, after the codebase was further refined. However, Wilson recommends in his HOW-TO that you disable aRts should you experience problems with your audio subsystem. You may configure this through the KDE Control Center, as described here:

1. Click the red hat icon and select Control Center.

2. In the Sound & Multimedia menu, select Sound System.

3. Deselect the entry "Start aRts soundserver on KDE startup" (this message has changed to "Enable the sound system" in KDE version 3.3 and later).

4. Click Apply.

Some cards may not be properly identified during installation; this can happen for a number of reasons. Perhaps your sound card is too new or driver support is considered too immature for inclusion among the main distribution packages. For these less common situations, the Fedora HOW-TO offers this remedy:

```
# export KVER=`uname -r`
# yum -y install alsa-kmdl-$KVER
# yum -y install alsa-driver
```

Wilson goes on to provide you with an example taken from his /etc/modprobe.conf file for the SB Live!, Audigy2, and nForce2 Audigy series sound solutions. These are a bit too long and complex to present here (and leave too many opportunities for error should you try to key them in by hand). Instead, you should grab these configurations on an Internet-enabled machine at the following URL:

www.wilsonet.com/mythtv/fcmyth.php#firstboot

Digital sound support in MythTV is possible, and a document that Mike Dean created describes how to use digital sound with your MythTV PC:

www.mythtv.org/wiki/index.php/Configuring_Digital_Sound

With any luck (or some well-informed product advice) your audio hardware will be working by the time you get a usable desktop. Originally, establishing audio support for Linux was something of a black art, but the unflinching persistence of the Red Hat development team has made much of the previously impossible (such as simplifying the Linux installation process) quite possible indeed.

Obtaining and Installing MythTV

In Chapter 2 you learned how to install MythTV on an existing installation of Fedora Core; this chapter gets you to that point. If you haven't already done so, install the Yum Extender, a graphical user interface wrapper to the command-line Yellowdog Updater, Modified (see the "Using yumex" sidebar). The Yum Extender gives you an intuitive graphical user interface to install or update systemwide packages in a central console and greatly simplifies the process. We continue to provide command-line sequences mostly for the benefit of those who do not have the luxury of using the extender (given the rare possibility that your graphics card isn't working properly).

Using the Yum Extender interface, installing the MythTV suite is a no-brainer. A simple invocation (also described in "Get Up to Date"), a single keyword in the search bar ("myth"), and a dash of patience is all that's required. If you've used a previous edition of MythTV and browsed the Fedora repository, one thing that stands out is the growing number of recent entries, indicating that development not only continues, but is increasing over time.

Obtaining and Installing Capture Card Drivers

The instructions here for obtaining and installing capture card drivers are paraphrased from the Fedora Core MythTV guide, a collective body of wisdom. Only those items that apply to North America appear here; thus, there's no mention of PAL, SECAM, or other standards used elsewhere in the world. For more details on the topics addressed here, consult the Fedora Core MythTV guide at http://wilsonet.com/mythtv/. You can also find a detailed list of video capture cards identified to work with MythTV at http://mythtv.org/wiki/index.php/Video_capture_card.

BTTV-Based Chips

The bt848 and bt878 Brooktree chipsets (found in a variety of older capture card products) are well supported and automatically identified by kudzu, Fedora's hardware manager. You won't have much fiddling to do here. Newer Brooktree chipsets (now Conexant) require — in Wilson's words — a "much-less-stable" cx88 driver to work.

If you happen to use a Brooktree chipset, you may not get the full functionality of the card using the defaults that Fedora assigns. However, there is a script called Find TV Card Options that can assist you in tuning parameters to help you establish a suitable configuration for your card. You may obtain this script here:

www.mind.lu/~yg/ftvco

Wilson adds that his bt-based card requires an audio jumper cable to multiplex audio and video properly into streaming MPEG-2 captures. For this, you must configure MythTV accordingly:

1. Click the fedora (red hat) icon on the taskbar.

2. Select Sound & Video.

3. Click Volume Control.

4. Identify the Line-In properties for your card.

5. Check the boxes for Mute and Record.

He then suggests that newer kernels (2.6) provide better ALSA support with the `snd-bt8x8` driver code, but this had not been tested as of this writing.

IVTV-Based Chipsets

Several products sport IVTV-based chipset support, and some of the popular vendor products (Hauppauge PVR-150/250/350/500, AverMedia M179, and Yuan MPG160/600) are known to work under Linux. Install the IVTV driver set like this:

```
# yum -y install ivtv-firmware ivtv-firmware-audio
# yum -y install ivtv-kmdl-$KVER ivtv
```

Add the following entries to `/etc/modprobe.conf` specifically for IVTV cards:

```
alias char-major-81 videodev
alias char-major-81-0 ivtv
```

If you have a PVR-500, it appears as two cards, and requires the following additional line:

```
alias char-major-81-1 ivtv
```

Owners of Yuan models may have to manually input the following:

```
alias char-major-81 videodev
alias char-major-81-0 ivtv
options ivtv tuner=2
options msp3400 once=0 simpler=1 simple=0
```

Try to load the IVTV driver:

```
# /sbin/depmod -a
# /sbin/modprobe ivtv
```

Should you encounter a memory allocation problem, try the following instead:

```
# echo 16284 > /proc/sys/vm/min_free_kbytes
```

Try to load the IVTV driver again. If your problems persist, and you are using particularly new (or particularly unsupported) hardware, consult the Wilson HOW-TO (or check Chapter 18 in this book, which Wilson also wrote).

BTTV and IVTV Cards in Combination

Both BTTV and IVTV-based chipsets can peacefully coexist in the same system with a few adjustments to the `/etc/modprobe.conf` file. Wilson provides his configuration online, and we produce it here:

```
# ivtv modules setup
alias char-major-81 videodev
alias char-major-81-0 ivtv
# bttv
alias char-major-81-1 bttv
```

If you select a supported tuner, it will be set up for you automatically. The first tuner is named `/dev/video0`, and your second tuner is `/dev/video1`.

Multiple IVTV Cards

You must make one slight change in `/etc/modprobe.conf` to use both your IVTV-based cards. Wilson uses this sample configuration to show you how to do it:

```
alias char-major-81 videodev
alias char-major-81-0 ivtv
alias char-major-81-1 ivtv
```

You might have already noticed that the aliases that correspond to ivtv entries differ only in the last number of the middle column. That number corresponds to the position in the `/dev` devices listing where that card appears (`/dev/video0`, etc.), and may be repeated for multiple cards.

Wilson suggests one final optional parameter:

```
options ivtv tuner=-1,2
```

You should place this just after the last alias entry above. When you specify a value of `-1` for the `tuner` parameter, it tries to detect the tuner type automatically for the device attached to `/dev/video0`. When you specify a positive value you indicate a specific type of card; here, Wilson uses the number 2 to identify his second card, an Avermedia M179 tuner card. He goes on to state that while this line entry is necessary for combining a Hauppage PVR-350 and an Avermedia M179, it is not needed if you combine two PVR-350 cards.

PVR-350 with TV-Out

To make things simple, you need another video output device to configure PVR-350 TV-Out capability. Wilson mentions how he had to configure his PVR-350 remotely using ssh's X Windows forwarding feature, but it's a complicated setup for novice builders. You can read more about this under subheading 7 (Get and install video card drivers) located here:

```
http://wilsonet.com/mythtv/fcmyth.php
```

North American HDTV/ATSC Capture Cards

As with other supported card types, Fedora's installer tries its best to satisfy driver dependencies for all hardware it knows about.

Later chapters handle details specific to operating an HDTV display. One of the core authors, Matt Wright, contributes his hard-won experiences in dealing with HDTV playback and the Advanced Television Systems Committee (ATSC) specification for high-definition content.

An excellent write-up by Angel Li, dated March 29, 2005, describes how to establish Air2PC support with MythTV and Fedora Core 3. Currently, Fedora Core is in stable release version 5, so your mileage may vary. You can read about Angel Li's experiences at:

```
www.rsmas.miami.edu/personal/angel/mythtv/air2pc-howto.html
```

Supporting unsupported cards in the multimedia PC world is an exercise best left to the reader, who should turn to the Web for guidance, because this chapter cannot cover every possible scenario.

FireWire Capture from a Supported Cable Box

Less than a handful of FireWire-based set-top boxes are known to work with MythTV, but we do not cover them extensively in this book (a few examples appear in later chapters). Jarod Wilson, lead author for this book, and the maintainer of the phenomenal HOW-TO guide that serves as its basis, reports that he successfully (and easily) records HDTV programs with his Motorola DCT-6200, and notes that Scientific Atlanta's 3250 series FireWire units also work.

If you're interested in getting a FireWire unit working, check online resources for support — MythTV, though mature, is still under heavy development, and supported hardware is subject to regular change. The feeling you get from the exercise of building your own MythTV/Linux entertainment PC may be summarized as "Where there's a will, there's a way!"

Obtaining and Installing LIRC

Obtaining (and installing) the Linux Infra-Red Control (LIRC) daemon is simple. Installing the MythTV suite provides some of the LIRC package, but here's where you finish the job. You may use the Yum Extender if you like, but the following commands work at the command line:

```
# yum -y install lirc-kmdl-$KVER
# yum -y install lirc-kdml
```

Thanks are in order to Axel Thimms for his work on ATrpms to get the most compatibility crammed into third-party packages; he provides many common IR control profiles immediately usable for MythTV. More information about configuring a remote control (and finalizing installation) appears in Chapter 5.

Setting Up MySQL

MythTV needs MySQL front-and-center to maintain its dynamic list of program guide data. The following sequence illustrates how you should prepare MySQL:

1. Enable MySQL with system startup:

```
# /sbin/chkconfig mysqld on
# /sbin/service mysqld start
```

2. Set the MySQL root password (replace THISWORD with your administrator password):

```
# mysql -u root mysql
mysql> UPDATE user SET Password=('THISWORD') WHERE user='root'
mysql> FLUSH PRIVILEGES;
mysql> quit
```

3. Create the MythTV database:

```
# mysql -u root -p < /usr/share/doc/mythtv-0.19/database/mc.sql
(enter the administrator password when prompted)
```

You may tweak some optional parameters through the MySQL configuration file (/etc/my.cnf) to improve performance with MythTV, although these changes are not required. Wilson supplies the following parameters that improved his MythTV experience (they should work for yours as well):

```
[mysqld]
key_buffer = 16M
table_cache = 128
sort_buffer_size = 2M
myisam_sort_buffer_size = 8M
query_cache_size = 16M
```

He warns that these settings are specific to the 4.x series of MySQL; an earlier version can be found at http://wilsonet.com/mythtv/HOWTO-fc3.php#mysql. The MythTV database is populated later by mythfilldatabase through the frontend application.

Final Thoughts

With the instructions in this and previous chapters, you should now have a base MythTV system on a Linux machine. In the rest of the book, you learn how to configure and extend the base MythTV build to perform all the tricks you desire. The following sections steer you in specific directions you may travel from this point forward.

Setting Up MythTV

Subsequent chapters deal with establishing backend and frontend roles for your MythTV project build. Much of this targets Fedora Core users, but if you opted to install KnoppMyth, most of this preparation is already done.

In Chapter 6, you configure MythTV as a slave backend, interact (once again) with `mythfill database`, and get some expert advice on tweaking channel performance. In Chapter 7, you find guidance on configuring the `mythfrontend` controls (General, Appearance, Program Guide, Playback, and Recording). Shortly thereafter, MythTV keyboard commands and theme packages are explored, considerations for DirecTV and DishTV are examined, and further tuner options are explained.

Part IV introduces topics involved in personalizing the sights and sounds in your MythTV environment, including adding DVD support, customizing MythTV menu features, tweaking parameters for playback on widescreen displays, and advanced performance hacks. You also learn how to manipulate the MythTV environment — keybindings, exporting the native `.nuv` format to one playable in any reader, outputting to high-definition televisions (HDTV), and even how to rip old VHS tapes onto CD.

Configuring MythTV Add-Ons

Chapter 9 is where the real fun begins — this chapter kicks off discussion about the variety of plug-ins that substantiate MythTV's original mission statement to be the "mythical home convergence" theater PC. You learn how to interact with the usual cast of characters (the official plug-ins) and some well-known unofficial plug-ins that can extend your MythTV experience in innumerable ways. Plus, you might even be inspired to attempt your own personal modifications, an important catalyst for the MythTV initiative.

New plug-ins are adopted with each major revision (so far), and the MythTV development community has shown no signs of slowing down when it comes to producing clever and useful new additions. During the course of writing this book, MythTV has seen one major revision (from 0.18 to 0.19) with a wealth of enriched functionality and enhancements. For example, several recent utility applications are now available, including `mythlcdserver`, for handling LCD interaction with MythTV; `mythwelcome`, a heads-up display for the unit as it cranks through background tasks; and a variety of internal functions that expand playback and recording capabilities. MythControls, official in release 0.19, provides feedback on invalid key sequences (such as inputting key sequences that MythTV doesn't understand).

A full listing of features that appear in the latest MythTV release (as we write this book) resides at

`www.mythtv.org/wiki/index.php/Release_Notes_-_0.19`

The goal of this chapter has been to demonstrate the relative simplicity of installing, configuring, and customizing Linux. MythTV is free and open for anyone to use, modify, and redistribute. If you have any suggestions about how we might improve our installation coverage for either the KnoppMyth or Fedora Core, we would love to hear them. E-mail us at `MythTV@edtittel.com`.

Remote Control Setup

I n the Linux runtime environment, remote control support is the province of the Linux Infrared Remote Control system, otherwise known as LIRC. LIRC may be used with just about any remote input device, and it works with the infrared (IR) emitters (sometimes called IR blasters) often used to interact with set-top boxes, like those used with cable or satellite TV delivery systems.

Selecting a Remote Control and Remote Control Receiver Technology

MythTV can be controlled with nothing more than a keyboard, but most couch potatoes typically don't want to control their television with a keyboard. Fortunately, MythTV works with a wide range of remote controls and IR receivers. The following sections detail some popular options in these areas, with vendor details and Web sites provided in Table 5-1.

Hauppauge Remotes

Driver name: lirc_i2c

The remote receiver included with retail boxed Hauppauge cards (not MCE models) uses a proprietary port on the back of the card. This configuration is well supported and widely used with MythTV. Even better news is that the IR receiver that's bundled with this package is compatible with more remotes than just the Hauppauge model that's also included. This means that with a little extra advanced setup effort, you can use a different remote of your choosing — for example, something such as the Harmony 860 universal home theater remote, which will not only operate your MythTV PC, but can also be programmed to operate most other devices that support their own infrared (IR) remote controls — in place of the Hauppauge remote. Because Hauppauge remote support is part of the

---

TV capture card itself, using one of these products also requires that IVTV be loaded before LIRC (essentially because IVTV provides some capabilities that must be available to enable LIRC to work properly).

> **Tip** As noted, you must load the `lirc_i2c` driver *after* IVTV for the remote to work properly. Do this by adding the following line near the bottom of the `modprobe.conf` configuration file on your MythTV PC: `install lirc_i2c /sbin/modprobe ivtv; \ /sbin/ modprobe --ignore-install lirc_i2c`

Hauppauge has replaced the remote it includes with its TV capture cards at least three times since the popular PVR 250 and other related models were introduced. The oldest of these is an all-black model that is hardly seen anymore. The second is a first-generation gray/black remote, pictured in Figure 5-1. The second revision of the gray/black model is often called the 45-button model, to reflect the number of control buttons it provides. As we write this chapter, the 45-button model is the newest Hauppauge remote and is included in all current retail boxed products from this company.

A prefabricated `lircd.conf` file and `.lircrc` file for the 45-button gray/black remote is available on Jarod Wilson's Web pages, at the following URLs:

- `wilsonet.com/mythtv/lircd-g3.conf.txt`
- `wilsonet.com/mythtv/lircrc-haupgrey-g3.txt`

A prefabricated `lircd.conf` file and `.lircrc` file for the first-generation gray/black remote is included with the IVTV and MythTV documentation and may be found at either of the following two locations on your computer:

- `/usr/share/doc/ivtv-[version number]/lircd-g.conf`
- `/usr/share/doc/mythtv-[version number]/configfiles/ hauppauge-lircrc-nativelirc`

Streamzap PC Remote

Driver name: `lirc_streamzap`

The Streamzap is an inexpensive, popular USB remote for Windows, but it also supports LIRC version 1.7.1 and newer versions for Linux use. A prefabricated `lircd.conf` file is included with the remote, along with the latest LIRC (at least, at the time the box was put together and shrink-wrapped).

Just as with the Hauppauge TV capture card, the IR receiver included with the Streamzap is compatible with other remotes. Later in this chapter, you learn how to create the custom remote profile that will be necessary in order to use something different if that's your choice.

FIGURE 5-1: Hauppauge first-generation "gray/black" remote

SoundGraph iMON

Driver name: `lirc_imon`

The SoundGraph iMON is a multi-function video fluorescent display (VFD) device that also includes an optional remote. It's designed to slide into a 5.25" drive bay inside a PC, so that the VFD is visible on the front of the case. The iMON comes in several versions, however, including an external model called the Knob that attaches to a PC through a USB connection and lacks a VFD (these even work with laptops and provide a handy way to add remote control to such computers). There's even a radio frequency (RF) version of the iMON now available, but we don't cover it in this book.

Some HTPC cases even feature built-in iMON VFD units. The best-known case builder to offer models with integrated iMONs is probably SilverStone, but Thermaltake, 3R Systems, and others also integrate this popular VFD/remote control solution with their cases. The newest iMON receiver models are not universal; they only work with the remote that's bundled with the iMON itself, which is called the iMon PAD. Prefabricated `lircd.conf` files are also included, along with the latest LIRC.

IRTrans

Driver name: `lirc_irtrans`

This kit comes from a small German company, and is mostly likely to crop up in the United States in an OrigenAE (an HTPC case manufacturer formerly named Uneed International) X11 case. The IRTrans module is a universal IR receiver that is compatible with just about any consumer electronics remote, including the well-designed Windows Media Center remote that is included in newer OrigenAE case bundles instead of the IRTrans. If you have an IRTrans but don't have the most current LIRC driver to go with it, you can download it from `www.irtrans.de/en/download/linux.php`.

ATI/X10 RF Remotes

Driver name: `lirc_atiusb`

For the most part, these remotes are all variations on a reference design by home automation company X10. These remotes are radio-frequency-based, which offers a few advantages compared to infrared remotes: RF works over longer distances, and a clear line of sight between the remote and the device you want to control is not necessary. Thus, using an RF remote, you could control your MythTV PC from another room. The most common such remote is the ATI Remote Wonder, but at various times nVidia, Niveus Media, and Marmitek have also used the X10 design in their products. Sadly, most of these have been discontinued, but they may often be obtained inexpensively from various auction or surplus goods Web sites. The more modern SnapStream Firefly, shown in Figure 5-2, is a very nice remote that has a good reputation in the Windows world; it's also based on X10 protocols.

Prefabricated `lircd.conf` and `.lircrc` files for the ATI Remote Wonder are available at

- `http://knoppmythwiki.org/index.php?page=ATIRemote`

Prefabricated `lircd.conf` and `.lircrc` files for the ATI Remote Wonder II are available at

- `www.mythtv.org/wiki/index.php/ATI_Remote_Wonder_II`

Prefabricated `lircd.conf` and `.lircrc` files for the Firefly are available at

- `www.fedoraforum.org/forum/showthread.php?t=47489`

Windows Media Center Edition 2005 Remote

Driver name: `lirc_mceusb2`

The Microsoft Windows XP Media Center Edition 2005 reference design remote, shown in Figure 5-3, is one of the nicest remotes to use for multimedia PC control, both from an ergonomic perspective (it fits nicely in the hand, and has a nice, user-friendly button layout) and for its longer-than-average IR range. A prefabricated `lircd.conf` file is included, along with the latest LIRC, on the CD that ships with this device.

A prefabricated `.lircrc` designed for this remote and MythTV use can be found at

`www.blatter.com/mceusb/lircrc_MYTH_EXAMPLE`

FIGURE 5-2: SnapStream's
FireFly remote

FIGURE 5-3: Microsoft Media
Center 2005 remote

USB-UIRT

Driver name: `lirc_usb-uirt2_raw`

The USB-UIRT, which stands for Universal Serial Bus (USB)-Universal Infrared Receiver Transmitter (UIRT) is a commercial USB model of an older RS232 serial port UIRT whose specifications have been floating around the Web for years. The USB-UIRT is widely used in the Windows PVR world but is also supported with the latest LIRC releases. A truly versatile tool, this one now also works well on MythTV PCs.

Vendor Contacts

Table 5-1 provides product information and Web sites for a variety of remote vendors.

Table 5-1   Remote Vendors

Name	Technology	Price Range	URL
Hauppauge	IR	N/A included in retail box bundles	www.hauppauge.com
SoundGraph iMon	IR	$75–$130 Also integrated into select chassis	www.soundgraph.com/index_e.asp www.silverstonetek.com
IRTrans	Universal IR receiver	$70 Also integrated into select chassis	www.irtrans.de/en/index.php www.origenae.com
Logitech Harmony	Universal IR	$200–$250	www.logitech.com
Microsoft Media Center 2005 Remote	IR	Approx. $35	OEM-only kit made specifically for MCE 2005
Philips Pronto	Universal IR	$150–$600	www.pronto.philips.com
SnapStream Firefly	RF	$50	www.snapstream.com
Streamzap PC Remote	IR	$40	www.streamzap.com
USB-UIRT	Universal IR receiver	$50	www.usbuirt.com

Loading LIRC Modules

Proper setup of your modprobe.conf file requires an alias char-major-61 declaration at the top of the configuration file that appends the name of your remote control driver to the statement in order to make things work. Thus, if your system uses the ATI Remote Wonder driver, you create the following line at the head of the `modprobe.conf` file:

```
alias char-major-61 lirc_atiusb
```

Later in the same configuration file, you must also load an actual LIRC driver module. In keeping with our Remote Wonder example, this means you add the following command:

```
modprobe lirc_atiusb
```

You can create this directive in the modprobe.conf file by adding the following line (of course, it has to occur after the preceding directive in order to work properly):

```
install lirc_atiusb /sbin/modprobe lirc_atiusb
```

 Tip   Sometimes the preceding method doesn't work properly. If that happens to you, instead of trying to load LIRC in the `modprobe.conf` file, you should add the last portion of the preceding command—namely, `modprobe lirc_atiusb`—to the `rc.local` file in `/etc/rc.d/`.

Remote Profiles

After LIRC is properly installed, you need some way to tell Linux how to interpret the raw IR codes that your remote emits. This essentially creates a unique text label for each individual such code. To make life easy for you, we included links to predefined configuration files for most of common remotes in their respective sections in this chapter. If your remote isn't mentioned here, or the predefined configuration file doesn't work on your MythTV PC, the next place to check is in the LIRC documentation directory. In a standard package installation this resides at

```
/usr/share/doc/lirc-0.8.0/remotes
```

Here, most common remote profiles are included, such as the MCE remote, iMon remotes, Streamzap, and a basic Hauppauge profile. Another place to check is the LIRC Web site; it may just have a profile for your remote archived at

```
http://lirc.sourceforge.net/remotes/
```

To use a predefined profile you must rename a copy of that file to lircd.conf, and place it in the `/etc` directory on your MythTV PC.

Creating a Custom Remote Configuration

Typing the command `irrecord filename` starts an interactive process that asks you to first press a remote control button, and then type a corresponding name for it at the keyboard. After working completely through this process, you will have built a freshly minted `lircd.conf` configuration file ready to go, and saved under whatever name you specified at the command line when you started this process. Copy that file as /etc/lircd.conf to test it out.

Completing Your LIRC Install

Next, start the LIRC daemon (system service). You will need to run as root with su and then issue the following command:

```
/sbin/service lircd start
```

You should see an [OK] response. If so, you are ready to test your remote and move on to MythTV setup. If not, you'll need to go back and repeat the process just described in this chapter.

Testing It Out

The command `/usr/bin/irw` enables you to test LIRC. With a proper configuration file available, it shows you whatever text string is associated with the IR code for each key press. You may need to run irw as root to make it work properly.

If it works as expected, go ahead and run `/sbin/chkconfig lircd on` to enable lircd to run automatically at system boot time. If it doesn't work as expected, check in `/var/log/messages` for clues as to why. See Chapter 18's "Troubleshooting Hardware/Driver Problems" section for further assistance.

MythTV Setup

You must now establish some way for your remote control buttons to mean something to MythTV. This file is copied to your home folder in a hidden file called `.lircrc`.

Many of the links mentioned earlier in this chapter for the various remotes we cover include an associated `.lircrc` file for you to use with MythTV. If you need to create one yourself, however, MythTV includes a default `.lircrc` file that you can easily customize inside a text editor to match your remote's button names.

Universal Remote Controls

While the remotes shipped with most capture cards work with MythTV, many people find them too small and flimsy. Furthermore, many MythTV enthusiasts already own several remotes for assorted HiFi equipment, so adding yet another one to the mix may not be desirable, regardless of how solid it is. Ideally, one remote should control all your devices. Luckily for you, LIRC really doesn't care what type of remote you point at it, as long as the remote sends signals it can decipher.

Universal remotes available on the market range from under $10 to around $400 (and possibly beyond). Obviously, not all are created equal. It's entirely possible to get a cheap universal remote and use it to control all of your equipment, including your MythTV box, but it may not be the easiest thing to configure.

Basic Remotes

For a typical low-end Universal Electronics (UEIC) One4All remote or RadioShack remote (typically re-branded UEIC remotes), you must find a device profile with functionality similar to what you want for MythTV. It must also match the infrared protocol (there are two different ones in common circulation) that the IR receiver on your MythTV box uses.

If you happen to use a Hauppauge capture card's IR receiver, or a USB receiver designed for Microsoft's Windows XP Media Center Edition, you'd configure your universal remote with a profile for a device that uses the RC-5 or RC-6 IR protocol. Something along the lines of a Philips VCR profile should provide a good starting point, but you're likely to have to do some combination of key moving, remapping, and IR learning (if that's possible with your remote), to get all keys working. In addition, you'll need to either find an LIRC remote profile (several generic ones appear in the LIRC add-on remotes archive, at www.lirc.org/remotes.tar.bz2) or build one from scratch using irrecord, distributed as part of LIRC. A process specifically tailored for the RadioShack 15-2115 and 15-2116 remote controls, along with pre-configured remote profiles and MythTV key mappings, resides at http://wilsonet.com/mythtv/remotes.php. These remotes used to cost about $30 but unfortunately they are no longer in production. However, the process should be at least somewhat similar for UEIC remotes currently available. The methodology for configuring other universal remotes varies from maker to maker.

High-End Remotes

There's another—and potentially much easier—route you might take to get your universal remote working with your MythTV box. It requires that you spend more money to acquire a more powerful universal remote with ample memory for IR learning, a technique whereby you use a single-purpose remote to teach the universal its tricks. Once you get the remote that comes with your capture card working, it can train your universal remote to use all of its IR commands. Typically, this is as simple as switching a universal remote into learning mode, selecting the button to which you want to assign a function, pointing the old remote at the new one, and then pressing the button on the old remote that you want the new one to learn. Logitech's Harmony remote series, while not cheap, comes highly recommended. We make use of a Harmony 880 remote these days quite happily. I configured it to work with MythTV simply by pointing an older remote at it to map all the keys over, so no tinkering with LIRC was needed.

Going one step further down the road of "no tinkering with LIRC," you can also purchase a wireless keyboard that transmits via infrared, and train a universal remote to emulate specific keys on that keyboard. The remote sends what amounts to keyboard button presses to the keyboard's IR receiver, which connects to your MythTV box through a PS/2 or USB port. The IR receiver then feeds that signal to the system as keyboard input, with no involvement (or need for) LIRC whatsoever.

Another cool feature with many universal remotes is their ability to map certain keys to a device other than the primary one you want to control (your MythTV box, we assume). A telling example occurs when all audio in your A/V stack goes through an amplifier, and you want the volume keys on your remote to control the volume level on the amplifier, rather than on your MythTV box, your TV, or other devices. Both the RadioShack 15-2115/6 and Harmony remotes have this feature.

The Harmony remotes are more expensive ($75 to $400, depending on which model you buy and where you buy it), but they are generally worth every penny because of their strong macro support, ease of programmability, and the way in which they use Activities, rather than just control raw devices. For example, a Harmony remote can be configured with a MythTV Activity, which knows that you need your TV on and set to a specific input, your amplifier on and set to a specific input, volume keys mapped to the amplifier, and all others mapped to control your MythTV box. The Harmony remotes are also state-aware, and can turn devices on and off as needed, when switching from one Activity to another. In these remotes all configuration occurs through a web-based interface and a USB cable to attach the computer to your remote. The only real downside is that Logitech's Harmony remote programming software doesn't work under Linux (and the Mac OS X software doesn't seem to work as well as its Windows equivalent), but these remotes are well worth the sacrifice! Figure 5-4 shows an example of a midrange Harmony remote, the model 680.

Within the MythTV community, other popular universal remotes include the Philips Pronto, the Niveus Media PC remote, TiVo remotes, and various One4All remotes.

The Keyboard Cheat

This last remote control method provides a nifty way around using a remote. With no remote to emulate, in fact, there's no need for LIRC either. The key is literally on your keyboard! If you install an IR-based wireless keyboard on your MythTV PC, you can simply instruct your universal remote to learn the appropriate keystrokes for MythTV control from the keyboard itself. Then, you can tuck the keyboard away for those times when you really need it. Because the remote sends keyboard IR codes to a keyboard connection, MythTV and other applications remain cheerfully oblivious to the fact that you're using a remote control. This method has the appeal of requiring relatively little effort and no special drivers or configuration files, and gets our simplicity award!

Cross-Reference   For a list of common MythTV keyboard commands, see Chapter 8.

FIGURE 5-4: The Logitech
Harmony 680 remote

Final Thoughts

There are a lot of remote control units out there from which to choose, so pick the one that best suits your armchair-centric lifestyle. After that, there's relatively little work involved in making a remote work well with your system. Doing some simple Internet research to find out what experienced users say about the various remotes — and checking your budget — should make your decision fairly simple.

MythTV Backend

The MythTV backend server is a cornerstone in the multi-layered framework upon which MythTV architecture rests. Without a working backend server, any MythTV frontend client is an empty shell devoid of content, if not also of purpose. That's why it's so important to pay close attention to what settings you apply to each backend server, and to understand how such settings can affect other applications or computers you configure to use them.

The MythTV framework is scalable. In other words, you can deploy a single monolithic MythTV box with native capture card capability as a stand-alone system. Later, you can add a second capture card, or possibly even a second computer. Later still, you can add more capture cards or systems to your growing MythTV empire if you choose to do so.

MythTV is also quite flexible. You can use it to define numerous input sources, and prioritize their usage by first availability or according to their order of appearance in a global manifest. Likewise, MythTV is coherent. Even when you create a hierarchy of interdependent secondary servers and frontend clients, a central authority maintains order across this entire domain.

A backend server supports two modes of operation predicated on the number of machines participating in your MythTV network. This might include one machine or several machines. The roles each machine takes on may be described best using a master/slave relationship, whereby a single central authority (the master) oversees the configuration, operation, and utilization of all subservient hosts (the slaves). With more than one capture card available at any given moment, you can record two programs independently and concurrently. You can also define fail-over cards in case a preferred device is unavailable when a recording is scheduled to begin.

In this chapter, you will discover how MythTV creates a bond between live television feed and its interactive frontend client. You'll also learn that the possibilities for any personal MythTV setup are bound only by your budget and imagination.

Over the course of a few months, this book has tracked the progress of the MythTV development project as it matures rapidly into a full-featured software suite. Many significant changes have occurred as some of these chapters were written, which indicates that the MythTV project is picking up strong momentum. If you migrate from an earlier MythTV revision to a newer one, you should be struck by the wealth of new features and functionality that were available only in crude or beta forms in earlier implementations, if not missing altogether.

in this chapter

- ☑ Key MythTV backend properties

- ☑ Master backend configuration

- ☑ Slave backend configuration

- ☑ Capture card configuration

- ☑ DataDirect and XMLTV listings

Here's a list of new feature highlights, paraphrased from the Release Notes for version 0.19:

■ LiveTV is now treated more like a normal recording, so you can press the R key while watching LiveTV and everything you've seen since you switched to that channel becomes a stored, named, recorded program. LiveTV recordings reside in a separate LiveTV recording group that's hidden from view by default, but you can enable viewing of these recordings if you wish. LiveTV recordings expire before any other content.

■ Recording ending times may be changed while recordings are in progress.

■ Recordings in progress on a slave backend will be discovered if the master restarts. In addition, the master can restart a recording on another card if a slave fails during a recording.

■ Added playgroups now allow default playback options (timestretch, skip, and jump intervals) to be set on a per-recording schedule basis.

■ Recordings in progress on a slave backend will be discovered if the master restarts and can restart a recording on another card if a slave fails during a recording.

■ Added support for changing channels across tuners during LiveTV without having to change tuners manually first

■ Added pop-up keyboard in text boxes

■ Added capability to control MythTV by telnetting to a TCP port on the frontend and typing text commands.

■ Filename changes. Recordings are now saved without ending times included in filenames. MPEG-2 recordings take an .mpg extension instead of .nuv (MPEG-4 or RTJPEG recordings).

■ Added support for DTS pass-through audio

■ Allows browse mode channel changing inside a picture-in-picture (PIP) window

You can obtain a complete list of changes from 0.18 to 0.19 (the current version as we write this chapter) at www.mythtv.org/wiki/index.php/Release_Notes_-_0.19.

Configuring the Backend Server

Once again, there are two primary roles a backend server can play for MythTV, with only minor differences in operation. At this level, a typical master/slave relationship describes the interaction between server and client (or server and server). Even if you only deploy a single computer, there is a weakly defined master/slave relationship; the real distinction is that the architecture is either unified or distributed.

What you must understand is that the MythTV framework operates in several discrete and interdependent parts, most of which is transparent to the end-user (as it should be). MythTV's backend server subsystem represents functionality that lays the foundation for higher-level features in the MythTV frontend client. Like an abstraction layer, the backend server architecture bridges user interface controls through hardware regulation. MythTV applications and plug-in modules rely on the backend server for timely and accurate delivery of information and resources. That's why you must take special care when configuring backend server parameters.

Whether you deploy one machine or many, you must define a master backend server. In a single machine setup, the master backend exercises no control over other machines, but it retains the same responsibilities nonetheless. Primarily, the master backend (MBE) server is responsible for pulling data from the program guide service provider and pushing it to any number of clients or secondary servers, called slave backend (SBE) servers. In addition, the MBE server centralizes global configuration data about the number and availability of capture cards installed throughout the system or network. The MBE schedules recordings on available capture cards, according to whatever priority you assign. It also performs any necessary commercial flagging or transcoding tasks. Thus, the existence and well-being of an MBE server is vital to a positive MythTV experience.

The Master Backend Role

In this capacity, the backend server primarily concerns itself with two main priorities: to populate the MythTV database with program guide listings and channel tuning information, and to inform MythTV which television capture/tuner card to use for any given task. In its master role, the MBE server manages a MythTV network. It serves as the authority figure for SBE servers and the frontend clients that use them. In multiple capture/tuner card arrangements, the MBE performs housekeeping duties and coordinates simultaneous concurrent threads of interaction for other MythTV elements (SBE servers and frontends/clients).

Because the MBE server centralizes and stores transactions, it's fitting to endow such a machine with the largest allocation of storage capacity. Separate staggered operations in rapid succession across a network can impact performance negatively. That's why keeping the most frequently used information centralized is essential to an efficient, low-maintenance network design. And you can forget about handling multiple multimedia clients over wireless links — there's barely enough bandwidth to stream a single multimedia feed over standard 802.11b/g radio equipment alongside moderate Internet traffic, let alone multiple such streams running simultaneously.

Ideally, for an off-server (remotely mounted) media repository, you should use Gigabit Ethernet (GbE) to enable the highest possible throughput affordable on your network. Unfortunately, this carries the not-so-obvious implication that all devices must support GbE to make this work. You might also be interested in store-bought Network Attached Storage (NAS) devices that excel at handling dedicated storage. Ultimately, your budget, your taste, and your experience dictate what works best for you.

The Slave Backend Role

When operating in a slave backend capacity, a server acts as a broker between a frontend client and the MBE server, with slightly fewer responsibilities than the master role entails. Instead of dictating which card is used, by whom that card may be used, how it is used, and when, a slave backend asks the master what actions are allowed. Likewise, a slave must also request channel guide listings from the MBE server because only the master interacts closely with the program listings provider.

Any number of slaves may be deployed in tandem and record in overlapped succession—a testament to the inherent scalability of the MythTV framework. The beauty of this arrangement is that you can schedule as many concurrent recordings as you have capture cards available for. Many other options are possible in a multi-tiered design, such as the capability to manage the wake and sleep cycles of all backend servers centrally, or to create a round-robin of capture card preferences among the array of devices defined in MBE global server settings.

Slave servers are important for large-scale deployments but have no bearing on single-box setups. If you are configuring a machine as a one-and-only MythTV box, you can safely disregard procedures related to slave backend assembly.

You may not run a MySQL daemon on any SBE server. Failure to heed this warning will clobber your MythTV configuration, and can be enormously frustrating. The SBE must rely strictly on the MBE for any MySQL-related data transactions.

Configuring and Running a MythTV Backend

Keep in mind the preceding concepts as you configure your MythTV backend server because a few crucial details are implemented at this stage. You must make a few preparations before configuring a MythTV backend system. Unlike ordinary applications and servers that utilize configuration files for runtime settings, MythTV uses a database scheme implemented entirely in MySQL.

If you are working from a previous version of MythTV—possibly from a distribution other than KnoppMyth or Fedora Core—you might want to consult online migration guides for the Debian, Gentoo, and Slackware distributions, located here:

www.mythtv.org/wiki/index.php/Category:Upgrading

Consult this documentation first to find answers to any questions and to resolve potential issues before you turn to public forums or real-time communications channels. Chances are good that someone has experienced a similar problem and documented it online for your benefit. This is also the beauty of a free and open software development cycle: You can interface directly with end-users and developers alike freely and openly (but good manners, and rules of engagement for most online forums, dictate that you consult available documentation before asking questions that others have already asked, and answered).

You must have the MySQL daemon running already, presumably on the MBE in a multi-tiered layout, or on the same host where your backend server resides. For thus running Fedora Core, open a console from the MythTV user account and execute the following commands:

```
$ su
# /sbin/service mysqld status
If the service binary reports the MySQL daemon status as stopped,
then start the necessary daemon as follows:
# /sbin/service mysqld start
# /sbin/chkconfig mysqld on
```

The first command starts the daemon, and the second ensures that it will restart when the system is rebooted or powered back on. The next sequence establishes a new working environment for MythTV within the MySQL database. Without these settings, your progress will cease, and profanity may follow!

```
# cd /usr/share/doc/mythtv-0.19/database
# /usr/bin/mysql -u root < mc.sql
```

Note The /usr/share/doc/mythtv-0.XX/ path is specific to your version of MythTV. As of this writing, 0.19 is in stable release, with 0.20 poised for future release.

Configuring MySQL on Multiple Clients

You must take special care to tailor your MySQL configuration to permit SBEs to access communal resources. For simplicity's sake, the default mc.sql script only authorizes the localhost to access this resource. Certain security implications arise with allowing general access to the MythTV/MySQL database but this is a book about hacking MythTV, not securing it from the bad guys. The bottom line on security is short and simple: Don't expose your MythTV network directly to the Internet!

The following examples are reproduced from the original MythTV-HOWTO guide maintained at the parent Web site. You are free to issue whichever of these commands best reflects your design goals.

Open a console window and issue the first command:

```
$ mysql -u root mythconverg
```

After this, you may use one of three distinct methods to handle the database. You may use an insecure method by specifying a percentile mark between the quotes, as in the string mythtv@"%". You may choose a top-level domain for external access to a named host, as in mythtv@"%.mydomain.com", which permits any host arriving from the mydomain.com name to access the database. The last method is recommended unless you really know what you are doing, because it restricts host access to a nonroutable (as far as the Internet is concerned, anyway) internal host address such as 192.168.1.3 (for example, mythtv@"192.168.1.%").

Issue a second command using one of the following three options.

The Insecure Method:

```
mysql> grant all on mythconverg.* to mythtv@"%" identified by "mythtv";
```

The Secure Method:

```
mysql> grant all on mythconverg.* to mythtv@"%.mydomain.com" identified by
"mythtv";
```

The Ideal Secure Method:

```
mysql> grant all on mythconverg.* to mythv@"192.168.1.%" identified by "mythtv";
```

Finally, you absolutely must issue a final command for these changes to take effect:

```
mysql> flush privileges;
```

You may have noticed the semicolon that trails the last character of every command — these are entirely necessary. Be sure to include them when you type these commands at the `mysql>` prompt. You may use other SQL database server daemons with MythTV but coverage is not extended to any kind other than MySQL. Your mileage will vary.

Before You Begin

When you navigate the configuration interface using a remote control it's always a challenge to enter text with a point-and-click hand tool. A new feature in MythTV version 0.19 helps resolve this problem, in the form of a pop-up on-screen keyboard accessible by striking the Enter key while the cursor is focused on an input field.

Read the information that's provided when you highlight any field for editing. A brief explanation for each field's purpose or significance is usually provided. This helps in understanding what you are configuring and why you should do so. MythTV's developers apparently recognize that not everybody finds Linux and MythTV intuitive, so they have kindly sprinkled in clues here and there for your benefit.

The following information describes configurations and settings for a MythTV backend server. You can navigate this interface without a mouse by using hotkey sequences much like you can in Microsoft Windows — select keys are underscored (Next, for example, means the combination of Alt+N continues to the next page). This applies to any underscored letter shown in the interface, regardless of location.

You need to find the Terminal application located on the Kicker bar (it's roughly analogous to the Windows taskbar) under Applications ➜ System Applications ➜ Terminal to accomplish some of the upcoming tasks. Don't let a lack of familiarity with the console application intimidate you; the instructions presented in this chapter spell out everything explicitly.

Database Configuration

Initially the MythTV database does not exist. You must create a MythTV database profile for MySQL before proceeding to real backend configuration tasks. When you first invoke the MythTV setup utility, it walks you through Database Configuration settings one time.

Starting from either the console or your Kicker bar, invoke the setup application (`mythtv-setup` or `mythtvsetup` for those of you on the command line; select Applications ➜ Sound & Video ➜ mythtv setup on the desktop) to begin the first of a series of configuration tasks for the MythTV backend server. The first prompt asks you to select your preferred language. The information in Table 6-1 summarizes the settings in the Database Configuration 1/2 screen, using the default values.

Table 6-1   Database Configuration 1/2

Setting	Default	Description
Host Name	localhost	Default IP address of this unit
Database	mythconverg	Default name for the MythTV database
User	mythtv	Default username for MythTV
Password	mythtv	Default password for MythTV user
Database Type	MySQL	Default MySQL database format

Alternatively, you can toggle between a graphical user interface and other console terminals by holding the Alt key and pressing one of the F*n* keys. Alt+F1 gets you to the first console, Alt+F2 to the second, and so on. Alt+F7 returns you to the GUI when you're done.

Note When running the MythTV setup utility, the configuration window can sometimes stretch beyond the parameters of your display. If you find this to be prohibitive to setting up MythTV, simply invoke the command-line application with the following additional parameter:

```
# mythtv-setup –geometry 640x480+0+0
```

Each of the fields listed in Table 6-1 is required. The host name may remain the default or you may specify an internal naming scheme of your choosing. This name must resolve to the IP address that's used later when you actually configure the MythTV backend server under the General Settings submenu. The MythTV User is the same one created for system usage, and its password should match that of the mythtv. Last, the database type defaults to MySQL.

Table 6-2 describes the settings in the Database Configuration 2/2 screen, using the default values.

Table 6-2   Database Configuration 2/2

Setting	Default	Description
Use custom identifier for frontend preferences	Unselected	This checkbox option enables the subsequent input option, allowing you to specify a naming prefix scheme for this unit (for multiple frontend clients).
Custom identifier	myth-frontend-	Default prefix name
Use Wake-on-LAN to wake database	Unselected	This option enables you to awaken a remote dedicated master backend with a WOL-compliant BIOS.

Continued

Table 6-2 *(continued)*

Setting	Default	Description
Reconnect Time	0	Time to pause between reconnects
Retry Attempts	5	Maximum number of retries
Wake command	`echo 'WOLsql ServerCommand not set'`	Default non-functional setting; this must be changed for WOL functionality to work properly.

The first option in Table 6-2 specifies whether to designate this unit as a frontend with a pre-fix, and what prefix should precede this name; this is extraordinarily helpful when working with multiple frontend clients. You can rename this however you like.

The remaining options pertain to Wake-on-LAN (WOL) settings that are useful for remotely waking your backend server from its restful sleep from the frontend client perspective. You may specify a reconnect time interval, the number of retry attempts, and you absolutely must change the `'WOLsqlServerCommand not set'` for this option to take effect. WOL settings for the master backend role are described later in Table 6-8.

You can find details for this procedure documented in the MythTV HOW-TO guide, section 11.5, "Using Shutdown/Wakeup," at www.mythtv.org/docs/mythtv-HOWTO-single html.html.

Specifying the Database Configuration settings is a one-time deal. You are not required to reconfigure these settings once you specify the values. These settings will persist throughout the lifetime of your MythTV build until you decide to restructure your MythTV network, beginning anew with a fresh install.

What follows are runtime configuration settings for the backend servers and frontend clients. After you are greeted by the opening graphical setup, you are provided the following five main categories:

- General
- Capture Cards
- Video Sources
- Input Connections
- Channel Editor

Each of these categories is described in the sections that follow, and is illustrated with tables that present options, buttons, and checkbox settings for important functions and features.

General

Variables that appear in this segment are called MythTV global values to describe their far-reaching effects over the entire environment. Indeed, any potential client of the MBE server must conform to these values to be useful. While some of these values should remain unaltered (such as stock port numbers that MythTV backend services use), others should conform to criteria you specify for your setup, be it a single-box setup or a vast network of participant devices. Consistency is key, because these settings affect all clients and servers that share communal resources. Table 6-3 describes settings that appear in the first of several pages of options that follow.

- **IP Address for localhost** — The value in this field should match your local IP address. By default, MythTV uses the loopback address (127.0.0.1), named localhost, but you may specify whatever you like as long as all parties agree to these settings.

    The localhost address specified in Table 6-3 should also map directly to the name specified earlier in the Database Configuration 1/2; otherwise, MythTV clients and slave backend servers won't point to a valid resource.

- **Port the Server Runs On** — This is the local port to match the local address you specified above. There is no immediate benefit to changing this value, so you may leave it alone.

Table 6-3   Host Address Backend Setup

Setting	Default	Description
IP Address for localhost	127.0.0.1	Enter the IP address of this machine. Use an externally accessible address (i.e., not 127.0.0.1) if you plan to run a frontend on a machine other than this one.
Port the Server Runs On	6543	Unless you've got a good reason, do not change this value.
Port the Server Shows Status On	6544	Port on which the server listens for HTTP status requests. Currently, it shows a little status information.
Master Server IP Address	127.0.0.1	The IP address of the master backend server. All frontend and nonmaster backend machines connect to this server. If you only have one backend, this should be the same IP address as the localhost.
Port the Master Server Runs On	6543	Port on which the server listens for HTTP requests

- **Port the Server Shows Status On** — This is the local port on which this server reports status to all your connecting clients. There is no immediate benefit to changing this value, so you may leave it alone.

- **Master Server IP Address** — Typical one-shot configurations do not require separate backend/frontend applications, so they coexist peacefully in the same physical machine. To enable one or more clients to access this machine, you must change the address to an internally routable address, like 192.168.1.2. Otherwise, leave the default setting alone.

- **Port the Master Server Runs On** — These settings are especially important later in this chapter when you discover the flexibility and freedom of deploying MythTV in multiple client/server arrangements. If this configuration is for the MBE, you must change both the Master Server IP and IP address for localhost entries for this backend server to make it accessible to others. These two numeric address values need to match up on the MBE server. As an SBE server, the localhost should be assigned a unique numeric address, and the Master Server IP should match the localhost IP for the MBE server.

  Unless you have good reason to change the port numbers, leave the default settings alone. The only consideration that remains is whether the Master server address is local, meaning a single unified backend/frontend setup or distributed across a network of MythTV constituents.

Table 6-4 details local configuration properties for your MythTV host. Use of these options is specific to your wants and needs, so configure these parameters accordingly. For example, you may wish to use a completely different directory path than the default (perhaps on a completely separate drive or computer!) to store recordings.

Table 6-4   Host-Specific Backend Setup

Setting	Default	Description
Directory to Hold Recordings	`/mnt/store`	All recordings are stored in this directory.
Save Original Files after Transcoding (Globally)	Unchecked	When set and the transcoder is active, the original nuv files are renamed to nuv.old once transcoding is complete.

- **Directory to Hold Recordings** — By default, MythTV assumes you intend to use `/mnt/store` as a repository for all recordings. To create this directory and assign the proper permissions, execute the following commands in a console window as the super-user:

```
# mkdir /mnt/store
# chown mythtv /mnt/store
```

You may insert a unique path in the preceding command sequence if you use a unique naming scheme. When creating a new volume for live-feed storage, you must also be sure to assign correct permissions to the directory and give ownership to the `mythtv` user.

■ **Save Original Files after Transcoding** — NuppleVideo formatted files (.nuv) are retained in the working directory once transcoding finalizes when you select a second Host-Specific Backend Setup option. The downside to enabling this feature is that you essentially end up with two sizeable files for every recording you create. You conserve storage space this way and avoid inevitable file proliferation problems. As part of the MBE's extensive housekeeping duties, one pertinent task it oversees is routine clean-up (removal by deletion) of this otherwise superfluous data.

The options in Table 6-5 are gone in 0.19 (the current version at the time this was authored). You will find these in MythTV versions 0.18 and earlier, but they are no longer in use. They're reproduced here solely to benefit those readers using prior editions.

Table 6-5   Host-Specific Backend Setup (versions prior to 0.19)

Setting	Default	Description
Directory to hold Live-TV buffers	`/mnt/store`	All Live-TV buffers are stored in this directory. These buffers are used to enable you to pause, fast-forward, and rewind through live TV.
Live TV Buffer (GB)	5	Indicates how large the TV buffer may grow
Minimum Free Live TV Buffer	50	Indicates how full the live TV buffer is allowed to grow before resuming play automatically

In a previous version (0.18) MythTV maintained a ring buffer for time-shifted live television feed. This is what enables you to pause, rewind, and fast-forward live television. You used to be able to specify a separate directory for live-TV buffers and restrict their growth properties but these options have disappeared as of version 0.19.

Global Backend Setup

Settings in this category, shown in Table 6-6, unilaterally influence all other capture devices and possible slave servers in your MythTV setup. You must select the right properties carefully for your particular configuration because they override local settings on any other machine.

Table 6-6   Global Backend Setup

Setting	Default	Description
TV Format	NTSC	The standard to use for viewing TV
VBI Format	None	VBI (Vertical Blanking Interrupt) is used to carry teletext and closed captioning data.
Channel Frequency Table	us-cable	Select the appropriate frequency table for your system. If you use an antenna, use a -bcast frequency.
Time Offset for XMLTV	None	Adjust the relative time zone of the XMLTV EPG data read by the mythfilldatabase application. Auto converts the XMLTV time to local time using your computer's time zone. None ignores the XMLTV time zone, interpreting all times as local.
EIT Transport Timeout (mins) (new in 0.19)	5	Maximum time to spend waiting for listings data on one DTV channel before checking for new listings data on the next channel
Master Backend Override	Checked	If enabled, the master backend will stream and delete files if it finds them in the video directory. This is useful if you use a central storage location, such as an NFS share, and the slave backend isn't running.
Follow Symbolic Links when Deleting Files (New in 0.19)	Unchecked	This causes Myth to follow symlinks when recordings and related files are deleted, instead of deleting the symlink and leaving the actual file alone.

- **TV Format** — This is specific to the terrestrial or satellite signal feed you receive from your communications provider. For the North American public broadcast region, this is NTSC for standard-definition television or ATSC for high-definition television.

- **VBI Format** — Enable this only for the closed caption or teletext on-screen display capability. These options are primarily of interest to the hearing impaired.

- **Channel Frequency Table and Time Offset for XMLTV** — TV and VBI Formats, the Channel Frequency Table, and the Time Offset for XMLTV are all specific to your locale. Because this book is written for a North American audience, we assume you use either National Television System Committee (NTSC) or Advanced Television System Committee (ATSC) formats. NTSC is the format for standard-definition television feeds, whereas the ATSC specification caters to high-definition (16:9 @ 1920 × 1080) broadcasts. If you display a high-resolution television feed by way of any compatible HDTV card, select ATSC; otherwise, select NTSC.

You also use the VBI Format and Channel Frequency Table accordingly. If you plan to use closed caption support, you must enable VBI Format.

Last, the Time Offset for XMLTV forces corrective action when the Electronic Program Guide (EPG) listings are desynchronized or don't match your local time zone.

- **The EIT Transport Timeout** — This is a timeout invoked when no response to a channel information request occurs. You enable this feature primarily for high-definition (DVB) signals.

- **Master Backend Override** — When the MBE server begins its routine housekeeping chores it is persistent about purging communal capture buffer directory paths when this option is enabled. Otherwise, the files will remain untouched, and you can even access centrally stored captures when the responsible capture card is unavailable. (Enable this if you want to use round-robin functionality from several machines, as described later in this chapter.)

- **Follow Symbolic Links** — Enable this option if you want the MythTV MBE server to traverse symbolic links to the original source file during deletion. Otherwise, only the link that represents the file is removed, while the much larger file remains resident on disk.

Some astute readers with prior MythTV experience may notice additional configurations in revision 19, such as EIT Transport Timeout and traversing symbolic links for file removal.

For high-definition TV-tuner/capture card solutions, you must make a few changes to factory settings. Instead of NTSC card type format, select ATSC and specify the Channel Frequency Table as us-bcast, not us-cable. Then select your unique device entry in the Capture Card setup screen (pcHDTV ATSC capture card, for example); and specify /dev/dtv0 as the Video Device, and Antenna-0 as the Default Input. Each of these variables varies according to the number and order in which those devices appear on the backend system.

Shutdown/Wakeup Options

Back when the VCR ruled the personal video recorder device market, you could schedule recording jobs for a specific time slot and the recorder set an alarm clock to wake itself up at the specified time. The challenge was figuring out a non-intuitive interface and deciphering a crudely translated user manual if you bothered to read it at all.

In the same vein, MythTV can intentionally be put to sleep to awaken at the next scheduled recording job, but in an extraordinarily simple and scalable way. The scheduler agent on the MBE server maintains a watch over all other media devices present on the network. During routine status checks that report back periods of inactivity to the MBE, that same scheduler agent begins a graceful shutdown process for all inactive systems. First it sets its alarm clock for the next scheduled recording, and then it notifies participant SBE servers to shutdown before shutting down itself.

Most of the settings that follow are beneficial largely in multi-machine networks and help their timely interoperation. While a single-box configuration benefits from default settings in small ways, these features illustrate the scalability of MythTV for multiple-box systems. Table 6-7 summarizes features you find in this General Settings subcategory.

Table 6-7   Shutdown/Wakeup Options

Setting	Default	Description
Startup Command (New to 0.19)	No default value assigned	This command is executed right after starting the backend. As a parameter, $status is replaced by either auto if the machine was started or user if a user switched it on.
Block Shutdown before Client Connects	Checked	If set, the automatic shutdown routine is disabled until a client connects.
Idle Timeout (secs)	0	The amount of time the master backend idles before it shuts down all backends. Set to 0 to disable auto shutdown.
Maximum Wait for Recording (min)	15	The amount of time the master backend waits for a recording. If it's idle but a recording starts within this interval, backends won't shut down.
Startup before Recording (secs)	120	The amount of time the master backend will be woken up before a recording starts.
Wakeup Time Format	hh-mm yyyy-MM-dd	The time string format passed to the setWakeuptime command as $time. See QT::QDateTime.toString() for details.
Set wakeuptime Command	No default value assigned	The command used to set the time (passed as $time) to wake up the master backend.*
Server halt Command	sudo /sbin/halt -p	The command used to halt backends.*
Pre-Shutdown Check Command	No default value assigned	A command executed before the backend shuts down. The return value determines whether the backend can shutdown. 0 = yes, 1 = restart idling, 2 = reset backend to wait for frontend.

*This command calls an external script.

- **Startup Command** — The Startup command appears in 0.19 and implements a feature similar to what Jarod Wilson implemented in his Fedora MythTV HOW-TO guide, by invoking a shell script with the bootstrapping of the GUI. Instead of relying upon the window manager (WM) of choice to invoke a post-startup batch command file, you may now plug directly into the backend for tighter integration.

- **Block Shutdown Until Client Connects** — When enabled, you are given a chance to connect your frontend client to the backend server before it forces a shutdown. This gives you an opportunity to stop and start frontend clients independently of the MBE, which does not shut down until the frontend client exits. The MythTV backend scheduler checks the source of the wakeup command to identify whether you invoked it or not. If so, your connection request will be honored before the MBE issues the Set Wakeuptime and Server Halt commands described below.

- **Idle Timeout** — When the MBE detects a lull in system-wide activity, it waits the specified number of seconds before shutting down all SBE servers. The MBE must either be recording, transcoding, or servicing clients in order for it to be considered active.

- **Maximum Wait for Recording** — This parameter safeguards against a premature MBE server shutdown when a scheduled recording is only minutes away. Instead of closing down promptly, the MBE stalls for the specified amount of time while awaiting the next scheduled recording.

- **Startup Before Recording** — How early do you want the MBE to awaken before a scheduled recording event occurs? Some programs start earlier or later than others and this parameter enables you to get a head start on early birds.

- **Wakeup Time Format** — This parameter is intimately coupled with the following parameter, Set Wakeuptime Command. The format is specific to the time format that the BIOS on your motherboard expects, and is used by the scripted Wakeuptime command.

- **Set Wakeuptime Command** — The Wakeuptime parameter issues the specified time at which your backend server should awaken. The process may be automated using the example script from the MythTV User Manual (see the subheading "Detailed Configuration: Backend").

Wakeuptime command:

```
sudo /usr/bin/mythsettime $time
```

Contents of script:

```
sudo echo $1 > /home/mythtv/myth.time
sudo echo $1 > /proc/acpi/alarm
```

Simply stated, this script issues the specified wakeup time on the MBE server.

- **Server Halt Command** — The MBE issues this command to shut down all SBE servers. If you are familiar with bash scripting or basic functional programming, you can supplant the standard `halt` command with a custom concoction of your own to handle a variety of tasks customized to fit your needs. You should change this only if you know what you're doing.

- **Pre-Shutdown Check Command** — This script follows up the shutdown process and returns a status of failure or success depending on the results.

  A MythTV system is considered to be idle if the following conditions are met:

  - No client is connected to the server
  - No scheduled recordings are active
  - No upcoming recording matches the Maximum Wait for Recording value
  - The Pre-Shutdown Check command returns a successful value (0)

  The following return values and response pairs are reproduced here for your benefit:

  - **0**–Regularly scheduled shutdown will occur
  - **1**–Reset the idle timeout and continue waiting
  - **2**–Reset the entire shutdown sequence if set to block until client connects

  That last return value is useful when you are actively logged into the MBE server or a scheduled task or background application is running.

To use the Wake-on-LAN (WOL) capability on your MBE and SBE servers you need a WOL-compliant motherboard BIOS and WOL utilities installed on the MBE machine. Both packages for this process are located at the following resources:

- `http://sourceforge.net/projects/nvram-wakeup`
- `www.malloc.de/tools/wakeup_clock.html`

For those interested in more information on similar subjects, check these resources:

- **TV Wakeup Timer** — `www.mythtv.org/wiki/index.php/TV_Wakeup_Timer`
- **Shutdown Wakeup** — `www.mythtv.org/wiki/index.php/Shutdown_Wakeup`
- **ACPI Wakeup** — `www.mythtv.org/wiki/index.php/ACPI_Wakeup`
- **How To Configure nvram-wakeup** — `http://svn.wilsonet.com/projects/mythtvology/ticket/40`

WakeOnLan Settings

Not to be confused with motherboard/NIC Wake-on-LAN functionality, the WakeOnLan settings in Table 6-8 are specifically geared toward the MythTV MBE subsystem. To fully utilize these WakeOnLan settings, you need at least one dedicated server to oversee all your MythTV devices. The beauty of this approach is that only one machine needs to run full time, while others may be powered off during inactivity, thereby conserving energy costs.

Table 6-8   WakeOnLan Settings (Master Backend)

Setting	Default	Description
Reconnect Wait Time (secs)	0	Length of time the frontend waits between retries to wake up the master backend. This should match the amount of time your master backend needs to start up.
Count of Reconnect Tries	5	The number of times a frontend will try to wake up the master backend
Wake Command	No default value assigned	The command used to wake up your master backend server
Wake Command for Slaves	No default value assigned	The command used to wake up your slave backends. Leave empty to disable.

- **Reconnect Wait Time** — How long should your frontend client pause after issuing the Wake command before attempting to reestablish contact with the remote MBE server? A default setting of 0 means *don't bother trying*, which is courteous to potentially slow-moving boxes such as the MBE server. Combine this parameter with the following parameter for greater effect.

- **Count of Reconnect Tries** — At what point should your MythTV frontend client give up and call it a day? You can keep trying to reconnect as long as you want (the default is five attempts) but without a responsive backend server what's the use? Eventually you will have to manually correct any runtime errors from which the MBE fails to recover. It's rude for the client interface to blithely pound away at a crippled server. This option is disabled by the preceding default setting anyway.

- **Wake Command** — MythTV's excellent setup utility gives you a single-line entry for an external command you can use to awaken your remote MBE server from its state of rest. Leave this entry empty to disable the command.

- **Wake Command for Slaves** — The same utility also gives you an entirely separate line entry to specify an external command to wake one or more SBE servers in unison. Leave this entry empty to disable the command.

Job Queue (Host-Specific)

A job queue provides the basic organizational unit by which a MythTV backend subsystem manages multiple independent SBE connections and scheduled tasks. This configuration window applies specifically to the host you are configuring and does not have global scope (as the options in Table 6-10 do). There are two primary jobs with which the backend server is concerned: automatic commercial detection (and extraction), and automatic transcoding (converting from one media format to another) jobs. Table 6-9 summarizes screen input for the MythTV version 0.19 backend setup utility.

Table 6-9 Job Queue (Host-Specific)

Setting	Default	Description
Maximum Simultaneous Jobs on this Backend	1	The job queue is limited to this many simultaneous jobs on this backend.
Job Queue Check Frequency (in seconds)	60	When looking for new jobs to process, the job queue waits this long between checks.
Job Queue Start Time	00:00	This setting controls the start of the job queue time window, which determines when new jobs start.
Job Queue End Time	23:59	This setting controls the end of the job queue time window, which determines when new jobs start.
CPU Usage	Low	This setting controls approximately how much CPU jobs in the queue may consume.
Allow Commercial Detection Jobs	Checked	Allows jobs of this type to run on this backend
Allow Transcoding Jobs	Checked	Allows jobs of this type to run on this backend
Allow 'User Job #1' Jobs	Unchecked	Allows jobs of this type to run on this backend
Allow 'User Job #2' Jobs	Unchecked	Allows jobs of this type to run on this backend
Allow 'User Job #3' Jobs	Unchecked	Allows jobs of this type to run on this backend
Allow 'User Job #4' Jobs	Unchecked	Allows jobs of this type to run on this backend

- **Maximum Simultaneous Jobs** — Currently set to 1, you may specify whatever value you desire provided the underlying hardware framework can support increased demand. Be especially careful with setting this value because it can have a tremendous impact on the performance of your MythTV system.

- **Job Queue Check Frequency** — This is the specified time interval between checks to the job queue for pending requests. At 60 seconds, the frequency is a bit high for a typical single-box setup for which only a handful of recordings may occur over the course of a week, meaning few jobs ever occur. Adjust this setting according to taste.

- **Job Queue Start Time** — When would you like to schedule your jobs? Should they start at night during lengthy periods of nonproductive downtime or while you are away at work? Use this parameter to control your MythTV job queue startup timeframe window.

- **Job Queue End Time** — Likewise, when should the jobs expire in that same window? When you come back from work and will most likely begin viewing television or just before you awake in the morning? Specify the time that works best for you using this parameter.

- **CPU Usage**—This parameter is set conservatively, on Low, out of consideration for the lowest common denominator. A higher setting can adversely impact MythTV systems with minimal resources. Modify this if you invest more money and/or hardware into your MythTV system and want to really exercise its resources.

- **Allow Commercial Detection Jobs**—Commonly called *commercial flagging,* this parameter enables your SBE servers to assume some of the duties of a possibly over-worked MBE server. Using this option you can detect and omit commercials from appearing in final MythTV recordings.

- **Allow Transcoding Jobs**—Transcoding jobs usually occur on the MBE server, but sometimes several transcoding jobs can occur all at once. This parameter allows the current SBE server to handle transcoding jobs locally if you desire.

- **Allow User Jobs**—User jobs are invocations made by your frontend clients to the backend server. Only four jobs are supported per machine.

For more information on scripting the shutdown/wakeup process, the KnoppMyth wiki features a WakeupToRecord article at `http://knoppmythwiki.org/index.php?page=WakeupToRecord` that explains such scripting in much greater detail and includes example scripts to illustrate the concept. You may find some of that information both insightful and applicable to your own MythTV project.

Job Queue (Global)

You should know that global settings override all others. This is important because you must maintain consistency across all SBE servers and frontend clients to ensure smooth operation. The parameters in Table 6-10 take precedence over the options listed in Table 6-9.

Table 6-10   Job Queue (Global)

Setting	Default	Description
Run Jobs only on Original Recording Host	Unchecked	When set, jobs in the queue are required to run on whichever backend made the original recording.
Run Transcode Jobs before Auto-Commercial Flagging	Unchecked	When set, if both Auto-Transcode and Auto-Commercial Flagging are turned on for a recording, then transcoding runs first; otherwise, commercial flagging runs first.
Start Auto-Commercial Flagging Jobs when Recording Starts	Unchecked	When set, if Auto-Commercial Flagging is on for a recording, then the flagging job is started as soon as recording begins. This is *not* recommended for underpowered systems.

- **Run Jobs only on Original Recording Host** — Instead of relegating tasks among available SBE servers, these settings force the original, correct behavior of having the party responsible for making your recording also perform any jobs you specified in the queue. The default setting is fine for most common MythTV uses.

- **Run Transcode Jobs before Auto-Commercial Flagging** — The question here is, do you want to convert the media format or cleanse the feed of commercial footage first? When you flag both Auto-Transcode and Auto-Commercial Flagging options on a scheduled recording, only one or the other may be performed at any given time. As a *job*, the implication is that this process runs only when your recording has completed, not while recording is underway.

- **Start Auto-Commercial Flagging Jobs when Recording Starts** — Enable this parameter if you would prefer to deal with the source of unwanted data at the point of origin. As stated in the MythTV setup dialog, this option is not for systems with limited resources. A sudden surge in resource consumption is enough to cause instability issues and might prevent you from being able to record at all.

The job queue services up to four local commands that can be scheduled to execute at whatever interval you specify. Perhaps you want to filter your scheduled recordings through a series of custom scripts kept locally. This is where you implement said scripts, each labeled with its own specific job description, as shown in Table 6-11.

Table 6-11   Job Queue (Job Commands)

Setting	Default	Description
User Job #1 Description	User Job #1	The description for this User Job.
User Job #1 Command	No default value assigned	The command to run whenever this User Job number is scheduled.
User Job #2 Description	User Job #2	The description for this User Job.
User Job #2 Command	No default value assigned	The command to run whenever this User Job number is scheduled.
User Job #3 Description	User Job #3	The description for this User Job.
User Job #3 Command	No default value assigned	The command to run whenever this User Job number is scheduled.
User Job #4 Description	User Job #4	The description for this User Job.
User Job #4 Command	No default value assigned	The command to run whenever this User Job number is scheduled.

Each of these line entries is reserved for options you specified in Table 6-9. These commands and descriptions correspond to the numeric entries in that configuration window. Like the Shutdown and Wakeup commands, these slots are provided for you to populate with external commands to perform any secondary tasks you require.

Capture Cards

No capture card is defined by default, so you must create one before proceeding in order for any backend to be useful. New to version 0.19 (much to the delight of users with older-generation MythTV boxes) is an option to delete all capture cards. Previously, when you defined an erroneous capture card entry, you could not delete it from this list, which left you with a list full of unnecessary duplicate or bogus entries. Table 6-12 briefly describes the two primary features in this initial configuration window.

By this point you should have already installed and established presence for your capture card; otherwise, your progress will come to an abrupt halt.

Table 6-12   Capture Cards Actions

Option	Action	Description
(New capture card)	Create a new capture card identity	Establish a new capture card entry on this host.
(Delete all capture cards)	Reset to factory defaults	Destroy all capture card entries on this host.

Readers new to the MythTV experience might wonder why there is a Delete All action but no specific Delete function. Previously (revision 0.18 and earlier) you could define new capture card entries but you could not delete them. Sure, you could change the properties of a card entry if something was set incorrectly, but that did nothing about bogus card entries that should have really been removed.

Unfortunately, lack of fine-grain control over what entries are deleted means you must exercise extreme care with entries you create in this context. Otherwise you will remove all entries, including perfectly valid ones. Table 6-13 shows the Capture Card Settings that appear when you elect to create a new entry.

Table 6-13   Capture Cards Settings

Setting	Default	Description
Card Type	Analog V4L capture card	Change card type to the appropriate type for the capture card you are configuring.
Video Device	No default value assigned	Specify the default video capture device entry.
VBI Device	No default value assigned	Specify the default VBI device entry (for close-captioning data).

Continued

Table 6-13 *(continued)*

Setting	Default	Description
Audio Device	/dev/dsp	Specify the default audio device entry.
Audio Sampling Rate Limit	No default value assigned	Specify the default audio sampling rate limit. Higher numbers indicate better sound quality.
Do Not Adjust Volume	Unchecked	Check this option for budget BT878-based DVB-T cards such as the AverTV DVB-T that require the audio volume be left alone.
Default Input	No default value assigned	Default Capture Card input source

- **Card Type** — This setting is specific to hardware you installed to capture video. Most commonly this is an analog Video 4 Linux (V4L) capture card device, which describes a typical PCI-based add-on card.

- **Video Device** — For the most common type of card (one using the standard V4L library) this will be /dev/video0. If you are using a digital broadcast card such as the pcHDTV, then you should specify /dev/dtv0. These entries are specific to the placement and number of cards present on the host you are configuring — that is, if you have two Hauppauge PVR series cards, you may have /dev/video0 and /dev/video1; if you have multiple HDTV cards, they may appear as /dev/dtv0, /dev/dtv1, /dev/dvt2, and so on.

- **VBI Device** — Unless you will display closed-caption support for television programming, you may disregard this option. This service displays textual information to represent the on-screen information for hearing-impaired viewers.

- **Audio Device** — Your audio input device is also represented in the Linux /dev tree as a raw device entry. Here, the default universal mapping is exposed using the /dev/dsp label.

- **Audio Sampling Rate Limit** — Measured in kHz, sampling rate is a measurement of signal quality when trying to reproduce analog sound accurately in an all-digital environment. Unless you know what you are doing, leave this value empty.

- **Do Not Adjust Volume** — As specified in the descriptive text, you should only enable this feature if you specifically use the BT878 series DVB card.

- **Default Input** — Capture cards commonly have several connection types: RCA, S-Video, Composite, Component, DVI, and HDMI, to name but a few. A single card may be represented internally to the backend server by several input device types, so you should specify which one you intend to use as the default.

Video Sources

No video source is defined by default, so you must configure settings in this category according to your region. Here, we assume you reside in the North American broadcast regions, as that is the target demographic for this book. Table 6-14 shows the two options presented in the first Video Sources screen.

Table 6-14   Video Sources Actions

Option	Action	Description
(New video source)	Create new entry	Create and configure a new video source.
(Delete all video sources)	Delete all entries	Delete all video sources.

These options are self-explanatory. The options that follow are a bit more involved and require a little explanation. For your benefit, Table 6-15 describes the Video Sources Settings page. The table is followed by a bulleted list that briefly summarizes each parameter.

Table 6-15   Video Sources Settings

Setting	Default	Description
Video Source Name	No default value assigned	Default Video Source name
XMLTV Listings Grabber	North America (DataDirect)	Default channel guide listings resource
User ID	No default value assigned	Subscription service account name
Password	No default value assigned	Subscription service password
Retrieve Lineups	No default value assigned	Force lineup retrieval now to ensure proper operation—from logging into the data source to pulling listings data from the server
DataDirect Lineup	No default value assigned	Identification string specific to the channel guide listings provider to which you subscribe
Perform EIT Scan	Unchecked	If this is enabled, data in this source is updated with listing data provided by channels themselves "over-the-air."
Channel Frequency Table	Default	Use default unless this source uses a different frequency table than the system-wide table defined in the General settings.

- **Video Source Name** — Designate the descriptive terminology by which you will identify this video source. This can be anything you like so long as it makes perfect sense to you. Time/Warner-Cable, HDTV-broadcast, and OTA-signal are just a few example names you might use.

- **XMLTV Listings Grabber** — If you plan to use the DataDirect service provided by Zap2it Labs (a subsidiary of Tribune Media Services), then this entry will read: North America (DataDirect). For any other service provider, you'll need to research and use the proper associated setting.

- **User ID** — In Chapter 3, you were instructed to sign up with a channel listings provider. This is where you input the account name you acquired for that service.

- **Password** — Likewise, this is the password by which you authenticate the account name for your channel guide listings provider.

- **Retrieve Lineups** — Although this appears in the settings window, the only settings you make here are to change the preceding User ID and Password if clicking this button fails to pull down channel guide listings from the provider.

- **DataDirect Lineup** — This identification string distinguishes the specific region that applies to listings you obtain. You should see your zip code included in this string, along with your subscription information.

- **Perform EIT Scan** — As noted earlier, this is specific to DVB. Enabling EIT scan functionality obviates any need for XMLTV listings from the service provider and instead seeks program guide information directly from the channel it tunes into.

- **Channel Frequency Table** — A frequency table corresponds to the bandwidth spectrum at which your cable service provider operates live television feeds. Each channel is tuned to its own frequency by the television tuner in your MythTV capture card. Use default settings unless you have a compelling reason to change them.

Input Connections

This option, summarized in Table 6-16, helps you map the Video Source to hardware input(s) on your card. To configure this portion of the MythTV backend, begin with a known, valid channel number. You can change this later if you must.

Table 6-16   Input Connections

Option	Action	Description
(New capture card)	Create a new capture card identity.	Create new Input Connection settings.
(Delete all capture cards)	Reset to factory defaults.	Delete all Input Connection settings.

Channel Editor

For the most part you won't have to tinker with the Channel Editor settings, shown in Table 6-17. These are handled automatically. However, when you need to block a channel from appearing in MythTV's channel lineups, or manipulate viewable information, start here. We recommend that you initially skip this setup and invoke the `mythfilldatabase` application before operating on any parameters that appear here.

Table 6-17   Channel Editor Settings

Setting	Default	Description
(New channel)	No default value assigned	Create a new Channel Settings.
Sort Mode	Channel Name	Default Sort Mode: either Channel Name or Channel Number
Video Source	(All)	Default Video Source(s) from which to obtain channel information
Hide channels without channel number	Unchecked	If set, the channels missing a number do appear in the EPG.
Channel Scanner	[Button]	Scan for channel lineup.
Transport Editor	[Button]	Simplifies ATSC setup so you don't have to edit the database directly

Table 6-18 lists the options in the Channel Options 1/2 screen, which you can adjust to modify the appearance of metadata that accompanies various channels you receive.

Table 6-18   Channel Options 1/2

Setting	Default	Description
Channel Name	No default value assigned	Specify a new channel name.
Channel Number	No default value assigned	Specify a new channel number.
Callsign	No default value assigned	Specify a new channel abbreviation.
Visible	Checked	If set, the channel will be visible in the EPG.
Commercial Free	Unchecked	If set, automatic commercial flagging will be skipped for this channel. Useful for premium channels such as HBO.

Continued

Table 6-18 *(continued)*

Setting	Default	Description
Video Source	[Not Selected]	Specify the input stream provider.
TV Format	Default	If this channel uses a format other than TV Format in the General Backend Setup screen, set it here.
Rank	0	Number of bonus points to be added to any recording on this channel during scheduling. Use a positive number as the rank if you want this to have a scheduled recording priority
Icon	No default value assigned	Image file to use as the icon for this channel on various MythTV displays
Video Filters	No default value assigned	Filters to be used when recording from this channel. Not used with hardware encoding cards.
Playback Filters	No default value assigned	Filters to be used when recordings from this channel are viewed. Start with a plus sign to append the global playback filters.
Use On Air Guide	Unchecked	When set, the guide information will be taken from the On Air Channel guide.
XMLTV ID	No default value assigned	ID used by listing services to get an exact correspondence between a channel in your lineup and a channel in their database. Normally this is set automatically when mythfilldatabase is run.

- **Channel Name** — The name of this channel according to the local broadcasting lineup for your region.

- **Channel Number** — The number of this channel according to the local broadcasting lineup for your region.

- **Callsign** — The abbreviated call letters for this particular station.

- **Visible** — If set, this channel is visible in the Electronic Programming Guide (EPG).

- **Commercial Free** — As stated, use this to avoid the commercial detection process for channels that do not carry them.

- **Video Source** — This is the name of the broadcast service provider.

- **TV Format** — This is the default broadcast type.

- **Rank** — This is the personal rank you assign to recordings on this channel, which comes into play later when you discover the power of MythTV personalization.

- **Icon** — The preferred icon for this channel.

- **Video Filters** — Because you are assumed to be using a hardware-based tuner card as outlined in this book, you will not be using this field.

- **Playback Filters** — Specify playback filters for this channel.

- **Use On Air Guide** — Instead of drawing on the information stored locally in the database, MythTV will pull information obtained directly from the tuner reading channel metadata.

- **XMLTV ID** — You won't have to specify anything here; running `mythfilldatabase` takes care of that for you.

Table 6-19 describes the options available in the Channel Options 2/2 screen.

Table 6-19   Channel Options 2/2

Setting	Default	Description
Frequency or Channel	No default value assigned	Specify either the exact frequency in kHz or a valid channel for your "TV Format."
Fine-tune (kHz)	No default value assigned	Value to be added to your desired frequency in kHz, for "fine-tuning."
Contrast	0	Default contrast setting
Brightness	0	Default brightness setting
Color	0	Default color setting
Hue	0	Default hue setting

These parameters have self-evident values and do not warrant further explanation. The only thing to keep in mind is that when specified on the MBE server, these settings override all others across the network for multiple-box MythTV networks.

Post-Configuration Tasks and Activities

A few final tweaks are all that's necessary to complete configuration and setup of the MythTV backend subsystem. You must first finalize the master backend process (or slave backend, whichever the case may be) by aggregating the service provider channel guide listings, tuner frequencies, capture cards, and global settings. This information represents core communal resources available to all MythTV devices, whether you have a single-box setup or several boxes working together.

Be sure to read through the final configuration suggestions at the end of the chapter before you continue on to the frontend client in the next chapter.

Configuring a Master Backend

Barring any errors in the preceding configurations (which you must repair first), you have two final details to address. First, the mythbackend server must persist across reboots. Second, you must invoke the mythfilldatabase application to populate the mythconverg database with channel guide and tuning information. On Fedora Core this is simply a matter of invoking system configuration utilities that handle all the dirty work for you. Use an existing terminal session or open a new one and issue the following commands:

```
/sbin/service mythbackend start
/sbin/chkconfig mythbackend on
```

You may also query the mythbackend server binary for its available parameters by issuing the following command:

```
$ mythbackend --help
```

That's the gist of it. The only task that remains for you to complete is to flesh out the MythTV database as covered in the following section.

Configuring and Running mythfilldatabase

Your MBE server will begin the process of pulling down channel guide metadata from the Video Source(s) you specified earlier during the backend configuration process. All this takes is a simple command-line invocation:

```
$ mythfilldatabase
```

Be patient; this can take a while. Many elements conspire to slow things down, such as the time of day (how many other users are currently active and sharing the same resources); optimum hardware capabilities; and the size of the data set you must acquire. Again, this must occur only once on the network (with the MBE).

Advanced Backend Configurations

While an MBE server is required to have a capture card present and configured, it need not be the first card defined (and therefore the default). Multi-tiered architectures can leverage round-robin functionality from a collection of SBE servers containing multiple capture cards by using a straightforward procedure outlined in the MythTV HOW-TO guide subsection 23.3, entitled "Advanced Backend Configurations."

The basic premise is this: Given an imaginary three-node network, you have an obligatory MBE server and two SBE servers. The MBE server includes two capture cards used as failover devices, as you will see momentarily. Each of the SBE servers has only a single capture card. The idea here is that you want to establish one SBE as the default capture card device server when configuring the MBE so that it takes precedence over all others.

Table 6-20 shows the three-way relationship between a single MBE and a pair of SBE servers.

Table 6-20   Advanced Backend Settings

Server	Value	Description
SBE card:1	#1	Default video input source
MBE card:1	#2	Failover #1 input source
SBE card:1	#3	Tertiary input source
MBE card:2	#4	Failover #2 input source

Starting with the MBE server, establish global values for General settings and Channel Lineup but skip the Host-Specific details, particularly the Capture Card settings. The same HOW-TO guide goes on to describe the set-up procedure, which is slightly modified for clarity here.

On the first SBE server:

1. Add the capture card on this host. The card receives card identity #1 in the global database.

2. Specify the first unique slave address for localhost.

3. Specify the Master IP address for the MBE server.

4. Connect the input source to the card.

5. Exit setup.

On the MBE server:

1. Add the first capture card on the MBE. The card receives card identity #2 in the global database.

2. Exit setup.

On the second SBE server:

1. Add the capture card on this host.

2. Specify a second unique slave address for localhost.

3. Specify the Master IP address for the MBE server.

4. Connect the input source to the card. The card receives card identity #3 in the global database.

5. Exit setup.

Return to the MBE server and complete these steps:

1. Add the second capture card on the MBE. The card receives card identity #4 in the global database.

2. Exit setup.

This example network illustrates how simple it is to operate a large-scale MythTV configuration that could easily incorporate all the computers in your household.

Configuring a Slave Backend Server

You won't be running `mythfilldatabase` on this machine, and running the MySQL daemon locally is not recommended. The only configuration you must make with regard to MySQL services is to grant access to all SBE servers as described earlier in this chapter in the section "Configuring MySQL on Multiple Clients," and ensure that proper connectivity can be established by your remote devices.

Open `/usr/local/share/mythtv/mysql.txt` in your favorite editor and find the line that contains a variable named `DBHostName`. Every participating SBE server on your network must contain the same MBE server address (where the MySQL server resides). You must also configure additional backend properties as follows:

- Specify the MBE server IP as the database server in Database Configuration (1/2).

- Configuration is similar to the MBE setup, except you do not define Video Sources here.

- Ensure that the IP addresses in General settings reflect the appropriate localhost and master.

- Change the variable `DBHostName` found in `/usr/local/share/mythtv/mysql.txt` to use the MBE address.

Because the bulk of configuration data is retained on the MBE server, the SBE focuses on less data.

Grabbing Channel Icons for DataDirect Users

One thing you cannot accomplish directly through DataDirect services is obtain channel logo icons for stations available to your subscription service. However, MythTV provides a means to obtain a default collection of icons if you have PERL installed, using the following command:

```
$ perl /usr/share/doc/mythtv-0.19/contrib/mkiconmap.pl
```

You are asked for your zip code and cable/satellite service provider, after which the `mkicon map.pl` utility creates a list called `iconmap.xml`. Then, you simply import these icons into the MythTV database using the following command:

```
$ mythfilldatabase -import-icon-map iconmap.xml -update-icon-map
```

If either you lack the PERL interpreter and its libraries on your MythTV box or the `mkicon map.pl` command fails, then you can copy the default icon map like this:

```
$ copy /usr/share/doc/mythtv-0.19/contrib/master_iconmap.xml iconmap.xml
$ mythfilldatabase -import-icon-map iconmap.xml -update-icon-map
```

And that's it. You're done.

Final Thoughts

For simplicity's sake, you may want the MythTV user to log in automatically whenever the unit is powered on. To do this, click on the Kicker bar (on the desktop) and follow the path for Desktop → System Settings → Login Screen (or from the command line launch gdmsetup). Locate the section entitled "Automatic Login" and then check the box next to the dialog that reads "Login a user automatically on first bootup." Select your MythTV user ID from the pop-up menu. If you prefer that the login times out before logging in the default user, you should configure the Timed Login option that permits you to log in using other credentials instead of MythTV if something should break on that account (such as a bad login shell).

In this chapter, you have only seen a small portion of the backend capability. There is enormous further potential for a variety of unusual implementations and obscure configurations, but we leave this topic behind as we advance into the next chapter, which delves into the backend's counterpart: the MythTV frontend client.

MythTV Frontend

MythTV exposes entry points into most of its real functionality at the interface level through the `mythfrontend` application. It gives you an action-oriented heads-up display that works with any or all of keyboard, mouse, or remote control inputs to interact with MythTV backend server(s) in completely autonomous fashion. But the most remarkable aspect about the MythTV frontend client is that it has the flexibility to take on nearly any conceivable form or function.

Because the client/server architecture divorces the user-end aspects of MythTV from its core backend services, you have plenty of freedom to exercise when it comes to the design, development, and deployment of frontend clients. Your frontend client can run concurrently on the same PC or a different machine than the backend server. In fact, the frontend PC needn't even be running Linux (nor must it absolutely be a PC, either, for that matter!).

Projects such as TapeWorm and WinMyth (introduced in Chapter 14) help diversify the MythTV user base by appealing to Windows-centric users. Even the Xbox has received the frontend treatment — the trick is to install Xebian or Gentoo (see also the "Enable Xbox Hardware" parameter mentioned later in this chapter). Of course, you can also use the KnoppMyth CD as a frontend client — provided you dedicate the hardware resources necessary for its installation.

Mythfrontend Overview

The MythTV frontend client provides a window into the features and functionality of the backend services and underlying hardware support. At the interface level, you can manipulate those underlying properties that make up your MythTV system(s) and exercise control over systemwide behavior from a single frontend unit. Whereas the backend server is more detail-oriented regarding the operational aspects of the MythTV framework, the frontend client is more detail-oriented about the client aspects — that is, what you see, how you see it, and when you see it. As you can imagine, this aspect of the configuration process contains much deeper and more diverse options than the previous chapter, which deals with backend server configuration.

As this book goes to press, the MythTV project continues to expand and assume a more refined look and feel, making it difficult to harness such a fast-moving target in the frozen words that fill a book while the subject matter keeps growing and changing. Progress made on the mythfrontend client between revisions 0.18 and 0.19 illustrates the enormous momentum behind MythTV development. It also completely reshaped (and sometimes restructured) MythTV's appearance and the placement of its settings and parameters.

As you go through this chapter, and follow along on your PC, you may observe that some options appear in other places than specified here. In large part, this depends upon which version of MythTV you run. Remember that more changes are likely to occur, and that some will create new options that we can't anticipate here. Nonetheless, noting these differences should illustrate just how rapidly MythTV keeps changing to serve you better. In the meantime, however, this chapter will get you started on your own MythTV system.

Your journey begins in the next section, the obligatory General Settings category. The finely detailed MythTV frontend application encompasses a breadth and depth of functionality that is sufficiently thorough to be exhausting to work through completely! We believe that with your support, MythTV will continue to grow and become better refined until it unilaterally and undeniably dominates the home theater landscape. It's already off to a great start.

General Settings

This order of oddfellows is too obscure to be categorized elsewhere, so they appear in a miscellaneous catchall category.

The first and second screens you encounter are reminiscent of the last chapter, which covers Database Configuration settings. Here again you'll find the very same two-page form that includes the same questions. Should the reason for this not be immediately obvious, please consider it a forcible reminder about the client/server (mutually exclusive, yet interdependent) nature of MythTV's operation.

Audio

MythTV provides you with excellent sound configuration properties to help you achieve the ultimate home entertainment experience. You may also specify global settings for the use of internal volume controls, specific mixer device entries, master mixer volume for audio playback, and enforce independent muting of left and right audio channels (useful for bi-lingual broadcasts).

- **Audio Output Device** — Specify which audio device entry you intend to use. According to the MythTV User Manual, you can identify Advanced Linux Sound Architecture (ALSA)–compliant devices with a special prefix and format, `ALSA:device`, where `device` is the label for a valid device. To use the next option, for example, you would specify `ALSA:spdif` and then enable the passthrough feature. The User Manual then goes on to suggest that you issue the command `aplay -l` in a console window to identify any ALSA devices you may have at your disposal.

- **Enable AC3 to SPDIF Passthrough** — If your audio equipment is Dolby Digital (AC3) certified (perhaps a digital television), then you can benefit from AC3 audio passthrough to the Sony/Philips Digital Interface (S/PDIF) output source. The AC3 specification provides you with enriched, theater-quality surround sound experiences to recreate an at-the-movies environment. S/PDIF connections appear in two forms: coaxial and optical

(TOSlink); these are the best connection types for high-fidelity audio playback. By offloading decoding tasks to an external unit using this option, you also free up host machine resources for other, possibly more important, chores.

- **Aggressive Soundcard Buffering** — The Aggressive Sound Card Buffering option enables MythTV to fake a more adequate sound card buffer than appears on the audio card in an attempt to speed up seeking at the expense of stability. Use this if you experience intermittent audio problems for programs that carry two discrete language signals.

- **Use Internal Volume Controls** — You can either have MythTV exercise exclusive control over Pulse-Code Modulation (PCM) and master mixer settings or delegate that responsibility to an external unit. PCM is a generic means of storing and broadcasting uncompressed digital audio, which commonly occurs on CD media containing commonly formatted WAV files.

- **Select Mixer Device** — Linux applications provide support for mixing multiple audio channels with independent volume control. For example, nVidia's `nvsound` module uses its special `nvmixer` utility to deliver on-board hardware mixing. Specify the native sound mixer device entry for your audio setup here.

- **Mixer Controls** — Using this option, when you change sound volume in MythTV you indirectly utilize the sound mixer specified above. Options are PCM (the default) and master.

- **Master Mixer Volume** — This parameter has a numeric value from zero to 100 (the default is 70) indicating the initial volume level output from the sound card. Because these are the master control settings, you should take care not to specify overly high or low numbers.

- **PCM Mixer Volume** — Like the master mixer volume control, this parameter is a numeric value from zero to 100 (the default is 70) that regulates initial volume level, but for PCM output. When you adjust the volume properties through MythTV, you indirectly influence this parameter. PCM audio arrives by way of your TV tuner/capture card.

- **Independent Muting of Left and Right Audio Channels** — Although this feature is useful mainly for European broadcasts, you should know its purpose. During some European broadcasts, a program may carry two discrete audio signals for native and translated languages by splitting each into left and right channels. By cleanly isolating each signal (via independent muting) you can tune in to whichever language you prefer.

General (1/2)

This section might as well be identified as basic remote interface commands, because that is precisely what best describes the following parameters. These actions represent some of the most primitive key sequences that map directly to remote control interaction.

- **System Exit Key** — It makes perfect sense that MythTV is designed to operate full-time, but when you want to quit the interface quickly and easily it should also require minimal effort. You can specify a number of exit key sequences (Esc, Ctrl+Esc, Alt+Esc, Meta+Esc) or none at all, but the important point is to choose one that doesn't interfere with desktop hotkeys.

- **Confirm Exit** — When you exit the `mythfrontend` interface, MythTV's default behavior is to ask: Do you really want to exit MythTV? If you find this more of a hindrance than a help, disable the default setting here and be done with it.

- **Halt Command** — The command you specify is called directly whenever you invoke the system exit key as declared above, which may be to halt the machine, power down, or exit.

- **Keypress Command** — You may specify a custom external script or binary application to be called upon receipt of a custom-defined keypress. The Linux Infrared Remote Control (LIRC) daemon can intercept commands wirelessly and invoke the application of your choice specified here or through the systemwide configuration file located at `/etc/lircd.conf` (which may not exist on clean implementations). That said, it's a simple matter to copy or create this configuration file.

- **Use Arrow Key Accelerators** — You probably want to leave this setting in its default position: On. This parameter enables you to use the left and right directional keys on your keyboard to exit or enter (or select) menu items, respectively. Then you can map these keys to the left and right keys (or analogous substitutes) on your remote control using the `lircd.conf` file and create an intuitive keypress sequence to navigate within the MythTV interface.

General (2/2)

This section deals primarily with basic access controls for three unrelated properties: Personal Identification Number codes, a CD-ROM autoloading type of functionality, and support for Xbox-specific hardware.

- **Require Setup PIN** — By enabling this option you restrict access to only those users who possess your secret code, which you supply in the next setting. This effectively defines a primitive authentication mechanism to prevent unauthorized tampering with your MythTV settings. Highly recommended for households with inquisitive (and quick) two-year-olds!

- **Setup PIN Code** — Once you enable the preceding option and supply this line entry, only holders of your PIN code may exercise control over setup menu configurations.

- **Monitor CD/DVD** — This option enables you to monitor the drive tray for newly inserted disks, and works something like the Windows CD-ROM autoload feature. Be sure to install the latest release for your distribution of choice when using this feature — older versions may not work very well.

- **Enable Xbox Hardware** — According to the MythTV User Guide, enabling this feature introduces a new entry into the settings menu. It permits you to take advantage of the Xbox LED. Using this feature requires you to run a specific non-native Linux utility called `blink.c`, which can be obtained at `http://xbox-linux.cvs.source forge.net/xbox-linux/tools/`.

Check out www.xbox-linux.org/wiki/MythTV_on_Xebian_HOWTO for details on how you can reuse an Xbox as a relatively cheap, full-fledged MythTV frontend. If you've got an Xbox and want to use MythTV, we predict you'll find it to be an irresistible combination.

Myth Database Logging

You can influence the way MythTV handles routine upkeep of its database and related database properties. MythTV will gladly report the activity of any of its loaded modules at your request, and you can even specify a window of time during which recorded events will remain available. Here are your options:

- **Log MythTV Events to Database** — MythTV can be quite informative about its database activities. By enabling this option, such events will be logged. You may then monitor these entries using MythLog, or instruct the software to e-mail these details to an administrative account. Use these features, particularly if you need or want to monitor long-term operation of your MythTV frontend.

- **Log Print Threshold** — The value you specify for this parameter effectively creates a sieve to control what types of messages are passed to your MythTV database. Use this to your advantage to regulate the size of the database to better conserve resources (including the time you must spend to plow through this stuff).

- **Automatic Log Cleaning Enabled** — You should probably enable this if you elect to do any logging at all. MythTV can get chatty, especially with several jobs and concurrent interactions in constant motion, so you should allow the subsystem to maintain house-keeping chores.

- **Log Cleanup Frequency** — By default, you get two weeks' worth of events, after which MythTV automatically flushes the log files and begins anew. You may tighten or loosen this window as you like.

- **Number of Days to Keep Acknowledged Entries** — When you acknowledge a log entry, it remains in the database for whatever amount of time you specify for this setting.

- **Number of Days to Keep Unacknowledged Entries** — Any log entry that goes unac-knowledged times out at a separate interval from that for acknowledged entries. By default, this is approximately double the time allotted to an acknowledged item.

- **Maximum Number of Entries per Module** — Setting this parameter triggers another cleanup interval on your mythfrontend client. If the number of log entries for a given module exceeds the maximum value you specify, MythTV automatically forces a routine clean-up and flushes the log file(s).

Mythfilldatabase

These are centralized settings that govern your MythTV database operation. Default values are fine if you intend to run stock settings, but you should adjust the following parameters for multi-client configurations:

- **Automatically Run mythfilldatabase** — As you can imagine, this automates the mythfilldatabase process. Doing so used to require that you enter a scheduled task manually into a job batching system, but this is a much better approach. You can also manipulate the parameters that influence mythfilldatabase operation directly. The following options are available only when this option is checked:

  - **mythfilldatabase Path** — Specify the full path (including binary) to your mythfilldatabase application if it appears somewhere other than the default location.

  - **mythfilldatabase Arguments** — As mentioned in Chapter 6, the mythfilldatabase application makes a variety of options available to you (see mythfilldatabase -help for more information). This is where you specify which options you need.

  - **mythfilldatabase Log Path** — When left blank, you get no log file; when filled in with a path and name of your choice, you can access a wealth of MythTV-related information in the log file.

  - **mythfilldatabase Execution Start** — As a convenience, the capability to specify downtime hours of operation for the MythTV database (so as not to interfere with your viewing) is available here. Specify what time you would like the database filling process to begin (for example, shortly after you go to sleep).

  - **mythfilldatabase Execution End** — Continuing the convenience factor, this option enables you to set a cut-off point for the mythfilldatabase process so that it doesn't interfere with your scheduled viewing time.

As of the current version (0.19), this list is a complete and accurate compilation of the General configuration settings.

From general settings to general appearance, the next options category treats you to the finer sensibilities of your frontend client: its aesthetics. Sight is clearly our most heavily used sense, and we naturally fixate on the physical appearances of objects and how they reflect our preferences. The settings in the next segment enable you to manage the visual properties that can make your frontend client unique compared to all others, if you choose to customize it to that extent.

Appearance Settings

When you want to change the look and feel of the MythTV interface, there's no more obvious place to come than here. The Appearance Settings dialog offers you a wealth of properties that affect just about every part of the aesthetic — from the way dialog windows appear to where they appear and the information they contain.

MythTV background themes, on-screen display themes, and even menu themes are available, in addition to localization settings such as date, time, and time zone. If you happen to use a Liquid Crystal Display (LCD), you can plug it in and access many of its properties as well. Figure 7-1 shows MythTV's TV Settings link.

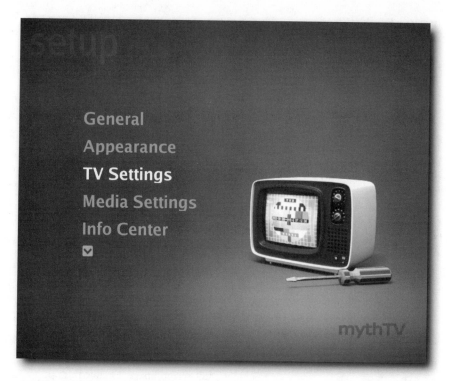

General

Appearance

TV Settings

Media Settings

Info Center

FIGURE 7-1: MythTV can be themed however you like.

Theme

You should be familiar with themed or skinnable interfaces by now — this is a facet of nearly all popular modern technology — from cell phones and handheld devices to the software applications that make them work. Your personal MythTV theme reflects your personality and completely influences the look and feel of your frontend client. Not only does MythTV offer theme options, but so too does the on-screen display (OSD). Visit the following URL for more details: www.mythtv.org/wiki/index.php/Category:Themes.

- **Qt Style** — The Qt style settings appear here and later again in Qt Settings. This dialog repeats information about properties that appear later in this chapter (and likewise, in the interface). Because these values have a far-reaching effect (read: global) you should take great care with how you set them; otherwise, your frontend client may become unusable.

- **Font Size** — This sets global font sizes for display through the MythTV frontend. Font Size defaults to TV, a small font whose size is determined later on the Qt Settings page. Use the big font for monitors and adjust size values according to your taste (and visual acuity).

- **Use a Random Theme** — Enable this option if you want the MythTV frontend to don a new disguise with each new invocation.

- **Menu Theme** — You may modify the appearance and organization of top-level menu options while retaining much of the same functionality by toggling this option. This is purely an aesthetic change.

Screen Settings

According to the MythTV User Guide (which is incomplete as of this writing, although the present information is quite insightful), a normal television operates with 5 to 10 percent over-scan, which occurs when the display removes the appearance of a border so that images appear continuous. Through a combination of the next five options, you can manage to recreate a display border by shrinking the GUI size so that it is no longer overscanned:

- **GUI Width (pix)** — Use this specifically if you intend to fine-tune the width of the GUI, represented in picture elements (pixels or pix) on your television. The default value is 0.

- **GUI Height (pix)** — Use this to modify the height of the GUI on your television. The default value is 0.

- **X Offset** — Change this option to modify where the GUI is aligned on the horizontal plane.

- **Y Offset** — Change this option to modify where the GUI is aligned on the vertical plane.

- **Use GUI Size for TV Playback** — This option uses the four preceding parameters for playback on your television, or to render a full-screen image. Disable this option if you intend to work around the overscan method.

- **Hide Mouse Cursor in Myth** — You might have noticed that your mouse, when dragged across the GUI, highlights fields but fails to show a cursor. This perplexing problem can be solved by disabling this option. Unfortunately, this is an all-or-nothing parameter because the majority of the MythTV interface is not receptive to mouse-driven actions. Once you turn the cursor on, it shows up everywhere — even where it's not needed (or useful).

- **Run the Frontend in a Window** — Enable this to run your MythTV frontend inside a window (such as an application) instead of filling the entire screen during normal operation.

Video Mode Settings

Use custom-specified video mode settings to tailor playback according to whichever output device is currently in use (which may be a computer monitor or some kind of television set, if not one or more of each):

- **Separate Modes for GUI and TV Playback** — To get resolution bias according to the display type, you must toggle this feature and set the following parameters. Each field is self-explanatory but the effects you will obtain vary according to your hardware.

  - **GUI** — Specify your default GUI settings for playback on a computer monitor.

  - **Video Output** — Specify your default television resolution for normal playback.

■ **Rate** — Your refresh rate can be set according to the resolution choices you made for the previous two settings.

■ **Aspect** — Finally, set the aspect ratio using this last field.

Additionally there is a subcategory of supplementary GUI/television mode profiles that can be crafted completely independent of each other.

Cross-Reference

Mode profiles are covered in detail in Chapter 17, which deals with custom modelines that permit you to tinker with display parameters at the lowest levels available. Check this out if you need (or want) to do some serious display tweaking!

Localization

The options specific to this configuration window tailor your language and time settings to your geographic region. Because they're both universal and well understood, you should have no problem determining the significance of each field given its brief description in the following sections.

■ **Language** — Set your preferred language.

■ **Date Format** — Specify your preferred date representation format (for example, Thu April 13).

■ **Short Date Format** — This is the preceding entry in abbreviated form (i.e., 4/13 Thu).

■ **Time Format** — Select your preferred time representation format. Options without AM/PM will appear in 24-hour military time format.

Qt Settings

Any changes you make here influence the frontend GUI appearance globally. The first three options concern only Qt font settings; the last two evoke the finer capabilities of Qt GUI properties such as transparency and shading.

You may find that the descriptions provided by the configuration parameters are too long to fit completely inside in the frontend windowpane that MythTV provides. This is where you correct that problem. Adjust the following parameters according to your needs:

■ **Small Font** — This sets the global interface theme font at the smallest setting to the specified value. You should adjust this according to your screen properties.

■ **Medium Font** — This sets the global interface theme font at the medium setting to the specified value. You should adjust this according to your screen properties.

■ **Big Font** — This sets the global interface theme font at the largest setting to the specified value. You should adjust this according to your screen properties.

■ **Use Transparent Boxes** — This feature is user-friendly in that the Watch Recording and Delete Recording screens will retain transparency when used. However, it isn't CPU-friendly in that it costs extra cycles to calculate the transparency properties. Disable this if you experience sluggish response from the interface while you use it.

Note This option is checked by default.

- **Popup Background Shading Method** — There are three methods for shading pop-up window backgrounds. They are listed in order from slowest (least resource intensive) to fastest (most resource intensive): No Shading, Fill, and Image. Low-power or especially conservative MythTV designs force you to consider how these impact overall system performance. On slower systems, in fact, No Shading or Fill are recommended, and are more likely to help deliver a positive MythTV experience.

LCD Device Display

Some MythTV boxes may use a virtual fluorescent display, or VFD, to view auxiliary information when the frontend client has status information to report. Using the next group of settings, you can enable a fair amount of capability for your MythTV client on a VFD or other small-format, low-resolution readout. Because most VFDs use LCD character elements or LEDs in their displays, MythTV's developers call such devices LCDs.

- **Enable LCD Device (checkbox)** — You should enable this option only if you use an LCD to display MythTV information and status. This option is *not* checked by default and requires a reboot to activate.

- **Display Time (checkbox)** — If the first option is enabled, when your LCD goes idle the MythTV frontend client displays the current time. This option is checked by default and requires a reboot to activate.

- **Display Menus (checkbox)** — If the first option is enabled, MythTV displays the selected menu option on the LCD readout. This option is checked by default and requires a reboot to activate.

- **Display Music Artist and Title (checkbox)** — When you have MythMusic active in the mythfrontend client, the currently playing artist and song title will be displayed. This option is checked by default and requires a reboot to activate.

- **Display Channel Information (checkbox)** — When you click or search through the channels on your MythTV box, you may instruct the LCD to display your current channel selection. This option is checked by default and requires a reboot to activate.

- **Display Recording Status (checkbox)** — When your client is preoccupied with a scheduled recording job, this option (when active) reports its status to the LCD. This option is checked by default and requires a reboot to activate.

- **Display Volume Information (checkbox)** — During operation, your MythTV frontend can report current volume information when this feature is in effect. This option is checked by default and requires a reboot to activate.

- **Display Generic Information (checkbox)** — Enable this option so your LCD can display generic information. This option is checked by default and requires a reboot to activate.

- **Backlight Always On (checkbox)** — Use this option if you want the LCD backlight to remain on constantly. This option is checked by default and requires a reboot to activate.

- **Heartbeat Always On (checkbox)** — Some LCDs have a heart icon that pulsates like a beating heart during operation; if your display offers this icon, then enable the heartbeat checkbox. This option is unchecked by default and requires a reboot to activate.

- **Menu Pop-Up Time (input)** — Specify the amount of time, in seconds, you want the menu to remain visible on the LCD readout after navigating through its options. This value is set to five seconds by default.

Once you finalize a perfect look, response, and feel for your MythTV frontend client, you can move on to configuring its television settings to better suit your viewing habits and preferences.

TV Settings

Without a doubt, the TV Settings category is the biggest and most robust set of configurable parameters included in the frontend Setup dialogs. This category encompasses all kinds of properties — from channel settings, ordering, and appearance to locally scheduled user jobs, program guide parameters, and personalization options. Figure 7-2 depicts one of the classier themes that accompany newer versions of MythTV.

FIGURE 7-2: TV Settings change the way you see everything.

General (Basic)

Set your channel ordering, preferred format, schedule priorities, and expiration thresholds for your viewing experience in the subcategories that follow. In addition, a wealth of commercial auto-detection methods become available when you enable the commercial flagging feature for recorded television feeds.

- **Channel Ordering** — This sets your preferred sort order for the appearance of channels based on channel number (alphabetic and numeric), database order, or channel name.

- **Channel Format** — Use this option to make MythTV display your preferred channel format. Your options are number-callsign, number-name, callsign, name, and number. (A callsign is the abbreviated station identification string, such as KVUE, just in case you were wondering.)

- **Long Channel Format** — Whereas the preceding format shows you an abbreviated form of station identification, this option provides you with a slightly longer format. Your choices are number-name, callsign, name, and number.

- **Change Channels Immediately without Select** — When you enter a complete channel number to the frontend it will switch over immediately without requiring you to confirm with the Select button. You probably want to enable this option.

- **Avoid Conflicts Between Live TV and Scheduled Shows** — If you enable this item, MythTV will default to a tuner card least likely to have scheduled jobs pending, rather than seek out the best card available.

- **Auto-Expire Method** — You run this as a thread on a backend server to automatically expire recordings based on a predetermined date. This option requires that the Disk Space Threshold setting is set to a value greater than zero; and when the threshold is reached, a worker thread will begin routine cleanup to free up extra room.

- **Auto-Expire Default** — To use the preceding functionality, you must enable this option. MythTV will then schedule the requisite housekeeping services for you. Should you choose to enable this, any recent recording can then be marked eligible for deletion (thus, Auto-Expired), while any existing recordings retain their predefined values.

- **LiveTV Recordings Maximum Age** — Specify the maximum age any given live television recording may reach before being slated for removal.

General (Jobs)

Using the Job Queue parameters, you can influence the runtime operation of scheduled jobs on this frontend client — from automatic commercial detection to the detection method used.

- **Commercial Flag New Recordings** — Every time you schedule a new recording, MythTV is right there with you, flagging for commercials (by default). Disable this feature to conserve CPU overhead.

- **Commercial Skip Method** — By default, this option functions only with Blank Frame Detection set, but when you enable the preceding checkbox, a variety of other options suddenly become available. The other features enable you to specify the many methods used to detect incoming commercials for immediate handling at the source. Scene Change Detection, Blank Frame with Scene Change Detection, and Logo Detection are made available to you, plus a combination of all the above.

- **Strict Commercial Detection** — You will find that some commercial interruptions appear to slip right by the preceding series of filters. Enable this property to exercise stricter control over commercial detection to help MythTV do its job a little better.

- **Default Auto-Transcode Setting** — Specify the default behavior for auto-transcoding jobs whether or not you wish to enable them by default.

- **Default Transcoder** — Either specify one of the transcoder device entries identified in your Linux installation or leave this at the default setting, in which case the software uses its own Auto-Detect feature. This sets the default transcoder for all jobs.

- **Run User Jobs** — In this dialog you encounter a set of four User Jobs profiles you can specify to handle that number of interrelated tasks. To schedule jobs for later execution or to take advantage of idle machines in multi-client environments, you should create a job script to pre-process files before handling their formats. See `www.mythtv.org/wiki/index.php/User_Jobs` for more details.

General (Advanced)

In this final General settings dialog you modify and fine-tune the little details about MythTV operation. Storage space considerations, start/stop record times, and signal settings are all available to you in this configuration window. The defaults are fine for most people, so only change these if you experience operational problems or discover that the defaults don't work for you.

- **Extra Disk Space** — You may use more than just MythTV on your frontend hardware, and this is where you should declare spare room for your personal recordings.

- **Time to Record Before Start of Show** — This global setting enables the recorder to start before a scheduled start time (without affecting the backend scheduler). It's ignored when you schedule two shows without sufficient time in between.

- **Time to Record After End of Show** — Similar to the preceding setting, this option enables you to specify how long to keep recording after the conclusion of a program (also without affecting the backend scheduler).

- **Category Record Overtime** — This submenu enables you to identify a specific group profile for recordings to allow a categorical bias for recordings you want to extend beyond the end of a show, as a whole.

- **ATSC Signal Threshold** — Not all signals are created equal, and you can separate the wheat from the chaff here. Beware: If you set this threshold too low, then stability issues arise; if you set it too high, you lose the ability to tune into perfectly valid signals.

- **Time Limit for ASC Signal Lock** — HDTV and Over-the-Air (OTA) digital-quality signals get automatic strength detection through MythTV when you activate this feature. Measured in milliseconds, this number is taken to represent the maximum time allocated to the auto-detection task before the frontend times out.

- **HD Ringbuffer Size (KB)** — A dedicated hard-disk ring-buffer enables your MythTV backend to get thrashed — that is, endure sudden loads of stress — and this buffer size is a measure of your server's threshold for pain. You must strike a delicate balance between time and space; otherwise, you can impose adverse effects on performance.

Program Guide (1/2)

The Electronic Program Guide (EPG) is your window into current and upcoming television programming. It also guides the MythTV framework through its daily routine. The parameters that follow influence the appearance of your EPG in various ways:

- **Guide Shading Method** — Shading methods enable the window to retain a level of transparency (or none at all) depending on your settings. Underpowered CPUs should specify more conservative settings (Solid, Eco), while beefier systems can use more demanding options (Blender, Alpha).

- **Display Genre Colors** — Enable this feature to supply a colorized context to the genres that appear in the EPG.

- **Display Genre Text** — Although this is not available for all grabbers, enabling this feature will permit you to give textual context to program genres that appear in the EPG.

- **Floating Program Guide Selector** — Your EPG selector is fixed at the center of your display unless you enable this option, freeing it to move throughout the guide.

- **Display the Channel Icon** — Where applicable, you may display a channel icon along with relevant station identification data.

- **Display Only Favorite Channels** — Set this option when you wish to exercise strict control over the channels that appear in your EPG. It restricts entries only to those channels you specify as favorites.

- **Show the Program Guide when Starting Live TV** — Enable this option and your EPG appears immediately upon starting live television.

- **Channels to Display** — Manipulate the number of rows (or channels) that appear in the EPG.

- **Time Blocks to Display** — Manipulate the number of columns (or time slots) that appear in the EPG.

Program Guide (2/2)

This second dialog handles the remainder of EPG settings. Use the following options to train your EPG to respond according to your preferred style of use:

- **What to Call Unknown Programs** — When your MythTV frontend cannot identify a program it is scheduled to record, it is branded with this catch-all label.

- **What Category to Give Unknown Programs** — Likewise, when your frontend client groups unidentifiable (or unknown) programs, they are filed away in this catch-all category.

- **Guide Starts at Channel** — Set your EPG to begin on a specified channel when the frontend operates outside of live television mode.

- **Use Select to Change Channel in Guide** — When enabled, you can activate channels within the guide using the Select button. Keybindings associated with the MythWeb plug-in switch the client out of live television mode, for example. The default behavior for the Select key is to bring up the Recording options screen.

- **Record Threshold** — When combined with the preceding option, your EPG will record a show that you Select if it is at least the specified value of time (measured in minutes) before airing.

- **Allow Channel Jumping in Guide** — Check this option to enable your remote control to enter numeric values and jump to an arbitrary channel selection within the EPG.

Playback

Control over just about every aspect of playback is provided in the following series of deeply nested menus and submenus. Some of them are too deep to accurately present in this book, and instead receive summary coverage to conserve space. This segment is perhaps the most appealing to the performance tuner in you, who's always looking to squeeze a little more out of where it really counts. Also available are a variety of options that serve as workarounds to known problems (not of MythTV origin), noted as such.

General Playback (1/2)

In this initial playback category you are granted control over a wide variety of parameters that govern the appearance and performance of video output on your frontend. These options are most helpful when you need to take corrective action to address problems with the way MythTV renders video output.

- **De-interlace Playback** — An image is considered interlaced when even and odd lines of resolution are drawn in alternating sequence, which tricks your eyes into perceiving a higher frame rate. Your television may produce flicker at the standard 30 frames per second (fps), for example. Enabling this option should ostensibly correct the issue.

- **Custom Filters** — You can enable additional video processing by way of external filters that you specify here. Visit the Web site at www.mythtv.org/wiki/index.php/Filter_Instructions for more information on playback or recording filters.

- **Use libmpeg2 for Decoding** — MythTV by and large relies upon the ffmpeg binary to get most of its heavy-lifting tasks (such as MPEG decoding) done. Enable this option if you prefer to default to libmpeg2 instead.

- **Enable Real-time Priority Threads** — Although we recommend you run MythTV as the specified self-named user, you can run with root privileges and earn extra performance points. During operation, some threads of execution are given a higher priority to access system resources, resulting in a perceived performance increase. However, you should disable this option as recommended in the prompt that appears should MythTV experience halting or jerky playback.

- **Use Video as Time-base** — Occasionally, video and audio channels will desynchronize and produce a noticeable difference between input arrival times. Enable this option to make your frontend take corrective action by forcing it to use the picture timing data to synchronize sound data.

- **Extra Audio Buffering** — Except for MPEG-4 or RTJPEG video encoders, crackling audio feedback can be corrected when your hardware encoding process behaves poorly. Enable this option to take corrective action when you experience noisy feedback.

- **Aspect Override** — You may specify a global aspect ratio that overrides the parameters-specified streams that you record. Several options are available: 4:3, 16:9, 4:3 Zoom, 16:9 Zoom, 16:9 Stretch, and Fill.

- **PIP Location** — Set a specific placement for the Picture-in-Picture element when you use it. Placement options at your disposal are Top Left, Bottom Left, Top Right, and Bottom Right.

General Playback (2/2)

The remainder of playback options encompass the behavioral aspects of your MythTV client. This includes all of its flagging and controlling options. We recommend that you enable those features that work best for you. That said, the defaults should be fine for most of your needs.

- **Action on Playback Exit** — Three values influence the choice your frontend client makes upon exiting playback mode: Just Exit (default), Save Position and Exit, or Always Prompt.

- **Prompt at End of Recording** — Selecting this option produces a prompt when recording completes.

- **Clear Saved Position on Playback** — If you set Save Positions on a file when you record it, this option clears them upon playback.

- **Alternate Clear Save Position** — When you operate the frontend in playback mode, the action keys (Select, Enter, Space) toggle between Position Saved and Position Cleared. Disable this option to use these action keys for individual keypresses.

- **Use Xv Picture Controls** — You should use this feature with extreme caution (in other words, set it independently of any other option and test it) because it operates the Xv picture controls completely independent of the Video4Linux (V4L) graphics library. This feature may not work in your particular setup.

- **Enable Channel Buffer Warnings** — MythTV will notify you when live television is not matched to data in the buffer when you change the channel. This option is disabled by default.

- **UDP Notify Port** — MythTV accepts inbound connections to this port from the `mythvosd` and `mythudprelay` applications for displaying status information such as Caller ID, e-mail notifications, etc. Point your browser at www.mythtv.org/wiki/index.php/Setting_up_MythNotify for more information on UDP-based notifications. The default port number is 6948.

- **View Recordings** — Your MythTV experience should cater to your every whim and fancy, even if it seems overly precise in how information is presented and summarized, or where your highlights and focal points are already set. These options enable you to modify many useful parameters to match the way you like to view recorded information:

  - **List Newest Recording First** — View your most recently recorded program first.

  - **Sort Episode** — Modify how your episodes are displayed.

  - **Generate Thumbnail Preview of Recordings** — Create a still image from your recordings to adorn the Watch a Recording menu.

  - **Time Offset for Thumbnail Preview Images** — Offset animated thumbnail creation a specified amount of time to avoid previews or commercials in your recordings.

  - **Generate Previous Image from Bookmark** — Make a best-effort attempt to grab an image from your bookmark.

  - **Display Live Preview of Recordings** — Enable a preview window to play a short trailer in the Watch a Recording window.

  - **CPU Friendly Preview of Recordings** — Operate your recording unit at a lower frame rate to achieve better resource conservation.

  - **Start in Title Section** — Point your selector to highlight the Programs entry in the titles window.

  - **Show Group Summary** — Display a group summary instead of summarizing the first episode in a group of your recordings.

  Although the following options map to all options present in revision 0.19, they may appear differently (or not at all) in your version. Indeed, they may appear alongside even more options.

- **View Recordings (Recording Groups)** — You may password-protect your recordings from unauthorized viewing, specify a default group policy filter, and always have MythTV prompt you for an initial group filter. You can also save the current group filter when any changes are made, show the filter name instead of the All Programs filter, and declare a global default view on the frontend.

- **Hardware Decoding Settings** — Unless you bought the Hauppage PVR-350 capture card, these options do not apply to you. A number of features appear only when you enable the first option. We recommended against enabling the following settings for any other TV capture card:

  - **Use the PVR-350's TV-Out/MPEG Decoder** — You get high-quality playback by setting MythTV to use the Hauppauge PVR-350 on-board MPEG decoder and TV-out capability.

  - **Video Device for the PVR-350 MPEG Decoder** — Specify the device name for your PVR-350 MPEG decoder card.

- **Program Guide Alpha** — Transparency blend your program guide over the background TV image for a classier look.

- **TV Audio through PVR-350 Only** — Externalize volume control by specifying that MythTV channel sound out through the PVR-350.

Evidently, those who purchase a PVR-350 have a decent set of options that are controlled directly on this settings page:

- **Seeking** — These properties affect the behavior of your playback unit when you engage the fast-forward (FWD) or rewind (REW) buttons. You can exercise greater control over the responsiveness MythTV exhibits when you invoke certain seeking functionality, as summarized in the following options:

  - **Smart Fast Forwarding** — After rewinding, skip forward the exact same amount.

  - **Sticky Keys** — Fast-forward/rewind continues after key is released, and subsequent keypresses increase directional speed.

  - **Fast-Forward/Rewind Repositioning** — Compensate for reaction time between seeing the resume point and quitting seek mode.

  - **Reverse Direction in Forward/Rewind** — Pressing a sticky rewind key in fast-forward mode switches to rewind, and vice-versa.

  - **Seek to Exact Frame** — Fine-grained seeking at the cost of speed

Provided you want to be ultra-precise (or forgiving, in the case of repositioning), these next options give you every ounce of control over the response MythTV exhibits when you search through your programs interactively.

- **Commercial Skip** — MythTV is incredibly flexible in the way you configure it to detect and handle commercials during real-time playback. Most of this functionality is exposed right here in the Commercial Skip settings page. A summary of available options follows:

  - **Automatically Skip Commercials** — Automatically skip commercials if you flagged Automatic Commercial Flagging or become notified of commercial detects.

  - **Commercial Skip Auto-Rewind Amount** — Reset your player to a specified amount of time (measured in seconds) after skipping through a commercial.

  - **Commercial Skip Notify Amount** — Set your MythTV client to preemptively skip a commercial in lieu of automatic skipping.

  - **Skip Blank Frames After Commercials** — When you specify Blank Frame Detection with Auto-Flagging, this will include the blank following the commercial break.

This gives you a fair amount of control over commercial detection on your frontend.

- **Overscan** — This screen enables you to specify your own overscan settings from vertical and horizontal overscan or underscan to vertical or horizontal axis image displacement. Use these properties to situate the MythTV GUI properly on your screen.

- **On-Screen Display** — Your OSD is a heads-up display of program metadata. Using these options, you can modify how this information appears onscreen.

  - **OSD Theme** — Your OSD has a theme completely independent of the MythTV frontend theme, and this is where you can set it.

  - **General OSD Timeout** — Specify how long you want MythTV to wait before making the OSD active after first initialization.

  - **Program Information OSD Timeout** — Likewise, specify how long after initialization program information should first become available.

  - **UDP Notify Timeout** — Specify how many seconds after initialization you want MythTV UDP Notify events to occur.

  - **Black Background for Closed Captioning** — If you need to see the words on the screen, then it helps to block out the background images.

  - **Always Display Closed Captioning** — Use this to dedicate your client to hearing-impaired tasks.

  - **Closed Captioning Font** — Change your font for displaying CC information.

  - **Font Size** — Specify the OSD font display size.

Configuring your OSD setup couldn't get any simpler than this.

Playback Groups

Playback groups provide you with a simpler means for grouping scheduled recording rules than using specific names or expressions. This page makes available properties for creating your own such groups to schedule similar recordings for a group of shows or programs. Create new groups or specify default settings for your hardware devices through this settings page.

Recording Profiles

Set profile properties for encoder cards and transcoder parameters you want MythTV to use during recording jobs. Where your capture card contains on-board encoder/decoder capability, you will find an entry (or two) in this window where you can specify such settings. You will have a group called MPEG-2 Encoders, and possibly another group called Transcoders, and a third option to create a new Profile Group.

Recording

MythTV tailors its grouping of options according to features available on your capture card. Different video cards have different levels of functionality, so this affects the types of options available to you for recording. Where your card lacks on-board MPEG encoder capability, MythTV is equipped to handle MPEG-4 and RTJPEG software encoding. There are trade-offs for hardware versus software encoding (hardware is clearly faster) and also between MPEG-4 and RTJPEG (the former takes up less disk space at the cost of more CPU cycles) so you must choose your options wisely.

- **Recording** — Use this option to set or reschedule higher recording priorities and avoid scheduling conflicts through a hierarchy of preferences. Some of the many priority setting options available include Single Recordings, Override Recordings, Week and Timeslot Recordings, and Channel Recordings. When combined, these options leverage a serious power over MythTV recording.

- **Channel Priorities** — Let's face it: You know all channels are created differently, to appeal to certain demographics, to fulfill certain cultural obligations, and to broadcast specific programming. You may like one channel more than another; and when it comes to scheduling conflict resolution, why should a lower priority channel get equal consideration? Set things up to reflect your preferences, and MythTV will behave as you would if and when conflicting priorities pop up.

Media Settings

All multimedia parameters are contained in this single category. From CD to DVD settings to the default and specified search paths, you can tailor every single aspect of media handling capability provided in the frontend setup. The following categories configure the four primary media plug-ins for the MythTV fronted client.

Music Settings

You can configure MythMusic settings here along with the default CD recording device, default player and playback settings, and visualization properties. This is where you control all video properties, where they get stored, and everything else about them. Player settings, default file extension types and handlers, and other configurable parameters appear here. The MythMusic plug-in is detailed in Chapter 12.

DVD Settings

Set the default storage path, DVD device entry, and rip settings for a variety of recordings. Basically, this is where you configure MythDVD (see Chapter 10 for more information).

Images Settings

Specify where MythTV should begin looking for your images and how it should handle specific formats. These properties will change the way MythGallery operates, as detailed in Chapter 11.

Game Settings

Use these properties to influence the way your MythGame plug-in operates.

Info Center

The Info Center ties together information from around the world about your environment, from the weather to news and culture, and even your online movie rental history (courtesy of Netflix). Though the functionality here may seem basic and leave you wanting more, the core capability is incredibly useful. In fact, we believe this category stands to gain in popularity as MythTV reaches ever-broader audiences.

Weather Settings

This module configures parameters for the MythWeather plug-in. When (and only when) you are finished setting these parameters, you may save them by pressing the i key (or the applicable remote control key you bind to). This invokes the MythWeather module for pulling down information it needs to flesh out a series of screens used to display Doppler Weather reports, daily/weekly forecasts, and more.

- **Weather Units** — This option is a no-brainer: Do you want Imperial or Metric measurements? As a participant in the American broadcast region, the clear choice here is Imperial, which displays temperature in Fahrenheit, among other things.

- **Location** — This option coincides with localization settings but is kept in a completely separate module from the main MythTV codebase. You must walk through an extensive list of city, country, and state codes conveniently alphabetized to find the right settings for your locale. Otherwise, the MythWeather module will complain and fail. Use the left and right arrows to ascend and descend into subcategories, and PageUp/PageDown to cycle quickly through these lists.

- **Aggressiveness** — This setting specifies how enthusiastically your MythTV box will pull information from the NWS servers. By default, the setting is placed at a conservative Low Bandwidth value that you should adjust to match your taste for weather data. Values 1–15 begin with the slowest connection speed at the small end and increase with bandwidth available.

News Settings

For your MythBrowser viewing pleasure, you may specify any number of RSS news feeds available through this configuration window. There are many types of news-feed category (Arts, Business, Computers, Media News, Magazines, International, and more) and many kinds of sites (Slashdot, KDE.org, Debian Security Advisories, and so on) to fulfill your needs. Navigate this interface by using right/left directional keys and using spacebar/Enter (or applicable remote keybindings) to select and deselect options.

Netflix Settings

MythTV's Netflix plug-in is a new kid on the block. As a result, a lot of configuration is needed for the current interface. However, you can't help but appreciate the functionality that this plug-in already provides. By default, you can view the Top 25 most popular hits from the default array of Netflix categories, and with a little elbow grease you can manage to configure its Queue and History listings as well. Press the Menu key to set update frequency — the rate at which the `mythbackend` process polls relevant information from the Netflix server. You can try the following process to get the MythTV frontend to interface with your account but be forewarned: This can be hairy if you aren't already somewhat familiar with Linux or MySQL. Figure 7-3 depicts the personalized Netflix queue you will see when you successfully configure the frontend plug-in.

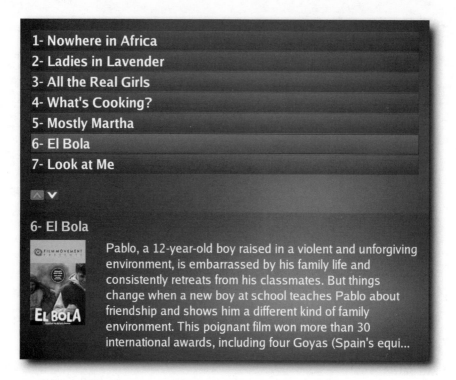

FIGURE 7-3: View your upcoming Netflix selections through MythTV.

Sign up and log into the Netflix Web site (www.netflix.com) and proceed immediately to the bottom of the first page where a series of links appear. The bottom row contains five items: Jobs, Media Center, Tell a Friend, RSS, and Settlement. Of these, you want to click the RSS link and note the two entries under the Personalized Feeds queue heading and Most Recent Rental Activity. This boils down to the following two links:

```
http://www.netflix.com/QueueRSS?id=<YOUR-NETFLIX-ID>
http://www.netflix.com/TrackingRSS?id=<YOUR-NETFLIX-ID>
```

These two links refer to what you have and what you want, respectively, from the Netflix video library. The italicized text is a unique number specific to your Netflix account, so be sure to insert your identity string here. You will need to insert these into the MythTV backend database in order for the Netflix plug-in to properly locate your data. Once you have identified your Netflix ID, open a terminal console and issue the following commands:

```
$ /usr/share/mythtv/mythflix/scripts/netflix.pl -L user pass
Status code: 200
```

```
$ mysql -u mythtv -p
Enter password: mythtv
mysql> INSERT INTO mythconverg.netflix VALUES (
'Queue', 'Netflix',
'http://rss.netflix.com/QueueRSS?id=<YOUR-NETFLIX-ID>',
'http://cdn.nflximg.com/us/icons/nficon.ico', null, 1) ;
mysql> INSERT INTO mythconverg.netflix VALUES (
'History', 'Netflix',
'http://rss.netflix.com/TrackingRSS?id=<YOUR-NETFLIX-ID>',
'http://cdn.nflximg.com/us/icons/nficon.ico', null, 2) ;
mysql> quit
```

Insert your personal user name and password in the first terminal command. According to the document this pointer is inspired by, there is something unusual about the way the Netflix cookie is obtained that requires you to invoke this twice. At any rate, upon reentry into the frontend Netflix menu, you should see your Queue and History/Tracking entries under their respective options, as illustrated in Figure 7-3.

Note   This works for MythTV on Fedora Core installations. Your mileage may vary on other distributions.

See www.mythtv.org/wiki/index.php/MythFlix_README for details on how to set up your Netflix account. Beware: The current method is not for inexperienced Linux users. See also the following sidebar, "Netflix: The New Age of Video Rental."

Web Settings

Your MythBrowser settings are specified on this page. Set your preferred bookmarks, specify the default zoom property (to adjust for a wide variety of Web site content), change the default Web browser (/usr/bin/mythbrowser), turn scroll bars and page scrolling on or off, and set your preferred scroll interval.

Netflix: The New Age of Video Rental

Netflix has the distinction of being both the first and the largest online DVD rental service, offering a flat rate for subscribers in the United States. To date, Netflix has amassed over 60,000 movie titles and upwards of 5 million subscribers. Rental choices are queued in order of preference (which can be dynamically reordered as you see fit), and you may keep a movie for as long as you like. New movies usually arrive in the mail within a few days upon return of your last selections, and the total number of movies you may rent at any one time is determined by your subscription type. See www.netflix.com for details.

Phone Settings

The MythPhone plug-in configuration settings are tucked away neatly in this little corner of the MythTV frontend settings menu. Your phone must support the Session Initiation Protocol (SIP) in order for an Internet telephony application to work with this plug-in.

SIP Proxy Settings

Use the following configuration settings to operate your SIP phone hardware:

- **Login to a SIP Server (checkbox)** — Enable this feature if you use an account name and password to authenticate with a SIP or Asterisk server. Changing this option requires you to restart the frontend client.

- **SIP Server DNS Name** — Set this to the name of your Free World Dialup or Asterisk server name.

- **Sign-in Name** — Specify your user account for authentication with the SIP server.

- **Password** — Specify your password to the preceding user account for authentication with the SIP server.

- **My Display Name** — You should specify the common display name used to identify yourself on SIP-based telephony.

- **Auto-Answer (checkbox)** — Answer all incoming calls when your MythPhone plug-in is active in the frontend client. Currently, no security is implemented for this feature.

IP Settings

Internet Protocol (IP) settings are specific to the SIP properties you use to establish phone calls. From Network Address Translation (NAT) to Real-Time Protocol (RTP), the settings you need to configure to establish Internet telephony through SIP are contained here.

- **SIP Network Interface (input)** — This refers to the network interface name by which you identify the SIP-server-facing network card. The default interface is eth0.

- **SIP Local Port (input)** — You should specify a separate port for each additional frontend client you deploy with SIP capability. Each port will be specific to the machine for which it is configured. The default is 5060.

- **NAT Traversal Method (input)** — Network Address Translation (NAT) is a popular way to provide the one-to-many mapping capability necessary to share a single Internet connection among multiple computers. If you have a router at home with a small network of computers, you may be using NAT and not even know it. The problem with NAT is that not all protocols make it cleanly through the mapping process, such as IPSec and, evidently, SIP. Choose None if you have a publicly addressable IP address, Manual if you are assigned a static IP address from your ISP, or Web Server for a dynamic IP assignment mapped to a top-level domain alias. Restart the mythfrontend client if you modify this setting.

- **NAT IP Address (input)** — This setting is entirely dependent upon the value you specify above. Enter a public IP address if you chose the Manual option, a URL for the Web Server option, and leave alone for None. The default entry is `http://checkip.dyndns.org`, which is an excellent resource for mapping your dynamic (constantly changing) IP address to a constant host name.

- **Audio RTP Port (input)** — Real Time Protocol (RTP) is basically a prioritization protocol that enables you to surf the Web and talk on the phone using the same Internet connection. This is the default audio port for the frontend you are configuring, which should end in an even number that is unique to each frontend client. The default port is 21232.

- **Video RTP Port (input)** — Similar to the audio RTP stream, this one is video only. You should treat this with the same consideration as the preceding option. The default port is 21234.

Audio Settings

This is where you specify your default microphone device, supported audio codecs, and audio and video anti-jitter buffering parameters for your SIP phone calls.

Webcam Settings

You might never have guessed that MythTV can also handle Webcams. In the true spirit of convergence, MythTV lets no device remain an island unto itself, and provides the glue necessary to use IP telephony and Webcam together. Plug your Webcam settings in here to further extend your MythTV experience.

- **Webcam Device** — Like the capture card entry you specify for your input device, this parameter corresponds to the Webcam device as identified by Linux. Thus, if your TV capture card is already designated as `/dev/video0`, you should try `/dev/video1` for your Webcam.

- **Transmit Resolution** — Use a smaller resolution to conserve bandwidth across the network, and a higher resolution to support better-quality images at the endpoints.

- **Transmit Frames/Second** — Specify the maximum number of frames that may be transmitted per second to regulate the impact streaming Webcam video imposes on your network. Valid values range from 1–30, where higher values create better-looking images at the expense of adding network overhead.

- **Maximum Transmit Bandwidth (Kbps)** — Specify the maximum uplink bandwidth for your wide area network (WAN) or Internet connection. The default value here is 256 Kbps.

- **Capture Resolution** — Specify the incoming resolution from the capture stream provided by the Webcam device. It is imperative that this number match your hardware specifications. You can digitally pan or zoom an image before transmission by setting a higher value here.

VXML Settings

Voice eXtensible Markup Language (VXML) scripts are the textual representations of voice dictation you might leave on an answering machine. The difference here is that you actually type the message as opposed to vocalizing it into a microphone. What you would like said, when you want it said, and how it is said can all be controlled here with the right know-how and a little poking around.

- **Time to Answer** — Specify the amount of time you want an incoming call to ring before automatically being diverted to one of the two Voice XML scripts specified.

- **Default XML URL** — This is the URL to the VXML script used as a prompt for callers to leave a voice message for you. If you leave this blank, the next option goes into effect.

- **Default Voicemail Prompt** — Customize your Voicemail prompt here. The default message is fairly standard: "I am not at home; please leave a message after the tone." Here, the message you create is filtered through the Text-to-Speech (TTS) library and synthesized into a voice for the caller.

- **Text-to-Speech Voice** — By default this option is blank. You can specify a pre-fabricated voice synthesis profile or insert your own. Example voice profiles ending in .scm are kept on the system on which you installed Festival. These usually reside in /usr/ share/festival, but your distribution may vary.

Final Thoughts

Whew! This comprehensive chapter introduced you to the concepts that drive your MythTV frontend interface and influence its operation. You may feel a little overwhelmed by all the options you can change (not all of which may be familiar). This might make the process of configuring your frontend seem daunting, but this need not be the case. While these properties represent what you can do with your mythfrontend client, there are no hard-and-fast rules governing what must be changed and what can be left alone. Try working with the defaults for a while, and let your experience guide you into configuration little by little as you learn more about the way MythTV works.

Where do you go from here? Several subsequent chapters deal with extra plug-ins (Chapters 9 and 14), advanced MythTV look/sound/feel hacks (Chapter 15), performance hacks (Chapter 16), and extending the environment (Chapter 17). If you have Internet access, we recommend that you read the MythTV Daily Use guide at www.mythtv.org/wiki/index.php/ User_Manual:Daily_Use. This presents a growing body of information and describes typical MythTV operation in both pictures and text.

Making MythTV Work

There's a definite series of activities involved in getting set up to use MythTV. First, you must get your MythTV PC put together, install Linux, and then install MythTV itself, plus your chosen plug-ins. After that you must install and get a remote control working, after which you must go through various configuration exercises with MythTV and its `mythfrontend`. After all that prep, you can finally start using and customizing your MythTV environment. Explaining those ins and outs is what this chapter is all about.

This is where you'll learn about running MythTV from the keyboard, should you choose to do so (and yes, there is a lot of stuff you can do by twiddling a few keys here). You learn about the visual themes that control MythTV's look and feel, starting with built-in options and progressing to other offerings— all the way to customizing or creating your own theme. You also learn how to integrate a set-top cable or satellite box with MythTV, and plumb the mysteries involved in integrating an IR blaster with MythTV. After that, it's on to teaching MythTV how to wake up when it's time to record something, and then digging deep into the details of scheduling and making TV recordings with your MythTV PC. This is where you finally get to put all your efforts so far to the test, and really start using MythTV to make things happen. Enjoy!

MythTV Keyboard Commands

MythTV supports keyboard sequences in more or less the same way that it permits you to drive around the interface with a remote control. Some people like one way better than the other, but the truth is that both ways work equally well, so you must pick a method and then learn how to make it work for you. If you are interested in driving MythTV from your keyboard, you'll find a whole series of tables from which you can find keys for everything you want to do—from the basics of the MythTV GUI all the way through managing TV viewing or recording, working with multiple TV tuner configurations, and using the program guide.

Tables 8-1 through 8-8 show you the keyboard commands for navigating in various modes. The tabular format is intended to let you see things at a glance and learn your way around. We understand that if you want to keep this information handy, you probably would like to keep it next to your keyboard—at least while you're learning your way around. Though real die-hards can copy the tables from this book with our blessing, you can also visit lead author Jarod Wilson's Web page that summarizes all this information as well. Find and print this puppy at `http://wilsonet.com/mythtv/keys.txt`.

Table 8-1   Standard mythfrontend Keys

Key	Explanation
Arrow keys	Use these to move the highlight point around.
ALT+F4	Exit from the application.
Space/Enter	Take action on the item under the highlight point.
P	Play in both Watch a Recording and Delete a Recording.
D	Delete in both Watch a Recording and Delete a Recording.
U	View details for the currently selected show on the Watch or Delete screens, EPG, Program Finder, Fix Scheduling Conflicts, and search results screens.
O	List the upcoming episodes for the currently selected show on the EPG, Program Finder, Program Recording Priorities, Fix Scheduling Conflicts, or search results screens.
I	Edit recording options from the EPG, Program Finder, Program Recording Priorities, or Fix Scheduling Conflicts screens. From the Playback and Delete screens, "I" presents options for recorded shows such as Auto Expire or Stop Recording. Pressing "I" while on the Recording Options screen will take you to the Advanced Recording Options screen.

Table 8-2   Watching or Recording TV

Key	Explanation
Page Up or Page Down	Use these to change the channel.
Num pad	Type a number to enter a channel number or jump amount (HHMM format).
P	Pause/play. You may also add an explicit keybinding for Play through MythWeb, returning you to normal speed if you are in slow motion, rewind fast forward, or pause mode.

Key	Explanation
C	Change inputs on TV Tuner card.
Esc	Quit TV activity.
I	Put the On-screen Display up again. During playback, "I" toggles between position and show description info. If a jump amount is entered, jump to that position.
M	Bring up the electronic program guide (Grid). See the EPG section.
Page Up	Jump back the configured number of minutes (the default is 10).
Page Down	Jump ahead the configured number of minutes (the default is 10).
End or Z	Skip to next commercial break marker.
Home or Q	Skip back to the previous commercial break marker.
T	Toggle close caption support. Pressing 0-9 (preferably 3 times) + T changes teletext page and turns on teletext.
F	Rotate between the various Picture Adjustments (Color, Hue, etc.) While Picture Adjustment is on-screen, use Left and Right arrows to adjust. These settings adjust the look of the video playback, and are independent of the G-key settings used at record-time.
[or F10	Decrease the volume.
] or F11	Increase the volume.
l or F9	Toggle mute.
/	Jump to the next "favorite" channel.
?	Mark/unmark the current channel as a "favorite."
U	Increase the play speed.
J	Decrease the play speed.
A	Adjust the time stretch (speed up or slow down normal play of audio and video).
W	Cycle through zoom and fill modes: 4:3 aspect ratio, 16:9, 4:3 Zoom (like Pan and Scan), 16:9 Zoom, and 16:9 Stretch (eliminates black sidebars in the TV signal).
F8	Toggle the sleep timer 30m->1hr->1hr30m->2hr->Off.
Ctrl-B	Jump to the beginning of the recording/ringbuffer.
+	Switch between audio streams.
Left	(If a jump amount is entered) to jump back that amount.
Right	(If a jump amount is entered) to jump ahead that amount.

Continued

Table 8-2 *(continued)*

Key	Explanation
In fast forward or rewind mode:	
Left/Right	Increases the ff/rew speed.
0	Plays at normal speed, but leaves the time indicator onscreen.
1 or 2	Plays back more slowly than normal ff/rew speed (1 is slowest).
3	Plays back at normal ff/rew speed.
4-9	Plays back faster than normal ff/rew speed (9 is fastest).
Space	Exits fast forward or rewind mode.
While video is paused:	
Left	Rewind 1 frame.
<	Rewind 1 second.
Right	Advance 1 frame.
>	Advance 1 second.

Table 8-3   Watching TV Only

Key	Explanation
G	Rotate between the various Picture Adjustments (Color, Hue, etc.) for recording. These values affect the look of the resulting .nuv file, and are independent of the playback picture settings. While Picture Adjustment is onscreen, use Left and Right arrows to adjust.
H	Channel history. Each repeat steps back through the previous channels.
O	Turns on Browse mode, enabling the user to browse channels and program info while watching the current show FullScreen.
Y	Switch between multiple capture cards. **Note:** You will lose your LiveTV buffer on your current card. Useful for different-sourced cards (such as Dish Network on one card, and HDTV over-the-air on another card).

Table 8-4   LiveTV Browse Mode

Key	Explanation
Left	Browse a program prior to the current listed program.
Right	Browse a program following the current listed program.
Up	Browse a program on the channel above the current listed channel/program.
Down	Browse a program on the channel below the current listed channel/program.
/	Browse a program on the next favorite channel.
0-9	Enter a channel number to browse.
Space/Enter	Change the channel to the channel of the current listed program.
R/r	Toggle recording of the current program (cycles through types).
ESC/O	Exit Browse mode.

Table 8-5   Playback Recording Zoom Mode

Key	Explanation
Left	Move video to left.
Right	Move video to right.
Up	Move video up.
Down	Move video down.
PageUp	Zoom in.
PageDown	Zoom out.
Space/Enter	Exit Zoom mode, leaving picture at current size and position.
ESC	Exit Zoom mode and return to original size.

Table 8-6   Using Two or More Tuner Cards

Key	Explanation
V	Toggles Picture-in-Picture on or off.
B	Toggles Window focus (lets you change channels in the PiP window).
N	Swaps the two channels by changing channels on both cards.

Table 8-7 Watching a Recording Only

Key	Explanation
Space/Enter	Sets a bookmark at that point. Next time you start the recording, you will automatically jump forward to this point and clear the bookmark.
X	Queues the current recording for transcoding.
O	Brings up the menu to allow toggling settings such as Commercial Auto-Skip, Auto-Expire, etc.
D	Exits the current recording and displays the Delete menu.
E or M	Enters or exits edit mode.

Table 8-8 Working with the Electronic Program Guide

Key	Explanation
Arrows	Moves the highlighted program point around.
A, D, S, W	Performs the same as left, right, down, and up.
PageUp/ PageDown	Moves the channel list up or down a page.
Home/End	Moves the highlight left or right by one day.
Ctrl+Left or <	Moves the highlight left by one page.
Ctrl+Right or >	Moves the highlight right by one page.
9, 3, 7, 1	(Like a numeric keypad) performs the same as PageUp, PageDown, Home, and End.
I	Brings up more information about a show. Also enables you to schedule a recording. If you select "Record this showing while watching Live TV," you can Instant Record a program.
Space/Enter	Allows you to resolve conflicts or change overrides. If the program is not already scheduled to record, it will instead act like pressing "I."
M	When on a channel, will change to that channel.
ESC or C	Exits without changing the channel.
R	Changes the current item from Recording/Not-Recording. Successive keypresses cycle through the scheduled recording type list.
X	Changes the channel to the currently selected channel without leaving the EPG (most useful in the alternate EPG).
?	Marks or unmarks the current channel as a favorite.
/ or 4	Toggles the guide listing between all channels and filtered favorites.

MythTV and Themes

Themes, often known as *skins*, are a way to change the look of the menus and dialogue boxes inside MythTV. You can stick with the default option, examine a set of pre-defined alternatives, find other themes elsewhere on the Web, or build your own themes. We lead you through this "theme park" in the sections that follow.

All About Themes

Three plain-text XML files define themes: theme.xml, qtlook.txt, and ui.xml. The theme is then rendered with source images such as a background, buttons, and more.

If you install the full MythTV package, a group of themes is included. You can choose among these in the MythTV frontend under Setup/Utilities → Setup → Appearance, on the first page, aptly titled Theme. Use the left and right arrow keys to preview themes via thumbnails, as shown in Figure 8-1. Once you've settled on a theme, navigate through to the end of the configuration pages and your selected theme will be applied.

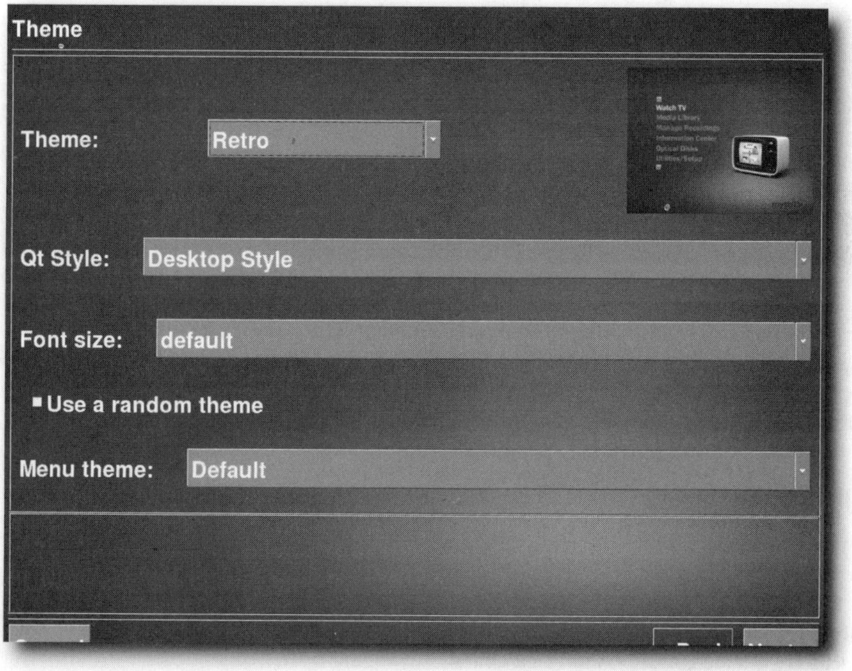

FIGURE 8-1: Select a theme

Hacking Out Your Own Themes

As we've already mentioned, themes really come from a group of XML files and images. Here's a little bit more information about what's what:

- `theme.xml` — This XML file describes the appearance of menus and specifies fonts.
- `qtlook.txt` — This file tells the Qt rendering library how to render basic controls and the main background image.
- `ui.xml` — This contains all the windows used by MythTV. There are separate `ui.xml` files for the plug-ins.

The images in a standard theme are optimized for 800 × 600 screen resolution. If you want to develop a theme for HDTV, use 1280 × 720 resolution instead. The fonts in MythTV are 100dpi to make them readable on a variety of display types. MythTV scales a theme to whatever resolution is currently in use.

Developing a theme can get quite complicated. For just about everything you'd need to know about theme construction, see www.mythtv.org/wiki/index.php/Theme_development_guide.

Adding Set-Top Box Support

Typically, with a cable television feed, you can get many of the channels you want simply by feeding a coaxial cable connection into a capture card and configuring it to use a cable frequency table. However, you will soon realize that there are many additional channels (typically, those numbered over 123) that you may also want to record, but you can only receive with them through your cable box. Satellite users must use their satellite boxes to tune in any channel. It's easy enough to output via S-Video or Composite video from your set-top box to an S-Video or Composite video input on a capture card (along with audio to appropriate inputs). The real trick lies in controlling the set-top box output (as in changing its channels). What's needed is a way for your MythTV box to send appropriate signals using one medium or another to your set-top box to run it remotely. As it turns out, there are several ways to accomplish this task.

FireWire

If you have either a Motorola 6000 series or a Scientific Atlanta 3250 series cable box, you should have at least one FireWire port on the box, which you can use to capture video and to transmit channel-change commands. If you've configured your cable box for capture over FireWire and defined the set-top box in `mythtv-setup`, you're already good to go. In that case, MythTV can already handle all channel-changing operations.

Serial-to-Serial

If you're not yet using a high-definition cable box, consider yourself lucky if your set-top box has a standard DB-9 serial port and your service provider has left it enabled. Some set-top boxes include the physical port but it isn't enabled. Alas, the only way to really know if it works is to try it. If you determine that the port is disabled, you may be able to call up your service provider and request them to enable it. It's probably simplest to tell them it's for your TiVo, rather than try to explain what MythTV is — regardless, some providers may still turn you down. Set-top boxes known to work nicely with a serial-to-serial setup include the fairly common Motorola DCT-2000 series cable boxes, which have standard DB-9 serial ports on them, and various DirecTV satellite boxes that have *data ports* on their rear panel, which are simply serial ports repackaged into a phone jack-like form factor.

If you do have access to a working serial port, changing channels is simple and cheap. You need a serial cable to connect from a serial port on the MythTV system that is recording to the serial port on the set-top box. In addition, of course, you need software that MythTV can use to send the necessary signals out of its serial port to the serial port on the set-top box. Several such programs are included with MythTV in its `contribs` directory (`/usr/share/doc/ mythtv-*/contribs/channel_changers/`).

A `dct2000serial.tar.gz` archive is distributed with MythTV. It works with the Motorola DCT-2000 series cable boxes. To use it, you'll need to install the `pyserial` package, which provides a serial port interface method written in the Python scripting language, which acts as a `dct2000serial` channel changer. This code may also be available in package form for your distribution as either `pyserial` or `python-serial`. If not, you can download and install it from `http://pyserial.sourceforge.net/` (documentation is also available on that site). Once the Python support is in place, expand the `dct2000serial.tar.gz` archive into `/usr/local/bin` as follows:

```
# cd /usr/local/bin
# tar xzvf /usr/share/doc/mythtv-*/contribs/channel_changers/
dct2000serial.tar.gz
```

Edit the `/usr/local/bin/changechannel.sh` SERIALPORT variable to reflect the correct serial port on the computer that you're using (it's likely to be either `/dev/ttyS0` or `ttyS1`, which equate to COM1 and COM2, respectively, in Windows-speak). With a serial cable in place, you can check whether your MythTV can control the set-top box by calling `channel change.sh` from the command line on your MythTV box, like this:

```
# changechannel.sh 005
```

If all goes well, your cable box should switch to channel 5 (the 00 padding is necessary to speed up the channel-change operation, assuming a cable box that handles channels into the 100s, but not into the 1000s — add another zero if the box handles four-digit channel numbers).

Fire up `mythtv-setup` and navigate to the Input connections section. For either the S-Video or Composite video input on the capture card that's tied to your set-top box's channel listings, adjust the field labeled External channel change command to read `/usr/local/bin/ changechannel.sh`, as shown in Figure 8-2.

For DirecTV receivers with a *data port*, you can make a simple 9-pin serial cable with this plug on one end, or you can buy one ready-made from various sources on the Internet.

For more information on serially controlled DirecTV receivers, visit the Direct Serial Control Utility page at `www.pcmx.net/dtvcon/`.

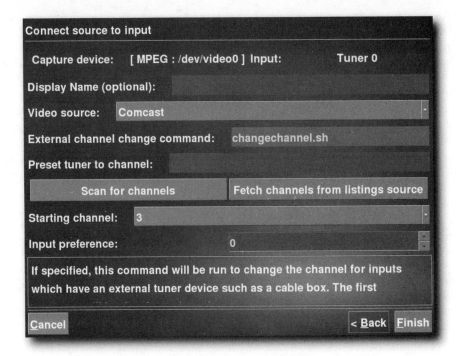

FIGURE 8-2: Configuring an external channel change command

For an alternative DirecTV channel change script that is updated regularly, visit www.pdp8 .net/directv/directv.shtml.

Serial-to-Infrared on Second LIRC Instance

Don't fret if you don't have a functioning serial port on your set-top box; there's hope for you yet! There exists a little device called an IR blaster you can use (see Figure 8-3). It's essentially a wire with a USB or serial connection on one end and an infrared transmitter on the other. You can buy one at a low cost ($15) from www.irblaster.info/ or any number of other online retailers. The official LIRC Web site even contains basic instructions if you wish to cobble together one on your own, at www.lirc.org/transmitters.html. The serial end plugs into an available serial port on your MythTV box, and the IR transmitter situated on your set-top box, near its infrared receiver. Commands go out the serial port and are converted to infrared, essentially making the set-top box think it's receiving instructions from its remote. Making this setup work isn't always the easiest thing to do, because you must juggle two instances of LIRC.

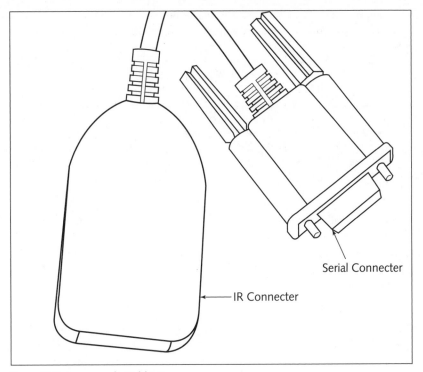

Serial Connecter

IR Connecter

FIGURE 8-3: An example IR blaster

The most common method to implement two LIRC instances is to clone and rename one instance from `lirc` to `remote`. This is actually pretty simple, courtesy of MythTV user Robert Wamble's HOW-TO (with lots of examples) on this subject. You can view all the details at `http://iwamble.net/IRBlaster_Howto.txt`, where you'll also find a script to convert an LIRC source tree into a `remote` source tree. There's even a preconverted source archive if you don't want to hassle with conversion yourself. Once you have the right set of sources, use the following setup process:

```
$ cd remote-<version>
$ ./setup.sh
```

First, select `1 Driver configuration` on the Mainmenu screen. Unfortunately, from here, the steps you need to follow vary quite a bit. For the `irblaster.info` variant, select `1 Home-brew (16x50 UART compatible serial port)`, then your COM port, and make sure that the With Transmitter Diode option is enabled. For the Actisys IR-200L/Act200L, select `6 IrDA hardware` after selecting `1 Driver configuration`, then `5 Actisys Act200L SIR driver support`, and finally your COM port. Other devices will require still other modifications.

Once you've returned to the Mainmenu screen, choose option 3, `Save configuration & run configure`. After you complete that step, you need to actually compile the `remote` source tree, as follows:

```
$ make
```

As we write this chapter, alas, the current `remote` source tree may encounter some interesting build failures. Luckily, they're easy to work around. The `make` will fail three times, each time on a `libtool: unrecognized option '--tag=CC'` error. If or when you get these errors, you should hit them first with `daemons/Makefile`, then `tools/Makefile`, and finally `doc/Makefile`. After the first failure, edit `daemons/Makefile`, removing both instances of `--tag=CC`, and rerun `make`. Rinse and repeat for the other two, and in the end you should be able to run the following:

```
# make install
```

Note that this will install a not-yet-renamed-so-as-not-to-collide-with-your-primary-LIRC utility into `/usr/local/bin/`, which you must fix immediately. Here's how:

```
# cd /usr/local/bin/
# for prog in ircat irexec irpty irrecord irsend irw irxevent
mode2 xmode2
> do
> mv $prog remote_$prog
> done
```

Next up, add some module setup options to `/etc/modprobe.conf` (or whatever your distribution uses). For the `irblaster.info-style` transmitter, add the following:

```
alias char-major-72 remote_serial
options remote_serial irq=4 io=0x3f8
install remote_serial /bin/setserial /dev/ttyS0 uart none; \
    /sbin/modprobe --ignore-install remote_serial
```

For the Actisys transmitter, make these `modprobe.conf` additions instead:

```
alias char-major-72 remote_sir
options remote_sir irq=4 io=0x3f8
install remote_sir /bin/setserial /dev/ttyS0 uart none; \
    /sbin/modprobe --ignore-install remote_sir
```

Note that both examples work with COM1. To use COM2, alter `irq` to 3, `io` to `0x2f8`, and switch to `ttyS1` instead of using `ttyS0`.

Out of the `contrib` subdirectory of your remote source tree, copy the appropriate initialization script (`remote.redhat` for Red Hat/Fedora, `remote.suse` for SUSE, and so on) into `/etc/init.d/`. You'll also need to locate the appropriate configuration file to emulate the right signals for your set-top box, which should be available in the archive available from `www.lirc.org/remotes.tar.bz2` (which contains more device files than the remotes subdirectory in the `lirc/remotes` main source archive). For example, if you have a Motorola DCT-2000-series cable box, the `motorola/DCT2000` file in the `remotes.tar.bz2` archive is what you're after. Move your appropriate `config` file to `/etc/remoted.conf`, and you should now be ready to fire up your transmitter for testing:

```
# /sbin/modprobe remote_serial
# /etc/init.d/remoted start
```

Replace `remote_serial` with `remote_sir` or whatever driver your transmitter requires.

To ensure that everything works and make it usable for MythTV, you'll need to scrape out the `change_channel.csh` and `channel.pl` scripts from `http://iwamble.net/IRBlaster_Howto.txt`. Copy their contents to new text files, place them in `/usr/local/bin/`, and make them executable like this:

```
# mv change_channel.csh /usr/local/bin/
# mv channel.pl /usr/local/bin/
# chmod +x /usr/local/bin/change_channel.csh
# chmod +x /usr/local/bin/channel.pl
```

In addition, be sure to edit `/usr/local/bin/channel.pl`, setting the `$remote_name` variable to the appropriate transmitter type, as defined in `/etc/remoted.conf` (in the preceding example, that would be `DCT2000`).

You should now be able to test your transmitter by running the `change_channel.csh` script from the command line. For example,

```
$ change_channel.csh 7
```

should switch your set-top box over to channel 7. Assuming it did, you've got everything you need to let MythTV control your set-top box. Fire up `mythtv-setup` and navigate into the Input connections section. For either the S-Video or Composite video input on the capture card that's tied to your set-top box's channel listings, adjust the field labeled External Channel Change Command to read `/usr/local/bin/change_channel.csh`. Be sure to enable your remoted transmitter daemon to run at system startup as well. On Fedora/Red Hat and SUSE, this should be as simple as the following:

```
# /sbin/chkconfig remoted on
```

Other distributions may use an init script management system other than `chkconfig` (Gentoo, Debian, Ubuntu, and KnoppMyth definitely do), so please consult your distribution documentation should you need any help on this front.

Serial-to-Infrared, Two Devices on One LIRC

A somewhat elusive setup — whose documentation went underground for a while, because the domain on which it resided (`lircsetup.com`) expired — is now detailed at www.htpcug.com/blaster.htm. This setup utilizes a single instance of LIRC to send and receive infrared signals. Rather than create a `remote` version of LIRC, build LIRC itself with the `--driver=any` and `--with-transmitter` options. Note that the `atrpms.net` LIRC binary packages for Fedora and Red Hat are built this way, too. Instead of configuring a `remote_serial` device, assign your receiver to LIRC's primary device number, and your transmitter to the second LIRC device number, using an `/etc/modprobe.conf` setup like the following, which assumes you're using the IR receiver on a PVR-250 and a serial IR transmitter on COM2:

```
alias char-major-61-0 lirc_i2c
alias char-major-61-1 lirc_serial
options lirc_serial irq=3 io=0x2f8
install lirc_serial setserial /dev/ttyS1 uart none; \
    modprobe --ignore-install lirc_serial
```

Put both your remote and transmitter definitions into /etc/lircd.conf, instead of splitting them between lircd.conf and remoted.conf, and then configure a second instance of lircd to start. The simplest way to do this is to fire it up from /etc/rc.local (for Fedora/Red Hat) or whatever works for your distribution, using this command:

```
/usr/sbin/lircd --driver=lirc_serial --device=/dev/lirc1 \
    --output=/dev/lircd1 --pidfile=/var/run/lircd1.pid
```

Set yourself up with a /usr/local/bin/change_chan.sh script that contains something like the following lines (here, we assume you're working with a Motorola DCT-2000 series cable box):

```
#!/bin/sh
REMOTE_NAME=DCT2000
For digit in $(echo $1 | sed -e 's/./& /g'); do
    irsend --device=/dev/lircd1 SEND_ONCE $REMOTE_NAME $digit
    sleep 0.4 # may need adjustment for your device
done
    irsend --device=/dev/lircd1 SEND_ONCE $REMOTE_NAME OK
```

Give it a try, and assuming it works, enter /usr/local/bin/change_chan.sh as your channel-change command in mythtv-setup. Please see www.htpcug.com/lircsetup_com.htm for additional assistance.

Note that you can also find patches to LIRC for some multi-function devices that support both receive and transmit capabilities, but none of them exist in LIRC itself as of this writing. Some of the more popular ones are the USB-UIRT and the IR Blaster shipped with some PVR-150 cards. You can find information about these using your friendly neighborhood Internet search engine.

Serial-to-Infrared without LIRC

If your set-top box lacks a serial port and you don't want to hassle with configuring multiple copies of lirc, there's still hope, though it comes at a price — it's roughly $45, instead of $15. The MyBlaster/Serial, from www.mytvstore.com/product_id_004.html, coupled with the scripts put together by an enterprising MythTV and MyBlaster user, will do the trick (the scripts are also now available from the manufacturer's site at www.mytvstore.com/mythtv_linux.html). You should buy the unit, configure it for your set-top box as per the MyBlaster manual, and then use the MyBlaster.pl script to change channels, in much the same way as you would for other devices previously covered in this section of the book.

Shutdown/Wakeup Commands

MythTV can shut itself down with nearly all power off, as a way to conserve power. This reduces heat output, and reduces possible wear and tear on your home theater PC, which makes it good for the machine as well as the environment. When it comes time to record something, MythTV boots up and prepares to record the program. Of course, MythTV won't fall asleep in the middle of a task: To use this option, no recording can be taking place, no client may be connected to the server (if you have more than one MythTV computer), and no recording can be scheduled during whatever sleep time you specify in your MythTV setup.

To wake up a MythTV system you have two options: Wake-on-LAN (WoL) or BIOS Wakeup. Configure these in mythtv-setup in the General settings on the fourth page:

- **Wake-on-LAN** is a feature found on just about any modern motherboard with an integrated network interface. The BIOS keeps a trickle of power flowing to the network connection and waits for a special packet type that triggers a boot-up. This means that you need another PC to be running 24/7, perhaps a file server or a custom firewall/router box, to send the wakeup packet when the time comes to prepare to record something.

- **BIOS wakeup** is easier to implement and requires no other PC to send a wakeup command. This method uses an entry in your motherboard's BIOS settings to set a wakeup time. Just about any motherboard made in the last eight years has this kind of power management option. The tool you need is called NVRAM WakeUp, available at `http://sourceforge.net/projects/nvram-wakeup`.

Not every motherboard has been tested but most should work. To help you decide whether this tool will work on your motherboard, the NVRAM WakeUp Website offers a listing of user-tested motherboards.

After installing nvram-wakeup, run `/usr/sbin/guess-helper` as root. This checks to ensure that nvram-wakeup works with your motherboard. If it does work properly, this program will write a configuration file for nvram-wakeup to use.

MythTV Setup for Wakeup

To access the wakeup options, run `mythtv-setup` and choose option 1, General. The setting to change is on the third page of settings; click Next until you arrive at the screen depicted in Figure 8-4.

Here's a rundown of the various parameters you can use with the wakeup utility:

- **Idle timeout (secs)** — This sets the time the server will wait after being idle until a shutdown occurs.

- **Max. wait for recording (min)** — This is used to give MythTV a rule about when to shut down if a recording is coming up. This value, in minutes, tells it not to shut down if a recording is x minutes away. For example: If this parameter is set to 20, then MythTV will not shut down your system at any time preceding an upcoming recording scheduled to start within the next 20 minutes.

- **Startup before rec. (secs)** — This option sets how long before a programmed recording the MythTV system will be woken up. You'll want to set this to slightly more than the time your HTPC takes to boot up.

- **Wakeup time format** — This is the format of the wakeup time for passing to the program you have set in the next option, Set wakeuptime command. The default of `time_t` works for our needs.

- **Set wakeuptime command** — This is the command executed to set the new `wakeuptime`. This is really just a pointer to a script, which is generally called `/usr/bin/mythsettime $time`.

- **Server halt command** — This is the script that will be called to stop your MythTV box and shut it down.

- **Pre Shutdown check-command** — This script is used to check for running tasks; if MythTV is busy doing something in the background such as converting a recording into another format, then the pre-shutdown check will pass an error and your system won't shut down.

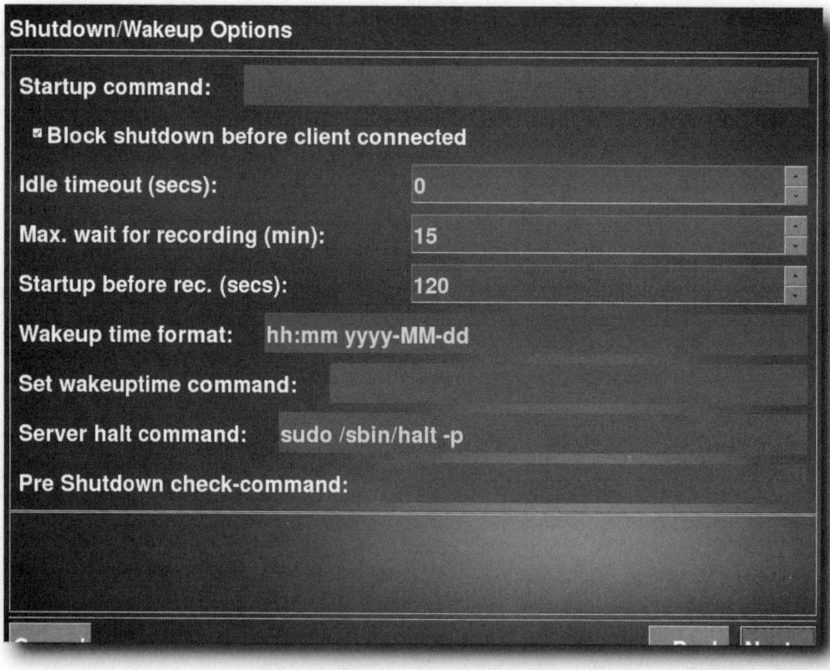

Shutdown/Wakeup Options

Startup command:

☑ **Block shutdown before client connected**

Idle timeout (secs):   0

Max. wait for recording (min):   15

Startup before rec. (secs):   120

Wakeup time format: hh:mm yyyy-MM-dd

Set wakeuptime command:

Server halt command: sudo /sbin/halt -p

Pre Shutdown check-command:

FIGURE 8-4: The Shutdown/Wakeup Options screen

For script examples and ideas for enabling the power button on your remote to shut down your MythTV HTPC, see http://svn.wilsonet.com/projects/mythtvology/ticket/40.

Recording with MythTV

When you select a show to record from the program guide, you have one of eight different types of recording options:

- **Single Record** — This option records the specific instance you choose from the TV guide.

- **Find One** — MythTV will find the first listing for the show you chose and record it, regardless of whether it is a new or repeat episode, or which channel it is on.

- **Record Weekly** — This option records a show on the specified channel and time of day once per week that you select. For example, if you selected a show that airs on Channel 5 at 11:00 A.M. on Tuesday, MythTV will record it every Tuesday at 11:00 A.M.

- **Find Weekly** — This option records a show once per week from any of the times that appear in the TV guide. This option just picks a showing of your TV program that ideally doesn't conflict with another scheduled recording, and records it once a week.

- **Record Daily** — This option records a show on the specified channel and time of day any day of the week. For example, if you want to record all episodes of *Friends* on TBS but only the 8:00 p.m. showings, you should use Record Daily.

- **Find Daily** — This option records a show once per day from any of the times that appear in the TV guide. Much like Find One, this finds a showing of your TV program from any point in time on any channel that ideally doesn't conflict, and records it once a day.

- **Channel Record** — This option records a show any time the title is listed on a chosen channel. For example, this would record *Friends* any time it is on TBS, but not on NBC, WGN, or my local WB affiliate that airs repeats.

- **Record All** — This is a wildcard; MythTV will record the show any time, any day, on any channel it finds in your TV guide.

Obviously, you'll want to use the option that represents the kind of recording you wish to make when you schedule a recording to occur.

Inevitably, most MythTV systems run into a situation where scheduled recordings conflict with one another. Until you have the chance to add additional tuner cards so that can't happen, you should be happy to note that MythTV has some smarts to help deal with such problems.

Priorities

By default, every scheduled recording takes the same priority — namely, zero (0). You can then set a numerical value higher or lower than zero to increase/decrease the priority of a show. You might want to make your "can't miss" shows twos (2), other shows you like ones (1), and any other shows you would prefer to have for fun minus ones (-1).

You can select the weighting in a few different ways:

- A priority field in the Scheduling Options section of the options page will show you all recordings with their associated priority values. You can set a priority for a specific show or per recording type. With the latter, you can give the highest priority to Single Record, for example, so that all your one-time recordings will get preference. To set this option, select Setup → TV Settings → Recording Priorities → General.

- Channel Priorities can be useful if you prefer to record a show or shows on certain channels. For example, on satellite TV there are often double feeds — one for the west coast and another for the east coast — and you may have a preference about which feed to use to avoid interrupting other recordings. The Channel Priorities are set in Setup → TV Settings → Recording Priorities → Channel Priorities.

- The last way to prioritize is to set the priority for a capture card. This has two major applications: First, you can set your HDTV tuner with a higher priority than your standard analog tuner so shows that broadcast in high definition always take priority over their analog brethren. Second, if you have a mixed-source setup with two tuners, whereby one is cable and the other is satellite, both may have access to the same channels (for example, both get Cartoon Network). In that case, you might prefer to record from the satellite if possible because the signal is cleaner. These are set in mythtv-setup under the Input Connections section, where the relevant setting is called Input preference.

Duplicates

Single recordings don't care about duplication because they are manual recordings that you set yourself, but other options such as Record Weekly, Record Daily, and Channel Record, do take repeats into account. By default, they will not record any shows that have aired within the last 14 days, on the assumption that later rebroadcasts are repeats of the same episode. However, if no specific episode information is provided, then MythTV records such rebroadcasts just to be safe because such "unmarked episodes" may be new ones. If, however, you specifically set Record New Episodes Only, when program listings do not include specific data, associated programs will indeed be skipped as repeats.

If you notice a show you wish to record that constantly lacks proper guide information, MythTV has an answer for that, too. The Find One, Find Daily, and Find Weekly options are oblivious to specific program details. They just look at the name of a TV show and record anything that matches.

Conflicts

If you have more than one capture card with a source that can record the scheduled program, MythTV tries to use whichever one is available. If none is free when the scheduled program is slated, MythTV falls back to the priority scheme mentioned earlier. This explains why more levels of prioritization enable MythTV to handle conflicts better, which makes it most likely to record what you want most, and skip what you want least.

Working with Upcoming Recordings

The Scheduled Recordings screen (see Figure 8-5) enables you to check whether there are any conflicts on your selections and manually resolve conflicts if you so choose. To use this option, select Manage Recordings → Scheduled Recordings.

You are presented with a list of recordings. List items (recordings) are color-coded to help you check at a glance how those recordings will proceed. The most important color is yellow, because it signifies that some kind of conflict has been detected.

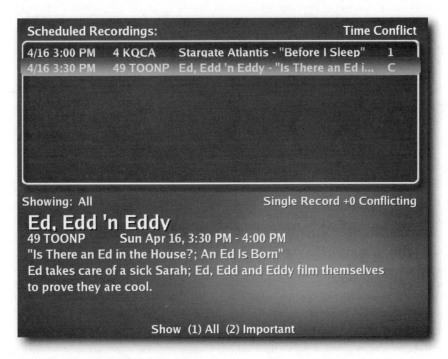

FIGURE 8-5: The Scheduled Recordings screen

To the right of the show's name you can see a status code. Numbers indicate which card has been assigned to record a show. Letters indicate a reason why something won't be recorded. Just below the box you'll find a short status message for the highlighted item, indicating what type of record rule was matched, the "total priority" for this show, and a one- or two-word explanation for the status code. If you highlight an entry with the arrow keys or your remote, you will see more information about its status.

The two codes to watch for are C and L. C means there are more shows than TV tuners available to record them. L means that MythTV knows a scheduled recording has a repeat later, which enables that show to be recorded later to avoid conflict.

Select a program and use the Info key (I on the keyboard) to see options available. The options screen enables you to resolve conflicts, extend recording length, and more. Edit Options changes options for an existing recording rule. That means changes apply to the rule as a whole, not just this single instance of its application. If you want to tweak only one upcoming recording, use Add Override instead. Afterward, Clear Override lets you undo any changes you made.

To cancel a single recording, select Don't Record. This cancels the current recording but doesn't cancel any rules that apply to future recordings. Never Record is an option that works when MythTV has access to valid episode information. It enables you to tell MythTV you don't want to record one specific episode, but other episodes will be recorded as rules apply.

For a recording in progress there is a Change Ending Time button. This enables you to extend the time window for a recording. It can come in handy when live events run long.

Note Changing the end time of a recording affects everything scheduled thereafter. Such a change may trigger new conflicts. If you make such changes on-the-fly, be prepared to sacrifice other recordings, especially if you only have one TV card installed in your MythTV PC.

Advanced Options

MythTV's TV listings are really just an SQL database. This infrastructure enables MythTV to offer a special query builder for finding and recording shows called Custom Record, shown in Figure 8-6. To access Custom Record, select Manage Recordings → Schedule Recordings → Custom Record.

The topmost field is Edit Rule. This is for selecting an existing rule or creating a new rule. Rule Name is an editable field in which you can give a query a nice name you'll remember, so you can reuse it later if desired. The next field has a drop-down list of pre-defined query strings to help you build whatever search you need. Most are quite useful, such as Only in Primetime and First Run Only. Just below the query strings field is a display of what your SQL query code looks like. Don't edit this text: It's just an illustration of your query in progress.

As the button name implies, Add This Example Clause adds the query clause displayed above it to the query builder field beneath it. In the bottom field of this window is a box for text editing, where you can edit the various statements to meet your needs.

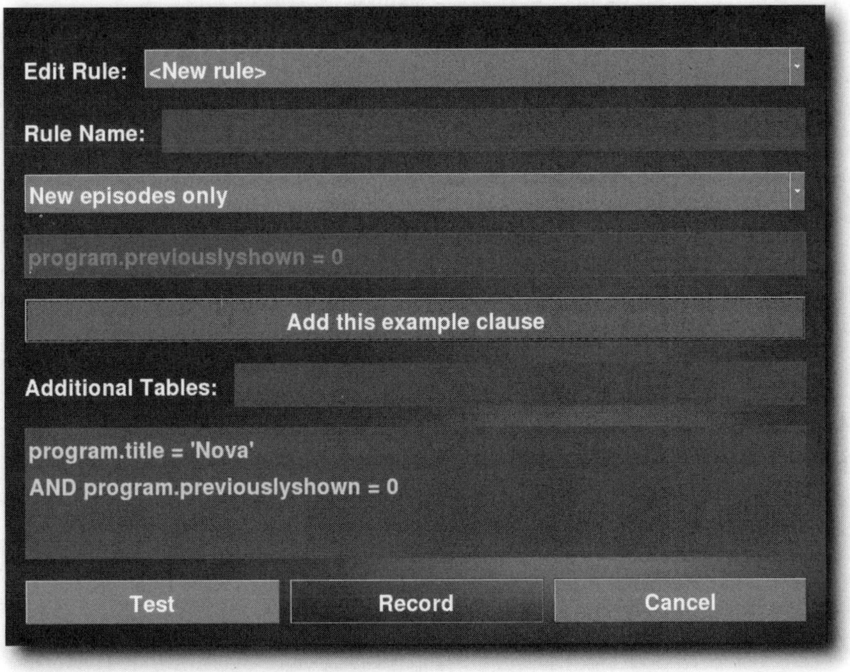

FIGURE 8-6: The Custom Recordings screen

When you are done, select the Test button. This tests the query and presents you with a list of what conforms to the rules you have defined. If this produces the results you expected, choose Record. If not, go back and add or remove rules until you get what you want. At any time, Cancel backs out of the Custom Recordings screen without saving any changes.

Some of the more advanced and less obvious statements include the following:

- `program.category_type` — This is one of four types: `movie`, `series`, `sports`, or `tvshow`.

- `program.stars` — This is a number from 0.0 to 1.0. On a four-star scale, 1.0 would be four stars, 0.75 would be three stars, and so on. This value derives from program guide ranking data. If that data is absent, no value will appear.

- `program.originalairdate` — Given valid program guide data, the original air date may be used to select a specific TV episode. A website such as www.TV.com should have this information for older shows.

- `program.previouslyshow` — This is a 0 or 1 flag. Zero means MythTV is not aware that the show has been aired, or that it hasn't aired in the past two weeks. This can be useful because you can either exclude repeats by matching on 0, or look only for repeats by matching on 1.

- `program.programid`—For entries other than EP, the last four digits are 0000. With EP, the last four digits match the episode number in a series. Tribune, not the show's producers, generate these, but they are usually in the same order as the episodes' original air dates.

Final Thoughts

There's a lot to learn about scheduling and managing recordings in MythTV. But there's no lack of expressive capability or power; the real trick is to learn how to make and use recording rules properly.

MythTV Plug-ins

Although TV was the driving impetus behind the development of MythTV, there's more to this beast than recording and watching TV programs. MythTV gains its abilities to deal with digital music, photos, DVDs, newsfeeds, and more through the addition of plug-ins that extend the basic MythTV framework to support the necessary features and functions that these types of media or information require.

Chapter 9 provides an overview of all twelve of MythTV's built-in plug-ins, which cover a range of functions — from surfing the Web (MythBrowser) to keeping up with the latest newsfeeds (MythNews) and weather (MythWeather), along with information about unofficial plug-ins. Although we only have enough space to provide brief descriptions and representative screenshots to highlight what these plug-ins can do, you should emerge from this chapter reasonably aware that plugs-in account for much of MythTV's flair and panache.

Chapter 10 narrows its focus onto the MythDVD plug-in, which enables you to transcode (to decode from one digital video format and re-encode into another, usually from some non-native format into MythTV's native .nuv format, or vice versa) video files on-the-fly. This enables almost any media player to work well with MythTV, but the default choice (and the focus of much of our coverage in that chapter) is the xine player.

Chapter 11 digs into MythGallery, a tool for cataloging, organizing, and displaying digital photographs that works with most well-known digital image formats. You can use this to put your digital photo albums in order, or to test the tolerance of friends and family to extended shots of Junior and Fido sharing a meal together.

Chapter 12 opens your ears to the magic of MythMusic, MythTV's digital music manager. This tool helps you acquire, organize, catalog, and listen to digital music. Like MythGallery, it works with most major, well-recognized digital music formats.

Chapter 13 deals with MythVideo, MythTV's tool for acquiring, organizing, cataloging, and playing back videos of all kinds. As with several other components, MythVideo is format agnostic and works with most major, well-recognized digital formats

Chapter 14 tackles the marvelous and miscellaneous other plug-ins that MythTV supports. In addition to covering items from Chapter 9 that don't merit their own individual chapters, you'll also learn about some of the more interesting plug-ins and add-ons that you might want to include in your MythTV environment. And if that isn't enough to satisfy your appetite for such bells and whistles, we'll also tell you where to look for more plug-ins and add-ons as well.

Plug-Ins Overview

By now, you should be quite comfortable with the concept of a mythical home convergence system, and how MythTV fulfills that promise. A large part of that fulfillment is due to the modular framework underlying MythTV applications. This highly flexible, easily adaptable framework inclines MythTV systems to new and creative uses unthinkable in canned capture systems.

In this chapter, we explore the plug-in components for MythTV and describe the capacities and functions of each one. We also give you a small taste of what's possible using MythTV's plug-in architecture. Without a modular framework, MythTV would fail to qualify as a convergent technology appliance.

What Is a Plug-in?

A *plug-in* may be generically defined as a stand-alone, supplementary software component that modifies the behavior or functionality of an existing application by improving, extending, or adding to existing features or capabilities. Any plug-in architecture depends on a well-defined API and seeks to make use of existing program functionality by enhancing or extending its parameters. This modular framework frees the application from potential constraints, opens the architecture to new uses, and promotes rapid development of new software.

First popularized by industry-standard imaging and Web browsing programs, plug-ins have evolved into bustling market segments of their own. The ever-popular Mozilla Firefox Web browser is just one example of many whereby users routinely exploit a plug-in architecture to great benefit. Fortunately for you, MythTV implements its own plug-in API, which in turn provides much of MythTV's functionality.

Plug-ins List

Prior to MythTV release 0.18, users had no choice but to manually select among a handful of readily available plug-ins one at a time, as needed. Clearly, this arrangement leaves something to be desired because so many newcomers to Linux find the compilation process both tedious and challenging. Today, only three main packages make up the core MythTV system (there used to be 11 such packages), while a comprehensive top-level script coordinates configuration and compilation settings among the many MythTV plug-ins.

One of these three primary packages contains current, quasi-official MythTV plug-ins and is aptly named mythplugins. At present, the plug-ins in this package provide the most popular and frequently used functions, but more are under development all the time, and new ones are likely to be added to the official list from time to time as circumstances and public demand may decree.

Remember that MythTV is brought to you by the open-source community, and that means development happens less rapidly than you might expect in a commercial product. By the same token, you can take part in the development process (given the right qualifications) and can incorporate additional functionality however you see fit. To quote from the MythTV User Wish List page (`www.mythtv.org/wiki/index.php/User_Wish_List`), "MythTV is a project by developers, for developers." But even if you're not a developer, there's still a lot to gain from working with MythTV plug-ins, and from contributing your ideas and input to the total MythTV user (and developer) community).

Official MythTV Plug-in Components

The official core plug-in package for MythTV (mythplugins) bundles some of the more practical and accepted components to extend its frontend functionality. As core components, these plug-ins are available in a single archive directly from the distributor site either in the form of an RPM or as source code.

The following command sequence obtains the current development revision of the MythTV plug-ins package from the mythtv.org Subversion server:

```
$ svn co http://cvs.mythtv.org/svn/trunk/mythplugins
$ cd mythplugins
$ ./configure --enable-all --prefix=/usr
$ qmake mythplugins.pro
$ make all
$ /usr/bin/sudo make install
```

First you must check out the sources, change into the newly created mythplugins directory, and configure the local compiler scripts. Then, run qmake and make applications to begin the process of building each plug-in for your MythTV host. Finally, sudo enables you to execute administrative tasks from a lesser-capable account (such as the mythtv user) so you may install the newly created plug-ins package. All of the following plug-ins require a current MythTV installation in proper working order before you can install or use them:

- **MythBrowser** is a module that acts as a gateway for viewing Internet content. MythBrowser enables users to browse the Internet from inside the MythTV interface, and is designed to permit browsing under remote or keyboard control. Figure 9-1 demonstrates MythBrowser in action at the Freshmeat project repository.

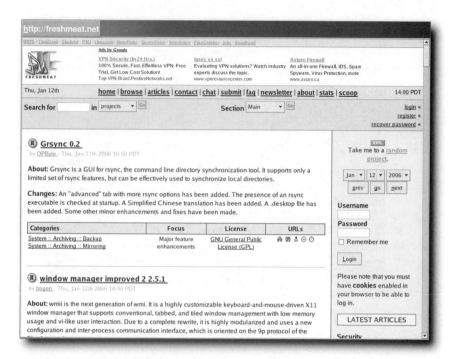

FIGURE 9-1: Browsing the Freshmeat project repository

- **MythControls** is a collection of top-level configuration settings for the MythTV frontend. The MythControls plug-in provides a top-level menu option to configure keybindings directly for MythTV. This is much simpler than having to go through MythWeb or editing configuration files by hand, and explains why many developers and users had trouble believing this capability wasn't already supported in MythTV. It is hoped that this item will go through testing quickly, and make its way into the official plug-ins collection soon.

- **MythDVD** is a plug-in that enables you to use `mythfrontend` as a DVD/VCD player and ripper. Playback is enabled through any number of Linux-compatible external players such as Xine, Ogle, or the ever-present mplayer. MythDVD can extract the volume title from a DVD image as an MPEG-4 AVI formatted file and introduce it to your MythVideo collection. A variety of options are available for MythDVD so that you can achieve a balance between storage space and playback quality (see Figure 9-2).

- **MythFlix** enables MythTV to interact with the Netflix online rental service. Subscribers to Netflix's online video rental services will rejoice once this new addition reaches production status. The MythFlix plug-in enables users to interact with the Netflix service through the MythTV interface.

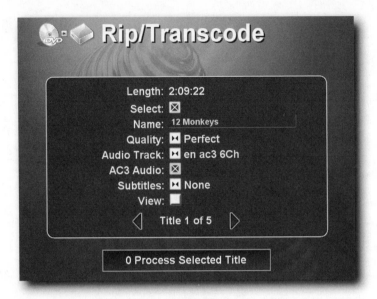

FIGURE 9-2: Transcoding a DVD in real time

- **MythGallery** is a plug-in that enables you to view your digital photos. MythGallery organizes a collection of on-disk images for display as an index of thumbnail images or a moving slide show (see Figure 9-3).

- **MythGame** is a plug-in that enables you to run different emulators and games from within MythTV. MythGame provides the interface between Linux-based game emulators (such as Xmame, Xmess, Snes9x, and others) so you can play old-school arcade games within MythTV (see Figure 9-4). See www.mameworld.net for more information on Mame.

Note   During our configuration of MythTV we encountered problems with the latest Xmame revisions. MythTV won't run the latest Xmame binaries. We found that backing away from the latest version to the last known good version (Xmame v0.97) was the only way to install a working game emulator plug-in. By the time you read this, it is hoped that the situation will have changed (either by fixing the v0.102 version that caused our heartburn, or by creating a newer working version).

FIGURE 9-3: MythGallery picture slide show and thumbnail index

FIGURE 9-4: Browse your game collection with the MythGame interface.

- **MythMusic** is a plug-in that enables you to listen to your MP3 collection (see Figure 9-5). You can even watch visualizations should you choose to turn them on. MythMusic permits nickelodeon-style audio playback for MPEG-3 compressed audio streams, and includes support for OGG Vorbis audio files as well.

- **MythNews** is a module that supplies MythTV users with ready access to RSS (Really Simple Syndication) newsfeeds, selecting newsfeeds, and so forth. MythNews permits you to sign up with XML/RSS newsfeeds that can stream breaking headlines in real time for viewing inside MythBrowser (see Figure 9-6).

- **MythPhone** is a plug-in that enables you to make and receive Internet-based phone calls (Voice over IP, aka VoIP) within MythTV. MythPhone combines Internet telephony services with the MythTV frontend so that MythTV end-users may place and receive audio and video phone calls through MythTV using the standard Session Initiation Protocol (SIP). MythPhone registers with the Free World Dial-up (FWD) service available through `http://pulver.com` and allows you to place phone calls through MythTV.

FIGURE 9-5: MythMusic playlist editor and music jukebox

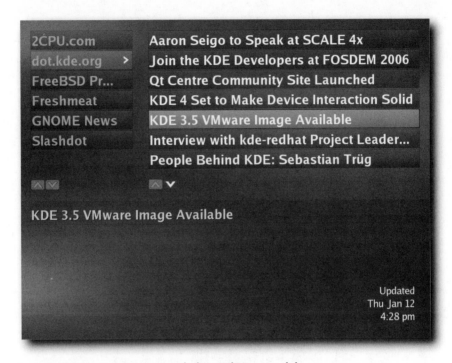

FIGURE 9-6: Browsing RSS news with the MythNews module

- **MythVideo** is a plug-in for managing video content not recorded inside MythTV itself.
  MythVideo catalogs video archives on disk, performs metadata look-ups from the
  IMDB (the international movie database, including poster art), and can even play a vari-
  ety of video file formats (see Figure 9-7). MythVideo provides Browse, Tree, and
  Category viewing of its cataloged content. It can use MythTV's internal playback
  engine, xine, or mplayer to display video.

- **MythWeather** is a plug-in you can use to obtain weather reports from online resources.
  MythWeather provides local weather forecasting for your locale (or wherever you specify
  in your MythTV configuration). You can grab the latest Doppler weather radar reports
  from online resources, daily and weekly forecasts, geographical map topographies, and
  much more (see Figure 9-8).

FIGURE 9-7: Grab IMDB movie metadata with MythVideo.

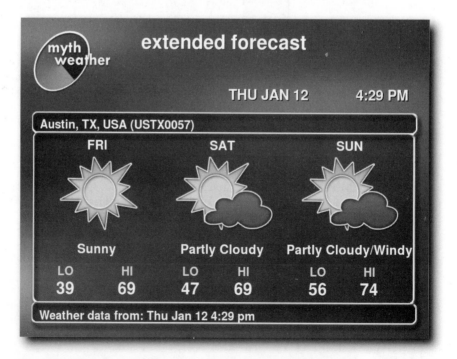

FIGURE 9-8: Obtain local Doppler radar weather data with MythWeather.

- **MythWeb** is a set of HTML pages and PHP scripts you can use to control MythTV, MythMusic, and MythVideo (see Figure 9-9). MythWeb acts as a frontend to the MythTV backend, and allows users to schedule and manage television recordings through a convenient Web interface. You can also use it to modify keybindings within MythWeb, and to interact with other plug-in modules within MythTV. You can even run these scripts as scheduled tasks, so you can drive MythTV without actually laying hands on the keyboard as those tasks are underway.

FIGURE 9-9: View and control MythTV from MythWeb.

Unofficial MythTV Plug-ins

A lot of developers have built plug-ins for MythTV, but only a fraction of these have attained official status, either as production or beta components. The items in this section are MythTV plug-ins available from sources other than MythTV.org but that may be worth digging into and using if you can get them to work and are happy with how they behave in your installation. We're especially keen on MythRecipe and MythFM; the others have their adherents and aficionados as well.

Frontend Plug-ins

- **MythBurnUI** (http://sourceforge.net/projects/mythburn/) enables you to burn recorded TV shows. You can also include menus, sound tracks, and chapter points.

- **MythMail** (http://mythextra.napsi.net/mythMail.html) is a Post Office Protocol 3 (POP3) client for mythfrontend, for browsing and deleting content from Web-based e-mail accounts.

- **MythRecipe** (http://mythextra.napsi.net/mythRecipe.html) enables you to view, bookmark, and filter Internet-obtained recipe collections selectively while listening to ambient background music (presumably, while preparing your favorite meals).

- **MythKaraoke** (http://mythextra.napsi.net/mythKaraoke.html) enables you to sing along to music with MythTV.

- **MythFM** (http://mythextra.napsi.net/mythFM.html) enables you to listen to FM radio using a Linux-compatible FM receiver.

- **MythStream** (http://home.kabelfoon.nl/~moongies/streamtuned.html) enables you to stream audio and video over the network using mplayer as a backend, and locate resources by URL, playlist, static Web page content, or XML/RSS newsfeeds.

- **MythCalendar** (www.wombatinvasion.com/pmwiki/pmwiki.php/MythTV/MythCalendar). The MythTV calendar system provides at-a-glance information based on the day, week, and month.

- **MythTiVo** (http://tivo-mplayer.sourceforge.net/mythtivo.html) is a GUI frontend for networking TiVo to MythTV and playing Now Showing items from anywhere within the network.

Add-ons for MythTV Plug-ins

Just to make things more interesting, plug-ins can themselves be extended by festooning these widgets with their own add-on code. Thus, the items detailed in this section can't really work by themselves, but can only do their thing if you've already installed the plug-in whose functionality they extend, enhance, or otherwise monkey around with.

- **MythNotify** is an add-on for onscreen display of Caller ID information inside MythTV. MythNotify notifies MythTV users about incoming phone calls and any relevant information provided by the Caller ID system. This happens in real time while live television is onscreen. While MythTV is part of the mythplugins core package, this item appears to be a supplemental component for the MythPhone plug-in. See www.mythtv.org/wiki/index.php/Setting_up_MythNotify for information on setting up your MythTV host to receive incoming phone calls.

- **MythBurn** is a collection of software and script extensions to MythTV for burning DVDs and creating DVD metadata content. MythBurn enables you to burn recordings onto DVD-R media, complete with animated menus, chapter points, and sound tracks. Check out the following sites for more details:

  `http://mythburn.sourceforge.net/`

  `http://sourceforge.net/projects/mythburn/`

  `http://mabene.icomedias.com/mythburn/`

  `www.knoppmythwiki.org/index.php?page=MythTVBurn_Scripts_HowTo`

- **MythStreamTV** (`http://mythstreamtv.sourceforge.net/`) is a module for manipulating and rebroadcasting live video streams. MythStreamTV transcodes and streams live MPEG-1/2 feeds to Windows Media Player or the Linux-based Media Player (mplayer), whereby all such streams may be controlled through the MythWeb interface.

Final Thoughts

This chapter has presented our overview of currently available plug-ins and add-ons that you may want to include in your MythTV system build. In subsequent chapters, we give more thorough treatment to what we believe are the most useful and popular MythTV plug-ins.

MythDVD

chapter

10

in this chapter

☑ Introducing MythDVD

☑ MythDVD prerequisites

☑ Understanding DVD playback options

☑ Working with xine

☑ Saving DVDs to your hard drive

MythDVD is one of the most important modules that enable the MythTV environment to deliver a complete media center feature set. MythDVD provides your portal to playing back DVD media, but it can also store DVDs on your hard drive, and offers something of a video kiosk's capabilities to let you choose and view any DVD on demand. MythDVD integrates with MythTV seamlessly inside the Optical Disks menu tree, and provides support for the Play DVD and Import DVD menu entries, as shown in Figure 10-1.

Prerequisites for MythDVD

Most Linux distributions are pretty good at detecting a DVD drive, and will typically create a link from the real device name for your DVD drive to /dev/dvd. If you have more than one optical device, however, this may be linked to a device other than the one you plan to use. If you've installed multiple optical drives in your MythTV system, stick a CD in each drive, and then check to see which one shows up when you mount /dev/dvd. If you don't see a /dev/dvd entry, you can make one for an appropriate optical device using a command like this one:

```
ln -s /dev/cdrom /dev/dvd
```

If your system includes multiple CD/DVD drives, the first device specification might look something like /dev/cdrom1 instead (or some number other than one, depending on which drive you actually want to use).

Before you can play back commercial DVD video discs, you must install LibDVDCSS, which allows proper CSS key exchange.

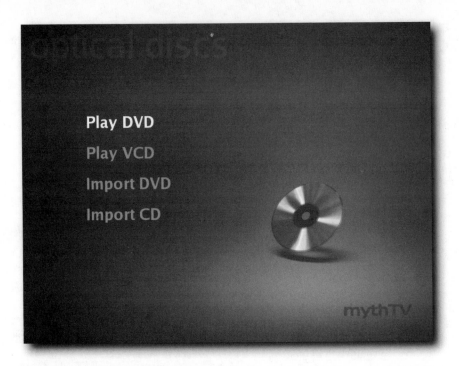

FIGURE 10-1: The MythTV Optical Discs menu

Note CSS stands for *content scrambling system*. According to most experts, it's a weak form of encryption used to alter the contents of commercial movie DVDs so that they can't be played back without accessing a special key that helps unscramble the encryption. Thus, tools such as LibDVDCSS are designed to enable proper playback of otherwise scrambled DVD content. For more information on this fascinating subject, visit DeCSS Central (`www.lemuria.org/ DeCSS`) and `developers.videolan.org/libdvdcss/`.

Understanding Your DVD Playback Options

MythTV in and of itself doesn't play DVDs. Rather, it is a frontend that harnesses a media player for behind-the-scenes duty. MythDVD has preset command-line launchers for three different DVD player programs: MPlayer, xine, and ogle. You specify your preferred DVD player in the DVD Player Settings screen, as shown in Figure 10-2.

FIGURE 10-2: The MythDVD Player Settings screen

MPlayer is a rudimentary media player. It even lacks its own configuration screen — all options must be supplied as command-line parameters — and MPlayer does not support a complete range of DVD playback features. When you choose Play, MPlayer simply starts the main feature. To obtain access to menus, introductions, side commentary, or outtakes and other features, you'll want to use a different media player instead. Fortunately, there are two candidates for MythTV that do support such capabilities, ogle and xine.

Ogle was developed as a cross-platform open-source DVD player program, and includes all proper support for DVD menus and navigation. It is still under development, however, and still missing some important features — such as advanced deinterlacing — that xine does support.

Xine is a mature, advanced media player. Among other features, it includes DVD menu and navigation support, robust onscreen display information, plus a handy configuration screen that enables access to options such as post-processing deinterlacing and S/PDIF passthrough. Today, xine is probably your best choice for DVD playback inside MythTV, so the following sections provide more detail on this media player.

Tip To replace `MPlayer` with `xine` on your MythTV system, use this command: `xine -pfhq --no-splash dvd://`.

Enter the command in Utilities/Setup → Setup → Media Settings → DVD Settings → Play Settings.

Working with xine

`xine` consists of two basic components. `xine-lib` is the core. You'll also need to get `xine-ui`, which gives xine a proper user interface so you can configure the software, and troubleshoot it outside of MythTV if necessary.

Setting Up xine for S/PDIF Passthrough

Most users will integrate their new MythTV HTPC into an existing home theater setup with surround-sound speakers. The best way to play back your DVD's soundtrack through a home theater system is to maintain a pure digital signal until it is decoded and sent to the speakers. That explains why S/PDIF (Sony/Philips Digital InterFace) digital output is the method that works best, and is therefore the method that most people will use. To set xine to use S/PDIF passthrough, you need to open the xine setup screen by right-clicking the video display. The xine setup screen appears with tabs across the top for various options, as shown in Figure 10-3.

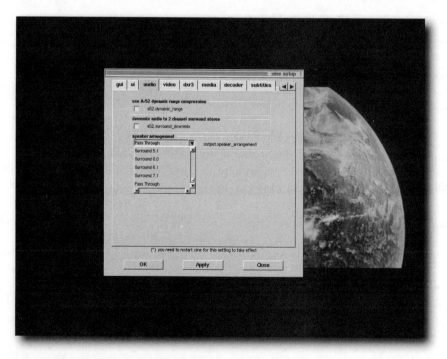

FIGURE 10-3: xine S/PDIF setup screen

xine Keyboard Commands

Table 10-1 shows a list of xine keyboard commands and shortcuts you can use to drive this valuable, full-featured program.

Table 10-1   xine Keyboard Commands

Key	Command
Enter	Play
Spacebar	Pause
Up/Down	Fast forward/slow motion
0-9	Enter the corresponding digit
/	Seek the % relative to the number previously entered
Left/Right	Seek -+ 15 sec (+Ctrl: 60 sec)
PageUp/Prior	Jump to previous playlist entry
PageDown/Next	Jump to next playlist entry
f	Toggle fullscreen mode
a	Toggle aspect ratio (AUTO/16:9/4:3/DVB)
i	Toggle interlaced mode
p	Pause/play
z / Shift+Z	Zoom into/out of video (add Ctrl to zoom horizontally or Alt to zoom vertically)
"<", ">"	Modify output window size
+ -	Change audio channel
, .	Change subtitle channel
n m	Adjust a/v sync
Home	Reset a/v sync
Insert	Toggle mouse cursor grabbing in the video output window
Esc or q	Quit

Saving DVDs to Your Hard Drive

To save a DVD's contents on your hard drive, you must start the Myth Transcoding Daemon (MTD). Add a line like the following to your `rc.local` file to make the daemon load during system startup:

```
/usr/bin/mtd --daemon
```

Now when you insert a DVD, you can choose to play it or save it to your hard drive by selecting Rip DVD from the Optical Discs menu. The Rip/Transcode screen is shown in Figure 10-4.

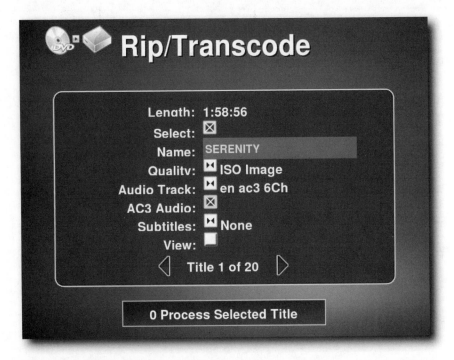

FIGURE 10-4: Saving a DVD to your hard drive

By default, MythDVD pulls the movie from the DVD and leaves it essentially in the same format it took on the DVD. If you select a quality level other than Perfect, MythDVD can recompress the DVD content, using a more efficient compression algorithm — namely, the MPEG4-derived digital video format known as XviD.

Here's a list of options that you will probably want to work with when taking advantage of this capability:

- **Select**—Toggles whether the currently displayed title will be copied

- **Quality**—Switches among the levels of compression

- **Audio Track**—Enables you to choose which audio track you want to use when copying

- **AC3 Audio**—With this setting checked, the standard Dolby Digital soundtrack will be preserved. If this setting is unchecked, the audio will be converted to standard stereo wave audio.

- **Subtitles**—You may choose to extract subtitles for use with the appropriate media player.

- **View**—This starts a preview of the selected title, which enables you to verify you have the right title to save.

When you are done making your selections, you can use MythVideo to watch your stored DVDs and even get information about the movies, movie posters, or DVD box cover art from IMDB. We cover this in more detail in Chapter 13.

Final Thoughts

By now you should be up and running with your MythDVD player of choice. The next few chapters focus on imagery and music. Chapter 11 covers the MythGallery plug-in, which, in a nutshell, enables you to manipulate and display images. Chapter 12 dives into MythMusic, which you can use to play music files, create playlists, and a whole lot more. You'll pop back into video mode once you get to Chapter 13, which covers MythVideo—a companion application to MythDVD.

MythGallery

Chapter 9 provides a general introduction to the core plug-ins package for MythTV feature extensions. This chapter delves further into the capability of the all-purpose image manipulation add-on that helps refine the spirit of MythTV — the MythGallery plug-in. In this chapter, you learn how to command MythGallery by remote and by keyboard, reconfigure the MythGallery settings, and generate HTML index pages from a directory of images for use with your personal gallery.

MythGallery Plug-in Overview

The MythGallery plug-in is among the core plug-ins package distributed with MythTV. It is described by the developers quite simply as a photo and slide-show application. The interface is very self explanatory, and provides you with five options:

- Random
- Rotate Clockwise (90)
- Rotate Counter-clockwise (90)
- Import
- Settings

The Random option performs as its name indicates — it randomly draws from a collection of images that you specify using the Import option. Rotate Clockwise reorients a tilted image 90 degrees, and Rotate Counter-clockwise spins the image in the opposite direction. Import provides a single-click solution for introducing new images into your existing gallery, and the Settings tab (sometimes obscured and hidden beneath the Import tab depending on the settings and theme you use) delivers quick-and-easy access to the configuration panel.

MythGallery does not require a restart to put its images at your disposal. In fact, you can create a new directory while the MythTV frontend is loaded with MythGallery active and in the foreground, back out and reenter the Image Gallery, and then continue browsing with your latest additions ready to go.

By default, each image is displayed as a thumbnail and treated with a simple rounded border, while subdirectory paths are clearly indicated by a tabbed file folder. You may traverse in any given direction using the arrow keys (or your numeric 10-key pad with Num Lock off) in the appropriate order, and get a full-screen view or descend into subdirectories using either the spacebar or the Enter key.

MythGallery Keyboard Commands

A common thread throughout the MythTV experience is one of ultimate freedom in options and configurability. Each plug-in is no exception, and virtually everything is controllable both with the click of a remote control button or the press of a keyboard key. There may come a time when your remote battery expires or for some reason conspires against you to exercise control over the MythTV frontend, however, so you should be at least vaguely familiar with the keyboard sequences.

Table 11-1 presents a complete list of the default key sequences as provided by the MythGallery plug-in README help file that accompanies installation of this MythTV plug-in.

Table 11-1   MythGallery Default Key Commands

Key	Action
Thumbnail View Keys	
M	Toggle the menu
P	Start SlideShow
Home	Go to the first image in thumbnail view
End	Go to the last image in thumbnail view
Enter/SpaceBar	Open a Directory/View an image
Left, Right, Up, Down	Navigate through images/directories
Image View Keys	
P	Start/Stop SlideShow
],3	Rotate image right 90 degrees
[,1	Rotate image left 90 degrees
7	Zoom out of image
9	Zoom into image
2	Scroll image up
4	Scroll image left

Key	Action
6	Scroll image right
8	Scroll image down
5	Recenter image
0	Full-size (unzoom) image
Page Up	Go to the upper-left corner of the image
Page Down	Go to the lower-right corner of the image
I	Toggle showing information about the image

You may also acquire a recent copy of the README help file online at the MythTV Subversion repository at `http://svn.mythtv.org/svn/trunk/mythplugins/mythgallery/README`.

The "m" key activates the control panel positioned in the upper left-hand corner of the onscreen display. You can then enable MythGallery's slide-show functionality, select random images with the click of a button, rotate images both clockwise and counterclockwise, and import images. Further discussion of the import feature follows later in this chapter, with an example bash shell script to facilitate its use.

MythGallery's slide-show functionality does come with a few caveats that may be minor for your purposes but worth considering or bearing in mind nevertheless. Slideshow currently won't descend into subdirectories — an oversight that's been documented since version 0.15. Using MythGallery's import function also requires special attention, as it does not browse many forms of removable media automatically. You can correct this behavior by knowing in advance where you want MythGallery to search for image data, and then plugging in the correct values within the MythTV Utilities Setup screen.

There are two places where you can find the MythGallery settings interface. First, and most easily accessible, is the Settings option situated in the MythGallery menu context. Activate this menu context (keyboard letter "m"), and then use the down arrow key to reveal the Settings option hidden beneath Import. Otherwise, you can start from the MythTV frontend main menu selection, and choose Utilities/Setup → Setup → Media Settings → Images Settings.

The first option you see points MythGallery to the area where it expects to find its image repository (by default, this is the `/var/lib/pictures/` folder, as shown in Figure 11-1). You may prefer to redirect MythGallery to search elsewhere, such as `/home/mythtv/images`. This way you avoid the possibility of MythGallery overfilling a critical portion of the Linux directory tree `/var`, which houses many special log files. These log files are quickly populated by systemwide services and applications, particularly the warnings, errors, and failure conditions they encounter during their operation. Because it's entirely too easy to go overboard when storing pictures in your personal gallery, it might be wise to designate another portion of the hard disk for this task and reserve the `/var` space for more important uses.

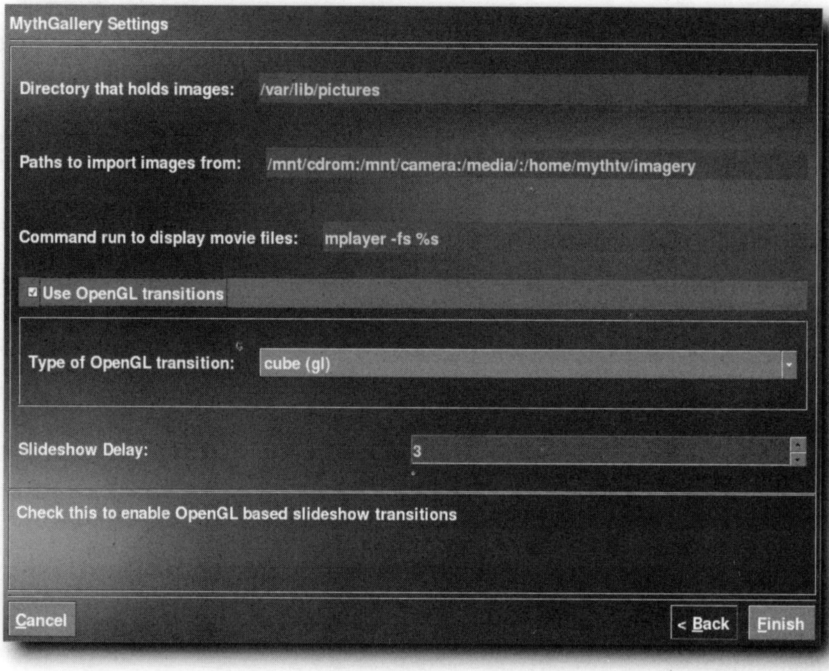

FIGURE 11-1: The MythGallery Settings page

Next follows a colon-delimited list of subdirectory branches that the plug-in will traverse as it imports image data. The first two defaults represent the general case, and draw upon devices located in the /mnt directory path. Usually, these entries serve as placeholders for devices that are meant to be removable in some way, such as CD-ROM or DVD-ROM drives or digital cameras. Fedora also uses the /media directory, which is populated with hot-pluggable storage devices such as USB thumb (flash memory) drives and external hard disk drives. These are both common and quite popular, and if you find yourself currently using a USB-based storage device or see this as a great method for transferring images, go ahead and append :/media (the colon is intentional, and required) to this string. This is particularly appropriate if your digital camera uses a compact flash (CF) memory card or some other removable memory and you insert that memory into a card reader that remains hooked up to your MythTV PC.

Finding USB Devices Under Linux

USB devices are represented in the device directory /dev as the letters sd followed by a letter (a–f) and a number (0–99). USB drives are automatically handled by the Hardware Abstraction Layer (HAL) daemon—or by automount if HAL is disabled—in all the latest versions of Fedora, and will be mounted without your manual input. If you have a USB-based device and would like to know its device name, issue the following command to a terminal window:

```
$ /sbin/fdisk -l


Disk /dev/hdc: 160.0 GB, 160041885696 bytes

255 heads, 63 sectors/track, 19457 cylinders

Units = cylinders of 16065 * 512 = 8225280 bytes


   Device Boot        Start         End      Blocks   Id  System

/dev/hdc1                 1        2433    19543041   83  Linux

/dev/hdc2              2434        9121    53721360    5  Extended

/dev/hdc3              9122       18240   73248367+   83  Linux

/dev/hdc4             18241       19457    9775552+   83  Linux

/dev/hdc5       *      2434        3477    8385898+   83  Linux


Disk /dev/sda: 520 MB, 520093696 bytes

1 heads, 32 sectors/track, 31744 cylinders

Units = cylinders of 32 * 512 = 16384 bytes


   Device Boot        Start         End      Blocks   Id  System

/dev/sda1       *         2       31744      507888    6  FAT16

/dev/sdb1       *         1       24321   195358401    7  HPFS/NTFS
```

Typical hard drive entries are indicated by the `/dev/hdc` naming convention (though this could just as easily be `/dev/hda` or `/dev/hdb`). In the preceding example, a Corsair flash memory storage device is indicated by `/dev/sda1` and labeled with the FAT16 file format. You can then determine where on the file system a given device entry is mapped by issuing the `mount` command with no parameters to a terminal window.

Upon completion of a successful import procedure, MythGallery presents you with new folder entries named according to the date and time during which the import took place. Figure 11-2 illustrates an updated MythGallery image repository with images imported from a USB flash device. This process is described in the MythGallery README file as follows:

When IMPORT is pressed in the menu each item in the import directory search path will be examined. If the item is a directory, its contents will be recursively copied to a new directory whose name is the current date and time. Using this method, removable devices can be put in the search path if they use an automount system (see the Linux documentation for info on how to use automount systems). If the item is an executable file, it will be executed with 1 argument consisting of the name of the new subdirectory. This way, import from a removable device can be accomplished without the use of an automount system.

FIGURE 11-2: Images picture data imported from USB flash

Empty folder entries are also copied, which creates the unfortunate side effect of populating your precious gallery with bogus data. Where image data is present in the subdirectory tree, a thumbnail image appears, framed by the folder border pattern. You may descend into new subdirectories by clicking Enter or Select on your remote, or by striking the Enter or spacebar key. Exit a subdirectory path by pressing Escape on the keyboard, or Exit on your remote.

If you use keyboard commands during the MythMusic configuration portion of the frontend, you may notice an inconsistency in how spacebar/Enter is interpreted. Even if you highlight an input field, either key causes the configuration window to close, instead of toggling a checkbox or drop-down list options such as the Use OpenGL transitions feature. Use the right or left arrow keys instead.

With the Type of OpenGL transition setting, MythGallery Settings provides 14 types of transition methods for use with slide-show galleries:

- chess board

- melt down

- sweep

- noise

- growing

- incoming edges

- horizontal lines

- vertical lines

- circle out

- multicircle out

- spiral in

- blobs

- random

- none

Additionally, the type of background used can be configured to use the current theme or an all-white or all-black backdrop.

Enable the OpenGL option to open another selection of methods for transitioning between images during slide-show displays. You may then blend, zoom, fade, rotate, bend, slide, and flutter from one image to the next. One cryptic entry labeled "inout" sends the current foreground image in a sharp arc into the background until it disappears into the horizon line, and then sends the next image zooming right back into focus. Perhaps you will find the cube method most appealing of all, as it maps several images onto an imaginary 3D cube, which then cycles through each picture with a quick spin and twirl in imaginary space.

Using the OpenGL blend option looks especially smooth with samples of topographical satellite imagery depicting Earth's continental bodies, each illustrated in various levels of detail. The OpenGL blend option smoothly transitions from one picture to the next by intermingling information from both and adjusting the transparency properties accordingly. Fade simply transitions into an all black background before presenting the next image.

The last setting, Slideshow Delay, adjusts the delay between transitions. Five seconds is the default, but you are free to adjust this value according to taste.

Finally, the option titled "Command run to display movies" enables you to view movie content from within MythGallery. Change this setting only if you have a specific reason. You are now ready to begin digging into the heart of this chapter: the MythGallery hacks.

MythGallery Hacks

Using MythGallery is a simple and straightforward affair. However, accessing MythGallery through anything other than the frontend client is not. The remainder of this chapter describes how to access your MythGallery repository through the MythWeb interface so you can view it with any Web-enabled browser.

Using MythGallery via MythWeb

Sometimes creativity must draw on the influence of others. An interesting and unintended use of the MythGallery plug-in is inspired by a message thread dated January 20, 2006 on the http://mysettopbox.tv MythTV forums.

Note For those interested in the original thread, you must sign up for an account and log in to the forum (http://mysettopbox.tv/phpBB2/) — unless you manage to find a cached version of the document — and search for the thread titled "MythGallery via MythWeb." Two users discuss the feasibility of accessing MythGallery from the MythWeb plug-in so that the images are Web-accessible and may then be viewed from any computer with a browser.

The mission is simple: define an automated, scriptable means to render an entire directory of MythGallery images into a browser-accessible index of images available through the MythWeb interface. For simplicity's sake, this example only processes JPEG format files but you can tailor this to work with other types if you'd like, or to work with multiple types of files. We leave the design and implementation of such features as an exercise for you.

Batch processing an entire directory of pictures into an indexed page of thumbnails is handled by wrapping a shell script around a freely available PERL script named iGal. Many built-in options other than those the following script uses are available, but they are irrelevant to this particular task. What follows is sufficient to prepare a basic HTML index page for MythWeb. You can obtain a copy of the iGal script at www.stanford.edu/~epop/igal/.

An example command-line sequence to process the default /var/lib/pictures directory appears here:

```
# /usr/local/bin/igal -C -d /var/lib/pictures/
# /usr/local/bin/igal -c -d /var/lib/pictures/
```

Once iGal has finished processing the directory content, you may create either a new directory or a symbolic link to an existing path in /var/www/html where MythWeb resides:

```
# /usr/bin/file /var/www/html/mythgallery
/var/www/html/mythgallery: symbolic link to '/home/mythtv/html'
```

Figure 11-3 depicts new image files indexed by iGal and made available to MythGallery.

FIGURE 11-3: HTML index created by iGal

To access MythGallery from the MythBrowser plug-in, you must first make an entry in the MythBrowser Bookmarks Settings control panel. The bookmark entry created for this example is shown in Figure 11-4.

Now that you know how to create a simple index using igal on a directory of picture files, you can apply that knowledge to fashioning a shell script to handle all the details. In the next section a script is used to prove by example how easy this is to achieve. Other useful software applications are introduced where necessary, with references to relevant online resources, to encourage you to explore further the potential inherent in MythGallery.

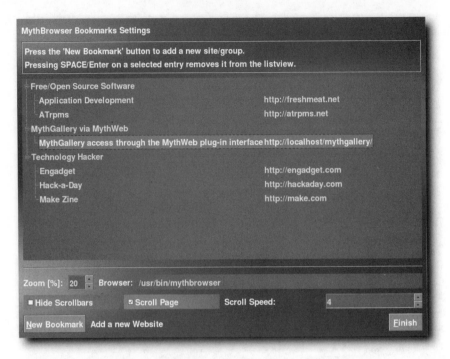

FIGURE 11-4: Configure MythWeb to access MythGallery using MythBrowser.

Using Scripted Gallery Creation

Automating this procedure to process entire directories is a simple matter for any common Linux shell scripting language. There are a number of ways to carry this out, but the simple demonstration we provide suffices to prove our point. Ideally, you would store Web page index data somewhere other than in MythGallery's default path. Otherwise, you create a redundancy problem that gets unmanageable from the MythTV frontend, where each image appears once as the index thumbnail and again as an original gallery image. This is especially bothersome should you wish to store hundreds or perhaps thousands of photographs or other digital images in your gallery.

There are numerous ways to copy the entire contents of a directory from one path into another using any of the common Linux command-line utilities. In some of the examples that follow, the symbolic link utility /bin/ln is used to create references to other files without recreating any of the actual data they contain. This same utility may be used to copy directory content by passing the –b parameter at runtime. Here's a sample command-line sequence that demonstrates this procedure:

```
/bin/ln -b /var/lib/pictures/*.jpg /home/mythtv/html/
```

Note   If you use /bin/ln with the -b flag, it will rename the original files contained in the target directory by appending a tilde symbol (~) to the end. You must clean these up; otherwise, large unnecessary files will accumulate, robbing the hard drive of valuable storage space.

Executing the link or ln binary with the -b flag invokes back-up behavior, which copies every single file from the source directory into the target directory. Unless you have a massive gallery of images, duplicating files will have only a negligible impact on storage space. However, one of the proper methods for duplicating directory content requires using the /bin/cp utility with the -R (recursive) option as follows:

```
/bin/cp -R /var/lib/pictures/  /home/mythtv/html/
```

Then it's simply a matter of pointing your Web browser to the following URL:

```
http://localhost/mythweb/pictures/
```

Occasionally you will come across images that are turned sideways or upside down. You may use /usr/bin/jpegtran to coerce JPEG images into their proper positions. Suppose you have a collection of images, some of which are arranged in various inconsistent directions. To prepare to make an image gallery, you should probably orient each image in the same direction, a job for which jpegtran is entirely up to handling. For example:

```
/usr/bin/jpegtran -flip vertical img-01.jpg > img-01.jpg.new
/usr/bin/jpegtran -flip horizontal img-02.jpg > img-02.jpg.new
```

The following is a quick-and-dirty shell script that can handle most of the details for batch processing our MythGallery index page. This script is a wrapper to the iGal PERL script, and handles all pre-processing details on your behalf. However, it does very little error checking and is unable to indicate what entry causes a problem, making it the very essence of a hack. Larger, more complex solutions are widely available — such as Gallery2 — that do a fantastic job of rendering professional-quality results, but they're not covered here.

```
#!/bin/sh
# $Id: myth-makegal.sh,v 0.1 2006/02/01 10:56:07 jkor Exp $
# quick-and-dirty hack for building an index of images from a
directory.

# This script relies upon igal which can be obtained here:
# http://www.stanford.edu/~epop/igal/ggate/

if [ $# != 2 ]
then
  /bin/echo 'Usage: $0 <PATH-TO-GALLERY> <PATH-TO-STORAGE>'
  /bin/echo 'Example: $0 /var/lib/pictures /home/mythtv/html/'
  /bin/echo 'Here /home/mythtv/html is symlinked as
/var/www/htm/mythweb/mythgallery.'
  exit 1
fi

if [ ! -d ${1} ]
```

```
then
  echo ${1}: No such directory.
  exit 1
fi

if [ ! -d ${2} ]
then
  /bin/echo "Making directory: ${2}"
  /bin/mkdir -p ${2}
fi

cd ${1}

/bin/echo "Creating symbolic links against ${1} (target: ${2})"

for file in *.jpg
do
  # Create a symbolic link of every file in the target directory.
  # That way you don't clutter up MythGallery with redundant Web
images.
  /bin/ln -sf ${1}/${file} ${2}/${file}
done

if [ $? != 0 ]
then
  /bin/echo 'Failed to link against ${1}.'
  exit 1
fi

/bin/echo Running initial pass against directory ${2}.
# Change this if you installed igal to /home/mythtv/bin
$(/usr/local/bin/igal -C -d ${2} 1 > /dev/null)
if [ $? != 0 ]
then
  /bin/echo 'igal returned an error during processing'
  exit 1
fi

/bin/echo Creating index content from gallery data.
$(/usr/local/bin/igal -c -d ${2} 1 > /dev/null)
if [ $? != 0 ]
then
  /bin/echo 'igal returned an error during processing'
  exit 1
fi
```

Note   For more information about shell scripting languages on Linux platforms, visit the Linux Documentation Project (TLDP) and look for Bash scripting guides; you'll find a beginner's guide as well as an advanced guide at www.tldp.org/guides.html. TLDP is an archive of many authoritative and definitive HOW-TOs, guides, and articles about all aspects of the Linux platform, and represents valuable input and information from the global Linux community.

Make sure appropriate permissions are set for each directory in which you intend to store image data for whichever user account is assigned the task of harvesting such data. For example, the default MythTV user cannot write to any other user's home directory unless you explicitly assign the necessary permissions on a case-by-case basis. With multiple users to draw picture files from and multiple mount points for potential picture repositories, this can easily become complicated, if not downright unmanageable. The best solution is to create a centralized directory designed expressly for storing pictures for use with MythGallery. This obviates the tedious process of reassigning permissions across the file system. You don't necessarily have to follow this practice and there is certainly no compelling reason to do so other than to isolate the activities of the MythTV user to a well-defined domain.

Gallery2

If you are feeling particularly adventurous, why not give the Gallery2 Web-based photo album organizer a spin? Gallery2 is much more user-friendly and integrates nicely with the MythWeb interface because it uses a Web-based configuration wizard. Plus, Gallery2 is a full-fledged content-management framework, whereas iGal is a minimalist solution.

Gallery2 is available free for download under the GNU Public License (GPL) and most of the basic requirements (Apache HTTP Web server, ImageMagick image processing library, MySQL database, and PHP) are already satisfied in your MythTV installation. Browse the following screenshots and decide for yourself:

```
http://gallery.menalto.com/gallery/screenshots
```

For a detailed description of the full requirements necessary to build Gallery2, point your browser at the following URL:

```
http://codex.gallery2.org/index.php/Gallery2:Installation_Requirements
```

Final Thoughts

This concludes our coverage of the MythGallery plug-in's capabilities. Ideally, this chapter will serve as a jumping off point for finding your own inventive and clever new uses for a MythGallery image collection. You now know how to teach the MythGallery plug-in a new trick, and in the next chapter you learn how to trick out the MythMusic plug-in.

MythMusic

chapter

12

in this chapter

☑ MythMusic plug-in
   overview

☑ Keyboard
   commands

☑ Smart playlists

☑ MythMusic hacks

☑ Scripted audio
   conversions

MythMusic is perhaps the one core plug-in with the most potential going for it today. Next to its video-handling capability — the bread and butter of any MythTV project box — audio capability runs a close second in terms of usefulness and hack value. As it stands, the MythMusic plug-in handles a wide variety of audio formats, and allows you to manipulate and re-encode audio samples entirely to your liking.

This chapter explores the nature of the MythMusic interface, the various ways to get at its underlying configuration, and how to modify certain transparent components (such as the utilities for which this plug-in acts as a harness) in creative and interesting ways.

We continue exploring and explaining the MythMusic plug-in as first described in Chapter 9. You will learn how to operate the MythMusic plug-in through the MythTV frontend using the keyboard commands, how to change corresponding key mappings for those commands, how to script the process of converting an entire directory from one audio format into another, and be introduced to a few extra software packages to further enhance your MythMusic experience.

MythMusic Keyboard Commands

Apart from the remote control profile you specify to the LIRC daemon for use with MythTV, there are several commands available to navigate within or interact with the MythMusic plug-in. Table 12-1 presents a complete set of MythMusic keyboard commands.

Each of these commands is accessible through the plaintext file contained in /usr/share/doc/mythtv-0.18.1/keys.txt or through the MythWeb plug-in interface using the browser of your choice. Simply point your Web browser to your MythTV box:

http://localhost/mythweb

Table 12-1 MythMusic Keyboard Commands

Key	Command
1	Shuffle tracks—Submenu options: Random, Start, None
2	Repeat—Submenu options: Track, All, None
3	Edit Playlist
4	Visualize
5	Blank screen
6	Cycle Visualizer mode
7	Decrease rating
8	Refresh music tree
9	Increase rating
D	Delete track from playlist
I	Track information
M	Stop playlist
O	Stop track
P	Play/Pause track
Q	Previous track
Z	Next track
<	Previous track
>	Next track
\	Mute
Home	Move to previous track
End	Move to next track
F9	Mute
F11	Volume up
F12	Volume down
PageUp	Rewind
PageDown	Fast-forward

There you will be presented with your most current program listings along with a series of icons gracing the top of the page, to provide easy access to the most commonly used configuration settings pages. An icon that looks like an automotive ignition key with monkey wrench—perhaps a hint that it's time to pop the hood—leads you to the configuration settings index page with a single click. Although the interface leaves much to be desired, this page will link you to configuration settings for the following items:

- MythWeb Settings: `http://localhost/mythweb/settings_mythweb.php`
- MythTV Channels: `http://localhost/mythweb/settings_channels.php`
- MythTV Key Bindings: `http://localhost/mythweb/settings_keys.php`

MythTV Key Bindings opens a highly experimental control panel for both the Jump Points and Keybindings Editors. Here, the terminology "highly experimental" is used to describe the beta release quality of the API (that is, it's not yet thoroughly tested). In fact, the first entry on this page reads as follows:

```
Note: This settings page has absolutely no error checking yet. You
can easily screw things up if you're not careful.
```

Don't feel too intimidated by that message. Its only purpose is to convey a very common and well-accepted principle: If it ain't broke, don't fix it. Scroll down through to the Keybindings Editor, locate the entries for MythMusic, and edit the fields to the far right of the corresponding value you wish to modify. We personally find the default values to be perfectly well suited for general-purpose use, and therefore urge that no changes be made to their existing state. In the next segment we describe a more interesting place to begin hacking around with MythMusic: the Smart Playlist Editor.

MythMusic Smart Playlists

One undeniably cool feature of the MythMusic plug-in interface is the Smart Playlist capability that permits you to sort, modify, delete, and queue up tracks according to multiple, flexible user-specified criteria, accessible from the drop-down Category list. First is the Decades category, a catch-all label encompassing a variety of genres sorted according to release date within a given ten-year span, from the 1960s to the 2000s. MythMusic also keeps track of how many times you replay a given track (or whether a given track has ever been played at all), which is then used in another Smart Playlist feature called Favourite Tracks (notice the British spelling). Invoking this feature from the Smart Playlist Editor provides you with the means for quick and easy access to your most enjoyable music selections.

Of course, these are only the defaults serving as placeholders for your own creative input, and you are at liberty to add, edit, change, and delete entries to your liking. Figure 12-1 shows the Smart Playlist Editor.

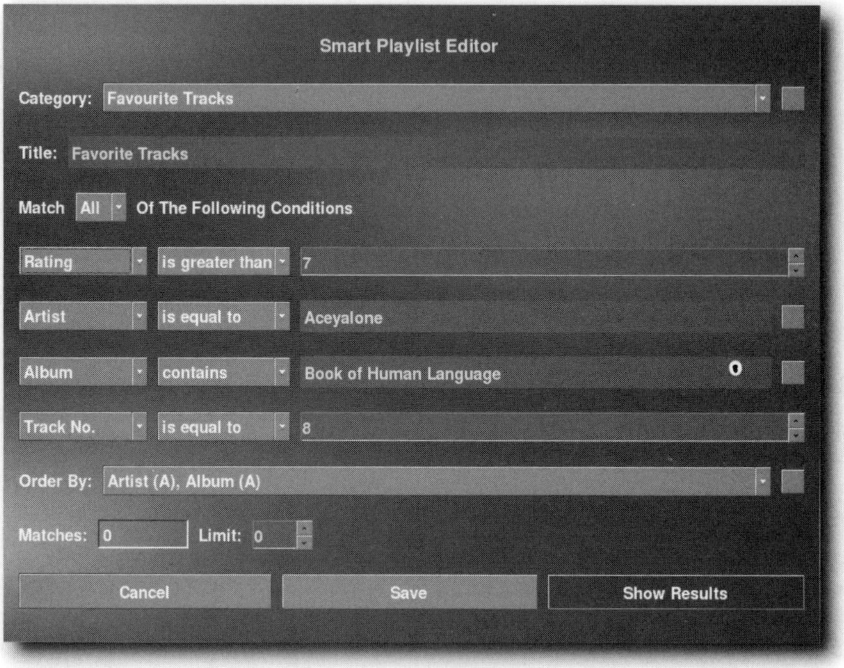

FIGURE 12-1: The Smart Playlist Editor handles ID3 metadata.

The Smart Playlist Editor also provides a wealth of other optional functionality, such as sorting favorite tracks by information contained in the ID3 headers. You can search for and filter selections by artist or album name, play count, personal rating factor, or import date, to describe a few of the criteria at your disposal. Each of these fields may be modified using a basic regular expression syntax. This gives the Playlist Editor a lot of leverage in how it manages and categorizes your song collection. The following list shows each of the available ID3 or metadata entries:

- Artist
- Album
- Title
- Genre
- Year
- Track Number
- Rating

- Play Count
- Compilation
- Comp. Artists
- Last Play
- Date Imported

Finally, the New Tracks category encompasses all tracks available to MythMusic that have not yet been played. This is a wonderful addition for those of us who possess large or complex music collections whereby some songs are so deeply nested they may never see rotation. MythMusic's Track Information subcontext menu also gives you the capability to modify audio file property tags, and you can dynamically increase or decrease popularity ratings for a given track from within the plug-in by issuing the corresponding keyboard or remote control commands.

Figure 12-2 illustrates an ID3 tag from a simple OGG-formatted audio sample.

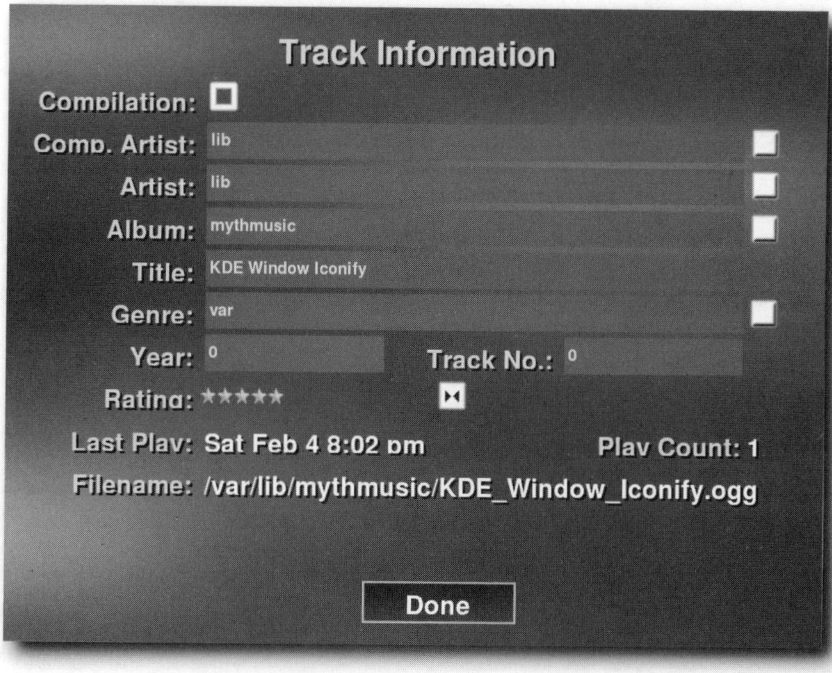

FIGURE 12-2: Example of an OGG audio format header in MythMusic

MythMusic Hacks

With so much power and built-in capability already present in the MythMusic plug-in, you might wonder what hasn't been considered. For starters, you cannot decode MP3s from the MythMusic interface by default, though you can play them just fine. In addition, there is no well-defined interface to batch up conversion when transcoding music files from one audio format into another.

You will need to install the requisite LAME and MPEG Audio Decoder (MAD) MP3 library headers to take full advantage of MP3 encoding and decoding capabilities (for our purposes, only LAME is required, but MAD is recommended). Both may be acquired and installed easily using the Fedora package manager yum or its corresponding graphical frontend yumex.

Using either method, grab the latest distribution set of the following items:

- `glame`
- `glame-devel`
- `gstreamer-plugins-extra-audio`
- `lame-devel`
- `libmad0`
- `libmad-devel`

Note   When using yumex, you may not always have access to the packages you want. Check the Repos icon on the left-hand windowpane of the yumex interface and make sure both release and updates are checked, and then click the Refresh button. Next, go to Profiles on the main toolbar and select New, and name this profile something unique. Select Profiles once again and click the unique name you just created for this profile. Every action from this point forward will include the release and update packages.

Now select the Install icon, begin typing in the preceding package names to the Filter input field, and then click Search. Click each package as it appears, and then click the Install button once you've gathered all of them together. The yumex utility will get to work, resolve dependencies, and then install all requested packages.

Once these packages have been installed successfully, you may rebuild several audio utilities for use with MP3 encoding or decoding. We walk you through a demonstration of rebuilding the Sound eXchange (SoX) audio conversion utility because it is readily available on most Fedora Core installations running MythTV and is relatively easy to use.

Our initial version lacks MP3 capability; you can verify this for your own installation by issuing this simple command:

```
# /usr/bin/sox -h

[ ... OMITTED FOR BREVITY ... ]

Supported file formats: aiff al au auto avr cdr cvs dat vms gsm
hcom la lu maud nul ossdsp prc raw sb sf sl smp sndt sph 8svx sw
txw ub ul uw voc vorbis vox wav wve
```

Astute readers will notice that among the variety of audio formats shown, both familiar and unfamiliar, MP3 does not appear. Therefore, you must obtain source code for SoX and compile this feature into the code so that you can burn MP3s using MythTV's frontend.

To begin this process, you must acquire the latest source archive from the SoX CVS archive stored on the sourceforge.net servers, as shown in the following sequence of commands:

```
$ /bin/mkdir ~/src && cd ~/src
$ export CVSROOT=":pserver:anonymous@cvs.sourceforget.net:/cvsroot/sox"
$ /usr/bin/cvs -d ${CVSROOT} login
Logging in to :pserver:anonymous@cvs.sourceforge.net:2401/cvsroot/sox
CVS password:
$ /usr/bin/cvs -z3 -d ${CVSROOT} checkout sox
[ Several files scroll down the screen ]
$ /bin/ls -l
drwxr-xr-x  7 mythtv mythtv 4096 Feb  4 19:46 sox
$ cd sox/
$ ./configure --enable-lirc --enable-lircc --enable-menu
$ /usr/bin/make
$ /usr/bin/sudo /usr/bin/make install
Password:
```

In this example, the password is blank, so just press the Enter key when prompted.

Note that during the SoX pre-compilation phase, you want one or more of the following entries to appear enabled so that you get MP3 decoding capability:

```
. . .
Ogg Vorbis support...............  yes
MAD MP3 Decoder..................  no
LAME MP3 Encoder.................  yes
. . .
```

Here again, MAD MP3 decoder support is optional. You specifically want LAME Encoding capability to achieve your goal—namely, to transform various formats into MP3 samples. Expect to see this information just after executing `./configure`.

Now you are ready to convert from just about any audio format you can throw at your MythTV Linux box. The following example is provided to jump-start your own experimentation. This example uses Sound eXchange to convert an MP3 audio sample into a raw format:

```
$ sox -V -r 44100 -w -c 2 -s sample.mp3 sample.raw
sox: Detected file format type: mp3
sox: Input file sample.mp3: using sample rate 44100
     size longs, encoding MPEG audio (layer I, III or III), 2
     channels
sox: Input file sample.mp3: comment "sample.mp3"
sox: Output file sample.raw: using sample rate 44100
     size shorts, encoding signed (2's complement), 2 channels
sox: Output file: comment "sample.mp3"
```

Next, check that both files now exist:

```
$ /bin/ls -l sample.???
total 306
-rw-r--r--    1 mythtv  mythtv    11764530 Jun 28 00:27 sample.mp3
```

```
-rw-------    1 mythtv  mythtv    129645121 Aug  5 10:13 sample.raw
```

You may also convert raw mono audio formats into stereo using Sound eXchange:

```
$ /usr/bin/sox -V -r 44100 -w -c 1 -s sample.raw -c 2 sample.wav
```

Now that you know what you can do with a simple audio transcoder, we show you how to write a script to automate batch processing of entire directories. Our first example demonstrates batch conversions for WMA to MP3 format for whatever directory you specify as the first input parameter to the script, and writes it to the second input parameter you provide:

```
#!/bin/bash
# $Id: myth-wma2mp3-lame.sh,v 0.1 2006/01/29 jkor Exp $
# Convert WMA to MP3 in bulk.

if [ $# < 2 ]
then
  echo 'Usage: $0 <PATH-TO-WMA>'
  exit 1
fi

if [ ! -d $1 ]
then
  echo Directory $1 does not exist.
   exit 1
fi

for file in *.wma
do
  name = ${file%.wma}
  # Does the FIFO already exist?
  if [ -f $name ]
  then
    /bin/rm -f $name
  fi

  # Make a FIFO
  /usr/bin/mkfifo $name

  # Transcode with LAME.
  /usr/bin/lame -quiet -m s $name -o $name.mp3 &

  # Rip with MPlayer
  /usr/bin/mplayer -quiet -vo null -vc dummy -af \
  volume=0,resample=441100:0:1 -ao pcm:waveheader \
  $file -ao pcm:file=$name

  /bin/rm -f $name
done
```

You invoke the preceding shell script with only one parameter: the location to your WMA directory. This script will iterate through every file identified and batch convert from WMA to MP3 format. There is no default directory for WMA files — these are a Windows-specific format, and can be found in the directory to which you import them.

Tip   If the preceding code gives you problems, particularly if error messages report that MPlayer cannot find Windows DLL files, you may need to install the Windows 32-bit CODECs package using either `yum` or its GUI frontend `yumex`. If that happens, install a package named `w32codec` to fix such problems.

The following sample script illustrates how you can batch process an entire directory of WMA-formatted files and convert them into OGG, an open-source alternative to MP3. This code is quite simpleminded in that it neither descends into subdirectories nor includes error checking to ensure that proper values and contents are supplied:

```sh
#!/bin/sh
# $Id: myth-wma2ogg.sh
# Batch process WMA-to-OGG on a directory

if [ $# < 2 ]
then
  echo 'Usage: $0 <PATH-TO-WMA>'
  exit 1
fi

if [ ! -d $1 ]
then
  echo Directory $1 does not exist.
  exit 1
fi

for file in *.wma
do
  name = ${file%.wma}
  if [ -f $name ]
  then
    /bin/rm -f $name
  fi
  # Make a FIFO.
  /usr/bin/mkfifo $name

  # Background the OGG Encoder for PIPE input.
  /usr/bin/oggenc $name &
  # Convert the WMA format into WAV and resample.
  # Send the output of MPlayer to the PIPE.
  /usr/bin/mplayer -really-quiet -vo null -vc dummy -af \
  volume=0,resample=441100:0:1 \
  -ao pcm:waveheader $file -ao pcm:file=$name

  # Remove the PIPE.
  /bin/rm -f $name
done
```

Encoding and decoding between pairs of various other audio formats is entirely possible. Most or all of the tools necessary for conversion are probably present on your system by way of the MythTV dependencies. If not, they may be easily obtained using any of a variety of package managers and third-party repository Web sites.

MythMusic Odds and Ends

In addition to the features already covered, the cover art for a collection of albums can be harvested in bulk using a third-party application called Album Covert Art Downloader (aka ACAD, it's currently at version 1.6.0 as we write this chapter). ACAD makes a best-effort attempt to identify cover art based on information gleaned from ID3 tags and file metadata, and searches the Internet for all applicable entries. Download your copy of the Album Cover Art Downloader for Linux from

```
http://louihi.kempele.fi/~skyostil/projects/albumart/
```

Also worthy of mention is the amp3mythtv "theme" geared toward "making mythmusic easier to manipulate large mp3 collections" (in the words of the developer). This color scheme consists mostly of red and orange with shades of blue to highlight active interface segments, but its functionality is what really makes this add-on stand out.

Final Thoughts

This concludes our coverage of the MythMusic plug-in and the potential uses you may find by poking around under its hood. From stock settings to modifying parameters and source code, you have seen how you can tweak and twiddle the MythMusic environment to better meet your needs. If you happen to discover a new or unusual way to use your MythMusic plug-in, please feel free to share it with the rest of the community. We hope this has inspired some of you to a greater sense of adventure — the very same feeling that beats at the heart of MythTV.

MythVideo

chapter

13

in this chapter

- ☑ Introducing MythVideo
- ☑ Initial setup
- ☑ Advanced settings
- ☑ Displaying your video collection
- ☑ Adding metadata to your videos

MythVideo is a complement of sorts to MythDVD. Whereas MythDVD is made specifically for DVD playback, MythVideo is a general-purpose video file player and video library tool. MythVideo is integrated into the MythTV menu structure as part of the Media Library. Figure 13-1 shows the MythTV Media Library menu; when you choose Watch Videos from the menu, you are using MythVideo.

In this chapter you'll learn how to set up MythVideo, add information to saved movies, such as those saved with MythDVD, and then learn the various ways to manage your video collection.

Initial Setup of MythVideo

MythVideo is generally a simple and straightforward component. From within MythTV, choose Utilities/Setup → Media Settings → Video Settings → General Settings. From this screen, you point MythVideo to the folders where your collection of videos is stored, or accept the default and begin building your library from scratch.

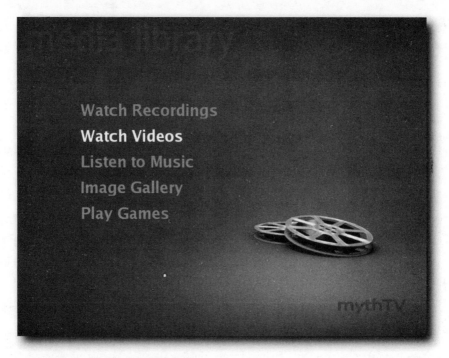

FIGURE 13-1: The MythTV video library

Choosing Your Default Media Player

As you learned in Chapter 10, the default DVD player software that MythTV uses is named MPlayer.

MPlayer is a rudimentary media player, and lacks an explicit configuration screen. Instead, it gets all its runtime option settings in the form of command-line parameters. Just as with MythDVD, however, you can use an alternate player known as xine.

xine is an advanced media player that includes robust onscreen display information, with a configuration screen that provides access to options such as deinterlacing and S/PDIF passthrough settings. If you want more control over the playback of your videos, xine comes highly recommended for the job.

To choose your default player, select Utilities/Setup → Setup → Media Settings → Videos Settings → Player Settings.

To use xine rather than MPlayer, substitute the following command in place of the default mplayer line:

```
xine -pfhq --no-splash %s
```

Figure 13-2 shows the Player Settings screen.

Player Settings

Default Player: xine -pfhq --no-splash %s

Cancel   < Back Finish

FIGURE 13-2: Setting the default media player

To get xine up and running, you'll need `xine-lib`, the core application code, and `xine-ui`, which gives xine a graphical interface to configure the program, and troubleshoot it outside of MythTV should you need to do so. You can visit the developer headquarters at `xinehq.de` to learn more about this software, or you can download a copy and other materials (such as plug-ins) from numerous other sites as well, including `dvd.sourceforge.net` and `freshrpms.net`.

Displaying Your Video Collection

MythVideo can be configured to represent your video files in three different ways. The Browse view, shown in Figure 13-3, shows a single video onscreen immediately, along with its metadata.

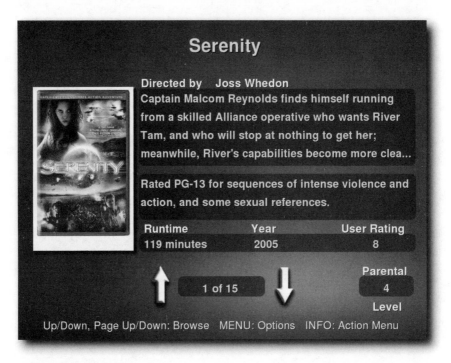

FIGURE 13-3: Browse view

The Tree view, shown in Figure 13-4, presents your videos in a list form that runs down the screen. This view can be configured to show file and subdirectory/path information as well.

The Gallery presents you with numerous titles at once, laid out in a tile view, as shown in Figure 13-5.

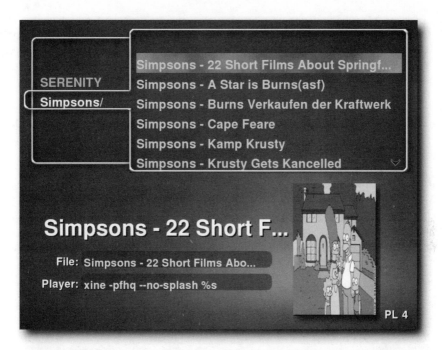

FIGURE 13-4: Tree view

FIGURE 13-5: Gallery view

Tip

To change views on-the-fly, bring up the menu (press the "m" key on the keyboard). From there, you can choose between the views on the pop-up menu. To change the view MythVideo uses by default, from the main menu select Utilities/Setup → Setup → Media Settings → Video Settings → General Settings. On its second property page, you can change the Default View to whatever you prefer.

New in revision 0.19 is the capability for MythVideo to scan DVD subdirectories when scanning for fresh content, and an option to disable loading program metadata when viewing the video list. This eases the burden on your MythTV unit when loading large collections of videos.

Adding Descriptive Metadata to Your Videos

MythVideo uses a special script that attempts to read the filenames for video files and then download related information from IMDB.com on the Internet. To manage your videos and configure how they use such information, head to the Utilities/Setup menu and select Video Manager, shown in Figure 13-6.

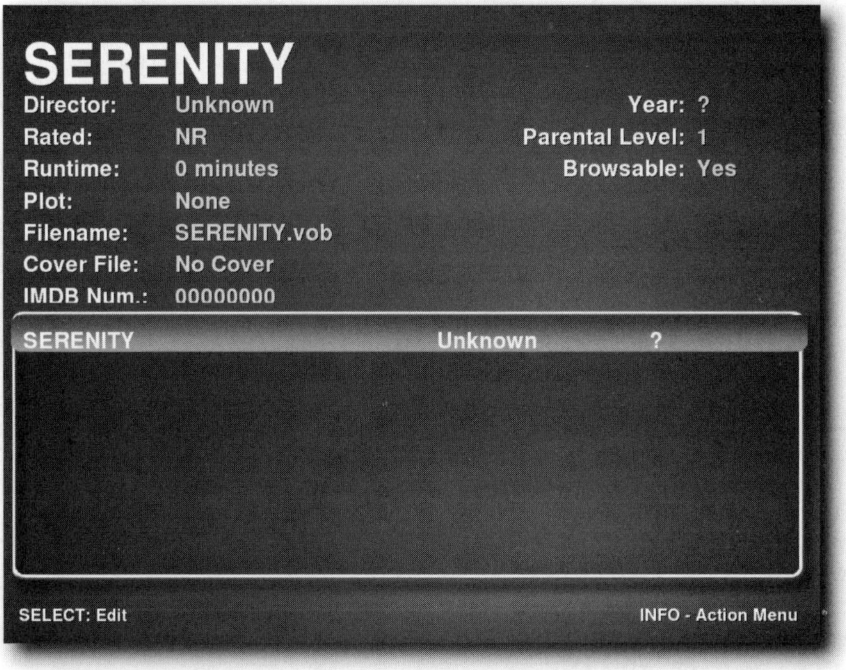

SERENITY

Director:	Unknown	Year: ?
Rated:	NR	Parental Level: 1
Runtime:	0 minutes	Browsable: Yes
Plot:	None	
Filename:	SERENITY.vob	
Cover File:	No Cover	
IMDB Num.:	00000000	

SERENITY   Unknown   ?

SELECT: Edit   INFO - Action Menu

FIGURE 13-6: The Video Manager

By default, there isn't really any useful metadata about the video. When you select a video inside this view, you can bring up an Information window (press "i" on the keyboard) in which you can find an option to Search IMDB (IMDB stands for Internet Movie Database, which advertises itself as "earth's biggest movie database"). When that option is selected, MythVideo tries to use the video filename to perform a keyword search on IMDB. When that's completed, you are presented with a list of possible matches in the results of that search, from which you can select the correct movie if it in fact appears. Once you select the IMDB database entry you want, MythVideo will download the cover art and details about that movie, including its rating, run time, a brief plot description, cast, director, producer, and more. If the IMDB search gets it wrong, you may also find the correct movie yourself using a Web browser, and then return to this interface to enter the correct IMDB number in the Manually Enter IMDB # field. This dialog box is shown in Figure 13-7.

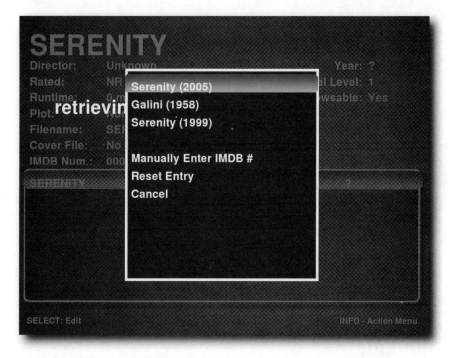

FIGURE 13-7: Choosing an IMDB entry

Tip

The IMDB database number appears as part of the URL in a movie's information page. For example, the recent science fiction film *Serenity* appears on www.imdb.com/title/tt0379786/, from which you can correctly infer that the IMDB database number must be related to the letters/numbers tt0379786. Actually, the database number is the last portion without the tt characters, so that IMDB number is 0379786.

An IMDB search is really only useful for movies. Unfortunately, the IMDB search feature doesn't really handle look-ups for episodic TV shows or video clips. Thankfully, you can edit IMDB information or make your own from scratch in the Video Manager by selecting an item (press the spacebar or Enter key on the keyboard) and then editing it in the Edit Video Information screen, shown in Figure 13-8. You can add rudimentary information to help catalog your video.

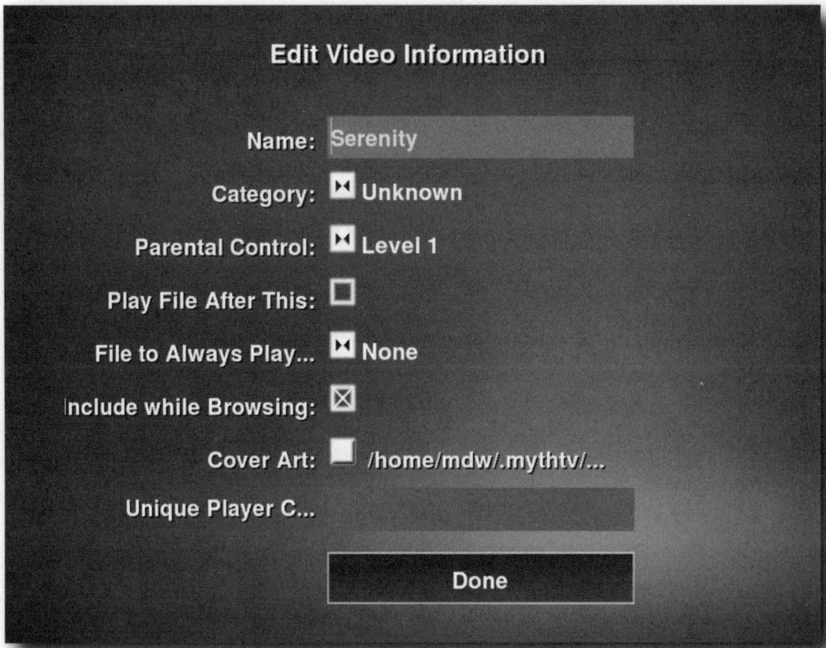

FIGURE 13-8: Create a manual entry in the Edit Video Information screen.

Final Thoughts

In addition to the information provided in this chapter, the "Tweaking MythVideo" section in Chapter 15 offers more tips for configuring MythVideo just the way you want it, and the "Maximizing mplayer and xine" section in Chapter 16 gives you some additional insights in using MythVideo as your default player. If you still have some VHS tape lying around, then Check out the section "Mythifying Home Movies and VHS Tapes" in Chapter 17. First, however, Chapter 14 covers must-have plug-ins for MythTV from your developer community. Read on.

Plug-Ins from the MythTV Community

Since its inception just four years ago, MythTV has blossomed into a bouquet of on-demand personalized content distribution and multimedia enhancements sufficient for anybody's digital lifestyle. No man is an island, as the saying goes, and no man's digital-age hardware should be one, either. Nowhere is this more evident than in the current digital marketplace, where MythTV represents a truly pioneering effort to merge all your media devices into a single cohesive system.

MythTV has a direct line into an emerging generation of do-it-yourself enthusiasts. These folks are no strangers to a little informed poking and prodding around inside modern computer systems. You, too, can delight in the fruits of their labors. Perhaps you may even become inspired to undertake your own projects, suggest improvements to existing applications, submit recommendations for feature inclusions with upcoming releases, or even find clever and creative new uses for current applications (several of your authors have taken this route). This certainly puts MythTV's mission statement into action, creating a mythic convergence box designed to usher in a new era of personal multimedia — for you, by those like you, and with you in mind.

Within the few short months during which this book took shape, the suite of MythTV applications has undergone a series of transformations in its appearance. Changes range from a restructuring of the application suite to an entire revamping of the MythTV Web site. Development has cycled quickly from MythTV 0.18 to 0.19, where the latter is currently a stable release. In addition, MythTV 0.20 is in CVS release status, which means this new project is not only alive and well, but that production has ramped up considerably since the transition from 0.17 to 0.18. The MythTV plug-in framework has also been reworked, and a few welcome entries have been added to the core plug-ins distribution, and more entries are poised for acceptance in each incremental revision.

A mushrooming contingent of feature-laden add-ons continues to appear. As end-users are inspired to reshape their experiences in ways that parallel the development of MythTV, more and more such plug-ins are bound to appear. Over time, some of these will also make their way into the core plug-ins distribution as well.

## chapter 14

in this chapter

☑ Exporting MythTV to other formats

☑ Personalizing MythTV properties

☑ Redefining MythTV remote controls

☑ Using Microsoft Windows as a MythTV frontend

The plug-ins covered in this chapter represent the community efforts of end-users turned developers in their attempts to incorporate "killer app" functionality into the MythTV framework for your personal enjoyment. The entries mentioned here are only a small fraction of the many MythTV plug-in projects active on the Web. By no means is this an exhaustive list, either. By the time this book goes to press and gets into your hands, new projects will have appeared. It is hoped that the exposure this book provides for MythTV will spawn even more new plug-ins.

Frontend Plug-ins

A frontend plug-in hooks into the main interface and provides embedded functionality usually accessible through configuration windows in the menu system. A handful of official frontend plug-ins ship with the current version of MythTV. Dozens of unofficial entries also crop up regularly. One such plug-in certain to gain increasing popularity is Torrentocracy, an application that refines the concept of convergence technology still further.

- **MythStormAlert** (www.knoppmythwiki.org/index.php?page= MythStormAlert)—MythTV's suite of applications already includes a comprehensive weather application, but MythStormAlert gleans weather alert information from the National Weather Service (NWS) at http://nws.noaa.gov (instead of weather.com). It uses your Federal Information Processing Standard (FIPS) state/county code (found at http://www.itl.nist.gov/fipspubs/ co-codes/states.htm) to localize weather for your immediate vicinity.

  MythStormAlert brokers XML-based information between the NWS system and your MythTV mythvosd for onscreen display in the frontend. Furthermore, it can be configured to work with the system scheduler for periodic weather updates. If you travel frequently, this plug-in might be invaluable. However, as of this writing, MythStormAlert is in alpha status and is deemed unsuitable for production use. Intrepid users need not let that deter them, of course, and by the time you read this that status may have changed as well.

- **Torrentocracy** (www.torrentocracy.com/)—Convergence is a wonderful thing when it's done right. A stellar example of such convergence comes from Torrentocracy, an amalgamation of an RSS news reader, a BitTorrent client, and seamless transition to Internet-based video feeds. In essence, Torrentocracy redefines how you view television, and continues the MythTV philosophy of convergence by merging grassroots Internet media distribution (through legal channels) and on-demand access to live television feeds.

  In the words of Torrentocracy's author Gary Lerhaupt:

  First, I should start off by saying that Torrentocracy will support and promote only sites that provide links to legal torrents. . . . Torrentocracy is not about railing against or stealing from big media.

  The Push: Windows Vista is poised to unleash a new era of digital rights management. Some users may also experience the crippling effects when it comes to viewing or listening to multimedia content, thanks to overzealous policymakers and profit-motivated corporate behavior designed to govern how you view, copy, and distribute material licensed for your use. Vista uses verifiable crypto hardware to validate and monitor use of digital media content in your possession, ensuring a high level of privacy and confidentiality between broadcast source and intended recipients. However, it also prevents viewing of such content on other devices, making (some) copies, and converting content into other digital forms.

The Pull: Torrentocracy represents one of many solutions for broadcasting live television media directly to Internet hosts. Some of this may be against policy or violate copyright, but much of it does not. You are authorized to view licensed material however you see fit, and Torrentocracy enables you to achieve such use on a greater scale. *Abusus non tollit usum* (wrong use does not preclude proper use).

For more information, read the Torrentocracy home page. You should educate yourself about any related legal issues involved with rebroadcasting copyrighted materials before distributing such content online.

MythWeb Plug-ins

Just when you thought things couldn't get any better, along comes something so innovative, so ingenious and clever, that you respond with the proverbial resounding smack to the forehead. In that vein, MythWeb functionality is a sleeping giant of potential just waiting to be roused from its slumber. One such stimulant might very well be MythWebRemote.

■ **MythWebRemote** (`http://sourceforge.net/projects/mythwebremote`)— MythWebRemote enables a higher level of interaction between a MythTV PC and the arsenal of portable entertainment and digital assistant devices in your possession.

The program grants an entirely different kind of "remote" remote-control access to MythTV—namely, through a laptop, PDA, or other network-aware input devices. Using MythWebRemote, you can control a MythTV box by sending interactive keypresses (by stylus or mouse) via TCP/IP to Apache/PHP running on the MythTV backend.

You might be surprised to learn that a simple PHP script provides this extensive functionality, nothing more. If you understand this easy-to-use scripting language, you can modify, enhance, and design just about anything you want, or it might inspire you enough to author your own MythWeb plug-in. Wrap this script in the same standard disclaimer that any inspired do-it-yourself project usually merits. As a consequence, you should expect experimental quality and a brush against the occasional unpolished edge or bug.

■ **MythWifi Remote Control** (`http://studwww.ugent.be/%7Eaveys/mythwifi/`)—MythWifi is yet another remote control application for MythTV. This one employs socket-based communications from a wireless device such as a PDA or a laptop. Furthermore, it delivers support for multiple frontends and backends, for supreme flexibility in multi-user environments.

Using a tiny custom database-oriented protocol framework, sent messages are handled as key-event sequences that correspond to a given action on the MythWifi Web interface control panel, shown in Figure 14-1. This offers tremendous advantages over an existing remote control set-up, and enables you to incorporate a variety of ordinary digital devices into a media center. You can pause, play, fast-forward, and rewind multimedia content, access menus and information, modify volume controls, and invoke the onscreen display (OSD) through this interface.

In addition, you can build client-side interfaces using any higher-level programming language you like, including C/C++, Java, Python, PHP, or PERL. This lends incredible freedom to the way users can develop and utilize their MythTV systems. MythWifi requires MySQL to work, but that requirement is already met in the MythTV base installation.

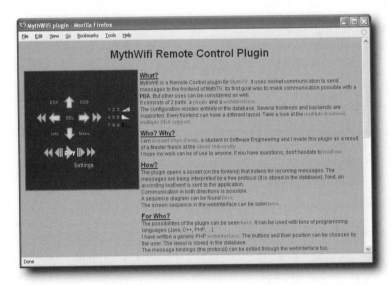

FIGURE 14-1: The MythWifi Remote Control Plugin Web page shows the plug-in interface.

General Add-Ons

General add-ons extend the usability and personalization of MythTV functionality. This involves either an overlay of features or a higher abstraction regarding how personal information may be viewed, measured, and manipulated. That's what drives TVWish, a preemptive, selective content personalization tool described in the following list:

- **Myth2iPod** (www.myth2ipod.com/myth2ipod.html) — Given a large array of portable media players and multimedia storage devices and rapidly growing do-it-yourself interest groups, it's only a matter of time before someone writes the missing software link between your desktop media repository and the modular peripheral components that represent the tokens of your digital lifestyle.

That's the motivation behind the Myth2iPod plug-in. It's a simple PERL script that ostensibly interfaces between MythTV and iPod. It creates an RSS feed for streaming content that the system scheduler can batch up for sharing using its latest installation script. Myth2iPod requires `nuvexport` (mentioned below) to work properly, so you should install it before installing this plug-in.

- **MythRecommend** (`http://ipso.snappymail.ca:8080/mythrecommend/`)— As another entry in the collection of personalization tools, MythRecommend provides a more abstract level of personal interaction with your MythTV domain. MythRecommend can enumerate a list of currently scheduled recordings and use that information to synthesize a new list of recommendations based on the popularity and frequency of similar programs in listings from other users who also view the same programming. It is also completely anonymous.

This functionality goes a long way toward personalizing your MythTV systems by making it unique and introducing a bit of personality beyond the typical skinnable themes and pluggable modularity. If you enjoy this kind of thing, check out TVWish, a complementary and much more robust framework for implementing much of the same capability.

- **NUVExport** (`https://svn.forevermore.net/nuvexport/`)— The response to a lack of NuppleVideo (.nuv) format files — the native format MythTV uses to store digital content — has been answered in numerous ways from various sources. NUVExport is one such answer, a simple PERL-based wrapper script that enables you to transcode between the .nuv format and something applicable to a broader range of playback devices.

You can export to DVD, VCD, DVCD, and Super Video CD (SVCD) media with support for many formats, including DivX, XviD, and MP3. Under the hood, `nuvexport` uses `ffmpeg`, `transcode`, and `mencoder` to get the job done. If you are already familiar with `ffmpeg`, then you know the immediate advantages this application exposes. If you're not, you should probably check it out!

- **TVWish** (`www.templetons.com/brad/myth/tvwish.html`)— Suppose you want to watch a show and possibly record it, rank it, and file it in sequence, and you want this to happen whenever the show comes on, yet MythTV only has a two-week memory (if you get your feeds from Zap2it Labs, anyway). Your solution? TVWish, a preemptive, rank-and-file, all-purpose wish-list creator. You can search and assign priority according to a number of criteria, from title popularity to chronological order, and create exclusion lists, imports, exports, and amalgamations.

TVWish gives your MythTV box real personality, for it continues to grow to know and understand you, anticipating your every move and obeying your slightest whim. Depending upon how particular you make your preferences, the program caters to your every wish. It can even selectively record episodes in the order you specify, regardless of their order of appearance on television. It can also filter out all but the best programs for you, and can even heed advice from a film critic of your choice in making future judgments about the programs it records.

Windows Programs

MythTV qualifies as the *mythical convergence box* for reasons entirely of its own. That it converges with commonplace Windows hosts is merely a modest exhibition of good form and proper social skills. A handful of projects merit special attention in this chapter, because you may want to interface to MythTV backend services remotely, from a Windows PC, without going through the trouble of installing Linux again (unless, of course, you run a Linux-only household).

The following applications represent a few of the offerings publicly available to you in this arena. By the time this book goes to press, more applications will undoubtedly crop up, so be sure to check in with the parent MythTV Web site (in particular, at `www.mythtv.org/wiki/index.php/Category:Plugins` and `www.mythtv.org/wiki/index.php/Unofficial_Plugins`) for a more complete list of current offerings.

- **DsMyth** (`http://dsmyth.sourceforge.net/`) — DirectShow is a Microsoft component designed to handle playback of digital audio and video streams (AVI, MPEG, and QuickTime) for Windows. DsMyth is a plug-in that enables you to unify the MythTV native file format with one that's more palatable across a wide variety of media playback systems. This plug-in also supports backend server streaming and viewing live feeds.

  DsMyth is blanketed with a few warnings about compatibility issues among MythTV core releases, indicating that the codebase remains experimental. Nonetheless, that should not deter you. Instead, it should encourage you to try the DsMyth plug-in and provide feedback to the developer, so that it may mature and become usable among a larger audience of MythTV end-users.

- **MythHelper** (`http://mythhelper.sourceforge.net/`) — With a name like MythHelper, you can't help but feel a sense of reassurance. This utility is one of the many transcoder applications and libraries available for MythTV to aid in the export of .nuv format files to Windows frontend devices. It provides a simple GUI interface with a listbox of entries for easy perusal of scheduled recordings maintained by the MythTV backend server.

  Using Normal and High-Quality (HQ) settings you can render XviD AVIs with a resolution of 640 × 480. At DVD-quality settings, it's easy to create an interlaced MPEG2 audio/video file for playback on any properly equipped machine. Hardware and software requirements are detailed on the MythHelper Web site to help you provide the elements necessary to its deployment on your network.

- **TapeWorm** (`http://david.spurgeonwoods.com/tapeworm/`) — The unusual moniker for this program has a subtle nuance that the original author may not have intended, related to its status as a Windows application. Experienced Linuxheads should latch on almost instantly. TapeWorm isn't malware, so no anti-virus software is necessary.

  TapeWorm exists to provide an alternative to the next item on our chopping block, WinMyth, but it has a very different agenda. Instead of acting like a well-mannered network object that communicates through proper channels (namely, the extensive MythTV API), TapeWorm attaches to the MythTV backend much like a parasitic organism, to leech out the information it needs to work. Your backend server will never know it exists, except for log entries and other latent prints that networked applications leave behind in /var/log.

Like the MythHelper application, TapeWorm also provides a simple graphical interface with an intuitive look and feel, as shown in Figure 14-2. The large main information pane describes all currently scheduled recordings for your viewing pleasure, with a smaller pane beneath it to summarize any highlighted line entry in the upper pane. Five buttons grace the bottom portion of the application window, to provide options for Play, Refresh, Configure, About, and Exit.

FIGURE 14-2: The TapeWorm program window is easy to use and navigate.

- **WinMyth** (http://winmyth.sourceforge.net/) — While MythHelper and TapeWorm appeal to minimalist sensibilities (otherwise known as the K.I.S.S principle), WinMyth goes one step further and gives you two tabbed windows and a mini-preview pane for a highlighted entry.

  The first tab, aptly named Recorded Shows, is a quick index to the recording schedule on your MythTV backend. The next tab to the right is TV Listings, a near match to the MythTV listings capability of the frontend and MythWeb applications. You may browse shows by time and channel, or preview the current selection in the same tab using a thumbnail window.

Four primary buttons describe the breadth of active interface properties: Set View Properties, Set TV List Properties, Watch Live, and Watch Show Full Screen. At last check, WinMyth is reported as working with version 0.19.0 on the SourceForge Web site.

Final Thoughts

Each of these applications embodies the MythTV initiative: a spirit of do-it-yourself with a bit of technical know-how. Add an inventive spark of inspiration that clicks, and you yourself could respond, "I can do that!" Indeed, you can do just about anything you can imagine using MythTV, and many people already have. These plug-ins are a testament to the viability of a modular framework that permits users to insert or remove functionality at will, and reap immediate results. This flexibility also enables you to adopt some, many, or none of the great ideas that make up the MythTV application suite. Either way, you can get what you want (and avoid what you don't want).

Advanced MythTV Hacks

part

IV

A s the title of Part IV is meant to emphasize, this part of the book is where we make good on the promise inherent in its title. Though we cover a lot of important, useful, and (it is hoped) informative material in the rest of the book, here's where the biggest, shiniest nuggets of "good stuff" reside. In fact, lead author Jarod Wilson wrote this part himself, just to make sure we didn't leave anything important out!

In Chapter 15, we tackle more and better ways to spruce up the way MythTV looks and behaves, starting with desktop themes. Then we walk through numerous other key topics, including adding DVD menu support, wide-screen HDTV tweaks and tricks, customizing mythfrontend menus, and more. Chapter 16 tackles MythTV under the hood and concentrates on important ways you can supercharge the performance of your MythTV PC.

Chapter 17 describes ways to extend your MythTV environment, including how to bring a cable or satellite set-top box into the picture (so to speak), and provides information about wireless networking with TV signals, ripping VHS tapes onto CD, and various ways to let your remote in on what's happening inside your PC.

Chapter 18 concludes this section with a discussion of MythTV troubleshooting that explains how to get past or steer clear of well-known pitfalls and potholes. Maybe you really can learn from someone else's mistakes!

By the time you finish this part of the book, you will understand a lot more about how to customize, tweak, and troubleshoot your MythTV system. We think this guidance should help you both develop a strong sense of proprietary pride in "your installation" and make the most of your multimedia experience.

MythTV Look, Sound, and Feel

MythTV is far more flexible than most commercial digital video recorder (DVR) options. Its open-source origins means that many talented individuals have already written code to add new features and expand the range of hardware supported for use with MythTV. MythTV also runs on a much wider range of hardware and operating systems than any other computer-based DVR. Over time, MythTV has evolved to include theme-based interfaces, a myriad of plug-ins, and support for HDTV video capture and digital audio output, to name just a few such additions. Many of these features require some tweaking before you can appreciate them fully; this chapter aims to guide you through some of the work involved.

More and Better Themes

These days, it seems like all the world loves a chameleon. There are countless different faceplates and carrying cases for cell phones and iPods, and different skins for your web browser and even your computer desktop, especially in the Linux world, where freedom reigns supreme. MythTV joined the bandwagon early on in its existence, and even ships with a few theme options in the core MythTV package itself.

However, there are also a lot of third-party themes floating about in the wild, which you can easily add to your system. Note that there are actually three types of themes for MythTV: user interface (UI) themes, on-screen display (OSD) themes, and menu layout themes. Some are designed to work together, but there's nothing to stop you from mixing and matching themes to your heart's content. Very few (if any) menu layout themes beyond those included with MythTV exist, but quite a few UI themes and a number of OSD themes are out there (see Figure 15-1 for one such example UI theme).

FIGURE 15-1: Abstract UI theme

Most themes outside those included with MythTV itself may be found in various places on the Internet, typically hosted by their creators. New and/or updated themes are periodically mentioned on the MythTV users mailing list, and ATrpms.net tries to package as many of them as possible for easy installation on Fedora Core (although they should work for any rpm-based Linux distribution). You can view the available pre-packaged themes at `http://atrpms .net/dist/common/mythtv-themes/`.

Additionally, at least one company, TechnoVera, briefly entered the fray, with a pilot program under the flag of the LxM Suite, which was a collection of additional subscription-based services and functionality for MythTV. Among the items available to subscribers were a few professionally crafted MythTV themes, primarily tailored for wide-screen televisions. The pilot program didn't meet TechnoVera's expectations, but the themes live on, now made available to the world at `http://jmeyer.us/`. Look for these themes to appear on ATrpms.net soon as well, if they aren't there already.

If none of the existing themes suits you, then you can try your hand at creating your own from scratch (or based on existing themes) — which is exactly how most third-party themes came into being. At the moment, themes consist of nothing more than graphics files (PNG or JPG format) along with xml files that describe how everything should be laid out. (A new OpenGL-based interface format is currently in the works as we write this chapter, but it has not yet been released).

If you're using Fedora Core, and installed MythTV following our directions in Part II of this book, you should have requested installation of the mythtv-suite. It's simply a meta-package that satisfies the dependencies for all MythTV components provided by ATrpms.net, and includes all packaged themes. If you see a new theme available at ATrpms.net — for example, mythtv-theme-foo-1.0.noarch.rpm, you can install it using the command `yum install mythtv-theme-foo`. If you're not running Fedora Core or want to install a new theme that isn't yet packaged, you can usually find it distributed as a tarball (for example, `themename.tar.gz`), which you can extract into your MythTV themes directory (typically `/usr/share/mythtv/themes/` for binary installs, or `/usr/local/share/mythtv/themes/` for source-based installs) to make it available for use.

So how do you actually go about using these themes once you have them in place? Well, just fire up MythTV and take a trip into the Setup section. The place to set the themes to use for the MythTV user interface and menus resides in a different location from the one where the on-screen display theme is set.

First up, take a look at the user-interface and menu theme settings. From the main MythTV menu, select Utilities/Setup → Setup → Appearance. The very first page, titled Theme, presents you with the opportunity to change the following settings: Theme (with a little preview), Qt Style, Font size, and Menu theme (see Figure 15-2). The UI themes Blue and G.A.N.T. are the stock themes included with MythTV itself, with a few additional ones provided in a separate download. Qt Style refers to the widget style of the Qt toolkit, which MythTV uses for most of its user interface elements (at least until the conversion to the previously mentioned OpenGL-based interface is complete).

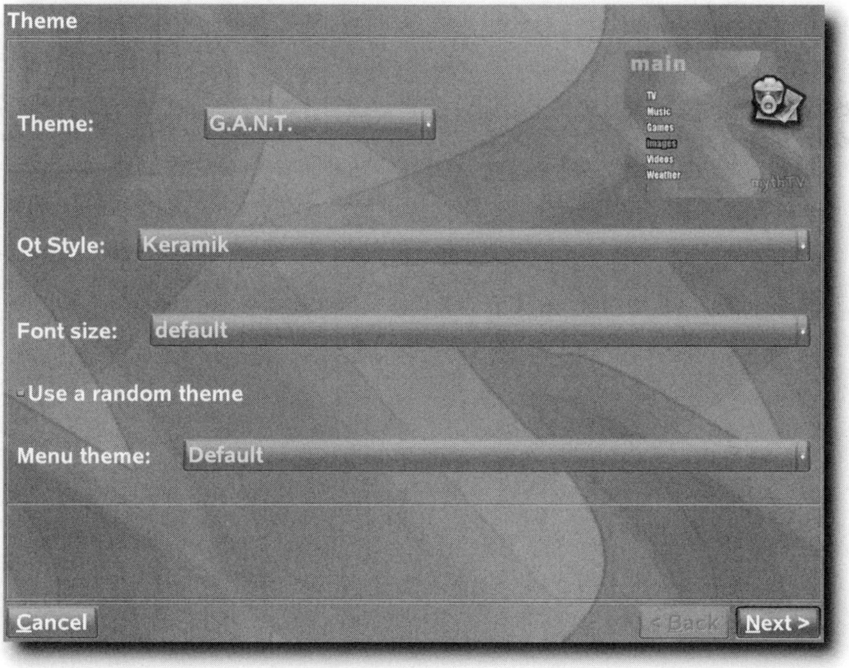

FIGURE 15-2: Configuring your MythTV UI

The default is Desktop Style (the default style sometimes varies from one Linux distribution to another), but many users find that the progress bars and buttons provided by the Keramik style are the most visually appealing. The Font size setting enables you to make some minor adjustments to how big the text appears within the UI. The Menu theme setting enables you to alter the way in which the various menus are laid out — the included options are default and classic, where classic identifies the old menu layout used in older MythTV releases, which has been dropped as the default in favor of a newer, more function-oriented layout.

You'll also notice the checkbox for "Use a random theme" on this page, which selects a random theme each time MythTV starts — though its utility is limited on a dedicated MythTV system, where MythTV typically never gets restarted. None of these settings are applied until you proceed through the rest of the configuration screens under the Appearance section, described next.

The Screen settings page enables you to adjust the width, height, and horizontal and vertical offsets of the UI; set TV playback to use the same screen area as the UI; hide or show the mouse cursor; and determine whether you run MythTV in a window or full screen. These options can be useful in various scenarios. You can use MythTV with any number of different display devices, including (obviously) a television set.

If you're using a connection other than DVI between your MythTV system and your TV, chances are good that your Linux desktop (which runs atop the X Window System, commonly called X) won't fill the screen perfectly. Most standard-definition televisions (and standard-definition inputs on high-definition televisions) overscan the incoming picture, which means that parts of the image lie outside the visible area onscreen. This has a legacy in standard-definition television broadcasts, which we won't go into right here, but it means that part of your UI can wind up outside your view. To compensate, you can shrink the UI size and shift it around to fit within the visible area.

For example, if you run your Linux desktop at a resolution of 800 × 600, upwards of 50 pixels can wind up offscreen in any direction. (If much more than that appears to be missing, you may need to adjust some video driver settings, which we cover in Chapter 18). Adjust the width to something like 760, and the height to 460, nudge it down 10 pixels and over 20 pixels, and you might have a better fit. You can also play back TV within that same confined area, though standard-definition television is formatted with overscan in mind, so this isn't recommended unless you're viewing high-definition television, but your HDTV (or SDTV) doesn't support fully digital input (namely, DVI), and it can't adjust overscan using the TV's (or computer display's) picture controls.

If you happen to run MythTV on your desktop, the options to run MythTV in a window and to unhide the mouse cursor are far more useful than on a dedicated system that's hooked up to your TV.

The next page in the Appearance section, titled Video Mode Settings, is entirely unused by default, and typically isn't something you should touch unless high-definition TV is in the picture (and even then, with some sets, it isn't necessary). Basically, if you run a version of the X Window System that supports the XRandR (X Resize and Rotate) extension, you can drive your display at different resolutions, depending on whether you're in the user interface and/or based on the resolution of the source material you're playing back. We cover this more in the "Wide-screen HDTV Tweaks" section later in this chapter.

On the Localization page, you can specify settings for Language, Date format, Short Date format and Time format to use within the user interface. The following QT page enables you to set the font sizes for the definitions Small, Medium and Big, which are used within themes as keywords to describe how big certain texts should be. Typically, there's no reason to stray from the defaults, and themes are designed with the defaults in mind, but feel free to adjust them to taste and/or eyesight. You can also toggle the use of transparent boxes and background shading methods used in various parts of the UI, which can have an impact on UI responsiveness, depending on how fast or slow your MythTV system is. The trade-off for more eye candy is degraded performance, so adjust with care.

If your MythTV case happens to have either a built-in LCD display, such as those in some high-end Ahanix (www.ahanix.com) and SilverStone (www.silverstonetek.com) cases, or an external LCD display, such as the ones from CrystalFontz (www.crystal fontz.com), you'll be happy to know that many of them work with Linux, and thus also become available for MythTV to use. You can configure what's displayed on your LCD using the LCD device display page.

This concludes our trip through the Appearance setup menu item screens. After pressing the Finish button on the LCD page, all your changes are applied. The most noticeable of these should be an immediate rescaling of UI graphics to match your new theme and/or display size preferences. Just rinse and repeat until you're happy with the way the UI looks, and then you can move on to adjusting your OSD theme.

You might have expected to find the OSD theme settings dialog mixed in somewhere with the rest of the appearance settings, but at the moment it resides under Utilities/Setup ➜ Setup ➜ TV Settings ➜ Playback, hidden on the ninth page (that's because you only see the OSD during TV playback). This page is fittingly entitled On-screen display, and contains options for the following: your OSD theme, Number of seconds for OSD information, OSD font, Closed Caption font, Font size, a toggle for black backgrounds behind closed captioning, whether or not to always display closed captioning, and whether you should always use browse mode when changing channels (see Figure 15-3).

The OSD theme option is fairly self-explanatory; it is here that you choose the OSD theme for MythTV to use. No previews are provided here, so you'll just have to try them out. The Number of seconds for OSD information option enables you to configure how long OSD information stays on screen after certain actions are taken (such as changing the channel, pressing the Program Info button, skipping forward, and so on). Out of the box, MythTV comes with two options for your OSD and CC fonts: FreeMono and FreeSans. There are some legal issues associated with distributing many other fonts, but you're welcome to try other TrueType fonts by placing them in MythTV's share directory (/usr/share/mythtv/ for binary installs; typically /usr/local/share/mythtv/ for source-based installs). FreeSans tends to be the more popular option, though FreeMono remains the default. Here again, you can adjust the relative size of the fonts you use.

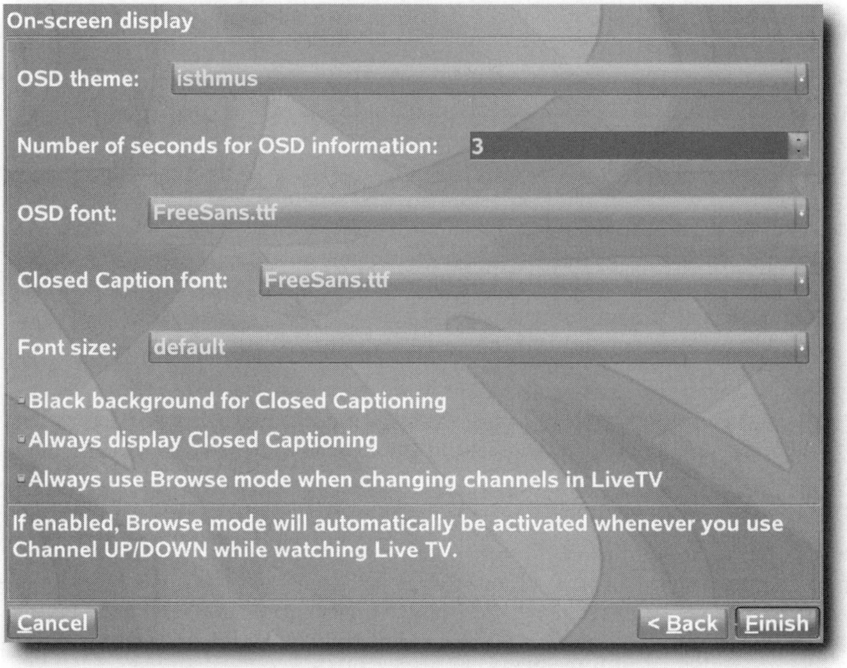

On-screen display

OSD theme: isthmus

Number of seconds for OSD information: 3

OSD font: FreeSans.ttf

Closed Caption font: FreeSans.ttf

Font size: default

° Black background for Closed Captioning

° Always display Closed Captioning

° Always use Browse mode when changing channels in LiveTV

If enabled, Browse mode will automatically be activated whenever you use Channel UP/DOWN while watching Live TV.

Cancel   < Back   Finish

FIGURE 15-3: Setting up your on-screen display

By default, if you use MythTV's built-in audio controls, when you mute the audio during TV playback, closed captioning (CC) data is displayed (if provided for that program, and if your video capture card supports closed captioning). You can even display CC data at all times with a black background, if you so choose. The somewhat misplaced option to use Browse mode versus changing channels directly while watching live TV also resides on this page. Browse mode essentially enables you to continue watching a show while paging through TV listings until you get to and directly select the program you want to watch instead.

Many folks are quite partial to G.A.N.T. out of all the UI themes available from mythtv.org (see Figure 15-4), and either Isthmus and Titivillus for the OSD theme, both of which tend to look best with the FreeSans font. In addition, a good number of third-party themes are coming along nicely, such as Justin Hornsby's Project Grayhem (`homepage.ntlworld.com/ justin.hornsby2`), as well as the former LxM Suite themes, at `http://jmeyer.us`.

FIGURE 15-4: The G.A.N.T. UI theme

Wide-screen HDTV Tweaks

Initially, the bulk of MythTV development centered around standard-definition television and the traditional 4:3 aspect ratio analog TV sets. These days, support is rapidly improving for high-definition televisions with a 16:9 aspect ratio. Multiple HDTV capture methods may be used with MythTV; several wide-screen themes have recently appeared, and MythTV does nothing to limit the sorts of devices to which you can direct output.

Driving Your HDTV

The first step toward optimal HDTV performance is to drive your HDTV at the best possible resolution. DVI is far and away the preferred interface over which to drive an HDTV, followed by VGA, Component Video, S-Video, and composite video. The first three can handle wide-aspect HDTV resolutions (interlaced and progressive-scan), while the last two can only handle standard-definition resolutions, which are always interlaced. (And no matter what you feed out of a computer to your TV over these two paths, it will be scaled to a 4:3 SDTV resolution, for maximum theoretical resolution of 720×480 for NTSC and 768×576 for PAL.)

You'll need to do a lot less tweaking if you can feed an actual wide-screen resolution to your TV. Likewise, the MythTV user interface looks much better when displayed inside a progressive-scan signal. The current best-case scenario is a television capable of accepting a 1920 × 1080 progressive-scan signal over DVI from your computer to your HDTV. See Chapter 3 for more details on configuring output to an HDTV.

Getting the Right Theme

The second step toward optimal HDTV performance is finding a wide-screen theme. They'll make better use of the extra screen width, and won't be subject to excessive horizontal stretching. Right now, at least four fairly well-polished wide-screen themes are available — namely, Minimalist-wide, Project Grayhem-wide, Syth-Lacquer-wide, and Midnight-wide.

Finding the Right Aspect

Assuming you've got a 16:9 aspect ratio feeding your TV, MythTV itself does a pretty good job of playing back material at the right aspect. Here, the definition of "right" is somewhat subjective, at least when it comes to playing back standard-definition TV on an HDTV. However, MythTV does offer multiple ways to override both playback and recording aspects. Depending on personal preferences, you might choose to leave your SDTV recordings to be captured with a 4:3 aspect ratio, which means black pillars will appear along the sides of your video. However, if you prefer, you can adjust your recording profiles for SDTV capture devices to a 16:9 aspect ratio, instead of 4:3 (change this at Utilities/Setup → Setup → TV Settings → Recording Profiles → MPEG-2 Encoders or Standard V4L Encoder → Default → third page, Aspect Ratio setting), though this can be problematic if you also view your recordings on a standard-definition TV from time to time. Another alternative is to set an aspect override of 16:9 for your HDTV-connected system (Utilities/Setup → Setup → TV Settings → Playback → first page, Aspect Override setting).

You can also adjust the playback aspect ratio while playing back a recording (or live TV), which can be extremely useful when viewing shows broadcast in HDTV, but actually only displayed within 4:3 on the screen (pillar-boxed), or for SDTV shows broadcast in a letter-boxed format. That's because in addition to offering 4:3 and 16:9 aspect override options, MythTV also enables you to apply a 16:9 zoom aspect override. Thus, you can take a pillar-boxed HDTV show and expand its 4:3 content out to fill 16:9, and you can apply a 4:3 zoom aspect override to SDTV letter-boxed shows (which have an actual video area of 16:9) to make them fill the full viewable area of your HDTV completely.

You can even rotate through aspects while watching a show using the w key on your keyboard (or whatever button it's mapped to on your remote). Alternately, you can press the m key (typically mapped to the Menu button on your remote) to bring up a menu of options, among which is Change Aspect Ratio.

Those forced to run a 16:9 display with a 4:3 signal can opt to set the `DisplaySize` property in the `Monitor` section of their `/etc/X11/xorg.conf` file per these guidelines, as excerpted from the `xorg.conf` man page:

```
DisplaySize  width height
```

```
This optional entry gives the width and height, in millimetres, of
the picture area of the monitor. If given this is used to
calculate the horizontal and vertical pitch (DPI) of the screen.
```

This setting is examined by both xine and MythTV to determine what aspect ratio your display really uses, regardless of resolution, and should make all of MythTV's aspect overrides operate as if you were running a 16:9 resolution.

For the most part, nothing special needs to be done with either MPlayer or xine to get movies to play back at the right aspect ratio if your display is recognized as being 16:9, either via a native 16:9 resolution or through the `DisplaySize` trick. However, MythVideo does allow you to set different command-line launch flags for whatever external playback engine you're using for movies, depending on the specific file extension, so you can set an arbitrary extension to trigger an aspect override that way, should you find such a need. (Follow the menu sequence Utilities/Setup ➔ Setup ➔ Media Settings ➔ Videos Settings ➔ File Types, and then create a new extension and assign it to use a specific playback command, rather than use the default player).

For whatever reason, you might want to launch xine with the `--aspect-ratio 4:3` flag to trick it into thinking your display is 4:3, not 16:9. Similarly, you can pass `-monitoraspect 4:3` to MPlayer (the respective man pages for both of these media playback engines contain complete lists of all the aspect override options available, should you happen upon another situation for which you need different overrides).

Finding the Right Resolution

In some cases, there are good reasons why you might want to use more than one resolution for some function or another on your MythTV box. For example, an HDTV with a native resolution of 1080i is actually capable of running 540p, which is electronically equivalent to 1080i (both send 540 lines of resolution per frame). Progressive-scan resolutions are far better if you have to read text, such as with MythTV's UI, but you want to make use of that full 1920 × 1080i to watch HDTV content. MythTV includes built-in support for the X resize and rotate (XRandR) extension, which offers the best of both worlds — your UI (and standard-definition programming) at 960 × 540p, and HDTV material at 1920 × 1080i, as well as a number of other combinations. If your set supports 480p, 720p and 1080i, you might opt to view standard-definition content at 480p, run the UI and watch 720p HDTV programming at 720p and watch 1080i HDTV programming at 1080i.

All of these settings are handled on the Video Mode Settings page within the Appearance section of the frontend setup (see Figure 15-5).

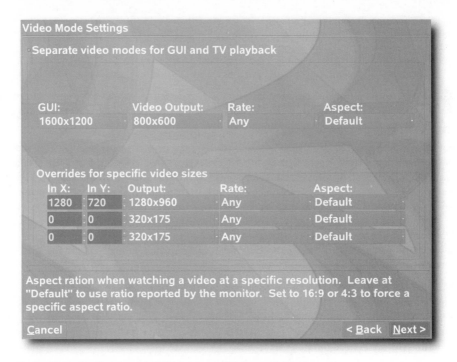

Figure 15-5: Configuring MythTV to use multiple resolutions

Using xine to Add DVD Menu Support

The current MythDVD plug-in release (0.19) includes native support for DVD playback, but does not support DVD menus. However, it's possible to configure MythDVD to use an external video playback application if you want DVD menu support. The most popular choice for DVD playback is xine (http://xinehq.de/). Among other things, xine already supports DVD playback with full support for DVD menus and Dolby Digital surround sound (including the capability to pass raw digital audio to your Dolby Digital decoding amplifier, covered later in this chapter).

Binaries are available for multiple Linux platforms, many of which are linked from the xine Web site. Alternatively, you can always download and compile from source yourself if you choose. Installing xine on Fedora Core is a simple matter of enabling the FreshRPMs repository in your yum configuration. For Fedora Core 5, just install the freshrpms-release-<version>.noarch.rpm package from http://ftp.freshrpms.net/pub/freshrpms/fedora/linux/5/freshrpms-release/, and then issue the command yum install xine.

Once you have xine installed, all that is left to do is configure MythDVD to launch xine for DVD playback. In Utilities/Setup → Setup → Media Settings → DVD Settings → Play Settings, use

```
xine -pfhq -no-splash dvd://
```

as your DVD Player command, and you should be greeted with full DVD menu support the next time you go to play a DVD in the MythTV frontend.

Note that if you ever pop in a DVD that contains episodes of your favorite TV show, you might find that the video looks absolutely horrid, with all sorts of jagged edges whenever any-thing moves, and/or looks like you're watching through a comb. If that's the case, it's likely the show was transcribed to DVD in its original standard-definition, interlaced format. However, the fix is simple: Bring up xine's setup UI and toggle on Enable deinterlacing by default on the gui tab (deinterlacing can also be toggled on-the-fly using the "i" key).

Tweaking MythVideo

The MythVideo plug-in simply provides a friendly interface for looking at your video library. Unlike MythTV itself, MythVideo relies on additional applications for the actual playback of your videos. This means you may need to use a little elbow grease in order to overcome a few limitations.

Share and Share Alike

MythVideo doesn't operate in the same client-server model that MythTV itself does, so there's no concept of a master backend MythVideo server that can stream movies to your frontends. You set up a storage location where you dump your movie files, and then point MythVideo at it. If you're running multiple frontends and want all of them to have access to the same movies, you probably don't want to put a copy of every movie on every frontend. Designating a single machine to house all the movies and then sharing them via NFS or Samba is highly recom-mended. NFS is recommended for simplicity's sake, though if you're also running Windows or Macintosh clients, Samba might be the route to take (configuring Samba is covered at www.mjmwired.net/resources/mjm-fedora-fc5.html; see especially the section entitled "Setup Samba").

We'll assume your movies all reside in /var/lib/mythvideo on your master MythTV backend server, called *mbe*, which has an IP address of 192.168.10.50 and a network mask of 255.255.255.0. We'll also assume you have a remote frontend machine, called *fe1*, with IP address 192.168.10.51, and that you'd like to be able to import new movies and their associated metadata, browse your movie library on both systems with all the cover art present, and watch all the movies on both systems (and this scales linearly with additional frontends).

First up, you need to configure *mbe* to share out `/var/lib/mythvideo` to your network. Add the following line to `/etc/exports`:

```
/var/lib/mythvideo 192.168.10.0/24(rw)
```

Make sure that `/var/lib/mythvideo` and everything in it are owned by the user you run MythTV as, so that both systems will have read and write privileges. Assuming you're running MythTV as the user `mythtv` on both your systems, the following command (run as root) should get you the necessary permissions:

```
# chown -R mythtv /var/lib/mythvideo
```

Next, start up your NFS server and enable it to run at system startup (`/sbin/service nfs start && /sbin/chkconfig nfs on`) on Fedora.

On *fe1*, add the following line to the file `/etc/hosts` (unless you've configured DNS for your internal network):

```
192.168.10.50  mbe
```

Then add a line to `/etc/fstab` that reads as follows:

```
mbe:/var/lib/mythvideo /var/lib/mythvideo nfs
  defaults 0 0
```

Now mount the share onto *fe1* using the following command (as root):

```
# mount /var/lib/mythvideo
```

As the `mythtv` user, try a simple directory creation on the share (which you'll actually need for some additional tweaks momentarily):

```
$ mkdir /var/lib/mythvideo/.artwork
```

By default, MythVideo is configured to store downloaded movie posters in `~/.mythtv/MythVideo`, but because this is a local file system path, if you were to download movie posters on one machine, then they wouldn't be available on other systems. To get around that, alter the location in which MythVideo looks for movie posters to `/var/lib/mythvideo/.artwork`, and they'll be available to all your systems. (Go to Utilities/Setup ➜ Setup ➜ Media Settings ➜ Videos Settings ➜ General Settings, "Directory that holds movie posters.")

With that all set up, you should be able to run the Video Manager (Utilities/Setup ➜ Video Manager) on any of your systems, have the resulting downloaded information and movie posters available to all systems, and be able to play your movies from any of your MythTV systems (see Figure 15-6).

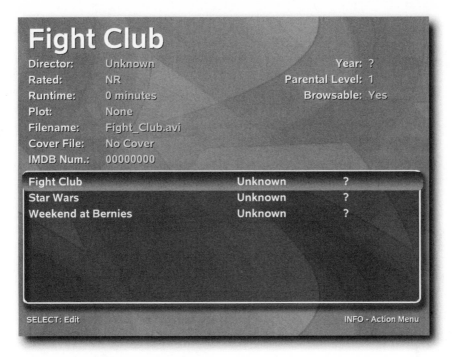

Fight Club

Director:	Unknown	Year:	?
Rated:	NR	Parental Level:	1
Runtime:	0 minutes	Browsable:	Yes
Plot:	None		
Filename:	Fight_Club.avi		
Cover File:	No Cover		
IMDB Num.:	00000000		

Fight Club	Unknown	?
Star Wars	Unknown	?
Weekend at Bernies	Unknown	?

SELECT: Edit   INFO - Action Menu

FIGURE 15-6: MythVideo's Video Manager

Keeping Things in Focus

A common MythTV problem when running within the de facto standard MythTV desktop environment, KDE, is that when you exit playback of a movie, your remote quits working. That's because KDE shifts focus to the Kicker (the panel at the bottom of the screen) for some reason, rather than to the MythTV window, so your remote control is now trying to work on the Kicker, and does nothing. One possible fix is to change to a different window manager, but that's a fair amount of work for such a trivial issue. The easy fix is to change KDE's window focus behavior, so that you make focus follow the mouse. This is a bit goofy for people who are trying to use the system as a normal computer, but it works well if you dump the cursor in the middle of the screen, because when MythVideo (MPlayer or xine) exits, focus will return to MythTV, and your remote keeps working. You can change window focus behavior by opening Control Center (off the menu button at the bottom left of the Kicker), navigating to Desktop ➜ Window Behavior, changing the focus policy to Focus Follows Mouse, and clicking Apply (see Figure 15-7).

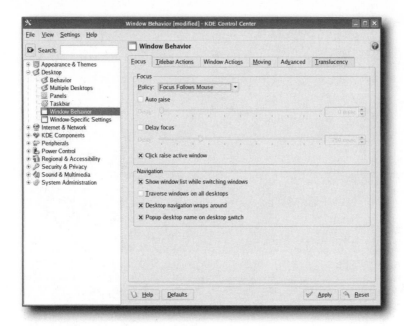

FIGURE 15-7: Configuring KDE's window focus behavior

Raw Digital Audio Output

Most DVD movies and HDTV programs include 5.1 channel Dolby Digital (aka AC3) audio. While you could let your computer decode Dolby Digital audio, and then output the resulting decoded audio, should you wish to integrate your MythTV system with a nice amplifier that can decode Dolby Digital audio, the amplifier usually produces higher quality audio (more accurate decoding and crisper playback) than if the computer decodes the digital stream and passes a PCM-encoded analog audio stream to the amp. Obviously, it's ideal to pass a raw digital stream to the amp and let it handle decoding.

Unfortunately, this is one of the areas that many folks find difficult to configure correctly, not only for MythTV, but under Linux in general. If you want a relatively surefire way to get raw digital audio output, get yourself a Creative Labs SoundBlaster Audigy sound card. They're now a few generations old, but that's OK because it means there has been ample time for most of the bugs to be worked out with these cards, and they are relatively cheap. SoundBlaster Live! 5.1 and Audigy 2 cards are also well supported by the same driver that the Audigy uses. All these cards have a mini-coaxial S/PDIF (Sony/Philips Digital Interface Format) on-board jack, or an optional add-on card or drive bay module that includes a standard coaxial or optical S/PDIF output. The mini-coax port requires a mono stereo mini-plug to an RCA-style connector adapter to connect to most amplifiers, while straight optical or coaxial cables can be used with the add-on cards or drive bay modules.

On the software side, you want a relatively new kernel with ALSA (Advanced Linux Sound Architecture) enabled. This should be the case for almost any Linux distribution's stock kernel these days (it definitely is for Fedora and Knoppix/KnoppMyth). You shouldn't need to do anything special to configure the Audigy driver itself (which is called `snd-emu10k1`); it should be detected automatically and configured by your distribution's hardware detection tools. Tweaking various audio mixer properties is a bigger task, and requires using a file and an audio mixer tool. The biggest job of all, however, is getting MythTV to use ALSA natively, rather than through an OSS emulation interface (OSS stands for Open Sound System, the audio framework that ALSA replaced).

Before tackling how to pass raw digital audio from MythTV, we focus on MPlayer, which offers more mature support for native ALSA and raw digital audio output. Running MPlayer from a terminal window spits out copious amounts of debugging information, which can be helpful when trying to ensure that things behave exactly as you want them to. You'll need a video clip with digital audio embedded, such as the ~31MB test clip available from the Downloads section of the pcHDTV website (`www.pchdtv.com/`). pcHDTV manufactures the HD-2000 and HD-3000 HDTV capture cards, designed exclusively for use with Linux; their configuration and use are covered in Chapter 3. To get started, download the `tst.ts` file and rename it from `tst.tar` to `tst.ts`. To ensure that you're playing the file back using an ALSA interface and passing raw digital audio, play the file back using the following MPlayer command line:

```
$ mplayer -ao alsa -ac hwac3 tst.ts
```

Among the output MPlayer spews to your console, you should see the following:

```
Forced audio codec: hwac3
Opening audio decoder: [hwac3] AC3/DTS pass-through S/PDIF
No accelerated IMDCT transform found
hwac3: switched to AC3, 384000 bps, 48000 Hz
AUDIO: 48000 Hz, 2 ch, ac3, 384.0 kbit/25.00% (ratio: 48000->192000)
Selected audio codec: [hwac3] afm:hwac3 (AC3 through S/PDIF)
```

If you're lucky, you'll actually hear something, but chances are good there's still some mixer tweaking left to do. The tried-and-true command-line mixer that ought to be on everyone's system is *alsamixer*. Fire it up from the command line by name:

```
$ alsamixer
```

You might find it convenient to launch alsamixer from a second console window, while leaving MPlayer playing back the test clip in another, so that you can see what difference mixer changes make in real time. Navigate from one slider to another using the left and right arrows, raise and lower sliders using the up and down arrows, and mute/unmute sliders or toggle them on and off using the "m" key. Make sure you've got the Master slider volume unmuted for starters (the volume level doesn't matter; that should be controlled by your external amp). In the case of the Audigy, one item you can toggle on and off in alsamixer is the Audigy Analog/Digital Output Jack. This must be turned on in order for raw digital audio output to work. The other mixer setting to watch out for is IEC958 Optical Raw, the proper setting for which seems to vary (at present, setting it to off works for an Audigy under Fedora Core 5 with kernel 2.6.16-1.2080_FC5 and alsamixer 1.0.10).

For those not using an Audigy, try twiddling any mixer settings that include IEC958 in their name, as IEC958 is the standard that encompasses the Sony/Philips Digital Interface Format, which is most likely what your amp utilizes for its digital audio interfaces (both coaxial or optical).

Once you've succeeded in getting digital audio passed correctly to your amp using MPlayer with the aforementioned command-line switches, it's time to set MPlayer and xine up to automatically output digital audio the same way. For MPlayer, edit /etc/mplayer/ mplayer.conf (or create it, if it doesn't exist), adding (if not already present) lines that read as follows:

```
# Default audio output is alsa, then try others
ao=alsa,alsa1x,
```

This tells MPlayer to try the alsa output module first, followed by the alsa1x module (it's named differently in some Linux distributions), and the trailing comma tells MPlayer to try anything it can think of if neither of the two specified methods work. Next, add the following lines (if they're not already present):

```
# Try outputting raw digital audio first, then fallback to auto-detection
ac=hwac3,
```

This tells MPlayer to try passing raw digital audio to an external hardware digital audio decoder first, and then fallback to auto-detecting what type of output it should use. Now that you've got all that set up, make sure you're still getting the right behavior by playing back your test file again, this time without the –ao and –ac parameters:

```
$ mplayer tst.ts
```

If all is well, you can move on to xine, which is trivial to get working by comparison. xine doesn't provide as much useful debug output as MPlayer does, but it generally works once the mixer settings are right. You can either edit ~/.xine/config or launch xine and configure raw digital audio pass-through using xine's setup GUI . Find the configuration option audio.output.speaker_arrangement: in ~/.xine/config and set the value after the colon to Pass Through, or select the audio tab in the xine setup GUI and choose Pass Through from the speaker arrangement drop-down menu (see Figure 15-8). If you play a file that doesn't contain digital audio, xine automatically falls back to properly decode and output the audio.

Now for the big one: configuring MythTV to output raw Dolby Digital/AC3 audio, if present, and fallback to decoding other types of audio, passing them out over the same S/PDIF connector it uses for PCM-encoded audio streams. Start off by heading into Utilities/Setup→ Setup → General within the MythTV frontend, and on page 3, set the audio output device to ALSA:spdif (sound cards other than the Audigy may need ALSA:default instead). You'll have to type it in manually; it isn't available on the drop-down menu. Now check the box for "Enable AC3 to SPDIF passthrough," uncheck Aggressive Soundcard Buffering (which causes problems with AC3 audio in some cases), and set the Mixer Device to default, which you'll have to type in manually (see Figure 15-9). Click through to the end of the settings screens, and then on to the next section.

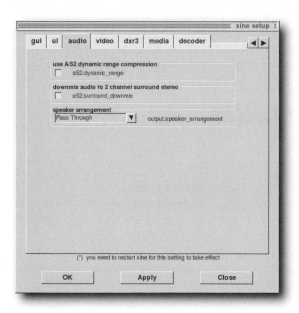

FIGURE 15-8: Configuring digital audio pass-through in xine

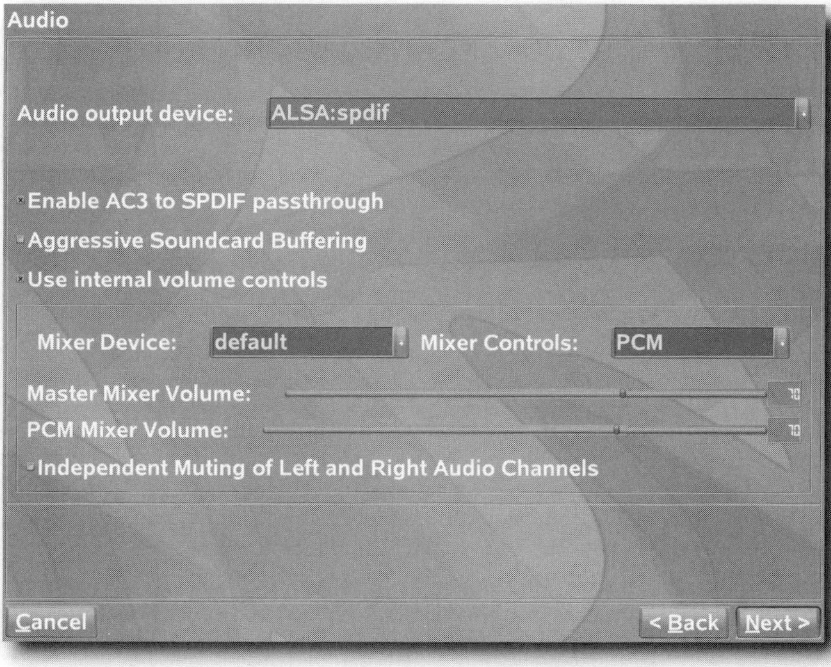

FIGURE 15-9: Configuring digital audio pass-through in MythTV

Navigate into TV Settings ➔ Playback, where you'll need to set a number of parameters with varying impacts on HDTV playback. For raw digital audio output, be sure to disable Use Video As Timebase, and to enable Extra Audio Buffering. With that done, it is hoped that the audio in your HDTV recordings will now pass to your external amplifier as raw digital streams.

Remote Power Button Tweaks

Most remote control configuration files map the off/power button on the remote to the same functionality as an exit or back button. If you already have a button for that, why duplicate it? Make the power button do something more interesting, such as enabling it to kill off or start up the MythTV frontend. This can be decidedly useful for nontechnical users who use MythTV on a regular basis, because even though frontend lockups are rare nowadays, they do occasionally happen. And when they do, it's a lot easier for nontechnical users to bring the frontend back up if they can simply double-tap the power button to perform that task.

So how do you do this? Well, it's simple enough to create a shell script that determines whether the frontend is running, and then takes certain actions based on the result of that check (plus a few other parameters). Create the following shell script as root, in /usr/local/bin/mythpowerbutton.sh:

```
#!/bin/bash
PROG=mythfrontend
RUNNING=`ps -e | grep -c $PROG`

if [ `echo $DISPLAY | grep -c ":0"` -ge 1 ]
then
    if [ $RUNNING -ge 1 ]
    then
        killall $PROG
    else
        ( $PROG & )
    fi
fi
exit 0
```

Next, make the script executable as follows:

```
# chmod +x /usr/local/bin/mythpowerbutton.sh
```

This script makes sure it's running on your primary display; and if a running mythfrontend process is found, it kills it off. If no mythfrontend process is running, a new one is fired up. In other words, if the frontend locks up but the system isn't completely locked up, the first time the script is launched, it'll kill off any running instances of mythfrontend. The next launch of the script can then launch a new mythfrontend process. Next, you must tie this script to the power button on your remote, first by adding the following stanza to ~/.lircrc:

```
# Power Button
begin
  prog = irexec
```

```
    button = POWER
    repeat = 4
    config = /usr/local/bin/mythpowerbutton.sh
end
```

Be sure to remove any other stanzas for the button Power, or, if your remote is configured for an Off button, rather than a Power button, adjust accordingly. (Double-check this by looking at the contents of /etc/lircd.conf.) Note the line prog = irexec, which indicates you need a program called irexec running when this button is pressed. irexec is part of the LIRC (Linux Infrared Remote Control) package, and it actually fires off the script you created, from the config = /usr/local/bin/mythpowerbutton.sh line. The next task is to ensure that irexec is running.

There are many ways to get irexec running. If you're running KDE, the simplest way is to create a symlink in ~/.kde/Autostart/, to cause irexec to start up every time you log in to your KDE desktop. Set the symlink up as follows, from within whatever user account in which you run mythfrontend:

```
$ ln -s /usr/bin/irexec ~/.kde/Autostart/
```

If you installed LIRC from source instead of a binary package, you'll want to modify the irexec location to /usr/local/bin/irxexc. The next time you log in, everything should be ready to run your new power button functions.

Customizing Frontend Menus

There are a few different ways to alter the menus within mythfrontend to make them more to your liking. The simplest instance enables you to get rid of menu components you don't use. For example, if you've installed every plug-in available but find that you never use MythPhone, you can remove all phone-related menu entries simply by uninstalling MythPhone.

As described earlier in this chapter, two different menu layout themes are available. If you don't like either one of them, you're welcome to create your own.

If you don't feel the urge to create an entirely new menu theme, simply copy main_settings .xml and mainmenu.xml out of /usr/share/mythtv/ into ~/.mythtv/, after which you can tweak them to your heart's content without screwing up your main install, and your changes will survive an upgrade. This is probably the easiest way to remove unwanted content from your menus, to rename things to your liking, and so forth, without breaking any actual packages.

Configuring Remote Frontends

While it may seem daunting at first, configuring a remote frontend system is relatively easy, if you know what to do. Once you've set up your first one, the rest are a piece of cake.

The road starts with some required configuration adjustments to your master backend system, on which (for simplicity's sake) we assume you also run MythTV's MySQL database. During initial setup of your MythTV database, permission is granted to the user mythtv to access the mythconverg database within MySQL using the password mythtv, from the local machine only. All remote frontend systems need access to the database as well, so some changes to our MySQL permissions are needed.

Once again, we assume your master backend is called *mbe*, with an IP address of 192.168.10.50 and a 255.255.255.0 network mask; and that your remote frontend, *fe1*, resides on the same network, with IP address 192.168.10.51. To grant *fe1* (and any other system on your network) remote access your database, do the following:

```
$ mysql -u root -p mythconverg
mysql> GRANT ALL on mythconverg.* TO mythtv@"192.168.10.%"
IDENTIFIED BY "mythtv";
mysql> flush privileges;
mysql> quit
```

The initial -p flag assumes you've got a password set for the MySQL root account (different from your system root account) to access your database, and invokes a password prompt. Omit the -p if no password is set (and then set one while you're in there). The IDENTIFIED BY "mythtv" part indicates that the password the mythtv user uses to access the database is also mythtv, so alter accordingly if you choose.

With the MySQL bits out of the way, it's time to fire up the mythtvsetup application on *mbe* and enter the General section, where you must alter the values for the variables IP address for mbe and Master Server IP address on the first page from their defaults of 127.0.0.1 to *mbe*'s network-accessible IP address (192.168.10.50). If you happen to run a firewall on *mbe*, then you must make ports 3306 (MySQL), 6543, and 6544 (MythTV) remotely accessible (left as an exercise for the reader).

Next, you can move on to configuring *fe1* itself. We assume you've already got all the necessary software (such as MythTV) installed. Just start up mythfrontend on *fe1*, which should have no pre-existing configuration, and you'll be greeted with an initial query to select your desired language. The next page should flash a message stating that "Myth could not connect to the database." On this page, either alter the Host name variable from localhost to *mbe* (if you have a corresponding entry in /etc/hosts or run DNS on your network) or simply input *mbe*'s numeric IP address (192.168.10.50). Alter the Password field to match what you specified if you used something different in the previous MySQL configuration bit (see Figure 15-10).

If you haven't configured a unique host name for *fe1*, or it happens to be a system with a host name that varies depending on the IP address assigned via DHCP, it might be useful to opt to set a custom identifier for the host, so you don't have to reconfigure the system every time the IP address changes. If you hadn't already guessed, settings are stored within and retrieved from your MythTV database based on system host names, unless overridden by a custom identifier.

At the conclusion of this brief configuration setup, when you first launch mythfrontend on *fe1*, you should be presented with MythTV's main menu, and your remote frontend can now interface with your master backend.

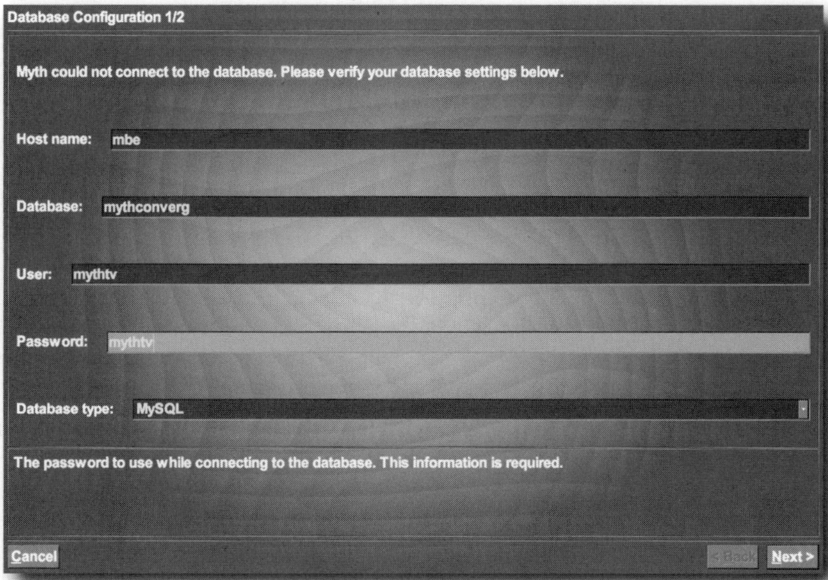

Database Configuration 1/2

Myth could not connect to the database. Please verify your database settings below.

Host name: mbe

Database: mythconverg

User: mythtv

Password: mythtv

Database type: MySQL

The password to use while connecting to the database. This information is required.

Cancel   < Back   Next >

FIGURE 15-10: Configuring a remote MythTV frontend system

Compiling Myth Components Individually

MythTV and all its (official) plug-ins use a slightly different compile/setup procedure than do some other open-source projects. The source for the MythTV core is in one tarball, and all plug-ins are in another. There's a fairly standard configure script within both tarballs that you can use to set up exactly which components and features you wish to enable.

You must start with the core MythTV tarball first, because all plug-ins must be built on top of the core, and they rely on libraries built from the core's source. You can either download an official release version of the core MythTV tarball from www.mythtv.org or you can fetch the latest development source directly from MythTV's source code repository (find directions at http://svn.mythtv.org/). Note that MythTV and its plug-ins use a number of libraries and software components outside of MythTV itself, so you'll also want to consult the official MythTV documentation at www.mythtv.org/modules.php?name=MythInstall to determine what you must install to enable those features you want.

In addition, note that for most rpm-based distributions (such as Red Hat, Fedora, and SUSE) and dpkg-based distributions (such as Debian and Ubuntu), you can likely obtain and install binary packages for all build dependencies from the same places that carry binary MythTV packages for those distributions. If you use apt as your automatic dependency resolver (available for almost all rpm- and dpkg-based distributions), you should be able to point it at the source repository for the binary MythTV package provider and use it to install all of MythTV's build dependencies. For example, users running 32-bit Fedora Core with apt installed can add the following two lines to their apt sources:

```
rpm http://dl.atrpms.net fc5-i386/atrpms stable
rpm-src http://dl.atrpms.net fc5-i386/atrpms stable
```

With those lines added, run the command `apt-get update` to refresh apt's metadata. Then, you should be able to run the command `apt-get build-dep mythtv mythplugins` to install all required dependencies of MythTV and all plug-ins on your system.

After you have all the dependencies taken care of and MythTV source in one form or another onto your system, move into the source directory and run the command `./configure -help` to see the full listing of available options. The configure script is pretty good at figuring out what it should and shouldn't enable, though some of the more advanced and/or occasionally unstable features (such as DVB support, XvMC decoding, and OpenGL vertical sync timing) require you to enable them explicitly. Another somewhat experimental option you might care to enable, especially if you think you might be a bit short on CPU power (especially relevant for HDTV), is `-enable-proc-opt`, which tries to auto-detect your exact CPU and set up compiler parameters optimized as much as possible for your CPU.

The next step is the one little place where MythTV's build procedure differs slightly from most other open-source projects. MythTV uses a good portion of the Qt toolkit, and thus requires a quick `qmake mythtv.pro`. After that, on with a standard `make`, followed by, as root, `make install`.

Once you've installed MythTV, you're ready to download the plug-ins source. The `mythplugins` tarball contains the source code of all the official MythTV plug-ins, but the configure script in the tarball enables you to build only those plug-ins (and features for those plug-ins) that you want. Once again, examine the output from `./configure -help"` to get the scoop on all the available options.

Tweaking Advanced Recording Schedules

Beyond the standard recording schedule options that enable you to record a particular show once, at a specific time slot every day, at a specific time slot on a specific day, or any time a show runs, to name a few possible scheduling options, you can also build more complex recording schedules, using the Custom Record option found on the Manage Recordings → Schedule Recordings page of the frontend.

Included on the Power Search Recording Rule Editor page under the Custom Record option are a number of canned examples for possible recording schedules (see Figure 15-11), which anyone with a bit of SQL experience can recognize essentially as SQL queries, run against data stored in MythTV's MySQL database. You can combine any number of the example queries on this page to build a very specific query; for example, you might want to record all movies showing on HBO that contain the word "Space" in their titles, subtitles, or program descriptions, and released after the year 2000. The custom query string for such a schedule is as follows:

```
program.title LIKE "%Space%" OR program.subtitle LIKE "%Space%" OR
program.description LIKE "%Space%" AND program.category_type = "movie"
AND
airdate >= 2000 AND channel.callsign LIKE "HBO%"
```

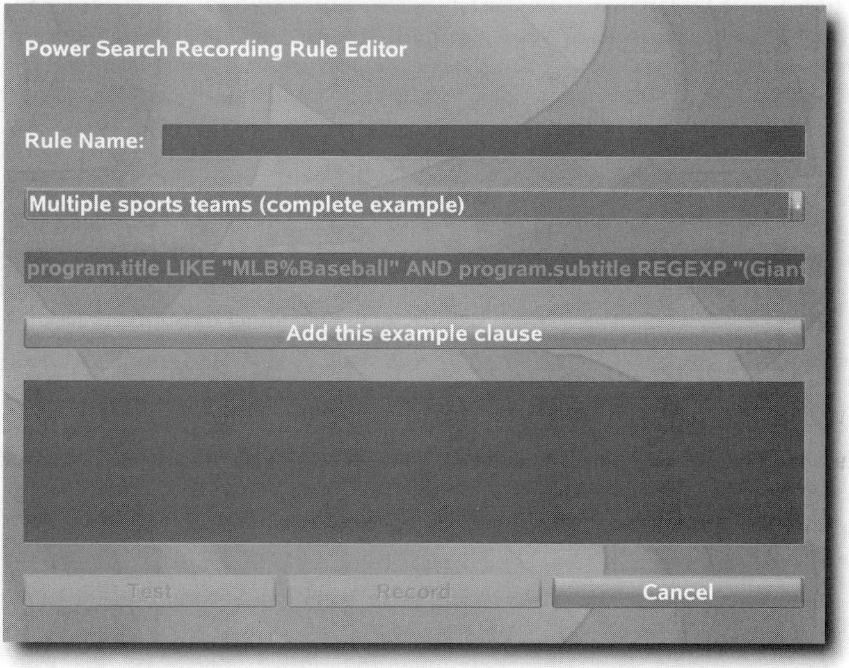

Figure 15-11: Configuring a custom recording schedule

The possibilities are pretty much endless once you get the hang of the syntax. With the examples provided within the Custom Record (not to mention the preceding example), you should be well on your way!

Adjusting Onscreen Font Sizes

MythTV was designed with 800 × 600 pixel display resolution in mind (at least, 800 × 600 before being converted by a TV-out encoder on a video card), with an analog television for display. Default font sizes are tailored for this setup, but for one reason or another, you might want or need to change them. The easiest place to make changes is within the MythTV frontend itself, under the Setup section, which contains a few places where you can adjust font sizes. The first page of the Appearance configuration section includes an option to move your relative font sizes from default, which you might recall is geared for use on a standard-definition TV, to small, designed for use on a computer monitor, and big, which might come in handy for anyone with limited vision. Page 5 of the same section enables you to set actual point sizes to small, medium, or big (medium == default). On the last page under TV Settings ➜ Playback, you can again select default, small, or big, this time for the OSD.

Note that MythTV UI themes and OSD themes are generally all (or are supposed to be) written without any definite font sizes specified, only small, medium, and big, so armed with the preceding locations, you should be able to alter any onscreen fonts to your liking without diving into any text files. However, it's possible you might find yourself diving into a theme's configuration file(s) to make slight changes to move an element around a little or possibly adjust a hard-coded font size. Within each theme's directory, you should find one or more .xml files, text files that define the layout for all the theme's elements.

If you think that font sizes don't display at the proper size, it's possible that your X server isn't properly determining the actual size of your display. Measure the size of your display (in millimeters) and then compare your measurements with the output of the command xdpyinfo, which should include something like the following amid its output:

```
screen #0:
  dimensions: 1920x1080 pixels (827x465 millimeters)
```

If your measurements and xdpyinfo don't match, set up `DisplaySize` parameters in your X config file, as described earlier in this chapter in the section "Wide-screen HDTV Tweaks."

```
DisplaySize   width height
This optional entry gives the width and height, in millimetres, of
the picture area of the monitor. If given this is used to
calculate the horizontal and vertical pitch (DPI) of the screen.
```

Add the `DisplaySize` parameter within the `Monitor` section of your X configuration file (`/etc/X11/xorg.conf` in most current distributions) and restart X to see the results. As an aside, you could also "lie" to X here to impact font sizing, but that's generally not recommended because it may have negative effects in other areas. It's best to set the `DisplaySize` exactly, and then use the available methods within MythTV to adjust font sizes further.

Finally, Fedora Core 3 and later users may find that many of the UI fonts show up with descending portions of characters such as g, p, y, and so forth missing. This stems from an issue with the latest urw-fonts packages from Red Hat. The easiest fix is to install the urw-fonts package that shipped with Fedora Core 2, and configure your package manager not to update urw-fonts. For example, download and install the FC2 urw-fonts package as follows:

```
# rpm -Uvh --oldpackage \
> http://mirrors.kernel.org/fedora/core/2/i386/\
> os/Fedora/RPMS/urw-fonts-2.1-7.noarch.rpm
```

Now configure Fedora's stock package manager, yum, to not upgrade urw-fonts (that is, not to reinstall the latest, but broken urw-fonts package), by adding the line exclude=urw-fonts* to /etc/yum.conf.

Final Thoughts

MythTV's open source, highly configurable nature makes it possible to get it to do just about anything (within reason) that anyone could want a DVR to do. You can output to virtually any audio and display devices, customizing everything to look and behave just the way you want.

MythTV Performance Hacks

chapter

16

in this chapter

☑ Running mythfrontend with elevated privileges

☑ Maximizing hard drive throughput

☑ Choosing the best file system(s) for MythTV

☑ Maximizing MPlayer and xine

☑ Throwing more hardware at your MythTV system

Generally, any computer built in the last three or four years has more than enough power to run MythTV, if all you're interested in is standard-definition television. The situation gets a little more interesting if you're trying to run MythTV on older hardware or a new but relatively slow EPIA Mini-ITX system, or you want to tackle high-definition television. In any case, it's always a good idea to maximize your system's performance. This chapter will help you do just that.

Running mythfrontend with Elevated Privileges

If a process is run with elevated privileges, it's possible to realize some performance gains. If you configure your system in just the right way, you can run the mythfrontend process at a higher processing priority than standard user processes get. This can be useful if your system is completely taxed during playback, which is usually the case when playing back high-definition recordings (unless you have a *really* fast processor, such as a 3.6GHz Pentium 4 or better). On some systems, altering your mythfrontend binary to run as set-uid root is sufficient:

```
# chmod u+s /usr/bin/mythfrontend
```

However, recent changes to the 2.6 Linux kernel have made that method obsolete, and favor another solution. For the latest kernels, you must run PAM 0.79 or later (PAM is an acronym for *pluggable authentication modules*), and then make a few changes to /etc/security/limits.conf. Assuming you're running mythfrontend as user *mythtv*, add the following to limits.conf:

```
Mythtv      -      rtprio      50
Mythtv      -      nice        0
```

These changes aren't dynamic, so you'll need to log out and log back in to have those changes applied to your mythtv user account.

Using either or both of the preceding privilege escalation methods, launch `mythfrontend` from a console window, navigate to Utilities → Setup → TV Settings → Playback, and check the box for "Enable realtime priority threads" (see Figure 16-1). Then work your way through the rest of the settings pages. At that point, you should be able to watch a recording with real-time priority enabled. Briefly start watching either a recording or live TV, and then exit out of `mythfrontend`. On the console from which you launched `mythfrontend`, you should see a message that looks something like the following:

```
2006-01-29 11:27:34.264 Using realtime priority.
```

If you haven't configured everything just right, you'll see the following instead:

```
2006-01-29 11:28:07.004 Realtime priority would require SUID as root.
```

Retrace your steps if you run into this error. If one privilege escalation method fails, try the other, or try enabling both at the same time, which should more or less guarantee success. Make sure you're running the latest PAM available for your system and be sure to completely log out and log back in (or even try a reboot, if you feel the urge).

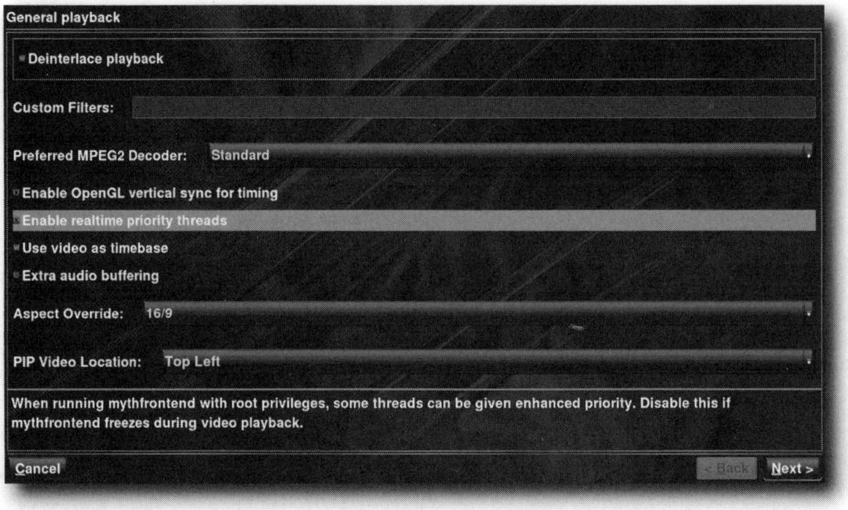

FIGURE 16-1: Enabling real-time priority threading in MythTV

Maximizing Hard Drive Throughput

Typically, modern Linux distributions do everything they can to make sure your hard disk drives operate at peak efficiency. However, for one reason or another, it's possible that direct memory access (DMA) mode might not be enabled for a given drive. This can cause a significant negative impact the performance of your MythTV system, as all video capture and playback happens on your drive(s).

Depending on the type of hard drive(s) you're using (and in the case of Serial ATA disks, the driver), your first hard drive should be either /dev/hda (for ATA and some SATA setups) or /dev/sda (for SCSI and some SATA setups). Generally, you should be able to determine what devices your disks are via the following command:

```
$ dmesg | grep "[h,s]d[a-z]"
```

Entering this command on a system with a single ATA hard drive and a DVD-ROM drive installed produces the following output (among other things):

```
hda: WDC WD1200JB-75CRA0, ATA DISK drive
hdc: SONY DVD-ROM DDU1612, ATAPI CD/DVD-ROM drive
hda: max request size: 128KiB
hda: 234441648 sectors (120034 MB) w/8192KiB Cache,
     CHS=65535/16/63, UDMA(100)
```

From this output, you know your hard disk is /dev/hda (and the DVD-ROM is /dev/hdc), and your hard drive should be able to run in DMA mode. To verify that DMA mode is actually enabled, execute the following command:

```
$ /sbin/hdparm /dev/hda | grep dma
```

If this command returns the following line, everything is OK:

```
using_dma = 1 (on)
```

If not, you can force it on by entering the following command (as root; if you're not logged in root you can use su to change your privileges):

```
# /sbin/hdparm -d1 /dev/hda
```

You can add this command to your system initialization scripts as well (on Fedora, tack it to the end of /etc/rc.local), to apply every time your system starts up. However, note that DMA isn't enabled on some drives in combination with certain motherboard chipsets for good reasons, so you do this at your own risk, and you should be aware that this can sometimes lead to system instability. If this tweak does cause instability, you may need to look into acquiring a different motherboard, another PCI hard disk controller, or a new disk drive.

Another great way to ramp up disk throughput is to use multiple disks configured in a redundant array of inexpensive/independent/individual (depends on who you ask) disks — called a *RAID array* for short. (RAID arrays were mentioned in Chapter 1). Obviously, if you're writing data across multiple disks simultaneously, their collective throughput capabilities can be aggregated (at least to a point — there are system limitations after which adding more drives to a RAID array may be detrimental).

Choosing the Best File System(s) for MythTV

A MythTV system typically produces a very lot of gigabyte or even multi-gigabyte files. Then, too, you've got core operating system components and database components to consider. To optimize all facets of your system, you definitely want to partition your disk(s), so that each of these elements may be housed in their own partitions. One caveat here is that much like many other debates in the Linux world (as in GNOME versus KDE, vi versus emacs, and so forth) there are differing schools of thought on the "best" file system for each of these tasks. Nevertheless, the following suggestions summarize quite a bit of real-world experience and discussion on the MythTV mailing lists.

Generally, Ext3 and ReiserFS are the file systems of choice for core operating system partitions because they are reasonably general-purpose file systems with relatively robust default journaling schemes that minimize any potential data loss, should your system lock up or spontaneously lose power. Some people swear by one of the two, and conversely, swear *at* the other. As a point of reference, Red Hat's default file system is Ext3, SUSE's is ReiserFS.

For the database partition, we recommend a single file system. You want Ext3 for this partition. There have been documented cases of random database corruption that only happen on ReiserFS, which may have been fixed by now, but do you really want to risk having that happen to you? The tried-and-true Ext3 is your safest bet here, and MySQL's performance isn't tied so much to the underlying file system as it is to the way you've configured MySQL itself.

For your video partition, there are a few considerations you'll want to keep in mind. If you're using the logical volume manager (LVM) underneath your video partition and anticipate that you might have need to reduce the size of that partition in the future, then note that neither SGI's XFS or IBM's JFS support shrinking a file system, whereas both Ext3 and ReiserFS do. In addition, note that both XFS and JFS are known to lead to stack overflows and system stability problems on some systems if a combination of software RAID, LVM, and XFS or JFS are stacked one on top of the other, particularly if you're using a kernel with 4K stacks (which all Red Hat-provided 2.6 kernels have), rather than an 8K-stacks kernel.

That said, XFS and JFS are the best file systems for your video partition, as far as performance goes. XFS and JFS are tailored for use with a lot of large files, which is exactly what will be on your MythTV video partition. This is also why they aren't so great for your OS and database partitions. Both are a bit more memory hungry and CPU intensive than either Ext3 or ReiserFS, and aggressively cache data, which, especially in the case of small files, can lead to data corruption in the event of a system lockup or power loss. XFS has slightly better write performance, while JFS has better file deletion performance, but both are quite good, assuming they don't cause your system to lock up and you don't care about shrinking your video partition (most folks find they only need to expand!). If XFS or JFS does lead to system instability, Ext3 is generally the next best file system (it performs well enough on one of our master backend systems to handle multiple recordings at once, anyhow).

Changing from one file system to another is relatively trivial, at least for your database and video partitions. For the purposes of this exercise, we assume your MythTV video partition is mounted as /video and resides on the partition /dev/hda5. Assuming you've got all the data from the partition backed up (or don't care about losing any of it), and have stopped all services accessing the partition (typically, mythbackend and mysqld are the two processes you need to stop), simply unmount the partition like this:

```
# umount /video
```

Note Those not familiar with Linux/UNIX, please note that *umount* (minus the first *n* in *unmount*) is in fact the correct spelling of the command. The n key on the keyboard of the programmer who wrote it must have been malfunctioning when the command originated many moons ago.

Next, reformat the partition:

```
# mkfs -t fstype /dev/hda5
```

Substitute ext3, reiserfs, xfs, or jfs for fstype to format the desired file system onto the partition. Note that you may have to install some additional software packages to use something other than your distribution's default file system type. For example, on Fedora systems (where Ext3 is the default), you'll probably need to run the following command:

```
# yum install fstoolpackage
```

In this case, fstoolpackage should be either reiserfs-utils, xfsprogs, or jfsu-tils. Once you have the necessary file system tools and have formatted the partition, edit /etc/fstab, and change the column for file system type to match the new one you just applied to the partition, and then mount the partition:

```
# mount /video
```

You should now be happily on your way with your new file system!

Maximizing MPlayer and xine

The default setups for MPlayer and xine essentially assume you're running them on a desktop computer, not on a dedicated media box, so there are a few tweaks to be made. Both media players have options that enable them to run full screen, suppress output, and identify specific video and audio output methods. We've already covered audio output methods in Chapter 15, but not the others; you'll find them covered right here.

The command-line options for these various features differ slightly for the two players. Table 16-1 details some of the available options and the command-line flags that enable them.

Table 16-1   MPlayer and xine Option Flags

Command	MPlayer	xine
Full screen	-fs	-f
Zoom video	-zoom	n/a
Quiet	-quiet	-q
Disable splash	n/a	--no-splash
Hide GUI	n/a	-h
Start playback	n/a	-p
Video output method	-vo <type>	-V <type>
Audio output method	-ao <type>	-A <type>

Without a full-screen flag, both MPlayer and xine start video playback inside a window (see Figure 16-2). In MPlayer's case, you must also specify a -zoom flag to scale video up to fill the screen, while this is xine's default behavior. The -quiet flag helps to suppress any unnecessary output from the media players. The splash screen in xine can optionally be disabled, as can on-screen graphical user interface (GUI) controls. You can also tell xine to start playback of a provided file immediately (this is actually its default behavior, but you'll see why we specify it momentarily). When launched from a command line, MPlayer has no splash screen or GUI, and starts playback of a given file immediately, thus there's no need for flags.

FIGURE 16-2: A freshly launched default instance of xine

You can also specify different audio and video output types, the full list of which can be found in the respective man pages for MPlayer and xine. Most of the time, there's very little reason to use anything but alsa for your audio output method and xv for your video output method (both MPlayer and xine take alsa as an argument to their audio output method flag and xv as an argument to their video output method flag). However, from time to time, you may find reason to try another output method. Note that MPlayer allows you to chain together a list of audio and video output methods, so if one fails the next one in the chain will be tried.

Typically, you'll want to start out working from a console window, testing various options to find a setup you like, but once you've got your ideal flag combination, input it into MythVideo's setup section (Utilities/Setup → Setup → Media Settings → Videos Settings → Player Settings) as your Default Player command. A relatively popular combination for xine is as follows:

```
xine -pfhq --no-splash %s
```

You'll notice several of the flags are combined into one, which is allowed when using xine's -p option. The preceding command starts playback immediately (-p), runs full screen (f), hides xine's on-screen graphical controls (h), suppresses debug output (q) and disables xine's start-up splash screen. The last argument, %s, is a MythVideo placeholder, which will automatically substitute the name of the file to be played back.

As well as command-line switches, most of these options may be set as defaults in MPlayer and xine's configuration files. The following is a snippet of an MPlayer configuration file (`/etc/mplayer/mplayer.conf` for a systemwide configuration, `~/.mplayer/config` for a user-specific configuration — which overrides a systemwide configuration), which achieves the same as specifying `mplayer -fs -zoom -quiet -vo xv -ao alsa filename` on the command line, using only `mplayer filename`:

```
# run full-screen
fs=yes
# zoom image to fill the screen
zoom=yes
# disable mplayer's usual verbosity
really-quiet=yes
# use XVideo for video output
vo=xv
# use alsa for audio output
ao=alsa
```

While MPlayer defaults to having almost nothing in its configuration files, if anything, xine is quite the opposite. Upon first launch, if a configuration file doesn't exist, one is written out for you, to `~/.xine/config`. As of this writing, a default xine configuration file is over 675 lines long, owing to copious amounts of documentation, describing what each configuration directive does. Surprisingly enough, configuration options to run in full-screen mode and suppress verbose output by default are not among them, while other relevant portions from the earlier xine `Default Player` line are:

```
# hide gui
gui.panel_visible:0
# no splash screen
gui.splash:0
```

Finally, please note that both MPlayer and xine may be controlled using the Linux Infrared Remote Control (LIRC) suite, which you should already have installed and configured for use with MythTV. MythTV looks for an LIRC configuration file in a slightly different location than either `mplayer` or `xine` (`~/.mythtv/lircrc` versus `~/.lircrc`), but for simplicity's sake, you can simply make these files one and the same with a symbolic link:

```
$ ln -s ~/.mythtv/lircrc ~/.lircrc
```

You can now put all your LIRC directives in a single file, and simply add new stanzas for each button for both MPlayer and xine. If you'd like to control MythTV, MPlayer, and xine via remote control, you would have three mappings in `~/.mythtv/lircrc` for each button, such as the following examples for the Play button:

```
begin
  prog = mythtv
  button = PLAY
  repeat = 4
  config = Space
end

begin
```

```
  prog = xine
  button = PLAY
  repeat = 4
  config = Play
end

begin
  prog = mplayer
  button = PLAY
  repeat = 4
  config = seek +1
end
```

Entire example configuration files for all three applications can be found in the wild on the Internet.

Throwing More Hardware at Your MythTV System

The core requirements for a MythTV system are a computer or computers, a video capture device or devices, and somewhere to store recorded video. While there are some limitations — a Pentium 133 is *not* a good platform on which to base your MythTV system, and some hardware just doesn't work very well under Linux — the exact specifications of such components are largely left to the user's discretion and/or budget. There are two main starting points for most folks' MythTV systems: an extra machine sitting around the house is slated for Mythification, or a brand-new machine is purchased specifically for use as a MythTV system. In the former case, chances are good that once you really dive into Myth, you'll want to expand or upgrade your old system. In the latter case, the burning question becomes "What exactly should I spend my hard-earned money on?" This section attempts to explain the benefits of throwing more hardware at specific resources in a MythTV system.

Central Processing Unit

As its name should suggest, the central component of any computer is its central processing unit (CPU), or processor. There's a fair amount of processing to be done in most MythTV systems. You need CPU cycles to run the `mythbackend` and `mythfrontend` processes, write video data out to disk, encode video (depending on capture card), post-process recordings (that is, run automatic commercial detection and flagging), play back video, and so forth.

The most processor-intensive tasks among this list include encoding video, post-processing recordings, and playing back video. Some video capture cards, such as the Hauppauge WinTV PVR-250 and any high-definition capture card, do not require much, if any, CPU cycles for encoding video, because the PVR-250 (and similar) cards have built-in hardware encoding chips, and HDTV is broadcast as an MPEG-2 transport stream that you simply write to disk. Post-processing recordings for transcoding or commercial-cutting isn't time sensitive (unless you just have to watch that show that just finished recording five minutes ago with the commercials automatically skipped). However, post-processing is rather CPU intensive, so be aware that if you do this on the same system on which you're trying to watch a recording on a Myth box, performance may be affected. This is especially true for HDTV playback, which is far more taxing on a system than standard-definition playback, owing to its significantly higher resolution. Any relatively modern processor, when paired with a decent video card, should pack enough punch for standard-definition television playback while handling other tasks in the background, but for HDTV, you really want at least 3GHz worth of processing power.

Another question is what type of processor you should use. The general consensus at the moment is that a 3GHz+ Intel Pentium 4 is still the best route, preferably one with Hyper-Threading enabled. AMD Athlon XP processors in the XP 3000+ range can also do the job, but seem to be a little less robust than a Pentium 4. Support for 64-bit processors, specifically optimizations in underlying video encoding and decoding libraries, is constantly improving as well. Thus, AMD Athlon 64 processors (as well as Intel EM64T processors) have become viable contenders, too. Note that as more and more code optimizations are made and more processing is offloaded to your video card, the required CPU power for decoding HDTV video will continue to decrease, but sticking with something in the 3GHz ballpark is a safe bet for now, though dual-core Athlon 64 X2s and FX-series chips are also entirely up to those tasks.

Video Output Card

Choosing a video output card is another big key to getting the kind of video playback experience you want. While in theory any card that supports the X Video (xv) extension (as well as some that don't) can be used with MythTV, not all cards and/or drivers are created equal. In about nine out of ten cases, a video card featuring an nVidia chipset in the GeForce 4 or newer series, driven by nVidia's own proprietary driver, is your best bet, particularly for HDTV. There are a few alternatives that work relatively well, but nothing as mature and reliable as an nVidia card.

However, please note that you don't need to spend an arm and a leg on the highest of high-end cards. Typically, high-end nVidia cards are high end because they offer superior 3D performance, and we're not doing anything with 3D here. Therefore, a lower-end GeForce 5200 or 6200 works at least as well as a brand-new high-end GeForce 7800, as far as MythTV is concerned. Furthermore, low-end cards can often be found in fanless, passively cooled (and thus silent-running) packages, while high-end cards typically require active cooling from relatively noisy high-speed fans.

Of possible interest is the trade-off between a 5000-series and a 6000-series nVidia card. There are certain video output capabilities MythTV takes advantage of in the 5000-series that were removed in the 6000-series and later, so if you can drive your display equally well with a 5000-series, it may actually perform a bit better than a 6000-series. However, the 6000-series is more HDTV-aware than the 5000-series. The 6000-series debuted a Component Video output dongle on some models, and can drive a display at $1920 \times 1080p$, while at least some of the 5000-series cards cannot (both support $1920 \times 1080i$ and $1280 \times 720p$).

Also of note is the bus interface for your card. For standard definition, PCI, AGP, and PCI-Express are all perfectly suitable, while HDTV playback requires AGP or PCI-Express, because the amount of data that has to be pushed to your video card can overwhelm a PCI bus. Note that most on-board video offerings (among which are some nVidia-based ones) are AGP-based, and are indeed HDTV-capable, though many of them utilize system memory, rather than having dedicated video memory, which does mean a bit of a performance hit versus a dedicated card. Keep this in mind if performance isn't quite where you'd like it, because most such systems can disable the on-board video in favor of a dedicated card, which might boost performance enough to deliver the sometimes elusive smooth HDTV playback.

The outputs available on the rear of the card are also of great interest, because your MythTV experience can definitely benefit from using the best interface method possible with your TV. Here again this is particularly relevant for HDTV. Various nVidia offerings pretty much run the gamut of possible interfaces, including DVI, VGA, Component Video, S-Video, and Composite Video, which not coincidentally, are listed here in order of descending preference for interfacing with your TV. A pure, all-digital DVI high-definition connection is far and away the best way to go, if you can, with the analog-but-still-HD connection types, VGA, and Component trailing behind. Standard-definition-only S-Video and Composite Video bring up the rear — HDTV will typically still look better than standard-definition recordings, but you're effectively tossing out three quarters (or more) of HD resolution, so this is a big no-no if you have an HDTV.

Video Capture Card(s)

Choice of video capture devices also impacts overall system performance. In the early days of MythTV, the best-supported capture cards were simple frame-grabbers, which required CPU time to encode captured video into a format for storage on disk. Today, quite a few more options are available, including standard-definition cards that encode video via on-board hardware MPEG-2 encoders, an external USB standard-definition tuner that encodes to MPEG-4 in hardware, and an ever-increasing number of digital/high-definition tuner cards. Because digital broadcasts are just that — digital data — no encoding is necessary: the bit stream is simply written to disk. For standard-definition television, you can choose between devices that require CPU time to encode and those that don't. It's highly recommended that you spend the extra money to get capture cards that encode video in hardware, as that frees up a hefty chunk of CPU power for other tasks (not to mention that video quality from hardware encoding generally seems superior).

Chances are also very good that if you start out with a single tuner in your MythTV system, you'll quickly find that you want at least one more. The more tuners you have, the more likely it is that you'll need hardware-encoding tuners, so as not to overwhelm your system. Note that hardware-encoding tuner cards exist with two encoders on a single board, which can be a very good thing if your system is low on expansion slots. While most high-definition capture cards can also tune in standard-definition channels, most folks who have high-definition capture cards find they also want a few standard-definition cards, because MythTV currently doesn't support using both the digital and analog modes of these cards in a sane or reasonable way.

Storage

Of course, as you ramp up the number of capture cards in your system and/or record more shows you'd like to keep long-term, you might find yourself running out of disk space faster than you thought. This becomes even more true once you start recording in high definition, because high-definition recordings take up significantly more disk space than encoded standard-definition recordings, owing to their higher resolution and bit rates. If you're recording multiple programs at once, it's also possible while trying to play back a recording or live TV that you may find your disk throughput just sufficient to keep up. Many MythTV users have found it essential to use multiple large disks in a RAID array, both to increase storage capacity and disk throughput.

However, please note that if you're running a RAID array, the more disks it has, the more likely it is that one of them will fail at some point. If your recordings are important to you, you might want to consider a RAID mode that provides some redundancy, such as RAID 5. Of course, more disks require more power (you may need a bigger power supply) and cooling, and the noise output from your MythTV system also tends to increase. Many people wind up running a dedicated master backend MythTV server that handles most video capture and all video storage, paired with a lightweight, low-power, low-noise frontend system for actual viewing, which plays video back from the backend system across the network. This dovetails nicely into a discussion about network bandwidth requirements and possible interface types, the subject of the section that follows.

Network Interfaces

Almost any new PC these days comes equipped with at least one RJ-45 Ethernet network interface, capable of network speeds of at least 100 Mbps. If your MythTV system is split across more than one machine, connecting them using at least 100 Mbps Ethernet over a hard-wired interface is definitely the best route to take. Technically, a 10 Mbps wired network has enough throughput to handle a single standard-definition video stream, but if your MythTV setup has a network involved, chances are good you'll frequently need to move more than one stream at a time, for which a 10 Mbps connection will likely be insufficient. High-definition streams are often around 19 Mbps by themselves, so if HDTV is involved, 10 Mbps definitely delivers too little bandwidth.

As for wireless, the old 802.11b standard, rated at 11 Mbps, might be able to handle a single standard-definition stream as well, but the lossy nature of wireless networking makes it suboptimal for streaming video at any significant resolution or bit rate. With a strong signal, 802.11g, rated at 54 Mbps, generally works well enough for streaming standard-definition video. Note that 54 Mbps is considerably higher than the bit rate typical for an HDTV stream at 19 Mbps, but 54 Mbps is somewhat misleading (it's a theoretical maximum that's seldom, if ever, attained in actual practice). Here again, wireless connections drop far more packets, requiring retransmissions, and don't work well with video. If packets are dropped and must be retransmitted, they don't arrive in time, and you wind up with video artifacts, skipping, pausing, and other unwanted effects. Moreover, of course, the problem gets worse if you try moving multiple streams at the same time, or try to use your wireless connection for anything else while trying to watch video.

In short, you really want at least a 100 Mbps wired network for your MythTV systems to use, if your system involves more than one computer. 1000 Mbps, or 1 Gbps (Gigabit Ethernet) is, of course, even better, though you'd have to move something like four or five HDTV streams simultaneously before it becomes a big winner over 100 Mbps.

Memory

MythTV isn't particularly memory hungry by today's standards. Many people run MythTV on systems with a modest 256 MB of RAM. That said, more and more users find that their systems may start swapping with only 256 MB, so 512 MB is quite common. This is typically more than enough RAM for MythTV to do its thing, though in at least one situation, more memory may be optimal. That situation occurs when powering a high-resolution display, such as an LCD or Plasma HDTV running with a progressive-scan resolution of 1920 × 1080 pixels. MythTV caches most of its graphical user interface elements into system memory, and at this resolution, they're scaled up quite a bit. With some of the more complex wide-screen themes, this can consume so much memory that even with 512 MB of RAM, the system must swap, which results in a somewhat laggy GUI. 1 GB of RAM is probably the most anyone could need in a MythTV system these days (and 768 MB is probably sufficient for the preceding case).

Sound Card

The last internal PC component addressed in this section is your sound card. On-board sound cards have been improving by leaps and bounds over the years, and many of them are now quite well supported under Linux. You should have no problems using on-board sound for stereo audio output. However, as mentioned in our earlier coverage on passing raw digital audio to an external Dolby Digital decoder/amplifier, not all of them work well when it comes to passing raw digital audio out an S/PDIF connection. If you want that kind of functionality, you might just want to save yourself some headache and buy a SoundBlaster Audigy PCI card, or some reasonable facsimile thereof.

Display

While you ought to be able to drive the majority of displays available with your MythTV system one way or another, there are certainly things to watch out for if you're in the market for a display — particularly an HDTV-capable one. As already mentioned, the best possible interface between a MythTV system and an HDTV display is through DVI (digital video interface), because it is the only way to establish a 100% digital connection from the video card all the way to the display. VGA and Component Video both require converting the signal from digital to analog. In other words: Definitely keep your eye out for a display with DVI inputs.

There's another variant of DVI called HDMI (high-definition multimedia interface) that is more or less a smaller form-factor DVI connection. This works, too, because you can get a DVI to HDMI adapter or cable relatively cheaply. One thing to watch out for, though, is displays whose DVI or HDMI ports *require* any device feeding them to support HDCP (a high-definition copy protection standard), because those inputs may not work with your MythTV system. HDCP is a non-issue with VGA and Component Video inputs (as well as S-Video and Composite), because the video data has already been converted from digital to analog.

Another thing to keep in mind is that MythTV's user interface looks far better when run in progressive-scan mode, so give more preference to displays that support either 1080p or 720p modes for the best overall viewing experience.

Hardware Miscellany

While you can definitely make do on the cheap, there is also something to be said for spending a bit of extra cash on a nicer case, cooling fans, and a high-quality power supply. There are many cases on the market these days geared toward home theater PC use. While they can be costly, they are often engineered to higher standards, especially where noise and vibration reduction are concerned. Similarly, numerous cooling fans and power supplies have been engineered for low-noise operation. Every little bit helps to make your MythTV viewing system as quiet and unobtrusive as possible. A few Web sites that cater to low-noise home theater PC systems that we highly recommended you visit include www.silentpcreview.com/, www.pcalchemy.com/, and www.digitalconnection.com/.

Final Thoughts

Quite a bit of tweaking can be done to optimize various aspects of your MythTV system, but in the end, it all comes down to having the right hardware for the job. For the most part, the best places to focus your MythTV budget are on storage capacity and capture cards. Of course, if some of those capture cards are of the HDTV persuasion, you'll also need to drop some cash on a relatively fast processor. For the remainder of your components, excessive spending isn't a requirement (but usually won't hurt anything, except your bank balance!).

Extending the MythTV Environment

here are numerous ways in which you can extend your MythTV environment beyond what we've covered so far. These range from exporting recordings for viewing on a video iPod to importing a home movie collection from VHS tapes or DVDs. In this chapter, we explore these and other ways to expand your MythTV system's capabilities. Get ready to wander down some interesting pathways as we explore this grab-bag of topics!

Exporting Recordings into Other Formats

There are several different ways you can export MythTV recordings to a different format for consumption by devices not running MythTV. This might be a Windows Media Center computer or it might be a portable device capable of playing digital video files, such as the Video iPod or a PlayStation Portable. You might also have reason to burn recordings onto either VCD or DVD. All these uses require you to convert MythTV native formats into something else.

If you simply want to be able to browse your recordings outside MythTV and be able to make sense of them based on filename alone, check out `mythrename.pl` in the `contribs` subdirectory of the official MythTV distribution. Copy `mythrename.pl` from the MythTV distribution `contribs` subdirectory to `/usr/local/bin/` and make it executable:

```
# cp mythrename.pl /usr/local/bin/
# chmod +x /usr/local/bin/mythrename.pl
```

MythTV stores recordings with a filename that is almost purely numeric, based on the channel from which the program was recorded, along with a date and time stamp. All `mythrename.pl` does is rename your recordings from their default numeric format into something more human-decipherable.

By default, `mythrename.pl` alters the filename in your file system and changes its reference in MythTV's database. If you prefer, you can use the `--links` flag with `mythrename.pl` to instruct it to create symbolic links instead, inside a `show_names` directory in your MythTV recordings directory. Either method should provide you with a directory of files you can browse easily and play from any other computer, if you share that recordings directory with your network (assuming you have video players on your other computers with the right decoding capabilities).

For example, recordings created with HDTV capture cards and hardware MPEG2-encoding cards are simply MPEG-2 files, with standard .mpg file extensions, so it should be possible to view them using any video player that supports MPEG-2 (and has enough CPU horsepower, especially relevant for HDTV content). The `mythrename.pl` script has a number of other options you can check out by running `mythrename.pl` with a `--help` flag.

If you find yourself running `mythrename.pl` frequently, you may want to schedule it to run as a cron job, perhaps on an hourly basis. Better yet, set it up as a recording post-processing job, which is addressed later in this section.

If you have a specific format in which you want to export your recordings, you have a few options, depending on exactly what it is you are trying to accomplish. You could use a format that compresses recordings more so you can save on disk space, or a format at a lower resolution that allows a less-powerful device to play it back.

MythTV includes native transcoding support, which you might be inclined to use on high-resolution, high-bit-rate recordings (such as HDTV) to scale their resolution and bit rate down and compress them with an MPEG-4 codec. If you don't have the budget for a high-end HDTV-viewing frontend, you might consider taking this route, which can convert recordings into a more manageable format that is much less CPU-intensive to decode and play back. If you run low on disk space, you might consider transcoding recordings with a higher bit rate to MPEG-4 to shrink their on-disk footprints. MPEG4-encoded recordings take up as little as one fourth of the disk space that MPEG-2 recordings require, with little or no perceptible losses in visual quality.

MythTV supports the concept of Recording Profiles, which you can use to advantage for format conversion. Within `mythfrontend`'s setup section (Utilities/Setup → Setup → TV Settings → Recording Profiles), for each recording device type (hardware MPEG-2 encoder, DVB capture, software encoder, and so on), you can use multiple profiles to define how recordings should be made. In addition to specifying bit rate and resolution for a given profile, you can also configure a profile to automatically transcode recordings when they're done, as shown in Figure 17-1.

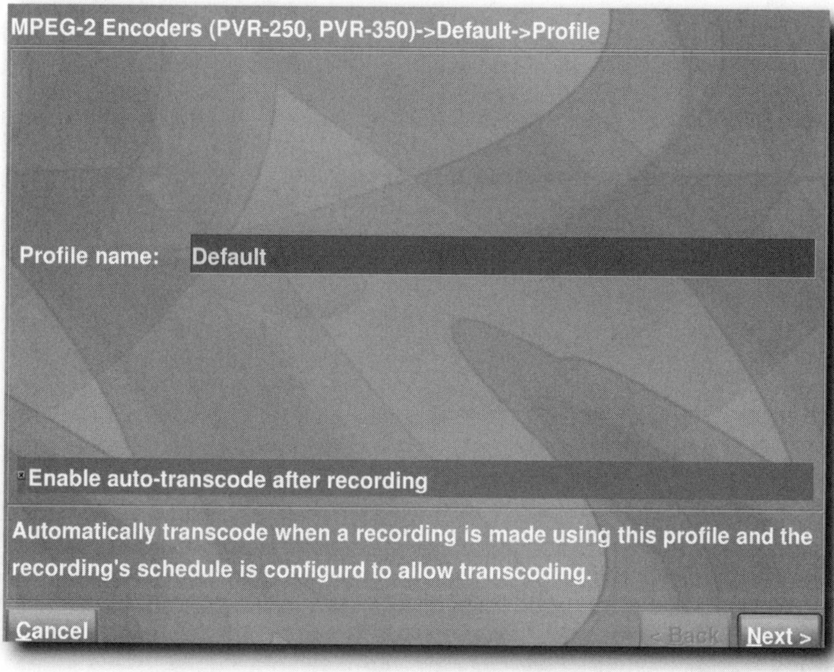

MPEG-2 Encoders (PVR-250, PVR-350)->Default->Profile

Profile name: Default

Enable auto-transcode after recording

Automatically transcode when a recording is made using this profile and the recording's schedule is configurd to allow transcoding.

Cancel   < Back   Next >

FIGURE **17-1**: Enabling automatic transcode in the Default profile

Now any programming configured to record using that profile will automatically be transcoded when it's finished recording. If you only want to transcode certain recordings (maybe you have only one particular series you plan to keep around for a long time), you can also configure automatic transcoding on a per-recording schedule basis. When configuring a recording schedule, select the Storage Options item to select a specific recording profile, such as the one you've configured to auto-transcode, or select the Post Recording Processing option, whereby you can tell MythTV to transcode the recording regardless of which profile it's using, as shown in Figure 17-2.

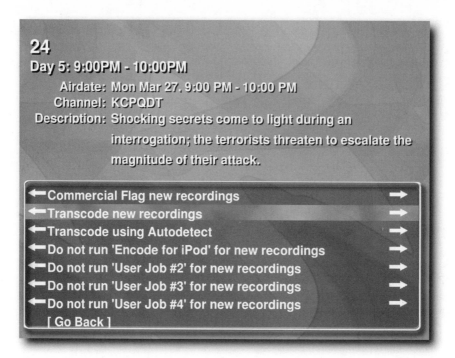

FIGURE 17-2: Recording details

Of course, it's possible what you're really after is a way to export your recordings to burn to DVD, Video CD, iPod, or other media, none of which MythTV's internal transcoding can handle. This is where nuvexport and possibly the myth2ipod script (if you have a Video iPod) come in handy. In the early days of MythTV, before hardware MPEG-2 encoder cards and HDTV/DVB became the rage, MythTV recording files were typically MPEG-4 files housed in the NuppleVideo container format, which not very many video players besides MythTV understand. Note that MythTV's internal transcoding process generates MPEG-4 files inside NuppleVideo containers as well. To make those recordings playable elsewhere, nuvexport was born (and now you know where the "nuv" part of its name comes from).

These days, nuvexport enables you to export any type of recording made within MythTV and convert it to VideoCD (VCD), SuperVideoCD (SVCD), DVD, DivX, or Xvid, just to name a few formats. This includes support for a format specifically tailored for use with Apple's Video iPod, if you choose to also install myth2ipod, part of which is an iPod plug-in for nuvexport. You can find nuvexport at https://svn.forevermore.net/nuvexport/, in both rpm and source tarball formats. Note that nuvexport relies heavily on ffmpeg, so make sure you have it installed on your system. If you'll be exporting recordings for your Video iPod, make sure your ffmpeg build supports Xvid and FAAC because the Video iPod requires use of specific codecs. You can check for the necessary support in ffmpeg simply by running the following at a command prompt:

```
$ ffmpeg --version
```

If you have the required support for the Video iPod, you should see `--with-xvid` and `--with-faac` in the output from the preceding command. If not, you'll have to figure out how to add that support (there's a decent tutorial available at `www.myth2ipod.com/myth2ipod.html`, though it is Debian/Ubuntu-specific).

Speaking of which, that link also gives you instructions on how to acquire and install the `myth2ipod` script. The beauty of using this script is that it can also generate the necessary xml feed to set up a podcast on your MythTV box to which Apple's iTunes subscribes, and subsequently, sync exported recordings out to your Video iPod.

Note that you can run `nuvexport` in two different ways: interactively, via a menu-driven interface (shown in Figure 17-3) or using a single command that specifies all required options to transcode a given recording or recordings (the `myth2ipod` script does the latter). The interactive mode is great if you don't typically transcode your recordings but you have a big trip coming up and want to prep a few recordings for mobile use.

FIGURE 17-3: Walking through nuvexport interactively

Configuring Third-Party Components as Post-Processing Jobs

MythTV's User jobs interface provides a simple way to make any of these commands available for MythTV to use. The same technique used to make all of the scripts covered in this section run as post-processing jobs for MythTV works for all third-party components. Run `mythtv-setup` and navigate to the last page of the `General` section. Several tokens have special meaning within the job command lines. There's more or less one of these for every important (and for some less important) piece of metadata associated with a recording. It may be necessary for you to pass some of these tokens to your post-processing job in order for it to work properly. The important ones needed by `nuvexport` and `myth2ipod` include `"%FILE%"`, which is the filename for the recording to which the job applies, and `"%DIR%"`, which is the directory path where the recording is stored. A full listing appears in the official MythTV documentation at `www.mythtv.org/modules.php?name=MythInstall`. You might find the following commands useful, shown as both plaintext below and within the appropriate MythTV configuration dialog in Figure 17-4.

- Transcode for iPod:

  ```
  myth2ipod "%DIR%" "%FILE%"
  ```

- Export to DVD-friendly format:

  ```
  nuvexport --nice 19 --input="%FILE%"
  ```

- Rename recorded files:

  ```
  mythrename.pl
  ```

Any of these custom jobs can now be assigned to run at the conclusion of any recording, or launched manually for a selected recording from the Job Options item in the information menu within the Watch Recordings area.

Once you have a DVD-friendly exported recording, just hit up any number of sites on the Internet that cover creating a DVD on whatever operating system you prefer. The results should be playable in any current consumer DVD player. A few ways to do it on Linux that might be of interest include the following:

- `http://gentoo-wiki.com/HOWTO_Create_a_DVD`
- `www.kravlor.com/node/118`
- `www.yhbt.com/article.php?story=20050204130636987`
- `www.mythtv.org/docs/mythtv-HOWTO-23.html#ss23.19`

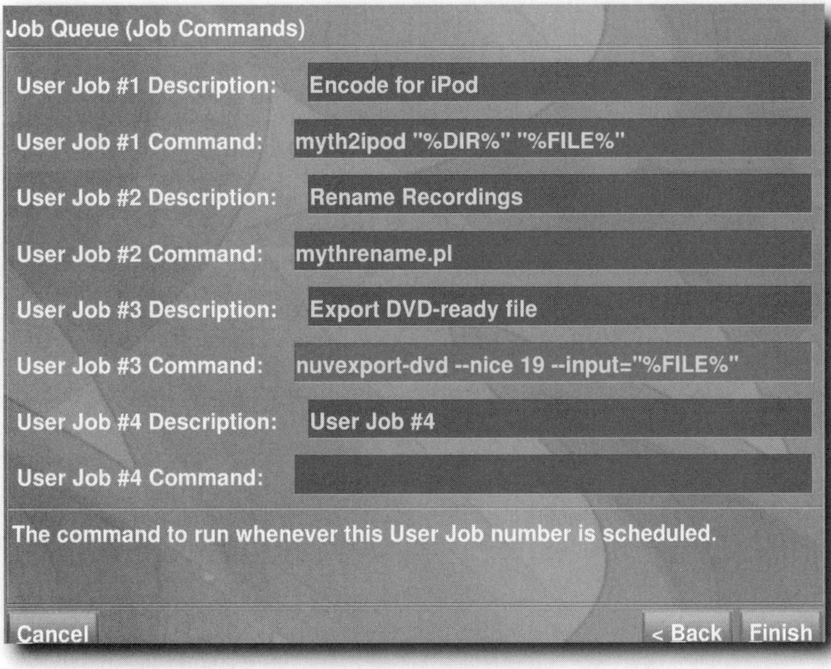

Job Queue (Job Commands)

User Job #1 Description:	Encode for iPod
User Job #1 Command:	myth2ipod "%DIR%" "%FILE%"
User Job #2 Description:	Rename Recordings
User Job #2 Command:	mythrename.pl
User Job #3 Description:	Export DVD-ready file
User Job #3 Command:	nuvexport-dvd --nice 19 --input="%FILE%"
User Job #4 Description:	User Job #4
User Job #4 Command:	

The command to run whenever this User Job number is scheduled.

Cancel   < Back   Finish

FIGURE 17-4: Setting up custom job commands

Customizing Key Bindings

There are three different methods to adjust what keys are bound to which functions within MythTV. One of them is not covered here because manually editing MythTV's MySQL database isn't something most people should tackle! The other two routes are far safer. The MythWeb add-on enables you to configure your key bindings using a web page (http://your.myth.box/mythweb/settings/keys), while the MythControls plug-in, added as of MythTV 0.19, enables configuration of keys within mythfrontend's Setup section (Utilities/Setup → Edit Keys). The MythWeb route merits a major warning regarding its lack of error-checking and how easily you can screw up a setup, so the MythControls route, which does incorporate some error-checking, is our recommended route.

The MythControls interface, shown in Figure 17-5, is fairly intuitive. The first column consists of key contexts, so start by selecting the context under which you'd like to configure a key. The next column provides a list of actions that can be performed in that context. Select the action you want to configure and you'll see four slots for keys that can be (or may already be) bound to that action. Select a specific slot and you'll be greeted with a menu that enables you to either set a new binding or remove an existing one. Select Set Binding, press the key you want to bind, and you're set. Note that among the available key contexts is one called Jump Points. Binding a Jump Point to a key enables you to jump straight to a particular function from anywhere within MythTV's UI.

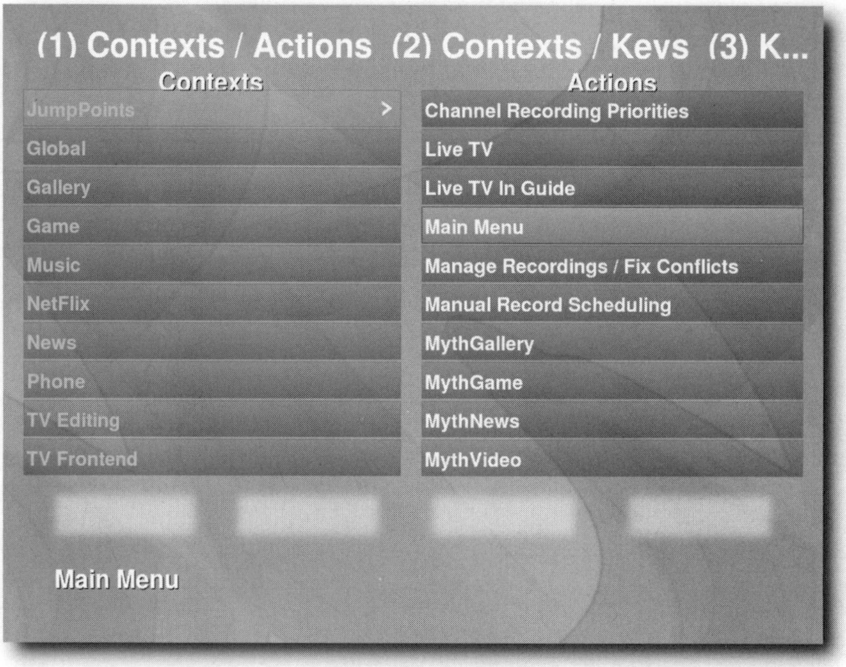

FIGURE 17-5: MythControls interface

MythControls is part of the `mythplugins` source archive available at `mythtv.org` or as a binary package for most distributions that provide MythTV packages, so chances are good you've already got it installed.

Wireless Networking

There is one critical distinction to make before discussing the impact of wireless networking (aka WiFi) with MythTV. If you're running a stand-alone, frontend and backend all-in-one box setup, even the slowest WiFi connection should suffice because the only network access the box requires is to fetch guide data updates (though this can also be done from files burned to CD, over dial-up, and so on), and assorted other bits of relatively small data for various MythTV plug-ins. WiFi can have a major impact if your setup splits the video capture backend and video playback frontend across multiple machines, and requires video to stream over your network.

Generally speaking, WiFi is considered a no-no for a remote frontend MythTV box. While 802.11b's official top speed of 11 Mbps and 802.11g's official top speed of 54 Mbps are enough to handle standard-definition television and high-definition television, respectively, in the real world, those numbers don't really hold water. Standard-definition recordings tend to max out at around 8 Mbps, and high-definition recordings at around 20 Mbps. Any number of electronic devices, cell phones, microwaves, and so forth can interfere with WiFi, and obstructions such as walls, floors, furniture and the like will quickly degrade signal strength.

By its very nature, WiFi networking is a lossy transmission medium. This is fine when you're simply reading e-mail or browsing the web, but it doesn't work so well when you're trying to watch TV, whereby all the data needs to get there on time. Any delays and/or dropped packets will result in a miserable viewing experience, so if you decide to tempt fate, you'll need a strong, clean signal and a bit of luck.

In addition, note that some wireless cards are better than others, especially under Linux. The group Seattle Wireless has compiled a listing of wireless adapters and their corresponding Linux drivers, at `http://seattlewireless.net/LinuxDrivers`, complete with feature comparisons and maturity ratings, so you might do well to consult their site if you haven't already acquired your wireless gear.

That said, you're certainly welcome to give wireless networking a shot if you're in a pinch, and/or if you're casually viewing video on a laptop. Standard-definition recordings tend to stream OK over 802.11g wireless connections, but you still need a fairly strong and clean signal to prevent stutter, frame drops, pixellation, and other unwanted effects. High-definition over WiFi is almost guaranteed to be unbearable for any extended viewing. If you don't believe us, you'll be able to see for yourself.

Outputting to an HDTV

As we explained in Chapter 16, there two major components on which you'll want to focus when attempting to display high-definition content on a high-definition display: the video output device in your MythTV box and whatever high-definition display you use — especially the inputs it makes available. In order from most to least preferable, the most desirable inputs you'll want to use on an HDTV are as follows:

1. DVI or HDMI (both rank more or less the same)
2. VGA
3. Component video

The distinctions between items two and three are fairly minimal, and some people actually prefer Component over VGA. In most cases, VGA is easier to use when interconnecting a computer and a high-definition display (unless you have an nVidia GeForce 6 or later model graphics card that comes with a Component dongle), while Component often delivers a slightly better picture. How you feed these various inputs is where things get interesting. Regardless of which type of input you feed, nVidia cards remain far and away the most popular and best-supported output devices for viewing HDTV content.

Remember also that high-end nVidia cards are high-end because of their superior 3D capabilities (which also contributes to their high cost). Because 3D has relatively little value for a MythTV system, currently available low-end GeForce 5200 or 6200 cards work about as well as a brand new high-end GeForce 7900, as far as MythTV is concerned. In addition, lower-end cards are often available in fanless, passively cooled (and thus silent) packages, whereas high-end cards require active cooling from a relatively noisy high-speed fan. In this context, note that certain video overlay features available on the 5000 series and earlier cards have actually been removed on newer models. This is of little concern to MythTV, which doesn't need those features, but this might have an impact on other applications you could run on a MythTV box.

DVI/HDMI Input

The Digital Visual Interface (DVI) and High Definition Multimedia Interface (HDMI) are the only purely digital interconnects available. Of all HDTV input types, they deliver the best picture quality. DVI and HDMI are pretty much identical except that they use different connectors, as far as video is concerned. In fact, you can buy a cable that has a DVI connector at one end with an HDMI connector on the other, to connect a DVI output on your MythTV box to an HDMI input on an HDTV. Although an HDMI-to-HDMI cable can carry audio and video on the same single cable, pure HDMI output from a computer isn't commonly available yet (if at all).

It's also true that copy protection is more likely to be part of the data that streams into HDMI inputs than into DVI inputs. That said, both types of digital data may be affected by copy protection so that output from a computer won't work with the input to an HDTV. To our way of thinking this reflects an unfortunate design choice that some HDTV manufacturers have made to support content providers at the expense of consumers, particularly where ease of use is concerned.

In theory at least, any video card with a DVI output should "just work" with any DVI or HDMI input on an HDTV. Any newer HDTV should send valid information over the Display Data Channel (DDC) in the video cable, and provide your MythTV PC's video card with information about its display capabilities (horizontal sync rate, vertical refresh rate, valid resolutions, and so forth). Using that information, the video card should be able to sync up with the television to produce output at 800 × 600 resolution or better.

Of course, common sense suggests (and empirical evidence confirms) that not all video cards are created equal. On my HDTV, a Westinghouse LVM-37w1 37-inch 1920 × 1080 progressive-scan LCD with DVI, VGA, and Component inputs, only one of three relatively new video cards sends a signal that uses the entire width of the display (via DVI). Both a GeForce 5200 and the -board GeForce 6150 graphics chips on an nVidia nForce 430 motherboard sent what looked like 4:3 signals starting at power on (during the BIOS POST). This situation remained unchanged even when the graphical user interface appeared. Neither card could drive the display at 1920 × 1080 (they maxed out at 1280 × 1024, and used only a 4:3 portion of screen). Conversely, a GeForce 6200 card sends a wide-screen signal all the way, and had no problems pushing a 1920 × 1080 progressive-scan signal, though a custom modeline is required (we'll get to custom modeline voodoo soon).

VGA Input

VGA (an acronym for Video Graphics Array) has the beauty of being the long-standing conventional way of connecting a computer to a display. It's an analog signal, which means there isn't any concern than you'll run into some kind of copy protection scheme that locks a computer out of using a VGA input, so again, in theory, any video card with a VGA output should just work with a VGA input on your HDTV. There may well be issues along the same lines of DVI with the display size not being correctly picked up on some sets, as well as the possible need for custom modelines.

Component Video Input

There are now three different ways to get Component video into your HDTV, if this is the only input type available. First, you should be aware that there are two different types of Component video, each of which uses three distinct connectors. One breaks the video signal out into separate red, green, and blue components; it's called RGB Component Video. The other breaks the video signal into a luminance (Y) component and two color-difference signals (Pb and Pr); it's called YPbPr Component Video. Of these two types, YPbPr is the most common.

Some of the nVidia GeForce 6 and later series graphics cards, as well as some cards with non-nVidia chipsets that don't work as well with MythTV, include an output jack to which a YPbPr Component video breakout cable may be attached. Generally, these tend to work well, and require little or no configuration work on your part to make them work. Using one of these cards, you should see all the BIOS POST information and your bootloader prompt, and the nVidia driver should auto-detect your display capabilities and drive it correctly at 1080i, 720p, or 480p. Worst-case scenario: You might have to specify a line in your X server configuration file to force the nVidia driver to use a particular HDTV standard, such as:

```
Option "TVStandard" "HD720p"
```

Place this within the `"Device"` configuration section in `/etc/X11/xorg.conf` to force use of 1280 × 720 progressive-scan mode. Similar options exist for 1080i, 1080p, 480p, and 576p (check out the appendixes in the nVidia driver documentation to learn about all the options available).

Before graphics cards began to ship with component output dongles in the box, some hearty souls had to purchase VGA-to-Component video transcoder devices to connect a MythTV box to a high-definition television. Though these early devices cost as much as $100, you'll find a wider (and cheaper) array of transcoders available today, should you need one. Two of the most popular models include the Audio Authority 9A60 and the Key Digital KD-VTCA3. Both are available new at numerous online outlets, such as Digital Connection, but may be purchased used for less on eBay. Digital Connection even provides some documentation on how to get things working, at `www.digitalconnection.com/FAQ/HDTV_4.asp` (although it's tailored to Windows, it provides useful information nevertheless).

Another top-notch source for information on how to make a transcoder device work, particularly under Linux, is Brandon Beattie's "Linux HTPC Howto," at www.linuxis.us/ linux/media/howto/linux-htpc/. You will find the Video Card Configuration page to be of great interest because using a transcoder means you must find and force a specific modeline to enable a viable signal to be displayed. Several standard modelines are defined on that page.

However, if none of those particular modelines work, you may be forced into scouring the Internet for alternatives, or building your own from scratch. This latter activity is a somewhat tedious process, documented online at http://wilsonet.com/mythtv/mythhd.php. This information also includes the modelines that ultimately worked on that original HDTV, and has worked on numerous other HDTVs as well.

If you have an RGB component input you want to feed, you can buy either a DVI-to-RGB Component or VGA-to-Component video adapter at low cost (roughly $20). Similar issues present with other input methods apply — especially the YPbPr Component transcoder route, but at least the adapter is cheaper!

A Bit about Custom Modelines

In theory, you can severely damage your display by playing around with custom modelines. You could end up sending some signal that does Very Bad Things to the circuitry in your set. Most modern sets have the smarts to ignore dangerous signals, but you've been warned. If you start playing around and you fry your set, you're on your own! Creating modelines is something of a black art to most folks; only a few people out there really understand all the components exactly.

Component dongles from an nVidia card probably represent the safest and easiest route, because no modeline tweaking should be required. Straight DVI and VGA may require custom modelines for optimal viewing, but one of the standard modes found in Brandon Beattie's Linux HTPC Howto should fit this bill. For my Westinghouse LVM-37w1 HDTV, the following modeline did the trick to create a perfect fit using DVI:

```
ModeLine "1920x1080p" 148.352 1920 1960 2016 2200 1080 1082 1088 1125
```

Custom modelines should be defined in the "Monitor" section of your X configuration file, and then referenced for use in the "Display" subsection of the "Screen" section of your configuration file. The following snippets come from the LVM-37w1 setup I use:

```
Section "Monitor"
        Identifier   "Monitor0"
        VendorName   "Westinghouse 37in LCD"
        ModelName    "LVM-37w1"
        DisplaySize  820         460
        HorizSync    30.0 - 80.0
        VertRefresh  50.0 - 75.0
        Mode
        ModeLine "1920x1080p" 148.352 1920 1960 2016 2200
                                      1080 1082 1088 1125
EndSection
[...]
```

```
Section "Screen"
        Identifier  "Screen0"
        Device      "Videocard0"
        Monitor     "Monitor0"
        DefaultDepth     24
        SubSection "Display"
                Viewport   0 0
                Depth      16
                Modes      "1920x1080p" "800x600"
        EndSubSection
        SubSection "Display"
                Viewport   0 0
                Depth      24
                Modes      "1920x1080p" "800x600"
        EndSubSection
EndSection
```

It's usually a good idea to put a new modeline you're trying out in your Modes stanza to begin with, with a known, good fallback resolution next in line. That way, you still see a viable desktop if the X environment determines that the new mode is invalid for some reason. If that happens, the first thing to do is consult your X server's log file to determine whether you can tell why it was thrown out. For the X.org X server, look in /var/log/Xorg.0.log; for the XFree86 X server, check /var/log/XFree86.0.log (or something similar). Within the log file, you should be able to find some evidence to help you figure out what's wrong. Normally, some error line states that either the horizontal sync or vertical refresh was outside the acceptable range for your display. If that's the case, try another modeline, rinse, and repeat.

If you need help, there's an excellent utility available called PowerStrip. It's very popular, especially among the Windows-based HTPC crowd, and it's available from EnTech (www.entechtaiwan.net/util/ps.shtm). Of course, using this tool means you'll have to install Windows on your MythTV box, at least for a little while. Once you've crafted an ideal setup through PowerStrip tweaking, you can instruct the program to output a Linux-friendly modeline. That ought to produce the same video signal when you return to the Linux operation. Several great PowerStrip guides are available online, should you need more assistance in using this tool. One our favorites is at www.audioholics.com/showcase/DIY/powerstriphtpcp1.htm.

Dealing with Overscan

Because of the inexact nature of analog signals, televisions and television signals have historically been designed to compensate by assuming that between 2 and 5 percent of the video data ends up offscreen, beyond the edges of the visible area on your television. This phenomenon is called *overscan*. It can be annoying for MythTV users, because a good part of your Linux desktop and MythTV user interface may end up offscreen. Should it occur, there are a few different ways to fix this problem.

First, your television may include settings to adjust its picture. This is probably the simplest route to take. Simply twist a few knobs until your output fits the screen as well as possible. Consult your TV user manual for clues about doing this.

Second, your video card driver may be able to adjust picture size and location. If you're using an nVidia card with nVidia's driver, you should also have a utility on your system called `nvidia-settings`. This tool enables you to tweak your TV picture. If you use the Component break-out dongle, one of the sliders available on your Display Device handle adjusts the overscan.

A third route involves modeline tweaking. It's possible that a similar modeline with minor tweaks here and there will produce a picture that fits your set a bit better. One may already be available, but it could also be the case that you have to come up with one on your own. This is where PowerStrip might come in very handy. Otherwise, you need to get familiar with mode-line structure and syntax. This means learning more about what all the parameters in a mode-line mean, and what changing particular values does to the picture. After that, you can start up the `xvidtune` program under Linux. Please carefully read the big warning that comes up when you launch it. Generally, any modern television set should have built-in safeguards. Thus, if you're only making small changes to a working mode, such as single clicks on any of Left, Right, Wider, Narrower, Up, Down, Shorter, or Taller (as shown in Figure 17-6), you shouldn't be able to get into trouble enough to cause any problems. Nevertheless, you've been warned (again).

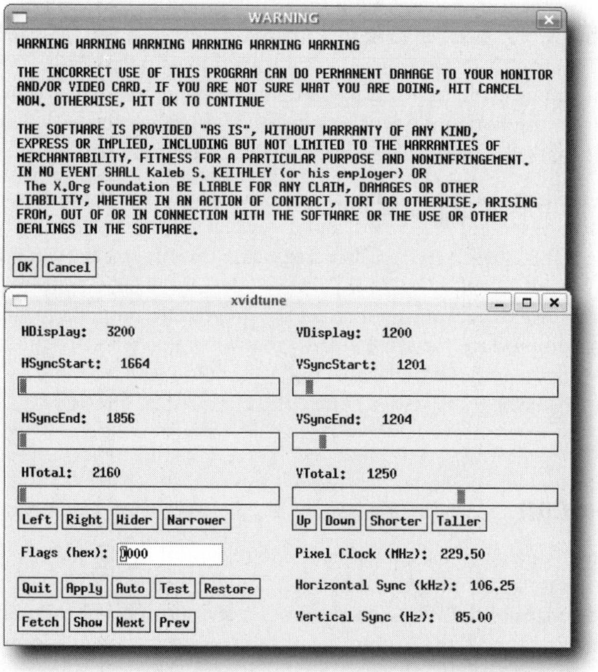

FIGURE 17-6: xvidtune: the power to shoot yourself in the foot!

Should you decide to use xvidtune, note that the numbers it displays correspond to your current modeline. With each alteration you make, at least one of those numbers should change. When you've tweaked to your heart's content, write down all the resulting values so you can use them to build a new modeline.

Another way to get that perfectly fit desktop through modeline tweaking is to reduce the resolution on the display. You must do this entirely by hand, but the long and short of it is that you keep essentially the same horizontal and vertical timings but try to output less pixels. This does offer another way to screw up your television, especially because it's a manual process. You're on your own here to figure out the exact details, but at least you now know it's a possibility.

A fourth route, if you simply don't feel like chancing damage to a perfectly good television, is to tell MythTV to compensate for you. MythTV offers built-in functionality to resize and nudge its GUI around to fit it to your viewable screen area. This has no impact on your desktop. It will still be overscanned, but most of the time, MythTV will be covering it completely! Navigate into MythTV's setup section, by selecting Utilities/Setup → Setup → Appearance, to the Screen settings page. Initially, values for GUI width, height, and X and Y offsets should all be zero. This tells MythTV to use everything your machine tells it is available, even though in this case, overscan means that some of it isn't visible.

Let's assume you're trying to compensate for, say, a 2 percent overscan on a 1280 × 720 display. A good place to start is to set your GUI width to 1264, height to 706, and then split the difference for X and Y offsets, so 13 and 7, respectively. Click through to the end of the configuration screens, and MythTV will adjust its GUI accordingly. Rinse and repeat until you get it just right. Note that you also have the option for MythTV to scale video output to play within this same area, or you can let it use the full screen (which is more or less what a television would normally do). The choice here may amount to personal preference and how much overscan you're dealing with. A tiny bit of overscan could actually be better than none, because some video streams have slightly ragged edges. This is particular true for SDTV, some of which you'll undoubtedly still be watching, because not all programming is available in HDTV format (yet!).

Managing mythfilldatabase

The mythfilldatabase program is essential to MythTV's ability to do its job. What this program does is update MythTV's database with the latest and greatest television programming data. MythTV needs this information to know what to record, to display guide data, and much more. After your initial run of mythfilldatabase, which should populate your database with several days' worth of guide data, subsequent runs pick up any changes for the current day, plus the next day in the future for which you don't yet have any guide data.

In the early days of MythTV, a cron job handled this task, and would typically run daily. Unfortunately, almost everyone (at least in the U.S.) ran mythfilldatabase at the same time, which overwhelmed the listing providers. Then, cron jobs started including a tweak to include a random delay before executing, which did stretch out listings requests a bit, but not enough. Enough of these cron jobs still started at the same time to bog the listing providers down. This route is no longer recommended, and is not covered here.

The new and improved, recommended way to get guide data listings is to use MythTV's built-in guide data fetching routine. Although it runs the very same `mythfilldatabase` command, it handles scheduling more intelligently. Navigate through `mythfrontend`, Utilities/Setup → Setup → General, to the Mythfilldatabase page, shown in Figure 17-7.

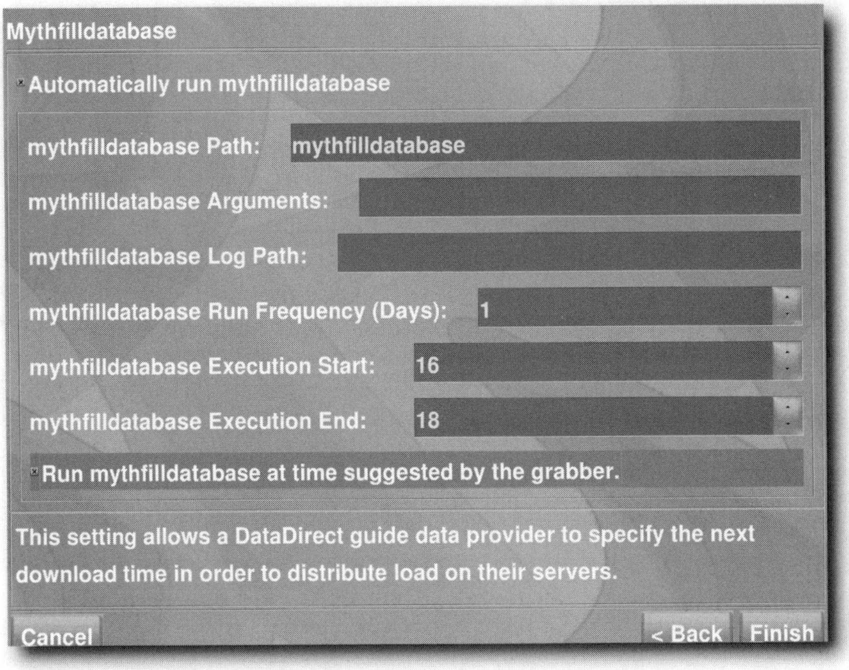

FIGURE 17-7: Configuring mythfilldatabase

Here, you define an initial window of time during which you'd like guide data to be collected. If you're in the U.S. or Canada, and use Zap2it's DataDirect service for guide data, enable the option to "Run mythfilldatabase at time suggested by the grabber." This was created in cooperation with Zap2it Labs (`http://labs.zap2it.com/`) to help distribute the load on their servers, which they're kind enough to let MythTV users use in exchange for completing a two-minute survey every three months. With that enabled, your `mythfilldatabase` execution window is then dynamically updated to match Zap2it's suggested time for your next run. On machines that don't use DataDirect, `mythfilldatabase` simply runs at some time during the initial execution window you define.

Mythifying Home Movies and VHS Tapes

MythTV offers no built-in way to pull video from a VHS collection for inclusion in your MythVideo library, nor does it offer any built-in way to pull video from a digital video camera. However, once you copy video onto your MythTV system in a suitable digital video format, MythTV will happily let you add that video to your MythVideo collection.

The simplest way to digitize a VHS tape onto your MythTV box is to hook up a VCR's S-Video and audio outputs to the S-Video and audio inputs on a PVR-150/250/350/500 (or similar) hardware MPEG-2 encoder card. The `ivtvctl` utility may be used to query the input to which your card is set, and learn what inputs it has, and then set up the correct S-Video input for use. Here's an example:

```
$ ivtvctl -P
ioctl VIDIOC_G_INPUT ok
Video input = 0

$ ivtvctl --list-inputs
ioctl: VIDIOC_ENUMINPUT
        Input    : 0
        Name     : Tuner 1
        Type     : 0x00000001
        Audioset: 0x00000007
        Tuner    : 0x00000000
        Standard: 0x000000000000B000 ( NTSC )
        Status   : 0

        Input    : 1
        Name     : S-Video 1
        Type     : 0x00000002
        Audioset: 0x00000007
        Tuner    : 0x00000000
        Standard: 0x0000000000FFFFFF ( PAL NTSC SECAM )
        Status   : 0

        Input    : 2
        Name     : Composite 1
        Type     : 0x00000002
        Audioset: 0x00000007
        Tuner    : 0x00000000
        Standard: 0x0000000000FFFFFF ( PAL NTSC SECAM )
        Status   : 0

        [...]
```

You want the primary S-Video input. From the preceding output, you can see that the capture input is set to input 0, which is the tuner, and you want to switch to input 1. Here's how to do that:

```
$ ivtvctl -p 1
ioctl VIDIOC_S_INPUT ok
```

```
Video input set to 1

$ ivtvctl -P
ioctl VIDIOC_G_INPUT ok
Video input = 1
```

Queue up the tape you want to import and set up the capture job on your MythTV box. This should be as simple as the following:

```
$ cat /dev/video0 > /path/to/storage/moviename.mpg
```

Right after you execute that command, press the Play button on the VCR. When the tape finishes rolling, press Ctrl+C to stop the capture job. Note that you might want to stop `myth-backend` during this process, or at least make sure that the capture card you're using for this process isn't scheduled to do any recording anytime soon. Otherwise, one recording or another may become corrupted, if it doesn't fail altogether. Unfortunately, there's no faster way to get video onto your system. More elegant software for importing video of this type is available, but capture time remains the same.

At the conclusion of the recording, you may want to open the resulting file in a video editor, such as `avidemux` (`http://fixounet.free.fr/avidemux/`). It can crop out ragged edges from the video, and you may also want to use it to clean up the lead-in and lead-out portions. Once you have a video you're happy with, save it to your MythVideo directory, where you can use the Video Manager (`mythfrontend` Utilities/Setup → Video Manager) to import it for viewing via MythVideo.

Importing digital video from a DV camera is much cleaner, partly because it's already digital, and partly because you can do it on a machine with no capture card, so long as it has a free FireWire port. A multitude of programs that can import DV exist for Windows and Macintosh, which you're certainly welcome to use, after which you can transport their finished products to your MythTV box. If you're working on your MythTV PC or another Linux box, Kino (`www.kinodv.org/`) comes highly recommended. Use it to pull in your video, do what you will with it, and save your work. Drop it into your MythVideo directory, use the Video Manager to import it, and it should now be available in your MythVideo library.

For a more heavy-duty video-editing suite, still 100% free, just like Linux, Cinelerra might be worth checking out, at `http://heroinewarrior.com/cinelerra.php3`.

Using Multiple Displays

Linux and X have supported multiple displays for some time now. There are a few different ways in which you can juggle multiple displays under Linux. Likewise, MythTV is multi-display aware, so you can configure it to use your displays however you like. The following paragraphs describe some possible and interesting usage scenarios.

One way to run multiple displays is to run two (or more) entirely independent X servers, each running its own desktop on its own display and with its own keyboard and mouse. However, this requires serious X server hacking we're not prepared to cover here. If you really want to try this, start your journey at `http://cambuca.ldhs.cetuc.puc-rio.br/multiuser/`, which includes at least one link to MythTV-specific usage for such a setup.

More standard approaches use the X server's generic Xinerama extension and nVidia's TwinView extension in its proprietary driver (which also exposes some Xinerama hooks). Generic Xinerama can be made to work with both multiple video cards (of the same or different types) and some dual-head video cards. We strongly recommend that nVidia card owners use TwinView in the binary nVidia driver. An example X server setup might feature a PVR-350 outputting your MythTV user interface and video playback to your television, while your video card outputs to a monitor that you use for normal desktop work. Similarly, one could use the nVidia driver to push a television from a GeForce series card's TV output and another display from its DVI or VGA output.

For the sake of brevity, and because an excellent, in-depth guide for doing all of these things already exists on the Internet, we'll simply point you to http://gentoo-wiki.com/HOWTO_Dual_Monitors. Despite residing in a Gentoo wiki, the information there should work on any Linux distribution for the most part, once you've installed appropriate video drivers (most should be included as part of your X server install, but nVidia's nVidia driver, ATI's fglrx, and the ivtv X driver all require separate installs).

Another common setup of interest uses multiple displays to show the same content. This is called *clone mode,* and it works quite well with an nVidia setup. Something along the lines of the following "Device" section in your X configuration, which assumes that a standard CRT capable of 1024 × 768 resolution and an NTSC television are both connected to a MythTV PC, should do just that:

```
Section "Device"
    Identifier  "Videocard0"
    Driver      "nvidia"
    VendorName  "nVidia"
    BoardName   " GeForce FX 5200"
    Option      "TwinView"
    Option      "TwinViewOrientation" "Clone"
    Option      "ConnectedMonitor" "CRT,TV"
    Option      "SecondMonitorHorizSync" "30.0 - 50.0"
    Option      "SecondMonitorVertRefresh" "60.0"
    Option      "MetaModes" "1024x768, 1024x768"
    Option      "TVStandard" "NTSC-M"
    Option      "TVOutFormat" "SVIDEO"
    Option      "NoTwinViewXineramaInfo" "true"
EndSection
```

Note that with TwinView setups, some hardware acceleration functionality is unavailable. This may lead to visual tearing of video during playback. Even if you drive two displays from a single nVidia card without using TwinView, those same hardware acceleration capabilities only work on the first display, so your second display may continue to suffer. Best practice is to run only a single display from an nVidia card for optimal MythTV performance (especially if HDTV is involved). Adding a second video card, nVidia or otherwise, should circumvent any of the problems mentioned here, so consider that option if you run into trouble trying to run two displays from a single graphics card.

If you do end up running multiple displays, you'll likely want to visit the Screen settings page, shown in Figure 17-8, under Utilities/Setup → Setup → Appearance, where you can specify which Xinerama screen or screens to use.

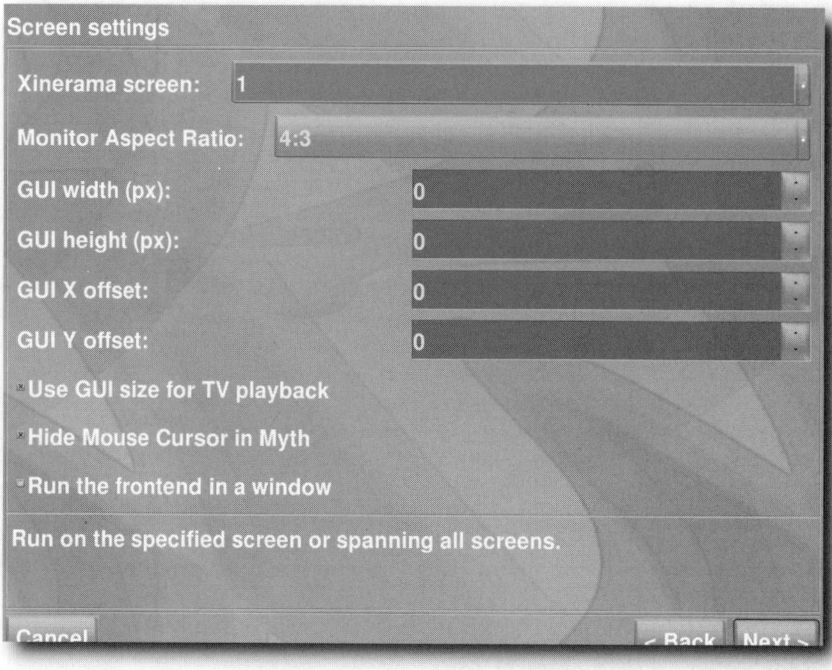

Screen settings

Xinerama screen: 1

Monitor Aspect Ratio: 4:3

GUI width (px):   0

GUI height (px):   0

GUI X offset: 0

GUI Y offset: 0

* Use GUI size for TV playback

* Hide Mouse Cursor in Myth

* Run the frontend in a window

Run on the specified screen or spanning all screens.

Cancel   < Back   Next >

FIGURE 17-8: Configuring Xinerama

Final Thoughts

This concludes a healthy, but by no means complete, sampling of ways in which you can extend your MythTV environment. We urge you to check out the MythTV users mailing list (www.mythtv.org/mailman/listinfo/mythtv-users/) and searchable archive (www.gossamer-threads.com/lists/mythtv/) for other ideas. In addition, feel free to consult your favorite Internet search engines if you have anything specific in mind. Someone may have already given it a shot, or maybe you can find some collaborators in learning a whole new way to use MythTV.

Next up in Chapter 18, we tackle some troubleshooting.

MythTV Troubleshooting

MythTV has umpteen different features, works with a huge range of hardware, and lets you customize things to your heart's content. However, along with such flexibility comes an increased likelihood that somewhere along the way something is bound to go wrong, and you'll have to fix it. This chapter addresses common pitfalls and frequently asked questions.

Restoring Missing Channel Icons

While using Zap2it Labs' DataDirect services in North America does offer several advantages over other means of acquiring programming data, it does not have any built-in means to pull down channel icons. The majority of the XMLTV-based grabbers (`http://xmltv.source forge.net/`) for other parts of the world have built-in functionality to grab channel icons. While not necessary, MythTV looks more polished if you have official channel icons displayed within the frontend along with your programming information, rather than just their call signs in text.

You'll need to get XMLTV installed on your system, regardless of whether you need it to grab programming data or not, and then generate an XML file that describes the stations in your channel lineup. This can be done rather easily via the `mkiconmap.pl` Perl script found in the MythTV `contrib` directory, like so:

```
$ perl mkiconmap.pl
```

The script will ask you a few questions about your service, make some calls to XMLTV, and then spit out an appropriate `iconmap.xml` file, which you'll then feed to `mythfilldatabase` to perform the actual channel icon import, as shown here:

```
$ mythfilldatabase --import-icon-map iconmap.xml \
> --update-icon-map
```

You can use this technique whether you use XMLTV or DataDirect to fetch your programming data. You can also run these commands any time after your initial import of icons. It will update any icons that have changed, add icons for new channels, and so on.

Handling Missing Plug-ins

The easiest way to be sure you have all of the available official MythTV plug-ins on hand is simply to install them all from the get-go. If you compile plug-ins from source code, by default all plug-ins should be built and installed. If you install them from binary packages, chances are good there's an umbrella `mythplugins` package that requires all the plug-ins. If you request such a `mythplugins` package and use an automatic dependency resolver, you get them all installed.

For Fedora Core systems utilizing the binary packages from `ATrpms.net`, if MythTV is installed using a `yum install mythtv-suite`, then everything you need is already in place. That's because the `mythtv-suite` package requires all of MythTV, along with all its official plug-ins, plus an assortment of themes.

That said, if you still end up missing some plug-ins, you'll need to start poking around to figure out what has gone wrong. For starters, make sure that you aren't mixing source-based and binary installs, because they (usually) place resulting executables into different locations on your system. For example, if you've installed core MythTV components from a binary package, then executables should reside in `/usr/bin/`, and your `mythfrontend` executable will look for plug-ins in `/usr/lib/mythtv/plugins/` (or `/usr/lib64/mythtv/plugins` on 64-bit systems).

Without making any alterations to default configuration options, a source-based install puts executables in `/usr/local/bin/`. Likewise, your `mythfrontend` executable looks for plug-ins in `/usr/local/lib/mythtv/plugins/`, or something similar.

Obviously, if a plug-in is installed in a location `mythfrontend` doesn't check, that plug-in won't load at runtime. Of course, you could configure a source-based install to put plug-ins where your binary base install can find them. Nevertheless, best practice calls for sticking with installs for MythTV base and plug-in components that are either all source-based or all binary-package-based.

If you do accidentally mix and match, it's typically much easier to remove binary-package-based components than to remove source-based components, because your package manager should be able to delete all packaged files for you. However, you can probably track down the locations of all source-based components to remove using a command like the following:

```
$ find / -name "*myth*" | grep local
```

If you remove pretty much everything in the list that this command returns, you should have purged your system of all source-installed bits and pieces.

Once you're positive you're running source-based or binary package-based components exclusively, with all components of the same type installed, determine whether that resolves your issues. Chances are good that they will be fixed.

If you still can't see all your plug-ins, the next best thing is to start up `mythfrontend` from a terminal window. When `mythfrontend` starts up, it tries to load any plug-ins it finds. Better still, if any plug-in fails to load for any reason, the program writes a useful blurb about exactly why it failed to the terminal window. If the output indicates no problem, or provides insufficient detail to clue you in to the problem, try starting `mythfrontend` with verbose logging turned on:

```
$ mythfrontend -v all -l mythdebug.log
```

The resulting `mythdebug.log` file should contain significantly more information to help you diagnose the problem. A common problem to watch for occurs when plug-ins weren't built against the same MythTV libraries as MythTV itself. Sometimes, users may have outdated source-based plug-ins installed that they forgot to update when they updated their core MythTV components. Another problem that may occur for one reason or another is specific to 64-bit systems, and involves mixing 32-bit and 64-bit components. If you think you might be in this boat, your best bet is to remove all MythTV and plug-in pieces and install them afresh. This time make sure they're all 32- or 64-bit, to avoid repeating the problem. You can run the `file` command against installed binaries and plug-ins to reveal whether they are 32-bit or 64-bit, as shown in the following example:

```
$ file libmythvideo.so
libmythvideo.so: ELF 64-bit LSB shared object, AMD x86-64,

    version 1 (SYSV), stripped
```

In this case, the MythVideo plug-in is obviously 64-bit, which ought to be the case with all your MythTV components if you're running a 64-bit distribution.

 Caution In earlier MythTV releases, some components were broken or didn't work very well, so people ran 32-bit versions of MythTV on 64-bit systems. This is no longer necessary or advisable.

Finally, if no debug output shows up, but you still don't see a plug-in, double-check to make sure you haven't simply altered your menu layout. This might, for example, omit the item needed to access that plug-in. If you've got a lingering `mainmenu.xml` file in `~/.mythtv/` from some prior menu customization, try removing it to see if that doesn't resolve the issue (but make a backup copy or rename the file just in case you must restore it).

If all else fails, visit the MythTV users mailing list. Search the list archive at `www .gossamer-threads.com/lists/mythtv/`. If you still can't find an answer to your problem, shoot a query to the list, which you can join at `www.mythtv.org/mailman/ listinfo/mythtv-users/`.

Eliminating Audio Crackles and Pops

Some sound cards (and/or their drivers) can be a bit finicky. This is most noticeable when you hear a lot of crackling and popping during audio playback.

On occasion, this results from excess output volume on one audio mixer setting or another. Especially if you're using an external amplifier of some sort, try lowering the Master and PCM Mixer Volume settings in `mythfrontend`, under Utilities/Setup ➜ Setup ➜ General (see Figure 18-1). Next, use your amp to raise the volume instead. Likewise, if you use a video capture card that requires feeding a loopback cable from the capture card to an input on your sound card, you may need to lower the volume on the sound card input.

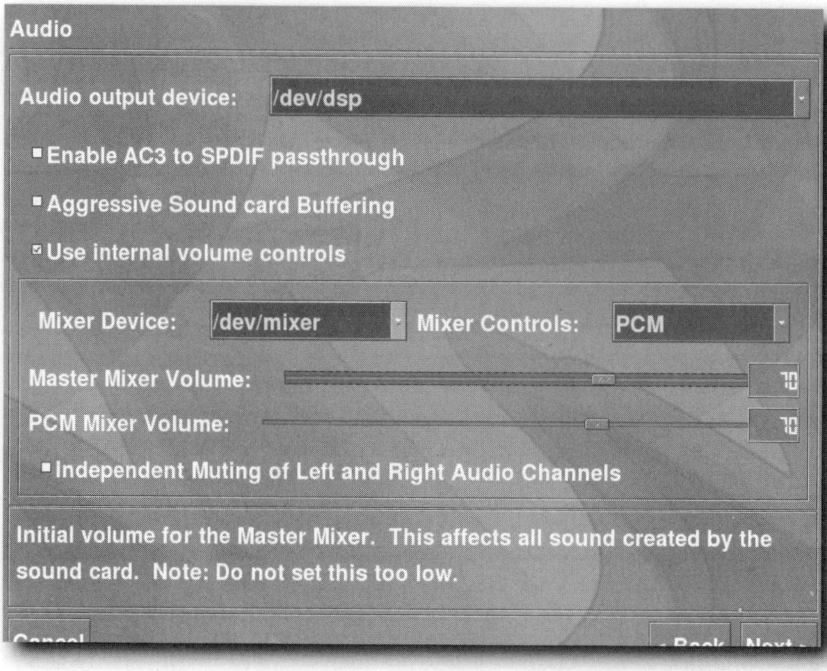

FIGURE 18-1: Adjusting output volumes

For hardware-encoding capture cards, the problem may be as simple as setting capture volume too high in your recording profile. Try backing that down a bit, in Utilities/Setup → Setup → TV Settings → Recording Profiles, for all your Recording Profiles (see Figure 18-2).

In addition, those who use hardware encoder cards may find they need to enable the Extra Audio Buffering option. It appears on the first page under Utilities/Setup → Setup → TV Settings → Playback (see Figure 18-3).

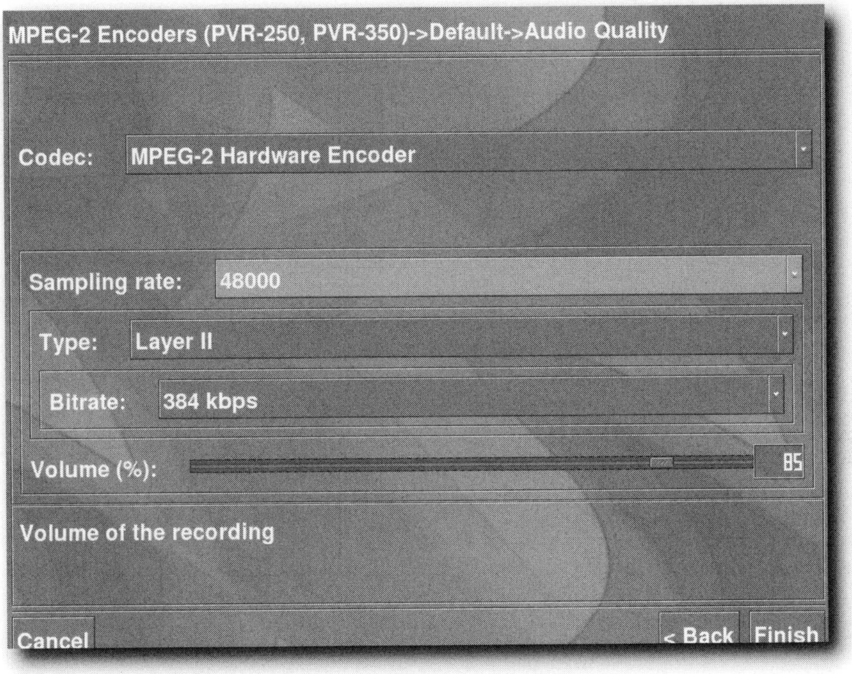

MPEG-2 Encoders (PVR-250, PVR-350)->Default->Audio Quality

Codec: MPEG-2 Hardware Encoder

Sampling rate: 48000

Type: Layer II

Bitrate: 384 kbps

Volume (%):   85

Volume of the recording

Cancel   < Back Finish

FIGURE 18-2: Adjusting recording volume levels

Finally, double-check all audio cabling. Fiddle with connections while audio is playing on your system. If you're lucky, you'll discover a loose connection or a bad cable. Cinch up the connection or replace any faulty cabling as needed.

If audio playback is typically fine for every output type except when you try to output raw digital audio from an HDTV recording to your amp, revisit the "Raw Digital Audio Output" section in Chapter 15.

If none of the preceding suggestions help your situation, yours may be another case worth taking to the MythTV users mailing list cited in the preceding section.

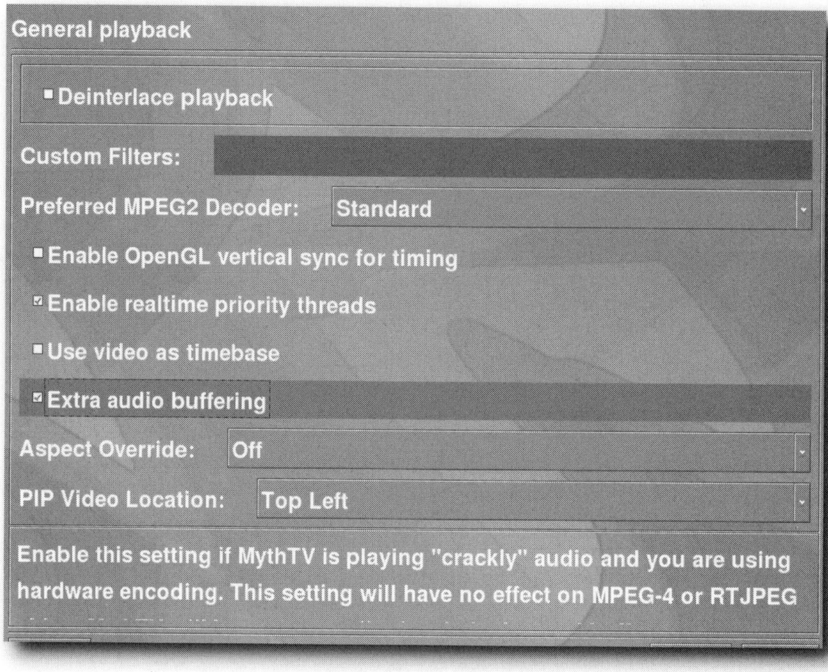

General playback

■ Deinterlace playback

Custom Filters:

Preferred MPEG2 Decoder: Standard

■ Enable OpenGL vertical sync for timing

☑ Enable realtime priority threads

■ Use video as timebase

☑ Extra audio buffering

Aspect Override: Off

PIP Video Location: Top Left

Enable this setting if MythTV is playing "crackly" audio and you are using
hardware encoding. This setting will have no effect on MPEG-4 or RTJPEG

FIGURE 18-3: Enabling extra audio buffering

Handling mythfilldatabase Errors

In earlier MythTV releases, mythfilldatabase didn't always handle errors very well. In
some cases, when it encountered an error connecting to a programming data server, it believed
there should be no programming information for that day. It would then proceed to remove all
programming data. This has since been fixed, and no programming data should be dropped
from your database anymore.

The only real issue to confront is what to do when a mythfilldatabase run fails. Given
that mythfilldatabase typically fills in between 7 and 14 days' worth of programming
data, a single failure is usually something you can ignore. You might miss out on some last-
minute lineup changes, but such things are rare and usually involve yanking a new episode for
some rerun filler content. Within mythfilldatabase, navigate to Information Center→
System Status, and the very first entry you'll see is Listings Status, which tells you when
mythfilldatabase last ran, whether it was successful, and how many days worth of programming data exist in the database, among other things (see Figure 18-4).

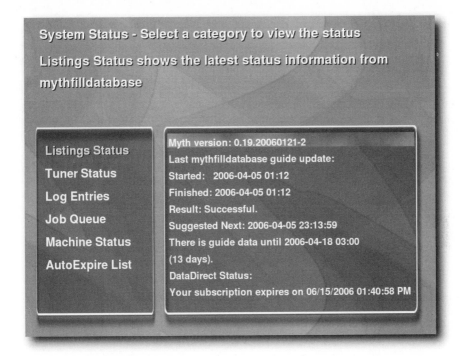

System Status - Select a category to view the status

Listings Status shows the latest status information from mythfilldatabase

Listings Status
Tuner Status
Log Entries
Job Queue
Machine Status
AutoExpire List

Myth version: 0.19.20060121-2
Last mythfilldatabase guide update:
Started: 2006-04-05 01:12
Finished: 2006-04-05 01:12
Result: Successful.
Suggested Next: 2006-04-05 23:13:59
There is guide data until 2006-04-18 03:00
(13 days).
DataDirect Status:
Your subscription expires on 06/15/2006 01:40:58 PM

FIGURE 18-4: Listings Status screen

If you happen to see a failed mythfilldatabase run, the fix is generally quite simple: Run it manually from the command line. In most cases, such a failure is a one-time glitch. Maybe your Internet connection was unavailable, or perhaps your guide data source was down for system maintenance. After allowing a bit of time for either end to recover, rerunning mythfilldatabase should put things right back on track.

If you've got a more systemic, longer-term problem, visit the MythTV users mailing list. If it's a widespread issue, it's bound to be under discussion there. Every once in a while, changes occur on the listing provider's end that may require an update to the mythfilldatabase or XMLTV code. Such updates usually follow quickly whenever something causes constant mythfilldatabase errors; they're also invariably discussed on MythTV mailing lists.

Troubleshooting mythfrontend

The vast majority of the complex and CPU-intensive work (such as video playback) done in a MythTV system happens in mythfrontend. Such being the case, this is likely the area where the greatest number and widest range of problems can occur.

Connectivity

First and foremost, when troubleshooting mythfrontend, you want to start up your myth-frontend process from a terminal window. For one thing, assorted messages about what mythfrontend is doing (or trying to do) will appear in the terminal window. Second, if for some reason mythfrontend locks up on you but isn't locking up the entire system, you can press Alt+Tab to jump over to the terminal window and enter Ctrl+C to kill off that hung mythfrontend process. Under ordinary circumstances, you should see nothing more than the following (though these lines are broken up for readability) when you fire up mythfrontend:

```
$ mythfrontend
2006-04-05 01:36:57.745 Using runtime prefix = /usr
2006-04-05 01:36:57.925 New DB connection, total: 1
2006-04-05 01:36:57.979 Connected to database 'mythconverg' at
    host: localhost
2006-04-05 01:36:57.981 Total desktop dim: 1600x1200, with 1
    screen[s].
2006-04-05 01:36:58.024 Using screen 0, 1600x1200 at 0,0
2006-04-05 01:36:58.033 Current Schema Version: 1123
2006-04-05 01:36:58.034 mythfrontend version: 0.19.20060121-2
    www.mythtv.org
2006-04-05 01:36:58.034 Enabled verbose msgs:  important
    general
2006-04-05 01:36:58.916 lang0: eng
2006-04-05 01:36:58.917 lang: eng
2006-04-05 01:36:58.923 lang1: eng
2006-04-05 01:36:58.924 lang: eng
2006-04-05 01:36:59.021 Total desktop dim: 1600x1200, with 1
    screen[s].
2006-04-05 01:36:59.023 Using screen 0, 1600x1200 at 0,0
2006-04-05 01:36:59.024 Switching to square mode
    (G.A.N.T.)
2006-04-05 01:36:59.841 New DB connection, total: 2
2006-04-05 01:36:59.842 Joystick disabled.
2006-04-05 01:36:59.900 Registering Internal as a media
    playback plugin.
2006-04-05 01:36:59.901 Connected to database 'mythconverg' at
    host: localhost
2006-04-05 01:37:00.019 Registering MythDVD DVD Media
    Handler as a media handler
2006-04-05 01:37:00.020 Registering MythDVD VCD Media
    Handler as a media handler
2006-04-05 01:37:00.657 Registering MythMusic Media
    Handler as a media handler
```

This output should suffice to indicate what's going wrong if the problem you're troubleshooting is mythfrontend's inability to connect to your mythbackend process. Take note of the portion of the output indicating that this instance of mythfrontend is connecting to database mythconverg on host localhost.

If this were a remote frontend, you should see a message about mythfrontend trying to connect to database mythconverg on your master backend host, either via DNS name or IP address, depending on how you've set things up in ~/.mythtv/mysql.txt. If you're not connecting to the host you think you should, that is the file to edit—specifically, the DBHostName parameter.

Additionally, make sure that you've configured your database server to permit remote connections, both at the firewall and in the database application. If you're running firewall software on your database server, you must ensure that port 3306 is open for MySQL database access, as well as port 6543 for remote mythbackend access. Remote access to your MySQL database must also be permitted within MySQL itself, per the instructions in the "Configuring Remote Frontends" section in Chapter 15.

Once you're sure the database side is all squared away, you'll have to do a bit of navigation within mythfrontend to trigger some additional output that may be necessary, as at this point you've contacted the database server but not the mythbackend server. The simplest test here is to go into Media Library→ Watch Recordings, which triggers an attempt to contact your mythbackend server. If all goes well, you should see something like the following:

```
2006-04-05 02:04:51.182 Connecting to backend server:
    127.0.0.1:6543 (try 1 of 5)
2006-04-05 02:04:51.193 Using protocol version 26
```

If the mythbackend process isn't running, or is running on a host other than the one to which it's trying to connect, you will see something like this:

```
2006-04-05 02:08:37.398 Connecting to backend server:
    127.0.0.1:6543 (try 1 of 5)
2006-04-05 02:08:37.399 Connection timed out.
        You probably should modify the Master Server
        settings in the setup program and set the
        proper IP address.
```

If the server is running but having technical difficulties, you could see multiple connection attempts that ultimately end in failure. This usually indicates a mythbackend problem, which is covered in the next section.

As mentioned in the "Handling Missing Plug-ins" section in this chapter, cranking up the verbosity of what mythfrontend reports, and redirecting it to a log file, may be useful, if the issue doesn't appear to lie with mythbackend:

```
$ mythfrontend -v all -l mythdebug.log
```

Don't forget to double-check all settings in mythfrontend under Utilities/Setup → Setup → General, to be sure everything looks correct. If it does, and you're positive mythbackend is running fine, it may once again be time to visit the MythTV users mailing list to solicit help in identifying the problem. If you think mythbackend is the culprit, jump down to the "Troubleshooting mythbackend" section later in this chapter for more fun and excitement.

One final connectivity issue worth noting crops up when you run multiple backends and some of them store recordings to your master backend using NFS. If the NFS share becomes unavailable or is unmounted on remote backend systems, and you happen to run mythfrontend on those same systems, mythfrontend may be unable to find its recordings. Typically, running a quick mount -a resolves this issue (assuming you've configured your NFS share(s) in /etc/fstab properly).

Audio Playback

MythTV started out supporting only the Open Sound System (OSS), the default Linux audio subsystem in the 2.4 kernel days. OSS has since been supplanted by the Advanced Linux Sound Architecture (ALSA) in the current 2.6 kernel. MythTV now includes native ALSA support, but it's not quite as mature as its OSS support. Fortunately, ALSA provides an OSS compatibility layer, which enables ALSA to emulate OSS, which MythTV can then use with its OSS support.

Of course, this all assumes your kernel's ALSA was built with OSS emulation bits enabled. All sane distributions have done this already, but if you're rolling your own kernel for whatever reason, make sure you have the `CONFIG_SND_OSSEMUL`, `CONFIG_SND_MIXER_OSS`, `CONFIG_SND_PCM_OSS`, and `CONFIG_SND_SEQUENCER_OSS` options set to `y`.

Assuming you run a modular kernel with the preceding options enabled (as is true for any stock Fedora kernel), kernel modules `snd-mixer-oss`, `snd-pcm-oss`, and `snd-seq-oss`, should all be present on your system. Make sure all of these are loaded if you want to minimize the fiddling necessary to get MythTV to output sound. With these modules loaded, on the Audio page in `mythfrontend` under Utilities/Setup → Setup → General, the default output device `/dev/dsp` and default mixer device `/dev/mixer` settings should work without modification.

Of course, using native ALSA is far more sexy. It's also essentially a requirement for optimal HDTV viewing and listening when you're feeding an external Dolby Digital decode-capable amplifier. Configuring and troubleshooting native ALSA output is covered in detail in the section "Raw Digital Audio Output" in Chapter 15. Native ALSA output is also covered quite a bit on the MythTV users mailing list, so search its archives as well. By the time you read this, it's possible that MythTV's native ALSA support will have improved. Hopefully that means it is now easily configurable, no longer requires manual input, and works just as well as using ALSA's OSS compatibility layer. MythTV's code is always changing, usually for the better.

Video Playback

For the most part, outside of people using output from a Hauppauge WinTV PVR-350, video playback "just works" with whatever video output device you use in your MythTV frontend system, at least if that's standard-definition television. Of course, there are some things you can do to optimize playback performance, and maybe a few things you can do to help eliminate playback glitches, artifacts, and the like.

For numerous cards, you are likely to obtain better performance using a video driver other than the one that ships with your X server. For nVidia and ATi cards, this means using proprietary drivers, from www.nvidia.com/object/unix.html and https://support.ati.com/, respectively. For SiS and XGI cards, this means getting the latest and greatest drivers from www.winischhofer.at/linuxsisvga.shtml. For Via Unichrome and Unichrome Pro video, you'll want the driver from http://unichrome.sourceforge.net/. Details on how to get each driver up and running also appear at the links provided, as well as in assorted tutorials around the Internet. In fact, you'll find nVidia and SiS details on one of the pages maintained by author Jarod Wilson at http://wilsonet.com/mythtv/fcmyth.php.

Once the driver is in place, additional tweaking may be necessary, sometimes at both driver and MythTV levels. Handy control panels are included with both the nVidia and SiS drivers. They may be used to adjust certain parameters that control how the video driver functions. Those who drive a television using S-Video or Composite video will find it worthwhile to check out the flicker filter controls in nVidia's `nvidia-settings` utility. The same thing goes for the antiflicker setting in the Winischhofer `sisctl` utility.

nVidia's utility also contains on/off switches to toggle video texture Sync To VBlank. This is typically a big advantage when it's turned on, because it helps to ensure that all video frames are played in the right order and at the right time. Similarly, you can turn on Sync To VBlank for OpenGL-specific operations. This is a plus, at least when using the 1.0-7676 nVidia driver, with OpenGL VSync enabled in `mythfrontend`. This enables MythTV to utilize the OpenGL vertical sync rate to synchronize audio and video, which often eliminates frame jitter.

Later versions of the nVidia driver (version 1.0-8178 is the latest as of this writing) are incompatible with MythTV's current OpenGL VSync implementation. Should you try to use these two items together, the CPU will be completely overwhelmed. Thus, this is something to check if your playback suffers greatly immediately following a driver update. In MythTV, use of OpenGL VSync may be toggled on or off in `mythfrontend`, under Utilities/Setup ➔ Setup ➔ TV Settings ➔ Playback.

For output resolution issues, see "Troubleshooting Output Resolution Issues" later in this chapter.

Remote Control

Assuming you use LIRC to convert IR signals into something MythTV understands, there are two common ways in which your ability to control MythTV using a remote may fall apart. First, always check to confirm that the LIRC daemon, `lircd`, is running. On Fedora Core, the following check as `root` suffices:

```
# /sbin/service lircd status
```

If all is well, the preceding command (or more generically, `/etc/init.d/lircd` status) returns the following:

```
lircd (pid 21856) is running...
```

If not, either you've forgotten to start up `lircd` or it tried to start but failed for some reason. Trying to start it up one more time is usually the next best thing, after which you should check its status again. If it returns OK, you must enable `lircd` to run at boot time (`/sbin/ chkconfig lircd on` for Fedora). If not, it's time to move on to further debugging.

Often, either the output of the `dmesg` command or the contents of `/var/log/messages` will provide clues as to why `lircd` fails to start, so be sure to examine both. The most common cause for this problem is when the proper LIRC driver never gets loaded for some reason. Output from `/sbin/lsmod` should contain one or more modules starting with `lirc`, if they are loading. If no such entries appear, load them manually (and see if you can't find a handy way to ensure they load during boot up the next time around). For example, you could load the `lirc_i2c` driver for use with a PVR-250's IR dongle as follows:

```
# /sbin/modprobe lirc_i2c
```

In addition, there should be an `lircd` socket and an `lirc0` character device in `/dev/`, with which `lircd` needs to interact. These are created automatically when you load an LIRC driver. You can use the following command to check this (it's shown here with sample representative output as well):

```
# ls -l /dev/lirc*
lrwxrwxrwx 1 root root      5 Apr  5 05:04 /dev/lirc -> lirc0
crw------- 1 root root 61, 0 Apr  5 05:04 /dev/lirc0
srw-rw-rw- 1 root root      0 Apr  5 05:02 /dev/lircd
```

If these devices still don't show up, something is probably wrong with your LIRC install. This is something you may need to take up with the packager who furnished your LIRC, if you're using binary packages. Possibly, it may be a fit topic for the LIRC mailing list, at `http://lists.sourceforge.net/lists/listinfo/lirc-list`. A quick poke into the MythTV users mailing list to determine whether it's a common issue can't hurt either. At this point, however, the problem isn't really MythTV-specific, which means it's best to start closer to the source.

A second way remote control ability typically falls down stems from a lack of proper LIRC configuration files. To get this ball rolling, you need an `/etc/lircd.conf` file that matches the remote you use. The easiest way to make sure this is indeed the case is to start up `lircd` with an appropriate `lircd.conf` in place. Next, fire up the `irw` tool, which simply spits out what buttons it thinks you pressed, based on corresponding labels in `lircd.conf`. If `irw` never spits out anything, you've got either dead batteries or the wrong `lircd.conf`. Press Ctrl+C to exit `irw`.

Once you have the right `lircd.conf` in place and `irw` happily spits out button presses, make sure you've got the configuration file in place that maps those button presses to MythTV functions. This is handled using a plaintext file in `~/.mythtv/lircrc`. A common pitfall here occurs when button labels between `lircrc` and `lircd.conf` don't match up properly. Every function mapping in `lircrc` must match a button defined in `lircd.conf` before it is actually able to do something productive.

Troubleshooting mythbackend

The first place to look when anything goes wrong with `mythbackend` is in its log. Of course, this assumes you're running `mythbackend` with logging enabled. Fortunately, this is its default behavior if you're using binary packages or a source-based install with one of the initialization scripts provided in the `contrib/` directory of the MythTV source distribution.

In the Fedora Core world at least, `mythbackend` logs to `/var/log/mythtv/mythbackend.log`. You'll definitely want to peruse this file when anything goes haywire. Common problems, including being unable to access a recording device, write to a directory, or read from a file (such as a recording), should be logged there. Note that in order to troubleshoot some of these `mythbackend` issues, you still need to use `mythfrontend`.

If you happen across an entry that states `mythbackend` is unable to open a certain video capture device, the most likely cause is that the driver for that capture device didn't load for some reason. We'll attempt to divine why that might happen in the next section of this chapter, "Troubleshooting Hardware/Driver Problems." If for some reason the `ivtv` driver fails to load for a PVR-250, you'll see something like this:

```
2006-04-05 05:41:21.948 TVRec(1): Changing from None to WatchingLiveTV
2006-04-05 05:41:22.008 Channel(/dev/video0)::Open(): Can't open video
    device, error "No such file or directory"
2006-04-05 05:41:22.009 ChannelBase: Could not find input: Tuner 1 on
    card when setting channel 60
```

These log entries should be accompanied by the following debug output from the `mythfrontend` instance that's trying to play back the video. For Live TV, that looks like this:

```
2006-04-05 05:41:21.845 TV: Attempting to change from
    None to WatchingLiveTV
2006-04-05 05:41:21.861 Using protocol version 26
2006-04-05 05:41:22.163 GetEntryAt(-1) failed.
2006-04-05 05:41:22.164 EntryToProgram(0@Wed Dec 31
    19:00:00 1969) failed to get pginfo
2006-04-05 05:41:22.164 TV Error: LiveTV not
    successfully started
2006-04-05 05:41:22.164 TV Error: LiveTV not
    successfully started
2006-04-05 05:41:22.168 TV: Deleting TV Chain in
    destructor
```

Another common failure occurs when required drivers load and configure the capture device properly but the user running `mythbackend` doesn't have sufficient permissions to access it. This isn't common on Fedora Core systems, because `mythbackend` is typically configured to run as `root` to avoid problems with the way device ownerships may be altered on-the-fly when a user logs in. `mythbackend` starts up before any user logs in, so devices are still all owned by `root`. Other distributions opt to configure groups with read/write permissions for recording devices, and then run `mythbackend` as a user in, for example, the `video` group. If you forget to add the user ID under which you run `mythbackend` to the `video` group, then you get the same effect — namely, an inability to use your capture device(s).

If `mythbackend` is unable to write to your MythTV recordings storage area, it may fail to start up. In that case, it will probably spew out an error message like this:

```
2006-04-05 05:55:55.907 Enabled verbose msgs:
    important general
/storage/MythTV/nfslockfile.lock: Permission denied
Unable to open lockfile!
Be sure that '/storage/MythTV' exists and that both
the directory and that file are writable by this user.
```

Do as the error messages say (make things writable by the user ID under which you run `mythbackend`, or change the user ID to one with appropriate permissions), and you should be back on track.

Slightly more cryptically, if `mythbackend` is able to start up but can't write recordings to your specified video storage area, you'll get something along these lines:

```
2006-04-05 05:57:10.086 TVRec(1): Changing from None
    to WatchingLiveTV
2006-04-05 05:57:10.299 TFW, Error: Opening file
    '/storage/MythTV/1060_20060405055710.mpg'.
                        eno: Permission denied (13)
2006-04-05 05:57:10.300 TVRec(1) Error: RingBuffer
    '/storage/MythTV/1060_20060405055710.mpg' not open...
2006-04-05 05:57:10.301 TVRec(1) Error:
    CreateLiveTVRingBuffer() failed
2006-04-05 05:57:10.302 TVRec(1) Error:
    Failed to create RingBuffer 2
2006-04-05 05:57:10.303 TVRec(1): Changing from
    WatchingLiveTV to None
```

If your recording storage area is simply not there, because you've pointed mythbackend at a non-existent location, moved a directory, or failed to mount an NFS share, mythbackend should fail to start up, and spit out the following:

```
2006-04-05 05:52:31.872 Enabled verbose msgs:
    important general
/storage/MythTV/nfslockfile.lock: No such file
    or directory
Unable to open lockfile!
Be sure that '/storage/MythTV' exists and that
    both the directory and that file are writeable
    by this user.
```

The easy fix is to make sure that the directory exists and/or is mounted.

Another problem that can be slightly more challenging to fix occurs when a file somehow ends up being entered into MythTV's database as having been recorded by mythbackend but the file doesn't actually exist anymore for some reason (maybe you deleted it or there were temporary permissions problems, or the planets were mis-aligned). When this happens, mythfrontend behaves sluggishly, and output such as the following appears in your terminal window:

```
[...]
2006-04-05 06:19:23.235
    RingBuf(/storage/MythTV/1060_20060405055432.mpg):
    Invalid file (fd 16) when opening
    '/storage/MythTV/1060_20060405055432.mpg'.
    1 retries remaining.
2006-04-05 06:19:23.739
    RingBuf(/storage/MythTV/1060_20060405055432.mpg):
    Invalid file (fd 16) when opening
    '/storage/MythTV/1060_20060405055432.mpg'.
    0 retries remaining.
[...]
2006-04-05 06:19:26.763 Could not open
    /storage/MythTV/1060_20060405055432.mpg.
    2 retries remaining.
2006-04-05 06:19:27.267 Could not open
```

```
    /storage/MythTV/1060_20060405055432.mpg.
    1 retries remaining.
2006-04-05 06:19:27.771 Could not open
    /storage/MythTV/1060_20060405055432.mpg.
    0 retries remaining.
```

At this juncture, deleting the recording from your database isn't as straightforward as simply using `mythfrontend` to delete it. MythTV has safeguards against removing programs from its database when it can't also remove the file referenced in the database. That's because this discrepancy can result in users with a ton of large recording files that MythTV no longer knows about. Unfortunately, manual intervention is then needed to recover gigabytes of disk space. Instead, when a file goes missing, you must create a dummy file in which the missing file should reside, and then perform a delete operation in `mythfrontend` (or via MythWeb). Fortunately, dummy file creation for a missing file cited in the preceding log is as easy as the following:

```
# touch /storage/MythTV/1060_20060405055432.mpg
```

Now, when you try to delete this file using `mythfrontend`, all should be right with the world again, at least in the limited scope of your personal MythTV world.

The final `mythbackend` troubleshooting area we cover involves protocol mismatches. MythTV's protocol version gets bumped up from time to time during its development (and almost always at least once between one release and the next) as the protocol is improved, more features are added, and so forth. To avoid wreaking havoc on a MythTV system, all components must use the same protocol version. The resulting log entries when this happens should contain the strings `Bad MYTH_PROTO_VERSION` or `Unexpected response to MYTH_PROTO_VERSION`.

So how do you end up with a protocol mismatch? This basically has to happen around the time a user upgrades MythTV software in one place or another on a MythTV system.

Suppose a user has split backend and frontend systems or multiple backends (or some combination) and forgets to upgrade one part or the other. Then, when newer and older components try to communicate, they'll abort, because they use different protocols. Simply upgrade all components to the same version and restart them to remedy this situation.

If you have upgraded a single system but fail to restart `mythbackend` after the upgrade, the older version could still be memory-resident. The same thing can happen if you restart `mythbackend` but leave the old `mythfrontend` running. Either way, there's a protocol mismatch. Restart all components, and all should be well.

A variant of this problem that's slightly more difficult to track down shouldn't happen, because we've already recommended that you not mix source- and package-based installs on the same system, but from time to time people still migrate from one to the other without cleaning up.

A typical situation occurs when an older `mythbackend` binary is left in `/usr/local/bin/` but a newer MythTV install resides in `/usr/bin/`. `/usr/local/bin/` tends to take execution path precedence over `/usr/bin/`. Thus, when users launch `mythbackend`, they're launching the older version. Then they click a desktop icon to launch `mythfrontend`, and the icon points to the new `mythfrontend`. Bam! Protocol mismatch.

Another thing to watch out for is which `mythbackend` you call from your initialization script, because they normally include full path specifications. You could easily have an old package-installed `mythbackend` launch from the initialization script, and then fire up a newer hand-compiled `mythfrontend` inside `/usr/local/bin/` from a terminal. Presto! Another protocol mismatch.

Again: Don't mix and match package- and source-based installs (unless you either truly know what you're doing or just really like pain and suffering)!

Troubleshooting Hardware/Driver Problems

With any new hardware, it's always a good idea to shake it down for a while before deploying it into production. Some of the drivers used with various components in many MythTV boxes are under active development. Thus, they're not always 100 percent stable. In addition, new revisions of hardware may come out that aren't yet perfectly supported. Typically, these devices *are* supported under Microsoft Windows, using drivers included in their retail packaging. Unfortunately, sometimes the best sanity check when starting in with new hardware is to try it out under Windows first.

That said, the array of hardware that is well-supported under Linux is quite substantial. This applies particularly to capture cards. If you stick to devices known to work well under Linux, you needn't endure the discomfort of installing Windows on your MythTV system just to sanity check your hardware.

Try to avoid absolute bleeding-edge hardware, because it often requires a bit of work to make it play nicely under Linux (and may not even be necessary for a quality MythTV system). For the most part, MythTV doesn't care what hardware it runs on, outside of its video capture and video output devices. As long as the rest works under Linux in general, it'll work with MythTV. Such being the case, troubleshooting hardware and driver problems outside of video capture cards, video output cards, IR receivers, and transmitters falls outside the scope of this book. We certainly spend some time focusing on these key items, though.

Video Capture Cards

There are really only three significant types of video capture cards, all of which are available in PCI card form. There are the dumb analog frame-grabbers that have been around for ages and ages, hardware-encoding analog capture cards, and digital TV capture cards.

With any of these capture cards, the show gets started with a kernel module, aka driver, that knows how to control the device. Most are automatically loaded at system startup without making you lift a finger. Alas, this can actually be a problem, because "automatic" doesn't always equate to "correct." Some of these devices do require manual intervention to make them work properly. In all cases, a driver is loaded at some point, and spits out initialization information. You can retrieve this sometimes valuable data by running `dmesg` or by looking at `/var/log/messages`.

If you run into problems, it can be useful to limit your system to a single capture device. That way, no guessing is required to determine specifically which one is in use. This makes it easier to narrow your focus and determine whether there's an issue specific to a certain card, or to troubleshoot something that crops up when more than one card is present in your system.

The dumb analog frame-grabber capture card family includes pretty much anything driven by the `bttv`, `cx88` and `saa7134` drivers. Most of these cards require a loopback cable that runs from an output on the capture card to a line-in input on your sound card to capture audio. Take note if you find recordings that lack audio. While configuring these cards for use with MythTV may require some tweaking, at a basic level, these cards should "just work."

The easiest way to test them involves using a television viewing application that's less complex than MythTV. For example, `tvtime` (http://tvtime.sourceforge.net/) works well for such use. Just fire it up and go to town — if you've only got one card, `tvtime` shouldn't have any problem finding it and making it work. This should enable you to determine whether you're getting any picture or audio from the channels you'd expect to see. If everything appears OK in `tvtime`, it's likely no driver issues are at work.

All the frame-grabber drivers are pushed upstream into the Linux kernel on a regular basis, so unless you have a brand-new card nobody's ever seen before, chances are good the in-kernel driver from a recent kernel will support it just fine. If things do *not* look good in `tvtime` — especially if ominous-looking output regarding the loading of your driver appears in `/var/log/messages` — head over to the video4linux mailing list, to which you can subscribe at `www.redhat.com/mailman/listinfo/video4linux-list`. The good folks there should be able to get you squared away.

Hardware-encoding analog capture cards (so-called because all video encoding is offloaded to the card from the system's CPU, unlike on frame-grabbers) are relatively new on the scene. They're immensely popular in MythTV circles. These cards are based on Conexant's CX23415 and CX23416 chipsets (formerly iTVC15 and iTVC16, respectively, before Conexant bought out the original maker). In homage to the iTVC legacy of these chips, the driver is dubbed `ivtv` (http://ivtvdriver.org/). The best-supported varieties of these cards come from Hauppauge — the PVR-150, -250, -350 and -500, to name just a few — but quite a few other such cards are supported as well.

We're assuming you followed some set of complete instructions to install and configure `ivtv` to start with, but because you may have problems with an older card, you should retrace your steps a little bit. If you followed something other than the official `ivtv` How-To (http://ivtvdriver.org/index.php/Howto), step through it as well, to double-check your work. If you've still got issues after that, visit the `ivtv` troubleshooting page, at http://ivtvdriver.org/index.php/Troubleshooting. This page includes a comprehensive list of things to try to get your card going. If you're out of luck after working through that page, there's still hope via ivtv's mailing lists. But before you tackle these, be sure to read over one more Web page, at http://ivtvdriver.org/index.php/Asking_for_help. In addition, be sure to search the `ivtv` mailing lists at www.gossamer-threads.com/lists/ivtv/ before you hit the Send button in your e-mail client.

If you've got problems with a relatively new card, you'll be happy to learn that the `ivtv` developers tend to stay current with new card revisions. They also continue to add and improve support for non-Hauppauge cards. Check out `http://ivtvdriver.org/index.php/Supported_hardware` for a current list of cards supported. Visit `http://ivtvdriver.org/trac/timeline` for an overview of recent action in `ivtv`'s development branch, to determine whether any of it might relate to your hardware. You'll probably want to start hanging out on the `ivtv-devel` mailing list too, for which you can find a subscription sign-up link at `http://ivtvdriver.org/index.php/Mailinglists`.

Typical `dmesg` output after loading the ivtv driver looks like this:

```
ivtv:  ==================== START INIT IVTV ====================
ivtv:  version 0.6.1 (development snapshot compiled on
       Wed Mar 29 19:14:09 2006) loading
ivtv:  Linux version: 2.6.16-1.2080_FC5 SMP gcc-4.1
ivtv:  In case of problems please include the debug info between
ivtv:  the START INIT IVTV and END INIT IVTV lines, along with
ivtv:  any module options, when mailing the ivtv-users mailinglist.
ivtv0: Autodetected Hauppauge WinTV PVR-250 card (cx23416 based)
ACPI: PCI Interrupt 0000:01:07.0[A] -> Link [APC4] -> GSI 19
      (level, low) -> IRQ 22
tuner 2-0061: chip found @ 0xc2 (ivtv i2c driver #0)
saa7115 2-0021: saa7115 found @ 0x42 (ivtv i2c driver #0)
msp3400 2-0040: MSP3435G-B6 found @ 0x80 (ivtv i2c driver #0)
msp3400 2-0040: MSP3435G-B6 supports radio, mode is autodetect and autoselect
lirc_i2c: chip found @ 0x18 (Hauppauge IR)
lirc_dev: lirc_register_plugin: sample_rate: 10
tveeprom 2-0050: Hauppauge model 32031, rev B210, serial# 6160296
tveeprom 2-0050: tuner model is Philips FI1236 MK2 (idx 10, type 2)
tveeprom 2-0050: TV standards NTSC(M) (eeprom 0x08)
tveeprom 2-0050: audio processor is MSP3435 (idx 10)
tveeprom 2-0050: decoder processor is SAA7115 (idx 19)
tveeprom 2-0050: has no radio, has IR remote
ivtv0: loaded v4l-cx2341x-enc.fw firmware (262144 bytes)
ivtv0: Encoder revision: 0x02040024
ivtv0: Allocate DMA encoder MPEG stream: 128 x 32768 buffers (4096KB total)
ivtv0: Allocate DMA encoder YUV stream: 194 x 10800 buffers (2048KB total)
ivtv0: Allocate DMA encoder VBI stream: 120 x 17472 buffers (2048KB total)
ivtv0: Allocate DMA encoder PCM audio stream: 455 x 4608 buffers (2048KB total)
tuner 2-0061: type set to 2 (Philips NTSC (FI1236,FM1236 and compatibles))
ivtv0: Initialized Hauppauge WinTV PVR-250, card #0
ivtv:  ==================== END INIT IVTV  ====================
```

Digital television capture cards, a blanket category that encompasses both North American ATSC/HDTV cards and non-North-American Digital Video Broadcast (DVB) and HDTV cards, are the wave of the future. They deliver digital television for the digital age. Pretty much everybody who makes an analog tuner has jumped onto this bandwagon and now offers a digital tuner card or is about to go to market with something new.

Of course, because some of these cards are so new, some aren't supported straight out of the box, or may not be perfectly supported just yet. Thus, when choosing a digital video card for a

MythTV box, you should either look for a card you know is supported or be prepared to join the DVB mailing list, at `http://linuxtv.org/lists.php`. The LinuxTV DVB wiki site, at `http://linuxtv.org/wiki/index.php/Main_Page`, includes a lot of information about what cards are supported and how to set up DVB drivers, links on how to use DVB cards with a wide array of software packages (including MythTV), and more.

For any card currently listed as supported in the LinuxTV DVB wiki, those drivers should be included in the latest 2.6 kernel. For some cards, however, you must make sure to acquire the appropriate firmware file(s) to put in `/lib/firmware`, or wherever your system's hotplug implementation looks for firmware files. For example, drivers for the pcHDTV HD-2000 and HD-3000 have been in the Linux kernel since release 2.6.12. Nevertheless, you must also download firmware files either from the DVB source code repository or from the pcHDTV Web site, where they reside at `http://pchdtv.com/downloads/firmware.tar.gz`.

Although drivers should load automatically and set up necessary devices for your card, please note that there may be some issues you must combat nonetheless. Following are a few you may encounter.

First up, on Fedora Core, at least in some initial implementations (this may be fixed by now, because author Jarod Wilson recently started work at Red Hat), the DVB devices created (in `/dev/dvb/adapterX/`) don't properly get their ownership changed to the logged in user as do other video devices. Therefore, you may need to either run `mythtv-setup` as root or perform a `# chown -R user /dev/dvb` operation, where `user` is the username under which you run `mythfrontend`, so you can actually access DVB devices to set them up properly.

Another gotcha crops up when using hybrid DVB cards. Some DVB cards receive nothing but digital TV signals, while others (the hybrids) handle both digital and analog signals. Some of these hybrid cards trigger assorted modules to load in ways that do Bad Things, making it necessary to compensate with a bit of manual intervention. For example, some hybrid cards use the `dvb-bt8xx` driver for their digital sides, which also loads the `bttv` driver for their analog sides. If left to its own devices, sometimes a system will load up the `bttv` driver first, and allocate a `dvb0` device as well, without also triggering a load of the `dvb-bt8xx` module. If your system includes another DVB card that uses a different driver and it is loaded before the `dvb-bt8xx` module, the card tries to occupy the DVB card #0 slot, to which the first `bttv` card has already partially laid claim. Then the `dvb-bt8xx` driver loads and thinks it must register as DVB card #1. To work around this problem, you must simply add a line to `/etc/modprobe.conf` that informs your module initialization tools that whenever `bttv` tries to load, `dvb-bt8xx` must load first. That line (broken across two lines of text here to fit on the page) is as follows:

```
install bttv /sbin/modprobe dvb-bt8xx; \
    /sbin/modprobe --ignore-install bttv
```

Example initialization output from `dmesg` for the cards in this scenario looks like the following:

```
bttv: driver version 0.9.16 loaded
bttv: using 8 buffers with 2080k (520 pages) each for capture
bttv: Bt8xx card found (0).
ACPI: PCI Interrupt 0000:02:07.0[A] -> GSI 19 (level, low) -> IRQ 19
bttv0: Bt878 (rev 17) at 0000:02:07.0, irq: 19, latency: 64, mmio: 0xf8100000
```

```
bttv0: detected: DViCO FusionHDTV 5 Lite [card=135], PCI
       subsystem ID is 18ac:d500
bttv0: using: DViCO FusionHDTV 5 Lite [card=135,autodetected]
bttv0: gpio: en=00000000, out=00000000 in=00ffffff [init]
tda9887 1-0043: chip found @ 0x86 (bt878 #0 [sw])
tuner 1-0061: chip found @ 0xc2 (bt878 #0 [sw])
bttv0: using tuner=64
tuner 1-0061: type set to 64 (LG TDVS-H062F/TUA6034)
bttv0: registered device video0
bttv0: registered device vbi0
bttv0: add subdevice "dvb0"
bt878: AUDIO driver version 0.0.0 loaded
bt878: Bt878 AUDIO function found (0).
ACPI: PCI Interrupt 0000:02:07.1[A] -> GSI 19 (level, low) -> IRQ 19
bt878_probe: card id=[0xd50018ac],[ DViCO FusionHDTV 5 Lite ] has DVB functions.
bt878(0): Bt878 (rev 17) at 02:07.1, irq: 19, latency: 64, memory: 0xf8101000
DVB: registering new adapter (bttv0).
DVB: registering frontend 0 (LG Electronics LGDT3303 VSB/QAM Frontend)...
b2c2-flexcop: B2C2 FlexcopII/II(b)/III digital TV receiver
              chip loaded successfully
flexcop-pci: will use the HW PID filter.
flexcop-pci: card revision 2
ACPI: PCI Interrupt 0000:02:06.0[A] -> GSI 18 (level, low) -> IRQ 20
DVB: registering new adapter (FlexCop Digital TV device).
b2c2-flexcop: MAC address = 00:d0:d7:0e:a5:e3
b2c2-flexcop: found the lgdt3303 at i2c address: 0x59
DVB: registering frontend 1 (LG Electronics LGDT3303 VSB/QAM Frontend)...
b2c2-flexcop: initialization of 'Air2PC/AirStar 2 ATSC 3rd generation
              (HD5000)' at the 'PCI' bus controlled by a
              'FlexCopIIb' complete
```

This output is verbose, but it can be extremely useful when determining what's going on. Without an install line added to `modprobe.conf`, `bttv0` added subdevice `dvb0`, but the `b2c2-flexcop` registered `frontend 0` and `dvb-bt8xx frontend 1`, which confused the system to the point where one or both cards are unable to tune in any stations. This output is also extremely helpful to developers who may offer to help you if you run into a problem like this one.

Documentation on DVB card setup, particularly for MythTV, continues to improve steadily as they become increasingly popular. While the LinuxTV wiki and mailing lists are good places to start looking for help, don't be afraid to bring DVB capture card issues to the MythTV users mailing list either.

Video Output Cards

By and large, the only times you're bound to run into driver issues with video output cards is when you either 1) have a brand-spankin' new video card that isn't yet recognized by the driver that handles it, or 2) you recently upgraded your kernel and forgot to upgrade the proprietary binary driver's kernel module component during that process.

For case #1, the answer is to sit and wait for a driver update to be released. Remember that the latest and greatest video card is probably not your best use of funds for a MythTV box.

In case #2, you must simply obtain the kernel module component for the updated proprietary binary driver. That process varies from driver to driver and from Linux distribution to Linux distribution. For Fedora Core systems using the nVidia driver that ATrpms.net packages by default, once booted into your new kernel, the update process is as simple as the following:

```
# yum install nvidia-graphicsversion-kmdl-`uname -r`
```

As we write this, *version* equals 8178, the latest available driver version number from nVidia. The `uname -r` part (those are back-ticks) supplies the information about whatever kernel you are currently using.

There are some other hardware issues you might encounter with MythTV, but they are relatively rare. In some cases — particularly where a switching amp or manual switch box sits between your video card and your TV input — the TV Out encoder on your video card won't auto-detect whether the connection is S-Video or Composite video. In that case, you must force the correct setting on the driver. This typically involves a one-line addition to /etc/X11/xorg.conf, in the "Monitor" section.

Another rare hardware problem involves a *really bad* TV Out encoder. There are a few reports of this in the wild. Some cards in a generally excellent line of video cards may use different TV Out encoders, and not all are created equal. At least one cheap GeForce 4 MX card has been observed to output all video with terrible moiré patterns. Replacing that card with another GeForce 4 MX but not changing anything else resolved the problem, which places the blame entirely on that particular card.

IR Receivers and Transmitters

IR receivers and transmitters usually either work (if you've followed the instructions) or they don't. One primary problem you'll encounter is related to an IR receiver's ability to receive IR signals. Many IR dongles don't have particularly wide reception angles (particularly those included with TV tuner cards). Thus, if they aren't firmly affixed somewhere and shift around a bit, you might have issues picking up button presses on your remote. This is one of the big reasons the USB Windows XP Media Center Edition IR receiver is highly recommended — it supports a much wider reception angle and picks up signals from greater distances. It also has a cable long enough to position the receiver just about anywhere you'd want, and costs under $40. Need we say more?

If a receiver or transmitter stops working and lircd is still running, make sure your receiver or transmitter is still plugged in and hasn't been damaged somehow.

Troubleshooting Output Resolution Issues

For the most part, output resolution issues don't crop up with standard-definition displays. People have been connecting computers to them for quite some time, and they simply aren't that complicated — they really only support maximum resolutions of 720 × 480 (in NTSC land) or 768 × 576 (in PAL land). Moreover, TV Out encoders on video cards know very well how to take whatever resolution you concoct between 640 × 480 and 1024 × 768 and output it in a way your television can handle. As long as you understand the resolution limits of a standard-definition television, there really isn't any room for output resolution problems to occur.

As you've probably figured out by now, HDTV is an entirely different story. Maximum display resolution varies wildly from one so-called HDTV to another. There are no less than 18 different HDTV "standards" in the North American ATSC specification, ranging from 640 × 480 up to 1920 × 1080. Refer to the section entitled "Outputting to an HDTV" in Chapter 17 for configuration and troubleshooting details.

Top Frequently Asked Questions (with Answers!)

Why is it called MythTV?

The name is based on MythTV's goal to become the *mythical* home media convergence box that so many folks have talked about for years.

How stable is MythTV?

MythTV is extremely stable. It *can* stress hardware a bit sometimes, however, so if your hardware is borderline, stability may suffer. On solid hardware, several months of uptime without a reboot is common — reboots usually only happen when updating kernels or adding more hardware.

Can my grandparents/parents/significant other/kids run MythTV?

MythTV probably isn't quite the thing for your grandparents, unless they like an occasional technical challenge. While MythTV is typically rock-solid, that doesn't mean there won't be occasional issues that must be solved. Parents are fairly safe as MythTV users, as long as you set it up for them. Most significant others and children are happy using MythTV (and in fact can't stand watching television without MythTV once they've developed a taste for it).

Can I buy a pre-built MythTV system?

Yes and no. In the United States, pre-built hardware packages exist from multiple vendors, including Storm Logic's MythTV store at http://mythic.tv/, but for assorted patent-related legal issues, they can't sell you a system with MythTV pre-installed. In Australia, (where patents aren't quite the roadblock they are in the U.S.), a company named D1 does sell a complete system based on MythTV. You can check it out at http://www.d1.com.au/hmc/welcome.php. Scour the Web and you'll turn up additional pre-built systems (check Appendix B in this book, too). Please note that many systems designed for Windows XP Media Center Edition work equally well running MythTV.

How many people are using MythTV?

That's hard to say. As of early April 2006, roughly two months after the release of MythTV 0.19, 62,685 downloads of the MythTV source have been recorded at www.mythtv.org/. The prior 0.18.1 release shows over 200,000 downloads. These numbers definitely don't come close to accurately reflecting the entire user base, however, because a large number of users install from binary packages that aren't tracked by mythtv.org's download counter, and another segment of users pulls their source code straight from MythTV's code development repository. A very conservative estimate might hazard a total of at least 500,000 MythTV users around the world, but a lot of people jump on this bandwagon daily.

What are minimal system requirements for MythTV?

This depends on exactly what you want to be able to do with a MythTV system, but at a bare minimum, you need something along the lines of a 600 MHz processor and a decent video card if you want to be able to play back what you record (just recording, with the right capture card, takes virtually no CPU power). Generally, 256 MB is the recommended minimum amount of RAM. You'll also need a hard drive (or drives) with DMA capabilities and enough room to store as much video as you want to be able to store. Note that all of these requirements increase significantly if you want to go the HDTV route. Oh, yeah, you need a video capture device too!

What are the recommended system requirements for MythTV?

A good starter system if you don't care about HDTV is something in the 1.0 to 2.0 GHz range with 256 to 512 MB of RAM and 120 to 250 GB of storage and two tuner cards (trust us, you'll quickly find one is almost never enough). If you're talking HDTV, a better starter system would bump the processor out to 3 GHz or more, and include 512 MB to 768 MB of RAM and 400 or more GB of storage.

On what operating systems does MythTV run?

MythTV runs on Linux, FreeBSD and Mac OS X. The vast majority of development occurs on Linux, so it's the best supported of all these options. FreeBSD and Mac OS X offer only limited backend recording capabilities, and Mac OS X also offers relatively immature support for hardware-accelerated video playback. No, MythTV does *not* run on Windows, nor do any of the developers have any good reason to make it do so.

What capture cards are supported?

Basically any device for which a Linux driver exists that fully implements the video4linux specification will do this trick. A few other devices also qualify, such as DVB cards, FireWire ports pulling from suitable cable boxes, some USB-connected external tuner devices, and an Ethernet-connected set-top box or two. Actually, answering what capture cards *aren't* supported is much easier.

OK, what capture cards *aren't* supported?

MythTV does not support the tuner on ATi All-in-Wonder video cards, because their driver doesn't fully implement the video4linux specification. In fact, one of the parts it doesn't do is critical for MythTV to do its thing. Certain TV tuners on nVidia's comparable cards are equally unsupported, also owing to incomplete driver support. No functional drivers exist for a number of other cards, all of which are listed in the hardware section of the official MythTV HOW-TO, at www.mythtv.org/docs/mythtv-HOWTO-3.html.

How many capture cards can I have?

How many do you need? Ten tuner systems (with tuners spread across multiple backends) have been seen in the wild, but there's no real reason you can't go bigger than that if you're looking for a line in *Guinness*. You'll more likely run out of PCI slots in your computers, or money for tuners to put in them, before you hit the maximum number of tuners a MythTV system can access. Some kernel drivers do set an upper limit of four capture cards of any given type per system, however.

Can I record from my set-top box?

Absolutely. Simply feed an S-Video or Composite video cable and an audio cable to a capture card with the necessary inputs (most analog ones have them), and off you go.

How much storage do I need?

That depends greatly on how many shows you want to record, how long you want to keep them, how much you care about quality, and so on. An hour-long high-definition recording typically consumes between 4 and 7 GB, while an hour-long reasonable-quality standard-definition recording uses anywhere from 1 to 4 GB of storage. Multiply those numbers by how many shows per week you think you'll record, factoring in how long you think you'll keep them, and so on . . . . In short, the more storage, the better!

How fast does my storage need to be?

You don't need anything spectacularly fast. A modern ATA hard drive is plenty fast enough to handle simultaneous recordings. You may find you need multiple drives configured in a RAID array of some type if you start moving more than two HDTV video streams around simultaneously.

Where can I get help with my MythTV system?

The best place to start is the official MythTV documentation, found at www.mythtv.org/modules.php?name=MythInstall. From there, slide on over to any distribution-specific HOW-TO documents, and then try poking the searchable MythTV mailing list archives for answers. After you've done that, sign up for the MythTV users mailing list and ask any unanswered questions you might have. The MythTV IRC channel, #mythtv-users, on irc.freenode.net, is another excellent resource as well.

Where are the searchable MythTV mailing list archives?

You can find them at www.gossamer-threads.com/lists/mythtv/.

Where do I sign up to join the MythTV mailing lists?

Visit www.mythtv.org/modules.php?name=MythInfo, on the bottom of the page.

How do I report a problem?

Go to http://svn.mythtv.org/trac/wiki/TicketHowTo to file a bug report.

How do I get someone to implement feature XYZ?

Convince a developer it's a great idea (good luck!), bribe a developer (known to work occasionally), or do it yourself (the solution is in your hands!).

How can I help MythTV?

Use it. Answer questions from other people on the mailing lists. Write some code. Help provide data for existing bug reports. Create new bug reports (see "How do I report a problem?").

Can I rip DVDs with MythTV?

Yes, the functionality exists in MythDVD if built with transcode support. The basics are documented at www.mythtv.org/docs/mythtv-HOWTO-20.html.

Can I burn recorded TV shows to DVD?

Definitely. Check out Chapter 17.

Can I share TV shows with others?

With other computers in your own house, yes, via remote frontends and/or simple file sharing. From a technical standpoint, it would be simple to share your recordings with others, but it's not legal (in the U.S., anyhow), so don't do it.

Can I use my universal remote with MythTV?

Absolutely! Give Chapter 17 another look.

Are antenna rotors supported?

Not natively, because they're problematic to deal with. That said, some enterprising folks have crafted "channel-change" shell scripts that rotate antennas as part of their channel changing operations.

What can I do to make my system quieter?

Buy a case designed for a Home Theater PC system. Get acoustic dampening material for the inside of your case. Slow down your fans. Go diskless. Check out the Silent PC Review Web site at www.silentpcreview.com/, or check out the *Extreme Tech* book *Build the Ultimate Home Theater PC* by this book's authors Ed Tittel and Matt Wright (Mike Chin is another author on that title, and he's also the guy behind SilentPCReview.com) for more ideas.

How many systems can watch the same live TV feed at the same time?

At present, only one. However, work is underway to implement live TV multicasting, to allow umpteen systems to watch the same recording at the same time.

Final Thoughts

If you haven't already figured out from the incessant repetition, the MythTV users mailing list is an excellent resource to tap when you run into problems with a MythTV system. Don't be afraid to use it, but at the same time, don't abuse it, either. Common courtesy dictates you should search the list archives for answers first, and *then* hit up the list with your problems, questions, concerns, and so forth. Another resource not mentioned as prominently as the mailing lists is the Internet Relay Chat (IRC) channel, #mythtv-users on irc.freenode.net, where you can hang out and interact with knowledgeable MythTV users who may be able to help you with issues you're having.

Appendixes

Though this part of the book takes its name from a vestigial body part that medical science is often called on to remove, that doesn't mean that the items you find here are either worthless or dangerous to your continued health and well-being. Far from it! What you'll find here is meant to provide a valuable supplement to the book's content, advising you "where to go" online to find various best-of-breed resources, downloads, information, and guidance.

Appendix A explains where to look for Linux distributions, especially those related to the two major focal points for this book — namely, Fedora and KnoppMyth. That's why you'll find it loaded with key primary points for obtaining information and guidance, plus documents and downloads.

Appendix B takes MythTV resources online as its primary subject, and thus spends some serious time describing what you'll find at the "mother of all MythTV sites" (MythTV.org) and at lead author Jarod Wilson's MythTV How-to site. But that's not all that's here, and what you do find here is guaranteed to spark your interest, if not result in a lost weekend or two spent Web-surfing.

Appendix C aims to help you stock your Linux system admin toolbox by pointing out important sources for diagnostics software of various kinds, as well as useful system monitoring tools. Our goal is to arm you with what you need to assess your system's health and to work toward improving it should that ever prove necessary.

By the time you finish this part of the book, you will understand a lot more about where to go and what to do to get your Linux system up and running with MythTV safely ensconced therein. You'll also have a good idea of the kinds of tools available to help you analyze and troubleshoot your MythTV system.

Linux Distros, Downloads, and Docs

This appendix covers distros and downloads in the same section, primarily because they normally occur on or are linked through the same Web sites. Another section describes the wide range of Linux documentation and self-help materials available online. Finally, we include pointers to popular portal sites that can expand the already considerable vistas herein still further.

If you have special sites or resources you find to be extremely or unusually helpful or informative, please share that information with us. We can't promise that we'll include everything that hits our mailbox in future updates, but we will respond to all suggestions and include those in online updates that we agree will benefit the book's general readership. You can e-mail us at mythtv@edtittel.com, but be sure to put **MythTV:** at the head of the subject line in your message, in order to get past Ed's spam filter. Thanks!

Linux Distros and Downloads

Because this book concentrates on Fedora Core 4 and KnoppMyth distros, we provide information for those sites in Table A-1; for completeness, we also include the Knoppix home site as well. Furthermore, you'll also find a link to an ultimate Linux distribution resource known as DistroWatch, which does its best to track every single Linux distribution known to humankind (there were 365 distributions named as we wrote this appendix; there will probably be even more named as you read it!)

Table A-1   Key MythTV Distros and Downloads

Distro	URL	Description
Fedora Core 5	`fedoraproject.org`	Ready access to download links, docs, FAQs, and more.
KnoppMyth	`www.mysettopbox.tv/knoppmyth.html`	Check the links at the middle of this page to access download sites.
Knoppix	`www.knoppix.org`	A bootable live Linux system that runs from DC or DVD; find info, download, and links info here.
DistroWatch	`distrowatch.com`	Use Search to look for any specific Linux distribution.

Of these sites, this book's readers are likely to find the first two items of greatest interest and relevance. Knoppix may come in handy for those seeking to learn more about the distribution upon which KnoppMyth is built. DistroWatch is a handy tool for checking status and update information about any and all Linux distros, so you'll certainly want to use it to make sure you're working from the latest and greatest version of your chosen distro.

Linux Docs and Information

Just as there are hundreds of Linux distributions that are known and tracked, there are also thousands of potential sources for documentation and information. Certainly, any good Linux distro site worth its salt will include or point to copious amounts of documentation, and then there are numerous sites that specialize in providing Linux documentation of all kinds. Much of this tends to focus on one distro or another (we list sites most relevant to this book in Table A-2), while some of these sites are actually omnibus documentation resources and cover many distributions along with all kinds of generally useful (and often extremely well-written) materials that they make freely available to their visitors.

You'll find all kinds of useful MythTV and Linux docs and information resources on and throughout these pages (more than you may have time or inclination to visit, in fact). That's why we summarize all the key items in Table A-2.

Table A-2 Key Linux and MythTV Docs and Info Sites

Page Title	URL	Description
The Linux Documentation Project	www.tldp.org	A vast clearinghouse of information, including subject-specific help, FAQs, command-line references, and guides
Linux Online Documentation	www.linux.org/docs/	Great pointers to HOW-TOs and guides (free online books on many subjects)
Fedora Documentation	http://fedora.project.org/wiki/Docs	Official release notes, installation guide, handy jargon buster, and package management guide
Knoppix Documentation Wiki	www.knoppix.net/wiki/	Large collection of FAQs, many of great potential interest, especially downloading, customizing, and hard drive installation
LinuxDocs.org	www.linuxdocs.org	Information of all kinds for Linux enthusiasts
The Pamphlet of KnoppMyth	www.mysettopbox.tv/doc.html	Brief but cogent information about all key aspects of KnoppMyth

As is so often true for Linux resources of all kinds, all of these sites include links to a virtual galaxy of potentially useful and nearly always interesting information. That's why we also recommend browsing around these sites as you start your MythTV project before you get too deeply enmeshed in the details. You'd be amazed at what you can learn by a bit of preliminary reconnaissance before really digging into your system, so we strongly suggest that you spend at least a few hours rooting around inside these sites (and other sites to which they lead) before you tackle installation and configuration too seriously. For one thing, you may find the very resource that bails you out of trouble later; for another, you will definitely get a much better idea about the volume, quality, and relevance of the information that awaits you on the Internet, both for Linux itself and for MythTV.

When Linux Trouble Comes Calling

Anybody who has dealt with Linux for any length of time knows that trouble with the system will occasionally arise. Be it hardware or software induced, inside or outside the Linux kernel, or simply the result of "operator error," you must be ready to pick up the pieces and put them back together should trouble cross the transom onto your Linux box (whether or not it's running MythTV). Beyond the resources we mention elsewhere in this book, at least some of the items in Table A-3 should help you find information and, it is hoped, insight. Related forums or message boards enable you to air your problems to your peers, in hopes that collective wisdom and ability exceeds your own—as it so frequently does (at least for your humble authors, whose collective bacon has been rescued from the flames by their community peers more times than they can remember).

Table A-3   Linux Troubleshooting Sites and Info

Site Name	URL	Description
Tutorialized.com	`www.tutorialized.com` `/tutorials/Linux/1`	Oodles of troubleshooting and problem-solving tutorials for all kinds of situations; see especially James Mohr's "Solving Problems"
Troubleshooting Professional Magazine	`www.troubleshooters.com`	Slightly dated, but still contains lots of useful suggestions and information about the process and particulars involved
Troubleshooting Building and Installing Packages	`www.tldp.org/HOWTO/` `Software-Building-` `HOWTO-7.html`	Helps diagnose and fix troubles compiling or installing Linux software packages
Troubleshooting with Syslog	`www.siliconvalleyccie` `.com/linux-hn/` `logging.htm`	Working with the built-in system logging (syslog) utility to detect and fix problems
Linux Troubleshooting	`www.linuxtroubleshooting` `.com/wiki/`	A comprehensive compendium of Linux troubleshooting tools, tips, and techniques
Linux Forums	`www.linuxforums.org`	Search on Linux Troubleshooting for access to forums and related links and info

Don't forget that your search engine of choice may also ultimately be your best source of information and insight when trouble comes gunning for you. If you can be as specific about what you're dealing with as possible, and learn how to state clear, unambiguous queries when using Google, Yahoo, MSN, or whatever, the odds are pretty good that you'll get just the help and information you need.

MythTV Resources

L inux is clearly the hacker's choice when it comes to feeding do-it-yourself ambitions. Nowhere is this more evident than in the innumerable distributions readily available in the multitude of forms tracked at DistroWatch, as discussed in Appendix A. The Linux user base is a global community of developers and users alike who commingle in online forums and in various channels online. As a result, plenty of interesting and inspirational input and feedback is available across a wide range of subjects.

Your success will depend in part on your ability to quickly and effectively locate all the information necessary to complete your MythTV project. This appendix covers only bare essential MythTV resources specific to the subjects covered in this book. You are advised to query the search engine of your choice for subject matter that goes above and beyond the exercises and experiences outlined in this text.

MythTV Core Resources

Here again, lead author Jarod Wilson's definitive Fedora MythTV HOW-TO guide makes an appearance, as it is the very foundation upon which this book was built. Without his insight and input (in fact, Wilson contributed numerous chapters), this book would not exist. The resources listed in Table B-1 are considered most beneficial to our readership and are therefore recommended as your first line of defense for finding consistent, reliable, and timely information when researching, implementing, tweaking, or hacking MythTV.

Table B-1   Key MythTV Resources

Resource	URL	Description
MythTV	`www.mythtv.org`	MythTV's original project page — the birthplace of convergence technology.
Fedora MythTV HOW-TO	`www.wilson.net/mythtv/`	The man, the MythTV, the legend. Wilson's site hosts the definitive guide to getting MythTV on Fedora.
MythTV Wiki	`www.mythtv.info/wiki/` `index.php.Main_Page`	MythTV information and comprehensive HOW-TO index. No *forums* in the typical online sense, just a lot of docs and links to outside stuff, which may include forums.
PVR Hardware Database	`http://pvrhw.goldfish` `.org/tiki-pvrhwdb.php`	An expansive and searchable database of MythTV-supported hardware.

Of the resources mentioned, the most in-depth coverage appears among the first three links. These alone can link you to the most common tips, tricks, and techniques to modify nearly every aspect of MythTV. The MythTV wiki and forums are also great places to start asking questions, or to post your experiences so that others may benefit from your findings. Finally, the PVR database is an unofficial listing of hardware components used in MythTV PCs by users around the globe.

Note Though not exactly a MythTV resource per se, Brandon Beattie's *Linux HTPC Howto* at `www` `.linuxis.us/linux/media/howto/linux-htpc/` does more than just provide a great overview of the process of building a Linux HTPC. It also digs into all the hardware issues at some length, with pointers to good resources where available, and with the down-and-dirty details where not. Definitely worth a visit! In the same vein, Till Harbaum's *Twonky: A MythTV based PVR* is a combination design guide/builder's journal that walks through the specifics involved in building his own MythTV system; read it at `www.harbaum.org/till/twonky/`.

MythTV Third-Party Plug-ins

The MythTV core plug-ins represent only the official extensions to the MythTV package and are by no means a complete collection of additional capabilities. The resources in Table B-2 point toward unofficial plug-in packages that several other do-it-yourselfers have taken the initiative to develop. Some of them are so useful you might find them essential to the operation of your own MythTV system. Ultimately, the choice is yours — find whatever works best for you, and don't be afraid to experiment. That's what MythTV is all about.

Table B-2   Third-Party Plug-ins

Page Title	URL	Description
MythWifi Remote Control	`http://studwww.ugent.be/~aveys/mythwifi/`	Use socket communications to control the MythTV frontend.
MythExtra Plug-ins Package	`http://mythextra.napsi.net/`	MythRecipe binder, MythFM radio, MythMail, MythKaraoke (experimental).
MythStormAlert	`http://www.knoppmythwiki.org/index.php?page=MythStormAlert`	Storm tracker originates from `www.noaa.gov`.
Torrentocracy	`http://www.torrentocracy.com`	RSS News, BitTorrent feeds, seamless transition to Internet video.
MythWebRemote	`http://sourceforge.net/projects/mythwebremote`	Provides remote network access via laptop or PDA to MythTV backend.
MythTiVo	`http://tivo-mplayer.sourceforge.net/mythtivo.html`	Interact remotely with your network-attached TiVo and MythTV boxes.
MythStream	`http://home.kabelfoon.nl/~moongies/streamtuned.html`	Based on StreamTuned; plays and records audio and video streams using MPlayer as the backend.
MythCalendar	`http://www.wombatinvasion.com/pmwiki/pmwiki.php/MythTV/MythCalendar`	A simple calendar application for the MythTV frontend.
MythBurn	`http://mythburn.sourceforge.net/`	Burn recorded shows to DVD from the MythTV frontend.
MythStreamTV	`http://mythstreamtv.sourceforge.net/`	Enables MythTV users to do live transcoding and streaming of MPEG-1 or-2 formats to Windows Media Player; also enables control via MythWeb.

None of the preceding plug-ins is vital to MythTV's operation. Indeed, many of them are experimental and should be treated with care and selectivity. But who knows? Given the bustling popularity of all things MythTV, some of these entries may one day find themselves among the core cast of Myth plug-ins.

Pre-fab MythTV Units

Not everyone has the time or patience to sift through the voluminous manual pages and online resources to get a viable MythTV installation up and running. So far, however, only a handful of vendors have taken the initiative to build and distribute turnkey solutions around MythTV and their own hardware choices, thereby eliminating most of the guesswork in the process. Such convenience does come at a price, however: At the time of this writing, the small number of MythTV-ready models available online *start* (in round numbers) between $700 and $1,000, with prices going up depending on features, functions, and hardware specifics. Table B-3 provides vendor sites and details.

Table B-3   Pre-fab MythTV Units

Site Title	URL	Description
HACKmyth Home Automation	`www.hackmyth.com/pages/products.htm`	The home automation control kit for MythTV. Pre-fab units and add-on modules for deploying home automation and security.
D1 HMC	`www.d1.com.au/hmc/welcome.php`	D1 Home Media Centre pre-fab MythTV entertainment box.
MythTV Store	`Mythic.tv/product_info.php?products_id=44`	A pre-fab PC system designed and ready for MythTV installation — self-tweaking, in fact!
Ubuntu PC	`http://ubuntupc.com`	Supports all the right hardware options and they'll pre-install MythTV for you (at extra cost).
Convert Xbox into MythTV frontend	`http://www.ehomeupgrade.com/entry/2077/convert_your_xbox`	Modify an existing Xbox to operate as a frontend control unit for your network-attached MythTV backend system.

As usual, your search engine of choice is surely the most valuable resource should you find yourself in any kind of a bind. Chances are good someone else has been there, done that, and lived to tell the experience. Why not benefit from somebody else's mistakes, trials, and tribulations whenever you can?

Linux System Diagnostics and Monitoring Tools

Sometimes you'll find your system acting oddly, erratically, or perhaps sluggishly or in fits and starts. That's when it's time to open up your toolbox and start digging into the Linux runtime environment to try to figure out what's up. Although your ultimate goal will always be to repair what you can, and work around what you can't, before you can take corrective action, you must first determine what's causing your system to misbehave. That's where diagnostics and tools come into their own, as you'll see in this handy little appendix.

What you'll find covered here is a set of pointers to some well-known and widely respected collections of Linux diagnostics (and other useful system tools). You'll also be led to tutorials and discussions about how to read and interpret Linux's invaluable system log (syslog) output, and other helpful monitoring tools. Finally, you'll be treated to a helping of cheerful guidance on the best way to administer a Linux system (such as your MythTV PC) to keep it running in tip-top shape.

Linux Diagnostics

The first and often the best place to dig for diagnostics is, of course, inside your own Linux distribution, and at sites where that distribution may be downloaded, but outside the tools and capabilities built into your own Linux environment, Table C-1 provides a set of nonpareil resources that can help you stuff your box of diagnostic tools as full as you'd like (or can stand).

Table C-1   Linux Diagnostics Resources

Resource	URL	Description
Linux Diagnostic Tools	`http://linux-diag` `.sourceforge.net`	A collection of tools and utilities for inspecting and documenting system devices, and for wrapping other popular diagnostic tools.
ethtool	`www.kernel.org/git/`	Linux network driver diagnostic and tuning tool (search on ethtool in URL).
sg3_utils	`http//sg.torque.net/sg/` `u_index.html`	SCSI device investigation, monitoring, and documentation.
HW Diagnostics	`www.linux-tutorial.info`	Click Table of Contents, The Computer Itself, and then HW Diagnostics (for a lot of other useful information on monitoring and other related topics).
Linux Test Project	`http://ltp.sourceforge.net`	Maintains a battery of Linux system testing tools, including useful file system, I/O, network, and load testing tools.
Lm_sensors	`http://secure.netroedge` `.com/~lm78/`	Monitoring tools for Linux systems containing hardware health monitoring chips.
nictools-nopci	`http://packages.debian` `.org/stable/net/` `nictools-nopci`	Diagnostics tools for selected non_PCI Ethernet cards.
smartmontools	`http://smartmontools` `.sourceforge.net`	Utility programs to monitor and control hard disks that use SMART technology built into most ATA and SCSI drives.
TCP/IP Diagnostics	`www.ianywhere.com/` `developer/technotes/` `tcp_ip_linux.html`	General advice on TCP/IP status and troubleshooting.
Ultimate Boot CD	`www.ultimatebootcd.com`	Instructions on building and maintaining a bootable CD with diagnostic utilities for system analysis and repair. Includes the best compendium of diagnostic tools we know of in one place.
Best Linux Hardware Diagnostics?	`http://ask.slashdot` `.org/article.pl?` `sid=05/08/02/165231`	Worth browsing in its entirety, but chewie's "suggested list of applications" alone makes the trip worthwhile.

Note Though you'll find "The Ultimate Boot CD" concept (and site) invaluable in helping you put a collection together, it's a great idea to burn a bootable CD or DVD with its own operating system and collection of tools on board. That way, even if your hard drives go wonky and your system won't or can't boot normally, you can still use this approach to get your PC up and running and to begin the process of troubleshooting and repair necessary to return it to normal working order.

More on Linux Monitoring and Logging

Digging into any Linux-based system invariably involves one or more trips to various directories where log files reside. In fact, some Linux aficionados argue that what monitors really do is log system activity, and that what savvy Linux system administrators do is inspect, massage, and zero in on critical information in log files. Though this may be stretching the point a bit, there's no doubt that knowing where the logs are, what they have to say, and how to interpret their content, are all key skills to develop if you want to make yourself entirely at home in the Linux world. That's where the resources and information in Table C-2 come into play, and where it is hoped that you'll be able to find guidance, advice, and support if and when you should need it.

Table C-2   Monitoring Resources

Resource	URL	Description
Linux Tutorial: System Logging	`www.linux-tutorial.info`	See entries for system logging, `syslogd`, and managing system logs.
Learn Linux Logging	`www.serverwatch.com/tutorials/article.php/3521746`	Finding, understanding, and using Linux logs.
Troubleshooting with Syslog	`www.silconvalleyccie.com/linux-hn/logging.htm`	Covers Linux logging basics.
Log Files	`http://linux.about.com/cs/linux101/g/Log_files.htm`	Basic definition and directory info about Linux logging.
Log files and other forms of monitoring	`www.seifried.org/lasg/logging/`	Description of operations and security for Linux logging.
Logcheck	`www.psionic.com/abacus/logcheck`	Program that scans system logs for unusual activity.
Log Analyzers	`www.linux.org/apps/all/Administration/Log_analyzers.html`	Comprehensive list of Linux log analysis tools.

Continued

Table C-2 *(continued)*

Resource	URL	Description
Building a Network Management System	`http://freshmeat` `.net/articles/view/` `1553`	Of particular interest are links to NMS and performance monitoring tools such as nagios, zabbix, big brother, ganglia, and so forth.
Working with Log Files	`http://weblog` `.infoworld.com/` `troubleshooter/` `archives/2006/04/` `working_with_lo.html`	Describes Linux logging basics, operation, and security issues.

The Art of Linux Administration

Ultimately, the care and feeding of Linux is something that all MythTV users must confront. There's actually a fairly well-established body of wisdom on the subject of Linux administration, along with a lot of information about best practices, routines, and caretaking rituals. You'll find all this information, and more, addressed in the resources in Table C-3.

Table C-3   Linux Administration Resources and Information

Resource	URL	Description
Linux System Administrator's Guide	`www.tldp.org/` `guides.html`	Follows equally great Installation and User Guides from a nonpareil Linux information source (see also LAME: Linux System Administration Made Easy).
Linux System Administration	`http://librenix.com/` `?inode=1917`	First of a four-part series to prep for the Linux Professional Institute LPI 101 exam, teaches all basic skills MythTV users are ever likely to need.
Linux HOW-TOs	`www.howtoforge.com`	Search on "Linux"; offers a ton of articles on system administration tools and tasks.
Linux Journal	`www.linuxjournal.com`	Search on Linux system administration and other topics and tools of interest.
Linux System Administrator's Guide	`www.faqs.org/docs/` `linux_admin/`	Good, general resource on the topics, tools, and activities involved in Linux system administration.

Again, consult your favorite search engine if what you find here isn't exactly what you need to deal with your particular situation. One of the many joys of open source is that nearly everything you might conceivably want or need for Linux, tool-related or otherwise, is probably tucked away in some remote corner of the Internet. All you have to do is find it!

Index

SYMBOLS AND NUMERICS

Continued

Continued

Continued

Continued